T0129187

Big Eye

Big Eye

The Preacher

LIAM WALSH

BIG EYE
THE PREACHER

iUniverse books may be ordered through booksellers or by contacting:

iUniverse
1663 Liberty Drive
Bloomington, IN 47403
www.iuniverse.com
1-800-Authors (1-800-288-4677)

ISBN: 978-1-5320-0986-0 (sc)
ISBN: 978-1-5320-0985-3 (e)

Library of Congress Control Number: 2016919187

Print information available on the last page.

iUniverse rev. date: 11/14/2016

Introduction

The book has two parts. The first is a dialogue with God. The second is a series of Golden Egg Meditations.

In order to enjoy this book a reader draws two circles and place words 'human mind' in one and the words 'Big Eye' in the other. The book is an effort to use the brain to communicate with Big Eye. It's in lengthy dialogue form. There are two characters, a person called Big Eye and a human being called Little Man.

Big Eye is God but I wanted to use a new name for God because people use it vainly and in a way that is over familiar. The word God is too common and is used disrespectfully by many. Big Eye is God the Father, God the Son and God the Holy Spirit.

Little Man is me the writer. I perceive myself to be a small dot living life in time on a large planet among billions of other finite living things. I'm anxious to tell the world about my aliveness or awareness of living.

I live on a quiet narrow road near the River Shannon and is conducive for retirement, reflection and writing. The drive inside me is to love Big Eye. I perceive him to be my Father based on Jesus Christ's encouragement on how to pray. I'm desperate to love dearly and deeply the Father of Jesus Christ. There is a lot of time and energy gone into writing this book.

The second part of the book consists of Golden Egg Meditation challenges based on Scriptural or Doctrinal nuggets. These pieces of treasure belong to Jesus and are classed as eggs for the mind to contemplate. The opportunity is there for everyone to build an internal Holy Nest for Golden Eggs to find a warm soul to nurture them into life. The reader picks his/her Golden Egg. I choose my Eggs. Each one has a title like Lamb of God, Body of Christ or I am the Way etc. Their nature is Divine as they originate from God's Son.

The Scriptural or Doctrinal Egg challenge could last for days, weeks, months or years. The Golden Words has infinite potential. The recipient of Holy Word Challenges must marry or love Jesus Christ. Holy Eggs come from Christ. They lie in the nest of the mind and grow through constant prayer, meditation and contemplation. The results are phenomenal.

The challenge is super spiritual. It has a high intensity rate. Any drop in interest may result in the death of the Egg. So it is up to the fervour of the individual to keep Golden Egg challenges alive and warm in the intellect. The success rate of an Egg surviving is only fifty/fifty.

The gist of the book is about one small Little Man's love for Big Eye and Big Eye's love for one single Little Man called Liam. It's a beautiful story. Hopefully ideas in the book might ignite a spark in each soul to transcend mundane living and find unity with Big Eye. My hope is to inspire people to find happiness.

In the book there is a strong emphasis on prayer. An hour spent in silence refresh the soul like water on a body. Prayer is invaluable. It's the only way to communicate with God. If you don't pray reading this book may be difficult.

The book makes you think about life as a journey and choices facing each person. You can live your life in this world and die or enrol for a future life in heaven by believing in Jesus Christ, the Son of the living God. A substantial part of this book is to encourage every human being to use their intellect in finding Big Eye who is an Almighty and Powerful God. Don't mind multitudes. Don't mind others. You are an adult. You have a life. I encourage you to find your Father. I encourage you to cement your love for Big Eye. A lack of response to this call is akin to being cut off.

The stall is set. Forget mob rule. Forget people power. Your first duty is to yourself. You can't blame others for the way you look, or the way you feel, or the way you think. So figure out what makes you happy or figure out what makes you miserable. At the end of the day all of us are small dots in motion and none of us are sure of eternal life or where our destiny lies.

The book shows that each human person has a capacity greater than any other living thing by having the ability to raise one's mind and heart upwards towards higher things. I'm confident and strong about my thinking and this work makes me extremely happy.

The book depicts a sincere religious man urging all to a life of heartfelt prayer with others in Church and through private reflection while out walking or while meditating on Sacred Scripture. Big Eye delights in any Little Man that's on his knees humbly expressing cries of love for him. Big Eye has radar vision for devout souls no matter whether they live in a jungle or in a populated city.

I hope my book is a joy to read. I urge all political powers and religious leaders to turn to God. And I urge each individual person in every country no matter what their religion to reject wrongdoing and choose a Sacred Way of Life with God. Spiritual life is hard work. The holy route could take a decade or two of strenuous efforts to shake of bad bits and replace them with Golden Eggs. The struggle is tough to find the straight road to heaven and it is just as tough to stay on it.

The book is an aid to grapple internal demons or wrestle with multiple irritations that prevent a clear vision of Big Eye. All thoughts from the Little Man came straight from the mind. The emphatic message has to be seen as an exploration of friendship with Truth Itself. The writer clearly has a love for God. But he is seen to struggle with unstable relationships and unstable intentions through the flawed reasoning of the human mind in comparison with Perfect Wisdom, Perfect Truth and Perfect Love that is inherent in God's nature.

Chapter One

Little Man

Hello! Hello! Good morning! Are you asleep, Big Eye? I'd like to talk to you. Are you busy? Are you tired? I love you. It's okay if you haven't time. I feel a nervous wreck. Forgive me if I'm pertinent. I'm a Little Man. I'm a dot in South West Limerick. Can you see me? I try by prayer to contact you, Big Eye. You are my Father and I love you. I know you have massive responsibilities in caring for seven billion people on earth not to mention other galaxies and created lumps of matter throughout space. Have you time for me personally? I'd love to talk to you. Is that possible?

Big Eye

Of course it is. I've time for everyone. You are precious, Little Man and I'm not asleep. I know you very well. You are under the microscope of my Big Eye as an aspirant writer. I'm aware of your good intentions to think about me and to love me. That's nice of you. So you desire to write a book. That's fine. I'm happy to give support and inspiration to work in your mind and heart for the purpose of a holy book. You like dialogue. Great, you can write that way. It's no problem. In fact, it is very thoughtful. I'm grateful to you. You are like a prophet from of old. The world knows about me already. But you can remind them again about their obligations to praise and love my Name. You make sure Liam that you express love for me in your book. I know you love me and that's mighty nice of you. Anything that helps a human being to love and respect me is appreciated. I support you Liam in your work. You

1

will find inspiration from my Holy Spirit. It's a high and noble intention that nothing else matters to you except me. It indicates Liam that I am important in your life. That's commendable. I'm very happy to have found a new soul willing to commit to me. I accept your mind Liam. Let the communication flow. I immensely look forward to interacting with you. It will be a joy. I advise though that you be patient with yourself and make steady progress. I await with interest themes formed in your intellect for discussion with me. I look forward to our endeavour together. You are a beautiful person Liam. I love you.

Little Man

Big Eye, thanks. I love you too. The promise of inspiration from the Holy Spirit deeply pleases me. I think of the Holy Spirit descending on the Apostles. It's a good start to my book with the promise of your Spirit inspiring me.

Big Eye I wrote this morning and it dawned on me that I would like to dialogue with you as my Holy Father. Is that okay? I love the idea of a Divine Father. The idea thrills me. I can call you my Big Eye Father. As an implication of that Holy Truth I am some kind of a son. That makes me happy. It doesn't matter if I'm fostered, adopted, an orphan or homeless. I have a Holy Father to provide for me and to care for me. I'm happy with that news. It's wonderful news. I'm proud to accept it. So hello Father. I'll try to make you proud of me through my writing.

Father, praise Jesus for me. Thank Jesus for me. He taught us to call you Abba Father. He is your Divine Son. I'm not. I'm part of humanity, mortal and sinful. So I accept Jesus prayer with great pride. I'm inspired to belief that I have access through prayer to a Sacred Father. Thank you Jesus for sharing your Father with us. It's lovely and reassuring. My genetic father passed away but the fact that there is a heavenly Father there for me is nothing more than a joy beyond telling.

Father, I pray to you, my love. I'm thrilled to bits with my discovery. I feel safe too in having a Sacred Father like you. The only thing is that I can't see you. You live in Heaven. I dialogue with you through faith and prayer. I visualise a Big Eye watching me. But from another angle I know what you are like through your Holy Word recorded by Biblical writers. You have been involved in the history of humanity for over four thousand years. That tells me that you are an ancient Father. That tells me that you are ageless. I'm glad that you don't die. I know too from descriptions in Sacred Scripture as to what kind of a Father you are. You are full of beauty, full of love and full of compassion. That will do for me. Attributes such as those attract me. You are the Greatest Father of All. And I feel honoured to be your son. For if you are my Father I have to be some kind of a son. Truth like that appeals to me. I want you Dad, my Father.

Father, I pray though about my shortcomings. What if I am a bad son or a rogue? What if I lack discipline, and am strong willed, and a slow learner? Or I maybe disloyal or distracted. I may not live up to the standard that you require Father or have the talent that you have need of to carry out work in the vineyard. But I trust your judgement. I can't imagine you would make a mistake. I can't see you choosing a rogue to preach Truth. You are too sharp. You see deep into the heart. You know of the scheming and unstable intentions in human minds. You discern my thoughts before I'm aware of them. For that Big Eye I love you. I'm nothing without your Love and Truth. Thank you Father. I'm like a little boy thrilled with a good Daddy who knows my history, my actions, my attitudes and my behaviours. I don't like myself sometimes and many doubts cross through my mind. I wonder if you are crazy to commit to a relationship with me. I was never the best student. Yet I love you because you accept me the way I am with my faults and shortcomings.

Father, I pray for the gift of intelligence and loyalty. For I wouldn't want to be a source of annoyance or embarrassment. You are honest and truthful Father whereas I'm unpredictable and odd. I've unstable intentions. So we could be a mismatch. I'm not good enough to mix with you my Divine Father because of the gulf in class between your Greatness and my Mediocrity. I'm out of my depth. How dare I try to walk with God. I'd feel miserable and embarrassed approaching the Throne of Grace where Holy Mary and St Thomas Aquinas sits in glory with the whole cohort of heaven. So I think of myself as been cheeky for desiring friendship with the Father of Jesus Christ. I can't imagine myself been plucked from the whole of humanity for special attention from you Big Eye.

Father, I intend to do my best to make myself pleasing to you. I start with honesty by hiding nothing from you. You can view me fully. I have always found telling the truth is the best policy. Hiding lies creates trouble. So I will tell you the truth Father.

Father, you know about my moody mind, my awful distractions and disrespectful negligence of you. I try to have high standards. I try to please you by having a high level of intensity in my efforts to worship you. But failures have hit me hard. I can't expect a Divine Person to hang around while I watch a hurling match. Nor can I expect Big Eye to get through to me while I worry about a whole series of little things like a broken toilet seat.

Father, I question my intelligence. I seek a unique union with you. You exist as a Creator. I exist as something made. I was once nothing, now I am something, and in the future I'm gone again. And the funniest thing is that I don't know myself. That is where you come in Father. I pray that you will teach me to know myself. There are things I do know. One is that I am a small insignificant little man. I'm irrelevant and unknown to everyone outside my home on the green isle. But that doesn't matter. My one true hope Father is for the tip of your All Powerful finger to touch me for I know that your Sacred Touch may heal me from my deficiencies. I need you to heal me. I need you to touch my heart with love. I need you to touch my mind with truth. I can then respond to you Father with more acumen and love.

Father I want to function fully and reach my full potential. It's only you Father that can bring that out of me. I'm lost to a certain extent because your Presence Father and heaven is not visible to me. It's crazy stuff if I write to a Father that I'm unaware of. So major emphasis has to be placed on prayer and faith as they are the only two eyes where God's Presence maybe possibly experienced.

Father, I call you by prayer. I'm used to calling you Our Father. But I call you my Father. It's more personal. I don't think you will let me stranded. So help my poor little mind. Increase memory levels. Increase awareness levels. Otherwise I can't reach my potential and praise you with distinction. The mind has to concentrate. I have to believe that you are there Father. I call your Holy Name. Make my mind beautiful. Come Father. Come Father. I'm a child of yours. Help me to adore you, my beautiful Father. I want more than anything to use my intelligence for the purpose of focusing on you Father.

Father, I find discipline tough going. In religious life I was able to keep my tongue quiet and devote my mind continually to prayer. But now I have to balance commitment to you with the distractions and demands of family life. I am not as free to worship. So please help me to balance the two. Disruptions are a daily occurrence. I have to listen patiently to aimless chatter. So my mind is distracted with responsibilities. So Father I have a question. What can I do when my eyes are forced away from focusing on you?

Big Eye

Liam my love I'd be a bit disappointed. Nothing should get in the way of love. I've a Super Mind. I'm Almighty God. I'm a Treasure. I'm Truth and Love. I Created you. It's worth your while to worship me. Believe me. I respect your desire and dilemma. I watch you analyse activities that affect you. I notice your mind at work and how you weigh up the balance between paltry and negligible things versus opting for my love. Well done. But Liam be careful. I wouldn't want you to turn your back on anyone in need. I wouldn't accept it. What you have to remember Liam is that I'm a Father for all Nations and no family or person is excluded from my care. If I'm rejected that is another story.

In answer to your question above Liam I agree that taking your eye of me is a distraction and no person on earth has ever had one hundred percent concentration when attempting to pray to me and love me. The ideal though Liam is to train your mind to focus on me. But in a family situation it is more difficult. You have to help at home with dish washing, ash removal, hoovering, caring for a wife, a child, and numerous other tasks. Liam, I prefer if you were more free. I'm God. I'm Big Eye. Perfect union with me comes first. So sit and listen to me. You call me Father every day. You invite me to be with you. I'm your guest because you pray to me. But I'm gone when your mind switches to something other than me and this is a problem. What you need to do Liam is reflect on your mind and prepare a place in there for me. Until that is done further dialogue and progress with me is painfully frustrating for you. There is a danger that you may never know me. Your lack of self-control lead to diversions and distraction. That happens a lot to you Liam.

Little Man

Big Eye don't sadden me. I'm human. You are Divine. My mind is the size of a marble in comparison to your Super Mind. I know very little. You know everything. There is no match between us. Your Intellect is big like a football whereas mine is small like a marble. There's no comparison between you and me. My marble mind is lifeless. Your Divine Mind is Super Perfect. My eye sees as far as the end of the road whereas you Big Eye sees the whole of Creation. You are Super Creative and has Super Knowledge. I struggle to understand a small thing like a silly wasp trying to escape through a glass window. Whereas you Father know the function and purpose of every living thing. I'm sorry Father. I'm no match for you. In fact, I feel pertinent in my attempts to approach you through faith, prayer and love. I'm feel uncomfortable about it. I know my place. A small marble like mind could <u>not</u> stand comfortable beside a Super Power. You are way above me. You are beyond what any human being can imagine.

Father, I concentrate on my intellectual ability in the hope that with your help faults are repaired. I'm spiritually blind and deaf. I pass myself off as an intellectual but deep down there's a realistic sense within me of a huge divide. My awareness of you Father could be better. I'm ashamed of myself. For my approach to you is arrogant. I'm nothing in comparison to Abraham, Moses, Elijah, and King David. I'm nothing in comparison to Jesus Christ, your Divine Son. I'm not fit to undo his sandal strap. I'm noting in comparison to St Dominic, St Patrick, St John, St Paul, St Thomas Aquinas, St Catherine, St Anselm or St Augustine.

Father, I promise whole hearted devotion. But I have intellectual weaknesses and this in turn scuppers holy devotion. I read Christ's Holy

Word that says I am the Way, the Truth and the Life. But my mind doesn't know where to start. What Life? What Way? What Truth? I need comprehension of the Holy Word.

Father, I promise honesty. The best way for me to develop spiritually is to examine intellectual performances. I must step out of my skin and view what's happening in my interior life. Intellectual faculties like memory, discernment, awareness and will must operate to a high level. Otherwise nothing remains in my mind about the Way, the Truth and the Life.

Father, this is a big test to my ability. And the quicker I stand up to it the better. I want to hear your Word. But I don't want to forget it a short time later. So what is missing? The answer to that question is the task of this book.

Father, I'm like a spider setting up a web to catch Divine Eggs. But I don't know how to nurture or spiritualise Golden Eggs like the Way, the Truth and the Life. I suspect one reason for this deficiency is a lack of awareness in the workings of the intellect. If I jumped out of my skin and viewed myself walking on road L0909 every morning what would stick in my memory – two hares playing in a field or prayer words calling your Holy Name.

Father this is where I win my battle with intelligence. During daily walks I train my mind to a greater level of intense prayer. I analyse interruptions and rejections that thwart holy intentions and deflate prayer. The Holy Spirit prompts. So I act with great alertness so as to block Satan's spawn from nesting internally and from interfering with saintly choices.

Father, there is a need in me to protect my soul from bad eggs. These are the kind that doesn't pray. Bad eggs breed vermin. These crack open and creep around in the nest of the soul by making a nuisance of themselves. Evil snowballs if prayer dries up. There is a better Way. It is the Way of prayer to you Father. I rely on it. It is prayer to you that protects and delivers from temptation and evil.

Father, you are sad with those who abandon you. But the Truth is they have nowhere to go. Many are stuck in a rut with the effects of spiritual poverty. Whose fault is it? It is their own. These people don't bother with Church and prayer. There is nothing as beautiful as a joyful face. Spirituality gives that beauty. All that matters are Holy Connections with Jesus Christ. Once that is done a well of bubbly grace gently erupts inside enabling us to worship in Spirit and Truth. Grace shines through such a body magnificently. Think about it. Open your heart to a Trinity of Love. It is available to you noble Christian. God's love is available to meek souls. How about that? A Trinity of Love trickles into every prayerful heart that says in the Name of the Father, and of the Son and of the Holy Spirit.

Father, godless people appear as blobs of matter. I pity them. They don't pray. They look unhealthy and there seems to be millions of them around the world. I see them. I don't like their demeanour. I don't like their spiritless attitude. I worry for the safety of their souls. I predict a lot of hardship for unspiritual people. Those who abandon their religion face trouble.

Father, I'm attracted to you. I love you. But you keep me on my toes. I pray every morning on road L0909. I find time for you. I give my all Big Eye. Do you see me? There is no division of time or hesitancy. I wholeheartedly pray to you. I hope my prayer and words reach you at your desk in heaven Father.

Father, I'm realistic though and

Father, I must be realistic here and avoid hypocrisy. There are tasks to be done and some of these are very mundane like hoovering the floor. There are problems to be managed. There are issues that can't be ignored. I can't run from basic human needs and argue for spending time with you Father. It would be a fatal oversight if I were indifferent to a sick loved one. A cloudy head has to clear. I have to balance Love of God with Love of Neighbour. Commitment to you is important but not if it is at the expense of the sick or poor.

Father, my desire is for you. I want you so much. I want nothing to disrupt my time with you. Often I sit and pray and find my mind grappling with boring issues. It takes so long to focus on you Big Eye. I want to write my feelings and thoughts. I want so much to love you.

Father, I obey and respect you. You are All-Powerful with a Big Eye to see everything. My desire is to give you as much time as possible.

And at the same time I shall be industrious with my time by fulfilling daily duties towards family. It's a question of switching from one mode of activity to another. There are many hours in a day and everyone has a little bit of time to turn to you Father.

Father, why should I complain? It's my fault that full dedication isn't possible. I'm an unimportant little man similar to an ant busy doing things. I'm just a dot among seven billion other living things moving about across the globe. Only a handful know of my existence. And I don't know how to serve others. So I'm concerned about my role in life. My chances of a call by you Father are slim. The best years of my life are gone. I can't see myself ever becoming a Saint.

Big Eye

Liam dear, don't complain. You had chances in religious life, retail, plastering and farming. You tried a few things but you don't know what you want. Your father compared you to a broken biscuit like a mind in disarray. You haven't changed by not knowing what you want from life. Learn to focus Liam.

Yesterday you spoke about forming Meditation Groups. It is a good idea and you did it before. Do you want to do that again? Oh! I know what you want. You want to be an author and write books.

Liam listen. The reality of your situation is that you are a family man with wife and child. They are your responsibility and are very important to you. I don't expect you to walk away from them and follow me. It wouldn't be fair. They love you but that doesn't say you can't love me too.

Liam, you have many faults so for you to become a saint is unrealistic at the moment. You irritate very easily. Three times in the last fifteen minutes I saw you annoyed over small things like your child asking for a shower. Come on Liam! A phone rang loudly and you didn't like it. A bedroom door was ajar and children talking distracted you. Come on Liam! A Saint is patient with people.

Little Man

Father, please, don't burst my bubble. I want to feel valuable and aspire to holiness. But the reality is different isn't it. I'm not as good as my ego makes myself out to be. You are right holy Father. I've done nothing for anyone. I can't be a saint by doing nothing for people. It's a form of delusion. If I can't love those living under my roof what chance is there of loving, you Big Eye who dwell far away in heaven?

Almighty Father you are right. I'm changeable and fickle like a broken biscuit. I dab into a bit of everything. My father was accurate in his assessment of me. A saint shows extraordinary love for others. I don't qualify. I haven't put the work in with poor people and sick people. I failed the test. God's friends help the broken-hearted. I haven't reached the needy.

Father of Life help. I pray to you for guidance. I try now to reach you directly. I try a different way than the conventional route. I shun everyone and everything in order to contemplate you. I plough away in prayer on my own. I love in my room reading about you and been quiet meditating about you. Over the years contact with family, school friends, work colleagues and brethren in religious life were kept to a minimal. I don't bother anyone and live in peace with all except for those who trespass and violate my solitude. My social life is you Father. You alone make me happy. I love you Big Eye. My walks are times with you. They are precious times. I love calling you in the morning. I pray to you Father, and to the Son and to the Holy Spirit. I love calling your Name. I bypass the whole human race in search of the wonder and awe that surrounds you, my Trinity of Divine Friends. My prayer walks in May are edifying.

Father, private worship is a good thing. Nobody need to know that I say the rosary, or offer a miniature Mass, or meditate on Sacred Scripture while walking on the road. Nobody needs to know that I gaze into the mysteries of eternity in search of my Divine Father and the Throne of Grace. I discreetly go about my business uninterrupted by avoiding poking my nose into anyone else's life.

Father, there is an exception to my private rule of exemption. I love my mother. I also pray for protection and blessings for close relatives. I include those who ask me for prayers. I wouldn't want anything bad to happen to loved ones. In fact, I pray for the spiritual welfare of everyone. I pursue a holy way of life through a single minded attitude. You are the Highest Father. You are the love of my life. Your Holy Name is on my lips.

Father, I hope to achieve in my lifetime my target of unifying my mind and heart to you. That for me would be the greatest and most sublime human act of all. Imagine being of one mind with your Father. Imagine being united with the Holy Spirit. Imagine being of one mind with Jesus Christ. Definitely that would be an achievement worthy of a celebration and eternal life.

Father, I know the commandment to love. But I can't love unless this holiest of virtues is given to me as a gift. I can't give what I don't have. I don't possess the gift of Perfect Love. There are cracks in my spiritual make-up. I'm not perfect. So God's love can't transfer from me to someone else because I never had it in the first place. I have to wait for the gift. Jesus must want me.

Father, I love the way that you are intertwined with your Son Jesus Christ and the Holy Spirit. You are a Divine Trinity united in heart and soul. I beg you to embed me into your Divine Way of Life. I have no other desire and I'm willing to do whatever it takes to fit me with a new suit of Divine Love, Divine Truth, Divine Peace, and Divine Trust. For if I don't have those Sacred Gifts than I have nothing to give to the world. I may as well wither away and die a grumpy old man.

Father, I'm more adamant than ever to find friendship with you. I'm passionate about it. Nobody distorts this holy desire. I place you Father, my Lord and God first in my life. I'm sorry to say and you might think I'm selfish but my firm believe is that you Most High Father come first. Family, friends or anything can't get in the way.

Father, for me I think the best way forward is through isolation. It is in isolated solitude that your Seed Father germinates productively in the eye of the intellect. A quiet environment also allows for proper concentration on what matters most in life. Proper and sincere prayer is never easy if surrounded by restless and noisy souls. Distractions torture the soul that is absorbed in meaningful prayer with Jesus Christ, the Son of Man. Answers to prayers will always come if proceeded by patience and quiet lengthy efforts of spiritual dialogue.

Father, I yearn for the Peace and Truth of Jesus Christ. Nothing is as precious. All the money in the world isn't as valuable. Friendship with the most beautiful woman on earth wouldn't suffice for the Peace of Jesus Christ, for the Truth of Jesus Christ and for the Love of Jesus Christ.

Chapter Two

Big Eye

Liam, I understand you. I understand your dilemma. You gave a chunk of your life to me and another chunk to family life. The blessed way of life is to commit to me. Priests and religious have opportunities to give all. But they often lose their way. They are encumbered by duties and bureaucracy. I desire more than anything the love of a human being. You are doing your best. By retiring from retail work you are more free to love me. However, your personal faults and problems block progress. The lack of fasting and your temper are your main culprits. Progress isn't easy Liam. The lashings on the flesh of my Son are symbolic of killing sins of the flesh. And the crown of thorns on my Son's head is symbolic of killing the sins of the mind. Wear that crown Liam. Feel those lashes Liam. Christ died for you because he loved you.

Liam, for me it is difficult communicating with a troubled soul. I provided many Church Doctors for you to teach the blessed way of life. And you should know by now that the best way to approach me is through the route of simplicity. You can see this quality in children through their enthusiasm and innocence. I like my Saints to be humble, gentle and straightforward with me. Always remember Liam that I am your Father and I like my children to approach me like a child. Adults think they can match me. And they are full of themselves. So Liam approach me on humble knees.

Liam, children flocked around my Son. He had time for them. He blessed them in my Name and he enjoyed their bubbliness and energy for life. Adults are not like that. I receive very little attention from them.

And a lot of them are like fussy Martha worrying about every little thing. I want you to sing and be happy. Come to me. I am your Father.

Liam, you are priceless. You have a wife and child and yet you desire special treatment. You haven't done anything Liam to gain merit. So what you ask is outside your remit. I can't replace Pope Francis or Bishops. They speak for me. It's their task to lead people. I hold Church leaders accountable for teaching the faith. I desire pastoral vibrancy and energy caring for and saving souls. My Spirit must be vibrant in the Church. I see spiritless ceremonies everywhere at the moment. I see unspiritual bodies everywhere walking aimlessly on city streets and country towns. I'm not a happy God looking at the death of my Son in vast numbers of bodies throughout the world, and in your own country in recent years. Pray Liam for vocations. Pray for a new generation of preachers to sprout up among people. I don't want to see the death of my Son in a country who produced Saints and scholars in the past.

Liam, you are not above Pope Francis, bishops, religious, monks and priests. As you say yourself you are my little man on earth. I'll put you in touch with the Son of Man who is on the lookout for loyal servants. The administration of the Eucharist is a top priority. So is preaching my Word. What have you to offer? You can't jump the queue. I fully support your effort to reach me through writing. And I fully appreciate your method in achieving that desire. You want to love me first, and then write to tell everyone to worship me. That's noble and honourable Liam.

Little Man

Holy Father! I don't look for favouritism. I look for something beautiful. It is to adore, love, pray and dialogue with you. I ask for what you desire and that is a commitment to love. I can achieve this desire in solitude and silence. I love long periods of time writing in my room. The habit of writing enriches peace mind. It also contributes to a lifelong dream of achieving a sweet union with you Most High Father. It makes my heart happy thinking about it.

Father, do you see what I planned? I retired from work to give time to you and write. I pushed away distractions so that nothing may be an obstacle. I cleaned out my mouth of trash so that nothing comes between us. The spade work is done. The road is clear. Everything is emptied from my mind.

Father, my gaze is only for you. I look at you. Hopefully you look at me. Big Eye, pour your Word into my empty vessel. Fill the void. Fill the emptiness. Your Word inside me is like a sweet. I love it more than life. It keeps me smiling.

Father, I'm not asking for something extraordinary or attempting to outdo anyone. My motive is not a Cardinals cap. I just want direct prayerful contact so as to give me a chance to tell you about my love for you. I want to sing and smile for you in appreciation for my life. I want to fly like a bird in the sky and chirp sounds of gratitude. For I can't be ungrateful for the egg or gene of my ancestors to have reached this decade through my existence and aliveness. I'm most grateful for my life. Credit is due to my ancestors who struggled and survived generations of hardship and pain to make me what I am today.

Father, I solemnly tell you of my passionate desire to love and obey you. Only a fool would bypass such an opportunity. O Fool would you reject such a Great Love as God. Go on. I dare you to reject God? The whole world has been given this Commandment to love God. It's clearly written. You must love God with all your soul, with all your heart and with all your strength. The power and meaning of this Commandment has to be obeyed and it entails complete dedication. I offer my whole being to that task.

Father, I love you. Your Big Eye sees me. To obey your will isn't too much to ask. You are my Perfect Divine Father. I want to breathe you, feel you and love you. I pray for inclusion in God's family and a high level of love. Only my heart and soul provide that desire. I have no control over another person's devotion.

However, there is one thing I do know. This concentration on heavenly worship makes me happy. This way of thinking makes me happy. I'm nothing without a burning desire for God. Father open my valves and allow the love to flow.

On my death bed I want this warm feeling for my Father to be known. My book is evidence. At the gates of heaven, I'd like Jesus to open my book and find the words where my declaration of love is recorded. I'm nervous at the thought of the day of transition and transformation when my soul flees from earth to heaven for judgement. It could be the most beautiful experience of all particularly if I'm welcomed by my Divine Friends and Body of Saints. I'll scream with delight and say, "O my God".

Big Eye

Liam, I keep my Word. I promised to make my home in anyone who loves me. I do that now with you. I make my home in you because you have welcomed me and keep my Word. I love you Liam. But you have work to do for me. I have used Scribes in the past to write accounts of the Holy Spirit at work among people. You honour me through writing. Preaching and spreading Good News about me, and my Son, and the Holy Spirit through writing is different and unconventional. But it is a good way to alert people to the Truth that I am the Father of every man, woman and child. The important point is that you are authentic and sincere. And I believe you are.

Liam, I give you my full support in your endeavours. I will help you. I'm so enthusiastic about you that I'll buy the brush for you to sweep away the cobwebs, distractions, irritations and worries in your life. I also supply you with the power to stand firm against dangerous demons lurking about to destroy you. The world has nothing to offer and it is your duty to climb the ladder of a blessed way of life.

Liam, don't be busy like a bee when I knock at your door. If you are tied up with worldly worries, I will call someone else. You have a chance Liam to establish your love for me. Drop everything when I call. Make no excuses. Don't hesitate. I'm well aware of your mental deficiencies and fragile ability to turn everything off so as to dialogue with me without disruption.

Liam, I draw up a contract with you and hopefully we can shake hands on it. Write for me. I had great writers in the past that pleased me. I recall King David and St Paul who did much to advance my Presence among Nations. I used St Jerome, St Thomas Aquinas, and St Augustine and a whole body of great Saints. The traditions that you benefit from today come from their rich spiritual minds and their writings. I'm always involved in the journey of humanity as Father and God of the whole of creation.

Liam, I therefore appoint you a writer. If you write well for me, you are a success. I know how dear that is to you. Liam, strengthen your relationship with me. My Truth cannot be flawed by your interpretation. I have serious issues concerning mankind at this present time and for the duration of the next century. Things need to be said. I have you now to write for me. I see you meditating on the road and begging me for a mission. I hear the words of praise on your lips and it is consistent. Even after experiencing demonic thunderstorms I see you bounce back strongly. Your prayer attempts Liam are turning up on my bureau for attention.

Liam, I Am who Am. I'm delighted to find a voice on earth to speak well of me. My Spirit work through people who take note of my Word. I use a spokesman to advise and guide the Church and Governments. The Son of Man has Authority to rule and guide. Liaise with him. He is your King. He is the King of Humanity.

Liam, I hope you are delighted with your contract. There is no rush to start. There is no pressure. The Three of us, Father, Son and Holy Spirit are with you. All that is required to make everything Catholic and official is to continue praying to us on the road and whenever you can. I can filter messages through to your mind through the Holy Spirit and the line of prayer. There are many messages I need posted to all Nations. One major concern for me is that the State in some Nations control individual freedom to opt for me. Another major concern in heaven during the last number of years is the absence of Church representatives in television programmes and debates. So write Liam but only in union with the Three of Us.

Liam, libraries are full of books. So why do you want to write? What is there to add? Some great books have been written about every human experience imaginable. Some have been turned into brilliant films. There have been hundreds of authors who wrote about me and my Son Jesus Christ. I see precious books in libraries covered with cobwebs. So why write another one Liam when the Holy Bible is the best book of all. You could argue that twenty sixteen is a different time with different needs from the start of time at zero, zero, zero, zero. You could also Liam update the world with Heavenly News for me. You could also be on an ego trip. These pray very little and write as if they had authority over my Name or were an equal to me.

Liam, tradition goes on. Today will be history tomorrow. Revelation doesn't stop. The continuation of human life presses on and you must bring a new freshness to it. New revelations can make the hairs on your head stand up. That is if you have any hair as you haven't. So don't be negative Liam. The written Word has a better chance of survival. Oral Words often die minutes' after departure from the lips.

Liam, take small steps and don't be anxious. Keep calm! There is no deadline. Don't rush into mistakes. Your mind is a small feeble little thing but at the same time it is the centre of thinking. The brain is a free intellectual system that processes knowledge that can be virtuous or evil. Liam use your brain to pray and treasure your mind. Think about its function. What is it for? Work Liam but not too hard and avoid forcing issues. I might not like it. The best progression for you is to work with my gifts of Peace, Love and Truth. I demand a high level of commitment and loyalty. And don't forget that not a day passes without trials, blows and tests. I warn you that loyalty comes at a price. People may hate you for preaching my Truth as it could act as a source of disapproval for those who live a lifestyle contrary to my will. Commitment is a big word for me. I question the integrity of flirts. These jump into my love when they feel like it, but often run away for a piece of cake elsewhere. You flirt sometimes.

Little Man

Sacred Father, thank you. Your advice is beautiful. I don't know what words to use in expressing my gratitude to you. I love your Holy Thoughts. No wisdom compares to your training of my soul. Thank you very much. I commit to you. I pray for the grace to remain steadfast. Sacred Authors pinpoint the Truth of your Sacred Word by urging us to commit to a Sacred Commandment. I accept your Decree Father. I understand it. To love you is our first duty. I have a steely attitude about carrying out this order. My mind is unruffled here. I fight tooth and nail to disallow anything that tries to side-track my concentration on you, heavenly Father. What you have pointed out above is adorable news. I'm overjoyed. I'm delighted. I'm thrilled. I feel like a Saint. On the road doing my walking prayer I felt as if the Queen of Peace and a troupe of Saints were beside me.

O Father I love you so much. Thank you for accepting me. Thank you for giving me this chance. I have a noble role. Big Eye you make me happy. Keep your Eye on me for I don't want to err or dishonour the Catholic Church. Sacred writing and preaching Truth always appealed to me. I love the world now through my dialogue with my adorable Father. This is a significant task. This is a substantial dialogue – me a Little Man communicating with Three Divine Beings. I'm absolutely humbled and honoured.

Father this is glorious news. I belong to a Trinity of Divine Friends. This holy realisation is more precious than winning half a million or buying a Mercedes. I'm among a circle of Divine Friends. Straightaway spiritual benefits lift me up. The blessed life becomes a reality. For nobody could stand in between Sacred Friends without being affected by their Holy Sanctity. I feel a surge of Holy Energy bursting through into my heart and moving upwards into my mind. My life has changed forever. The very thought of Divine contact tickles me with a holy joy and excites me beyond reason. I'm enkindled with a fire of love. Faults and sins melt away before my eyes. Thank you Father. I can't believe my luck.

O Father, I can't stop going on about this. Proximity to you is beautiful. I feel an aura of holiness and sacredness while around you. It's a life changing experience. I'm excited and there's a smile on my face as broad as the River Shannon which is the widest river in Ireland. A covenant with you Holy God and Almighty Father benefits more than me. It gives hope to humanity. It gives hope for National and personal renewal. Nothing would please me more than to resurrect belief in Jesus Christ. I write for everyone. It doesn't matter if you are a Muslim, a Christian or a Jew. There is no division in my message. There is no favouritism. I hate no one and love all. Nothing pleases God more than to see children of all Nations on their knees sincerely praying for discernment so as to make right decisions for the future of mankind in every country. I hope to be a Peacemaker. The trickling of graceful thoughts into my mind through my dialogue with you Father should benefit Nations, Cities, Families, Communities, and each individual.

Father I dedicate my life to you. I give you every minute of and am loyal. Even if I have to suffer and die I'll not budge a millimetre. For I have found a way to you who are the Highest and Greatest of all. I'll not waver from my task. The contract is signed and sealed.

Father, my great friend Fr William will be delighted. He was a rare and true friend during formation years. I'm sure you have him with you in heaven. He helped me through a dark period and his spiritual advice was second to none. Fr William thought I'd become a saint late in life. He had great faith in me. I pray to him now as I contemplate my new life as a Sacred Author. I remember his words to me on a postcard, "Give yourself to Jesus Christ". I try Fr William. If I satisfy you Big Eye maybe after the general resurrection, I'd meet Fr William again.

Father, my experiences in Religious Life was fruitful. I enjoyed study and prayer. I learnt a lot and it stood to me to this very day. I searched books for the meaning of sin so as to understand its abstract nature in the way it affects thoughts and actions. I also found religious life restrictive in the sense that I couldn't burst forth and become the flower that was within. I was kept back academically. My full potential was overlooked. My ambitions were hammered everything I tried to advance intellectually and equip myself with thousands of more words to use for writing. But I never stopped loving you Father or praying to you. The blessing of bread and wine meant a lot to me, and it still does to this very day. I wanted union with God. I had high levels of energy and would wilfully have used it to improve the Order. But I wasn't privy to the inner circle. My efforts to influence change was clamped. The men in charge were stuck in a rut and change to renew and refresh was close to impossible. Most Institutions are similar. Bad habits are hard to change.

Father, I'm sorry for my departure from religious life. I disappointed Fr William and those who had faith in me. I did love the chance to live a holy life. St Dominic's ideals of study, prayer and preaching are relevant.

It's just that the Orders vision to use my talents and energy didn't come anywhere near my expectations. I wanted a Degree in Spirituality by studying a Church mystic like St Catherine, or St Theresa of Avila, St John of the Cross.

Father, even though I departed the Order of St Dominic my faith has not wavered. I still love the Order. And I hope on the last day of my life my decision will not be held against me. I look forward to meeting the brethren. And I thoroughly admire great Saints that came through the Order of Preachers.

Father, my departure had nothing to do with you. I love you Father, Son and Holy Spirit. In Spirit and in Truth I acclaim you as my Lord and God. My faith in the Catholic Church is strong. But the Church need a downpour of grace to shake of lethargy and dull liturgy. The Church needs an evangelical revamp to reinvigorate the teaching of Doctrine handed down to us by the Apostles and Fathers of the Church.

Father, I'm happy. I have never stopped searching for you. I did this before I entered religious life, during my time in religious life, and my time after religious life. I have never stopped looking for you. I searched for you in every bone and muscle of my body. I concentrated on finding you in my heart and mind by chewing over your Word whenever possible. I found you, Father in one simple word and that is Abba. I'm very excited at last. I have no trust in psychologists, philosophers, intellectuals, politicians, builders, hotels, females, work colleagues or anyone. I trust one person alone and he is God our Father. I solve all upheavals in my life through prayerful reflection with the best Father that only meek and humble souls can find while living their lives.

Chapter Three

Big Eye

Liam well done. You don't need to apologise. I know the truth. You didn't reject my Son. You love Jesus Christ and your heart warms to the Eucharist. That's good enough for me. We have work to do. I'm not going to let you idle. There's more to life than to contemplate me or Big Eye all day.

Liam, my Sacred Office is in heaven and I communicate from there. You don't see me. But I can communicate with you in the same way as you can talk to someone in America by phone from hundreds of kilometres away. Once you call me Abba in prayer I dialogue with you. All I need is good soil or a good mind and a loving heart. My Word travels through my Son Jesus Christ and my Holy Spirit enlightens you. I travel through an imaginary spiritual line that originates in my Sacred Home and connects to human hearts and intellects that has a friendly welcome for me. You don't have to know anymore. My Holy transmission occurs while you are deep into lengthy prayer. My Sacred infusion deeply satisfies the soul. Fr William pointed out to you that the interior life is everything. So close your eyes, sit still and search for me in the quietness of your stillness. I come to you and make my home in you if you are patient.

Liam, I see you my little man. I love you. I love the whole of creation but I'm particularly proud of the achievements of human beings. Their industrious progress using raw resources to build cities, planes, trains, cars etc. has changed life for everyone. You have come a long way from the very start of life but Liam remind people to show gratitude. Those who do praise me are like precious flowers. But there isn't enough of them in the world. The ratio of people thanking me is one out of every seven as outlined in the story of the seven lepers.

Liam, I call you Saint Liam. I call you because you place all your hope in Christ. You seek Jesus Christ. I admire that Liam. Most people seek what they can get out of you. I'm happy with your progress. What I like now about the new Liam is that if you had nothing you would love me, and if riches came your way you would still love me. I like that. So I appoint you an overseer of others. You can prophesy against Bishops, priests, politicians, and every representative of people if they seek their own profits at the expense of the poor and vulnerable in society. You are in a lovely quiet location little man for prayer and dialogue with me. I watch you closely on your prayer walks and in your study room. You have a nice quiet habitat ideal for meditation. You are lovely Liam. Your mind is lovely. Your heart is sweet. It's about time I took your efforts to love me seriously. You set up a study room to seek Love and truth in your home. You kept Religious Books from the past because you didn't want to forget me. You read my Word and absorb it as well as any man on earth.

Liam, in reward for loyalty and commitment I pump a portion of Sacred Love into your heart because a union has been established between me your Father and you my little creature near the Atlantic Coast of the green isle. Continue Liam extracting juice through Sacred Reading from the Church Doctors.

Liam, my Holy Spirit beams directly into your room as you think. My Presence around you enkindles a fire of love inside you. All you have to do is relax. I repair damaged souls and make them beautiful. I do this for you. I'm well aware of your conscious effort to idolise me. Anyone who senses my Presence should feel happy. You have sensed that inner sweet taste of my Sacred Grace. It makes you feel good. I reward loyalty Liam. You have shown strong determination to stick with me when things go wrong. Whatever crisis comes your way you must be strong. There's great parties in heaven when an errant soul repents and returns home to his Father. I saw this happening with St Paul, St Augustine, Mary Magdalene and the prodigal son. I urge sinners to repent especially those who have done wicked things. Compassion and mercy is there for the contrite of heart. You cut out a lot of past sins Liam. Well done. You are like a dentist uprooting bad teeth. I am your Father and as such my care for you is of paramount importance. I watch you struggle with temper. I see you fall and fall several times a day indulging in eating unnecessary food. I will help you to fast and control your temper. Fight them vices with prayer. Together we will loosen their roots and pull them out.

Liam, I send gifts that may help you with anxiety. This experience is unpleasant. Overeating and temper causes inner turmoil. My gifts to you are Patience and Diligence. The gift of Patience will pave the way for keeping calm when pressurised to lose your temper. And the gift of Diligence will help you to control that little voice in your head that tempts you to overeat. You will need these Liam going forward. I am God your Father and I know what's good for you. This spiritual lesson Liam aims at creating inner calm as opposed to inner turmoil. It's vitally important that you grasp this teaching Liam because many towering waves of anxiety are on the way ready to batter your mind. If you are not ready to face down storms calmly you will drown. Stand solid on the rock.

Liam, proceed calmly. Do not be afraid of death, or storms, or exile, or loss of property. Stand firm with Jesus. Keep your eye on my Son. While Jesus slept during a storm anxiety flooded St Peter's mind. It was a matter of life and death and he didn't cope very well. I remind you of future tribulations. Storms will bash your mind. Corruption will infiltrate the Church but see it as an opportune time to stand firm in faith and love for me and my Son Jesus Christ.

Liam, I have another piece of advice for you. Be careful of those who put pressure on you and don't be too hard on yourself. Too much pressure cause inner turmoil. I am Big Eye and as such I see you doing hundreds of trivial tasks each day. I further observe that no space is allowed between the last task and the next one. And adding on to that I see multiple unimportant tasks pile up on top of each other within your mind. That builds up pressure. You must deal with it. People close to you use you the most. You must manage unfair expectations. An over reliance on one person isn't healthy. All must help and work together. You are caught to do small jobs before you have time to think. To tackle this issue Liam, I give you grace to exercise the virtue of Prudence. This helps you to be ready for unjust demands as well as delegate workloads. This virtue helps prepare for all likelihoods. Use it.

Little Man

Father, thank you for your care of me. It please me so much to have such a brilliant Father. I am anxious and pressurised a lot. Sometimes it is my own fault for not been clever enough. I thank you for the PDP written above. I love you Father as I can't stop thinking about you. You are a true Father to me. I can't see you but I know you dwell in heaven. Nobody has seen heaven. But you see us. You see me. I sense your Presence around me and in me. I never thought for one second that it would be possible for you to be intimate with me. You are powerful in comparison to me a tiny little thing on a green isle.

Father I can't imagine what you look like. Nobody has seen you. You could have human shape and be an old man. But I know that is not true. I think of you as a God of all creation who is eternally beautiful and holy. I think of your holy attributes. But what alarms me are people that know about you and speak about you but at the same time don't know you. Isn't it strange? It's crazy. People speak as if you are their great friend. They live a lie. They don't know you as an intimate Father. They are way of the mark if they think they are on personal terms with you. Words coming out of mouths is learnt knowledge.

Father, I'm aware of the gap between preaching and living the Word. To understand a word, I have to extract the juice from it. Otherwise words are shallow and meaningless. I could say I love Jesus but at the same time be unable to express it. Father you gave me a gift of Prudence. But I may be unable to use it. I'm like a child with a new toy unable to play with it. I pray hard Father. I want to enjoy my present. Prudence is a good choice. It's more precious than I realised at first. I had misgivings about it. But I now understand my holy present is about treading cautiously and making good decisions.

Father, thank you once more. Prudence has helped me make the best decision of my life and that is to accept the mark of the cross on my forehead. I declare myself to belong to Jesus Christ. I prudently dig deep into the sense of a word. In the praying about the Present of Prudence I have caught myself performing a whole string of imprudent actions. I unlock doors, dress beds, make cups of tea, fetch keys, close gates, light fires, cook dinners, wash up, fetch phones, etc. My point is that these ordinary little things take up time and drag me away from you Father. Little things cut in on my times of dialogue with you.

Father, I contemplate day and night. I wake early and call you straightaway. I try to rise above stress, worry and pressure. I see these things as the enemy of the human being. I see it in the faces of people and my heart goes out to them. They have lost their religion and are very poor spiritually.

Father, even though thousands upon thousands have lost their faith my belief grew stronger. Spiritual walks have a new dimension. A cohort from heaven join me on the road. While praying I feel a glorious Jesus Christ, and his Wonderful Mother with a body of high powered Saints flank me on my holy walks. My love has intensified. I adore my Catholic faith due to having a Sacred Father and a Sacred Mother caring for me. The Catholic Church is beautifully and spiritually rich. I honour a Wonderful Woman full of grace. My heart throbs with excitement thinking of the glorious moment of joy when my Blessed Mother and her Divine Son received Coronation Crowns as Queen and King in heaven. There arrival on that day must have been a scene of unbelievable beauty. I can only imagine the joy you felt Father at the arrival of Christ returning home after his mission on earth to save souls. I can see angels with trumpets line up to welcome home Jesus Christ. It was a new dawn. It was an unprecedented human experience. Your joy Father must have been indescribable when you met with your Sacred Son and his Holy Mother while being escorted to the Throne of Grace to receive their seats as Queen and King of heaven and earth. It was an exceptional step forward for human life as the possibility of heaven opened to mankind for the very first time. So I tell you little men and women around the world to honour and respect your King and Queen.

They hold the Golden Key to unlock the door of heaven for each one of us on the basis of spiritual leadership and simplicity of sincere worship.

Father, I'm delighted not only to have you but I have a Mother too. Your Son Jesus Christ was remarkable in establishing the role of a Woman, the role of a Female, and the role of a Mother in the heart of my religion and Catholic faith. I feel doubly secure by this fact of faith. My Sacred Mother Mary pray for me.

Father, I dislike reminding you of the sad moment when Jesus your Son was alive but doing on the Cross. Even though he was weak, and in fierce pain he cared for his Mother and St John. Jesus in agony said to St John, "Behold your Mother. And he said to his Mother, "Woman behold your son". Father, fit me with St John's shoes. I want Mary to be my Mother. I thank my mother Mary and my father Edward, and their grandparents, and great grandparents for the gift of life and Catholic faith. They claimed me for Christ through the gift of baptism when I was unable to choose. Now I can decide and my decision is to adopt Mary as my Spiritual Mother. My future as a Christian should be secure if I address and pray to my God Father and God Mother as much as possible every day.

Father, I hold my head high and worry about nothing. I smile and walk tall. I have a Super Father and Mother. By constantly calling the Mother of God we stamp on Satan's head every time he attempts to smother me with misery and depression. I love life. It's wonderfully beautiful. Birds tweet and are happy. I sing a psalm.

Father, sometimes I can't see the red mist coming. Yesterday a pile up of traffic, and slow drivers at roundabouts allowed a red mist envelope me. On top of that a couple of irritating spirits ran amok in the car. My gift of patience failed as the red mist thickened. I became very irritated and restless when a spirit that dislikes me challenged my authority. It is in these type of situations that I need a good mother to protect me. But I didn't call her. Holy Mary, Mother of God, pray for me. I find myself annoyed when I don't call you Father, or call you Holy Mary, or call you Jesus Christ when confronted with bad spirits that snap the head of you over something very small like opening or closing a car window. A sharp snappy bite from a demon isn't nice. The damage could take a few hours or longer to heal.

Father, what hurts you most? Hypocrites! These look good on the outside but are rotten internally. Unholy Intellectuals! These are eloquent with knowledge but lack intimacy with you. Filthy Practises! These live like dirty animals and never say a prayer. Fat Cats! These live for money and are so full of stealth that expensive Enquiries add to the woes due to greedy astronomical legal costs. Rejection! These simply don't want you Father and have lost their faith.

Father, true worshippers are rare. I haven't come across anyone. I haven't seen a Saint. In fact, I am inclined to think that everyone is a stranger because nobody knows what goes on in the mind and heart of another person. Nobody completely adores you Father.

Father, why is the human being so hard-hearted? You have an Almighty Big Eye and are All-Powerful. Your intelligence is second to none. I can't see behind me and am limited in seeing what's in front of me. But your All-Powerful gaze sees all in an instant. You see the citizens of North Korea. You view the happenings of New York. You observe Dublin City. Nothing escapes Big Eye. You see in detail every human act. The actions of each individual is known despite the fact that over seventy thousand people attend music gigs or sport events.

Father, I feel privileged that you watch me. I hide nothing. You see every thought. You are in tune with every feeling. You notice every stir. I'd expect a good Father to supervise a son and lead him to spiritual stardom. I'd like the Eye of my Father to see me as a little Lamb. Shepherd me Father. Watch me Father. I'm a Baby Lamb dependent on you. Your beautiful Eye is sensational as rays of glorious light beam through a hole in the clouds. I think you have something to do with the sun. Your beautiful brightness lit me up. I was thrilled with the sight and my spirit lifted. The sun sort of danced and shone straight into my heart. I think you were there Father. I think eternity has something to do with the sun.

Father, I feel privileged that your Eye shepherds me like a swan caring for cygnets. I'm safe under your care. You have a beautiful Eye. I see nothing but beauty in that Eye. There is a Sacred sparkle in that glorious Eye. And to think that your Great Eye focus on my home, my room, and my heart is extra special. Nothing substitutes for a Father's love. To feel his love and care is a dream. **Big Eye** is a wonderful description for you Father. I have a great Father. And I have nothing but praise for you. You are the Father of Jesus Christ and your glory is in him. Father this Realisation, this Truth is joyous beyond belief. I smile with joy. The Father's peace blesses me. There is a sparkle in my eye now as a result of knowing my heavenly Dad. I'm safe in the arms of my Father. My happiness has moved up a level. I'm completely at ease with the Greatest and Highest of All.

Father, a work colleague said girls are easily pleased. Her observation was interesting. She commented on a scene of excitement generated by young females receiving attention from guys. Well Lord, I'm easily pleased. I feel excited by calling you Father. It generates joy in my intellect. It swells love in my heart. You buzz about my head and body like a soldier bee ready to sting evil intruders. I love you and you make me feel a billion dollars.

Father, I'm further blown away by your Holy Word. The Truth enwraps me with rapture. A holy bliss rains through my senses while reading or hearing the Sacred Gospel. Your Son is a Master Teacher. Christ is a gem with a Golden Mouth. I could sit at his feet and listen to him all day long. No Teacher is his equal. His Wisdom and Truth is beyond compare. St Thomas Aquinas urged me to stay close to Christ if I want security. It was Christ who first told us to call you Father and I feed on this Truth.

Father, I struggled onto the straight path wounded and in pain. I have had my years of desert desolation until I came to the Well of Life. There I met Jesus. There I drank Jesus. The fresh water reenergised me. Grace bubbled up inside me. Jesus wonderfully refreshed me. I met Truth. He knew everything about me. I had a Divine experience. The brightest spark imaginable lit up in my mind.

Big Eye

Liam, you have written very well about me. Keep it up. I'm happy with your choice to choose spiritual things and desire a link with heaven. You humbly desire me. I'm glad you stopped wandering around the world by returning to me your Father. Be a model for the faithful and serve in my kingdom. Align yourself to the Catholic Church. Go to the Altar. Feed on the Body and Blood of my Son. Absorb his Glorious Word. I'm at work in the Church. My Divine Life is offered to you in my Word and Eucharist. My Divine Way is found by my Little Lambs who rise from their sleep and make their way to be fed in my house on Sunday mornings. My Divine Truth is sown in your soul by my Word. It please me immensely to see you in Church. My Son is lonely. Only a handful pop in during the day for prayer.

Liam, I regard you a great friend because you write about my Divine Truth. You have stepped up to the plate. You pray at my Sacred Altar. My Son is there all the time. I'm glad you chose Truth. You are now on my side of True Life with my Son Jesus, my Mother Holy Mary and all the Angels and Saints. Your name is inscribed as a member in my Kingdom. By doing this you abandoned filthy practises, evil living, and bad example. You stepped away from lies, hatred, and rebellion.

Liam, I appointed the Son of Man to a special role over mankind. My Christ has responsibility for past, present and future human beings. He will be in touch with you for heaven needs men and women like you. You have proven without doubt that you belong to me. Welcome Liam. You share now in Divine Life with Angels and Saints. And I have something else too. My Queen of Peace agrees to mother you in same way as I Father you.

Liam, I notice you reading a piece from St Thomas Aquinas regarding the way to reach true life. Listen to him. He is right. He advises you to stay close to my Son Jesus. This is highly recommended for all aspirants who want my Son. Jesus is the Way so walk straight Liam and don't veer off on to any other road under any circumstances. There are hundreds of tempting diversions. Don't go down them. You heard a voice in your head yesterday evening tempting you to stop for a treat in the shop. You spotted it and kept going. Well done.

Liam, read St John's Gospel. It's wonderful. He wrote beautifully. His love for my Son shone through his book. St John points to the Way of Life. My Word is Spirit and Life. Eat these words Liam. Drink them every day. The secret is to keep my Word. St John passed on that Word and it has stood the test of time. It has survived every generation and influenced millions. If my Word is in you my Spirit will be in you too. To keep my Word is to store it in the interior bedroom of your heart. The application of your intellect is huge Liam. Idlers don't want the bother of doing anything with my Word. Disinterested souls don't do anything with it either. But from you I want a response. Carry my Word around with you. You have to be a Word Carrier. You must be a Golden Egg carrier. Don't forget St John had Christ in his heart and he laid a multitude of Golden Gospel Eggs. So keep my Word Liam. Store them in your mind. My Holy Spirit wouldn't let his Word die. Instead he will enkindle every little Golden Egg into a bright continuous flame of spiritual growth. It's best Liam that your lamp is lit and shining bright for the world to see. Life is about spiritual quality. By your book Liam you might revive interest in a classic period of Green Isle history where Saints and Scholars blessed not only your own people and land but influenced the whole of Europe.

Liam, you remind me of St John. He was truly Jesus' friend. He is the Apostle of Love. You see for yourself intense love in his writing. You will love him Liam. Pray to him. St John has a unique relationship with Mary. He was with her at the moment a cruel lance pierced Jesus's side as he hung on the cross dying. Their anguish of mind exceeded bodily pain. Even as my Christ weakened he spoke in concern for his Beloved Mother and beloved St John. He ordered them to look after each other as mother and son.

Little Man

Sweet Lord above! This is too much for me. My brain will blow up with uncontrollable delight. Excitement levels have rocketed. This can't be happening to me. I'm encouraged to love St John – the Apostle of Love. O my God. Big Eye thank you. I'm on the straight path that leads to union with the Mother of Christ and the most loveable Apostle of all. Wonderful news! I cherish Holy Companions and none can be as close to you Father as Holy Mary and Saint John the Apostle.

Father, I'm blown apart but at the same time I'm humble enough to acknowledge my unworthiness. Battles have to be overcome every day. Trials approach like waves and are incessant. Father, I'm sorry for past sins and recent sins, and for sins that hurt your Son Jesus. I repent of evil actions that me as a man committed. I challenge myself to fight every trace of evil found stuck inside my intellect and flesh. I reject the Tempter. I don't want you Satan. Go away Devil. Get out of my home. Go away from our world. The greater the bloodshed the louder you laugh. No one can change you. You are an evil beast. You give mankind a bad name. You are at work corrupting religion and politics. Satan you are evil. You work every day to destroy human life. You instigate wicked acts. I have rejected you Satan. The world would be better off without you. Scram.

Father, I'm not a fool. The battle to shake off sin in the body and soul starts with me. I have no interest anymore in carnal actions. I aim for heaven. Pleasures of the flesh mean nothing to me. But I beg for past fleshly acts to be forgiven. I beg for mercy and compassion. My interest is Divine Truth. Fleshly pleasure drags a quarter of humanity into bed. It's a temporary source of happiness and is much different than eternal love that comes from loving you Big Eye.

Father, I must confess a major sin that has tormented me for years. It's deadly. It's anger Father. I'm afraid of it. I'm not proud of it. It is tied up with arrogance. I can't tolerate people who wrong me and irritate me. I've had huge outbursts of anger over the years. I blew a fuse with a little dictator who objected to me going for a walk. I blew up when quizzed over a robbery involving trusted friends. I see red when children irritate me by messing.

Father I wonder if you are wise in choosing me. I'm damaged and not good soil. I have physical ailments. I'm spiritually poor. I am cranky and tired. Please forgive me. You are a Great Father but I am a restless child. I rely on your Power to fix my mental and physical broken parts. As I am you could not possibly send me on a mission to preach like Ezekiel. But I have faith. You created me, therefore I believe you can recreate, refresh or renew me.

Father, I feel magnificent due to your acceptance of me an unworthy and damaged soul. Your healing hands can restore my self-worth. Your holy touch renews my evaluation of myself. For I was tarnished by the hands of a bad man and an evil predator.

Father, I write to express my love for you before my expiry date. The work is the dream of my life. I don't want faults to dominate. What I hope to achieve is to pass a message to everyone that there is a Father there for you no matter how sick you are, or how sinful you are, or what shortcomings you feel you have. I feel accepted by my Father even though I'm academically weak and had a virtuous blackout while a young man.

Big Eye

Liam, shut it! You wallow in self-pity. Stop feeling sorry for yourself and don't question me. I choose whom I desire. We have an agreement. Honour it. I forgive sins and don't hold them against you. So stop looking at the ground and hold your head high. You belong to me. You belong to Christ Jesus. So snap out of your cloudy, moody sadness. Trust your Father. I'm God. Stand up. Stand tall and show me you are a man of courage and let nothing get you down. I expect strong conviction from you. But what I see at times is a sheep-like man who lack courage and give in to temptation after temptation through a lack of incaution and unpreparedness. An alert holy man would be always ready for imminent temptations. In the last twelve hours you failed miserably to apply my gifts of Patience and Diligence by succumbing to three temptations.

Liam, you have to trust me. It's pointless moving forward one millimetre more if you mistrust or doubt me. You don't trust anyone. You have been hurt and let down by many. But I am your Father. I am different. You have to trust me. I don't give you a scorpion for a piece of bread. I don't trip you up when you do well. Because you are sheepish Satan slips into your mind and dismantles my gifts of Patience, Diligence and Prudence. Imminent temptations run riot in your head unless you trust me. It's impossible to fight Satan on your own. You can't successfully work for me if there isn't an unshakable bond between me your Father and you my Christian son. So Liam have strong faith in me. Without it you will be eaten alive by vermin as they feed on dead souls. I have faith in you Liam but yours is not solid all the time.

Liam I advised you to stay close to Christ. He gave all to me. He was obedient. He never wavered. My Christ is Truth. That fact is an inbuilt charisma that appeals to all except for those who side with evil doers. And above all Liam faith in my Son Jesus Christ is an irrevocable commandment.

Liam, there is not too much wrong with what you do. You qualify to be part of my team. You are well versed in Scripture. You are familiar with Church Fathers and Traditions of the Church. These things stand to you. I propose you stay close to Jesus Christ and all will be well. There is a slight concern of drifting in and out of consciousness. Your mind is vulnerable to attacks if you don't keep me in sight all the time. You are also allowing yourself to be carried along by the prospect of worldly prosperity. Liam I tell you solemnly purify your motives in regard to me before it is too late.

Little Man

Father, I long to stay close to Jesus. I'd jump into pages of the Gospel this minute if I thought I could accompany Jesus in his journeys around Israel. I could be Mary listening to Jesus at his feet. I could be one of the two disciples walking with Jesus along the road. I could be Peter in the boat on the night of the storm. I could be Zacchaeus in the tree. I could be St Dominic at the foot of the cross. I could be the prodigal son returning to his Father. Gospel scenes bring Jesus alive. I want that aliveness. I place myself in the shoes of St John in the scene of the transfiguration. Father, help me understand Divine Truth.

Father, I tell you my story too. Things hurt me in the Church. There were a few reasons. We went through a dark damaging time when media circles exposed a can of worms that damaged trust in priests. The truth came out. Paedophiles rocked the Church and sent scandalous shockwaves reverberating through every household. There were a few bad and unholy priests who pleasured themselves on children. Their actions caused enormous damage. Satan had a field day as he laughed at the destruction of fallen priests as well as the decline in Church worship caused by scandals. Weak priests capitulated to Satan.

Father, it was awful. Priests working with children became suspicious. Priests didn't trust each other. No one was trusted with a child anymore. I found the experience draining and sad that priests' friendship with little children was damaged beyond repair. The awful experience was mentally destructive too. Priests working with altar servers were observed. Unexpected checks were made. I couldn't be happy with that. The priest/child environment changed. I wasn't happy. I loved children and had time for them. They came to see me a lot. I loved their enthusiasm and energy for life. Clerical paedophilia ended it.

The Media took the high moral ground and applause. Politicians weren't far behind. All I can say is God help the country if Politicians and Media groups judge the Church and act instead of religious in their relations with you, God our Father. Some don't believe in you Father.

Father, I love children and never harmed them. I loved them and blessed them. I had time for them and would never turn them away, or allow anyone else turn them away. I gave a huge amount of my time to children and gave them a good time. I'm proud of my record.

Father, I was unhappy with aspects of religious life too. Community leaders didn't take seriously my talents. I wasn't in religion for a good time. I was in it to work in the vineyard and evangelise the Gospel of Jesus Christ. No one listened to me. No one took my commitment seriously. No one took my life seriously. No one took community meetings seriously. I didn't feel part of the hierarchy in Religious Life. I was a liturgical priest useful for Mass and confession. My average academic background kept me back.

Father, I loved Religious Life though. There were fine men in the Order. But they didn't have much time for me. The experience was like everything else in life with high points and low points. Mass, prayer and study were my strong points. St Dominic's ideals to pray, to study, and to preach are equal to the motto of any Religious Order. And more than anything Father, I loved the word Veritas. The search for Truth is dear to me. The Dominican branch of the Church is rich in spirituality. I highly recommend it. However, each religious priest or brother should be accountable. They must work hard to preach Jesus and save souls who found excuses to abandon the Church of Christ.

Chapter Four

Big Eye

Liam, you are at it again reflecting over your life. I don't want to know the past. It's gone. Today is new. The present day is what matters. In fact, this very minute is what's important. Dialogue will be monotonous if you keep referring to past years. It's obvious Liam that you carry unnecessary baggage in dialogue sessions with me. Your mind has garbage and its spilling into your writing. I don't want it. I am Holiness Personified. It is enough to condemn filthy practises like paedophilia and move on. Keep it out of your writing. Satan has no platform in my vocabulary. I want nothing to do with that Bad Spirit. My focus is to hear from those who give their lives to me and spread the Gospel of Jesus Christ. There is no doubt that the Church is vulnerable and weak. Storms often batter it. But a Soldier of Truth always emerges. I have never been short of a Saint to save the Church founded by my Queen of Purity and King of Love. My hope Liam is that you will work for Jesus Christ. You need a thick skin. You need to stick at it no matter how many times you fall each day. I'll train you to rise up every time you are tripped by the forces of evil. I am Good News Liam. I am Truth.

Liam, start fresh again. Pray to me your Father. I hold nothing against you. Your effort to repent has been approved. I'm happy with you. So jump for joy. My statement of approval is very significant. Your long search for me deserves merit. I am God and my calling of you Liam signifies that you belong to the Holy Family of Jesus Christ. There is no need for you to worry or be stressed by my call. I'm aware of your apprehension and fear worrying about your ability and worth to fight for souls around the world. I'm there to help you. Just trust Jesus. My Great Son outfoxed Satan. He gave you a Way. Satan hates pain and he wouldn't go near you if you suffer for me. My Jesus Christ is there for you Liam. You will love him. He looks deep into the eye. And you must stare deep at Truth Itself. Intense prayer will find him. Together we make our home in you. You are on a mission to conquer first of all your own internal conflicts before bringing the battle to the whole world. Your new Friend Jesus is Master General. He provides you with tips to overcome evil. He quells waves of evil that threaten to break-up your committed mind to work for my Kingdom.

Liam, I propose a challenge. Frequent your Meditation Shed. Sit straight and still. Close your eyes. Join hands. Now this is important. Call Jesus' Name. Always call Him. Call and wait. He may not come straightaway. He could come on the first watch, or the second watch, or the third watch. The important thing is that you are ready when he comes. That is the Way to have Jesus with you and in you. Pray regularly and quietly and my guarantee is that you will find it wonderfully refreshing and peaceful. Jesus will not turn away a potential spiritual friend. He has a Sacred Mind and Heart. You will be fascinated by him. Keep calling him. Wait for his knock. Let him in. In front of you, you will see Sacred Eyes staring at your troubled mind and unhappy heart. By the time the prayerful meeting conclude you may find yourself on cloud nine resulting from a Divine experience with me. People would see you tranquil and happy with a graceful lit up holy face.

Little Man

Father, thank you. I do what you tell me. It's obligatory because you are God and me a little man. I'm not properly doing your Will unless I obey you. It's contradictory saying I love you while at the same time do things that displease you.

Father, I'm afraid of not been able to please you. You are Divine and I am human. I can try though. I'll practise sitting still in a quiet place and invite Jesus to call. My hope is that Jesus will come to my home. He did visit homes in the Holy Land. I'd be honoured if he visited me. I'd give him my chair and welcome him. I'd give Christ my best chair while I sit listening at his feet. I cherish his Masterful Presence and beautiful Words. The Master is unique. Nobody is like him. His Word makes a lasting impression. A taste of this Holy Man makes me long for more of him.

Father I thank you for this directive to sit still. I feel blessed. Quiet prayer opens the door to the Lord. I'm honoured with his visit. I can't believe my luck. It's possible to spiritually experience Jesus Christ.

Oh dear! I'm not clever. The penny dropped. I'm on a par with two sisters named Martha and Mary whom Jesus visits. O dear! O dear. I can't fuss about the way the house is looking or as to who will do the serving. I can't complain. A Great Guest calls. I must stop fussing and attend to my Guest. He is God's Doctor who came into the world to save the lost and sinners. It's not the time to worry about a cobweb on the wall. Instead sit still to listen to our Great Guest.

Father, you are wonderful. I'm grateful that you gave me the ability to praise you. Nothing matters as much as praising you. I sit now like Mary at your Son's feet. I'm ready to change my life. Nothing compares with your intelligence and Truth. I'm sick of dishonest rogues. They grab quick money and vanish. It would take a mighty mood swing now for me to trust people again after been tricked many times by rogue dealers.

Sorry Father. I was side-tracked by a wrong done to me. The hurt of dishonesty lingers in my soul. I lost consciousness of you Jesus. I'm very sorry. I'm not on a par with Mary. It appears more like a double bogey. My mentality changed from being a good contemplative to deep sadness over a bad job done on my driveway.

Father, I regret taking my eye of you. My mind is like a balloon full of worries. I couldn't burst them. I acted like Martha plagued with a mentality incapable of enjoying my Master's visit. I worry about so many things whereas only one is needed. I have sick in-laws, an unwell wife, a dead uncle, a sick mother and an ill friend. And on top of that pile are files of domestic woes. So how can I concentrate on you Jesus?

Father, I refocus again. I'm sorry for the invite and then fail to love you while you visit my home. I love your mind Jesus. Grant me gifts Lord to understand you. Help me discern the better part. Teach me to entertain my visitor and shrug off distractions. Jesus deserves High King status. Train my mind to watch Jesus in the same way as a hurler has to keep his eye on the sliothar. Learn from Mary. Sit and listen at the Master's feet. Watch myself. Watch my intellect. Mental discrepancies can't ruin good intentions. Contemplate Jesus Christ. He likes a secure and loving home. I can't flip in and out of passionate listening. I can't slip off into another room to check something while the Master is somewhere else in the house. Such actions wouldn't please the Master. Practise consciousness. Practise awareness. Jesus sits on a chair. I sit on another chair. I'm sure Christ will occupy the chair. Pick the theme of the dialogue. Pray the theme of the dialogue. I train myself to concentrate and converse with Jesus.

Father, I love you. I go through events of each day and try my best to choose the better part. I reflect on Martha and Mary in order to analyse which sister is more like me at this point in time. I'm Martha at times when been fussy. Worry, agitation and anxiety are detrimental to peace of mind. Mental irritation and physical restlessness harm quality conversations. I say to myself, run little man, run to a quiet place and run from barking dogs. To choose the better part helps to quell storms. I tell myself to listen to Jesus. This helps to release pressure. There is nothing like a quiet time with Jesus.

Father, give me the gift of following through on my own words. I see an image of Mary sitting at the feet of your Son listening to him speak. I imprint this lovely image in my mind. As soon as Mary moves I jump in to replace her. This can be my way of being with Jesus. This practise is one of the first things to learn. I instruct my soul to approach Jesus with a single-minded love and with the highest respect due to his Divine Nature. Otherwise to enjoy his company could be difficult.

Father, I sit with Jesus. It's a nice feeling. I feel secure with the Son of Man. O my God, he is the pinnacle of Peace, Truth and Love. Whereas I'm shaking with bucketsful of nervous tensions. Jesus hold my hand. I'm sorry if I jumped into Mary's place. I desire to hear your Word by sitting with you. Your Father has told me to stay close to you. I want to study your Doctrine. And I can only do that by inviting you to my home. And I can't wait for you to walk through my door.

Father, it's a marvellous feeling shutting out everything except you. For I have to identify and control every thought except a thought about you. This is the way to spend time with Jesus. I often feel smothered by the demands of people. It's for that reason I want to go into my room, shut the door and turn to Jesus. If the mind has no room for Christ, then there is a major relationship problem.

Father, finding time to concentrate and love you isn't easy at all. I know my desire. I hunger for you. I thirst for you. And at the moment I'm unhappy with what's happening to me. I'm overrun with issue after issue. And it has severe consequences in having quality time with Jesus Christ through prayer and my appearances in Biblical scenes. I want to be with Jesus in the Garden of Gethsemane. I want to be with Jesus out in the boats. I want to be in Martha and Mary's house when Jesus visits.

Father, the problem with most of us living in the world is that we are busy like bees or industrious like a mound of ants. It's all about work and money. It's all about having a good time and enjoying the luxuries and pleasures of life. All work and little prayer result in physical bodies looking tattered. Human being take stock of your situation. The Spirit of Christ isn't in you if you don't worship and pray. I'm afraid of widespread spiritual poverty spreading across the globe. Human being change. The cows and the birds are happier than you. Human being shame on you. You have abandoned the Master. The little bit of heavenly grace that was in you has dried up.

Father, I urge a return to Christ and prayer. The effect of prayer transmits a nicer look. The difference is similar to the front of a house being refreshed by a coat of paint from a wall that look neglected and unclean. Prayer creates a shine in our appearance whereas grace oozes through the pores of our skin. This lovely feeling emerges in the personalities of those who spend time with Jesus. So I urge all to take Mary's place and sit at the feet of the Lord.

Father, I know this recommendation to pray isn't easy amid commitments like making cups of tea, cooking dinners, lighting fires, dressing beds, washing cups and plates, paying bills, cleaning, shopping, and multiple other little chores that's tasking on energy levels. Self-management of time is crucial if quality time is to be spent with the

Lord. I'd love to be a contemplative. Task irritations drag me away from this holy desire.

Father, I promise to keep trying to attain a high level of intensity in search of your Presence. I promise to knuckle down to prayer and dissolve the lorry load of trash that troubles me every time I approach you. I don't want my relationship with you to be shallow. I speak of a rare opportunity where it is possible for an individual human being to fall in love with the Father of all life, and with the Saviour of the world, Jesus Christ and with the wonderful gift of the Holy Spirit to enkindle a spark of Divine Love within the soul of each person.

Big Eye

Liam, it's never too late to love me. An old man could turn to me as was the case with Nicodemus. And in the course of each day you could drop everything and find refuge in a Church and pray quietly to me. My Churches throughout the world are free of charge. I'm Present in the tabernacle. All is necessary is careful reflection. There are ways to overcome every difficulty. I know it hurts when rogue dealers trick you. But swallow your pride. Money isn't everything. Liam, there are no excuses for you to allow days pass by without turning to me. I'm here to help you overcome problems. Instead of drifting through life and been tossed here and there by strong forceful waves plan a programme. I want some of your time and at the moment pressures from others have squeezed me out. That isn't good enough. Your spiritual reading has stopped. Your walks down road L0909 has stopped too.

Liam, you have a beautiful shed suitable for contemplation in your garden. Nothing stops you from praying quietly in that place. My Son Jesus waits for you. He wants you to go away from the hustle and bustle of life. You are a fool if you don't create space for my Son Jesus. The Prayer Shed is ideal for Christ to enter and be with you. Little Man spend time there. I'll send my Son to you to calm your battered brain and prevent amnesia from remembering me. I love you Liam. But I can only point the Way. And there is no other way to heaven except through my Son. I want you to absorb an image of my Son crucified. Your Prayer Shed is wasted. Clean it out. Turn it into a sanctuary for

Prayer. The clutter in your head is caused by the clutter in your shed. I want nothing but an image of my Son, lit candles, and silent prayer. Practise sitting before my Son in silence and read passages of St John's gospel. Do this without fail. Even when you are tempted to give it a miss make it happen. For all your writing Liam is worth nothing if you don't obey and spend time in the company of Divine Love. As soon as you stop praying and you do this quite often I watch as the tide of filthy rubbish flood your soul.

Liam, I tell you solemnly man's word frustrates me. I hear of pledges to love me every day but they are empty promises. Satan pulls at their legs and keeps them in murky waters. The Devil attacks subtly good intentions. It's a voice in the head that chops good thoughts in the soul of the human that frustrates and prevents commitment to Christ. When this occurs there is never a follow through on holy thoughts. I plead with you Liam to be strong. I'd like plenty of prayer. My Son and I, and the Holy Spirit must be in your life. Otherwise temptations and evils will suck the holy way of life out of you. My Divine Hand is there for you. I have it held out for you. But you must latch onto me Liam. I can't bring a demon to heaven. I'll save you and protect you if you are willing to obey me and work. My Love is offered. Don't succumb to beautiful women and the lure of riches in preference to me. If you do, I say adieu.

Little Man

Father, I sincerely thank you for your advice and patience. I regard your piece of dialogue with me invaluable. You know everything Big Eye. Nothing escapes your attention. I'm sorry for doing a runner. I strayed from the straight path and ran down an avenue with two beautiful and highly successful rich women. My mind entertained them. I'm sorry for side-lining you Father. They are no substitute for you. I prefer you Father.

Father, thank you. You help is priceless. I feel like a stray dog looking for a bitch. I'm sorry again. You are a marvellous Master. Please accept my apology. I return to you with my tail between my legs and hope for forgiveness. Hopefully you will accept my apology for indulging in a temptation. I knock for re-admittance into the house of Jesus so as to sit once again at the feet of my Master and learn the art of solitude in the company of my only Love Jesus Christ. I'm back on the chair of stillness and my scars and mistakes wouldn't hold me back.

Father, I'm back in the house. Your Son sees my wounds, he sees my pain, but he is a Good Samaritan and cares for me. I haven't seen an iota of disapproval from his caring glance. Yet my prodigal mind deserved a severe reprimand. There's a lovely atmosphere in the house due to Jesus's Presence. It's beautiful. There's a holy odour coming from Jesus. It's peaceful and quiet. Martha's anxiety has calmed too. She's stopped fussing about. I'm fascinated on the Son of Man in the house. Everything about him is wonderfully unique. The sweetness of his company is magnetic. It draws me to him.

Father, I'm mesmerised. I don't know what to say to him. I don't know what to discuss. He looks at my mind and I'm stunned. O Jesus, I love you. I'm glad to have found you in this house. I'm modest and on my best behaviour. Jesus look at this wounded man. I desire more than anything your gentle touch and for you to hold my hand. I can feel tension drop from my body. O dear Jesus heal me. Mary thank you for sharing Jesus with me. Thank you Martha for opening your door to me. I love this house which is the model for all future convents founded in your Name Jesus.

Father, time spent with you is the Source of Life. I thirst more and more for time with you. It refreshes me like water on a hot day. Contemplation invigorates me through and through. A still presence comes first. Dialogue follows.

Father, prayer is like water between me and you. It's the link between you and us on earth. The more prayer the further and deeper it reaches. A little trickle dries up fast. Prayer often fails to reach you because it lacks persistence and penetration. Prayer is the water that connects the river with the Ocean. Your super Mind is the Ocean Big Eye. And my little mind is the river. If there is a lot of dry weather water levels dry up. If there is little prayer grace dries up.

Father, prayer is an invisible form of communication. I can't see you Father, or see with the eye your Son Jesus or be aware of the Holy Spirit. There isn't a physical body. But prayer is an unbelievable form of communication that brings Divine Life into the very fabric of our substance. The key to the door into Martha and Mary's house is unattainable for those who don't pray. They are locked out.

Father, my heart goes out to dry and poverty stricken souls. There's no spiritual water welling up inside them. Their chances of sitting at Jesus' feet is zero. They will be washed away in a flood. They will bawl and scream for help. But it would be too late to save them. They rejected Jesus while they had breath in them. They passed by houses of prayer and never gave a minute to worship the Body and Blood of Christ. My heart goes out to those that live as if there is no God.

Father, I try to pray. A quiet hour with you helps me more than you. This holy activity highlights the mess in my mind. The recipients of prayer are Divine and that implies Perfection. The tone of voice is noted by Divine Intelligence. Straightaway the Lord picks up the sincerity of the prayer. The beauty of prayer is that it allows a Perfect Mind see into the state of a complicated bag of human contradictions that swing from evil to good, or good to evil at the click of a finger.

Father, it takes great concentration to pray. It's hugely different than talking to another person. And even talking to someone is difficult. The hardest part of prayer is the realisation that at the other end is an Invisible Person. Prayer is about reaching you Father. And access to you is not easy. I can't recall one person seeing you Father, or seeing Jesus, or experiencing the Holy Spirit in the last two thousand years. I have to rely on faith and prayer to be in union with you Almighty Father.

Lord, I'm very grateful for Jesus. He taught his disciples how to pray and in doing that he helped me too. For I'm addressing you as Father for many years. Very few will understand the spirituality of my writing unless they have a grasp of God as a Father. Jesus' prayer gave us the beautiful words that we use by saying, "Our Father". I try to keep my mind on you Father in heaven when I pray. I pray to a Sacred God. Holy is his name. And the beauty of it is that he is Father to all human beings even though a bulk of humanity are lost and don't know their heavenly Father.

Father, you are my God. I adore and worship you. I love you deeply. I pray for good use of my heart and mind so that my prayer is good quality. I don't want to come across as a child complaining and moaning all the time. I'd like my efforts to speak to you Father to be concentrated and continuous. It's all about a genuine connection. My prayer words have to be deep and sincere. They must travel a long distance to heaven. And what happens to most prayers is that they dry up before reaching the Father's ears because there isn't enough water in them to carry them through mazy jungles, fields of weeds and deserts of dry sand. In other words, the soul dries up and fails to make a connection.

Father, to keep a prayer line open to you is the life blood of a soul. Heaven is there. The Father lives there. He is eternally Present. The difficult part is the dumb soul. This has to be activated. Most human minds are asleep to God. People don't understand the head – the part of the body that is above the shoulders. It's a computer in itself. But most of them are turned off. A vast majority of human beings live on their history, and accept their culture and don't think for themselves. These people want to be led and most of the reasons behind this laid back approach to life is laziness.

Father, I pray now. Power hose my brain and wash the dirt out. Clogged up filth has to be powered out of the mind. The beautiful creation of a human mind isn't functional until its recreated and recycled from years of heavy laden and unnecessary human knowledge that blocked up the intellect and senses. I pray for a good mind like a new engine in a car that runs smoothly. And the first task of this new mind is to jump into the arms of my Father and adore him. For it is love that makes life a happy experience. And nobody can give this properly except a Perfect Father and God fits that description.

Father, I know of the problems that prevents perfect union with you. One reason is impatience with myself. Another reason is time. And you are aware of it. It is these type of things that result in failed attempts. Another reason is ignorance. My mind is placing Jesus as a holy and valuable friend. I failed to place Jesus above everyone and everything else. I try to rectify that now. The mentality of Mary in the house comes into play here. She sat and listened to Jesus. My failed attempts and frustrations with prayer are simply due to my reluctance to sit and relax with Jesus Christ, the Son of Man.

Father, I have come to realise pride and dependence on self has blocked my inclusion into your inner circle. I'm on the periphery. I pray to change that. All this writing is about a human life on road L0909 that longs for his Father. I'm desperate for inclusion into the heavenly family. I want to jump out of myself and find new life. I retired from retail work for this reason. I would give up everything for you Jesus. I dislike human life. There are too many sleepless nights, argumentative relationships, stalemate situations, spending errors, and dishonesty. I'm sick of earthly life and long for your love Father. I want you badly and should never have left you.

Father, how do I change? I want hours of meditation and contemplation every day. I want to sit still on my chair in the Prayer Shed and examine my conscience so as to find out what faces me. I know that in the course of praying issues bubble up and these are to be used to address spiritual growth. It's one of the beautiful facets of prayer that we learn to know ourselves.

Father, I regard prayer a treasure. Its greatest asset is a struggle to unify oneself with you Lord Jesus. And as mentioned above prayer goes after hidden problems and sins in the soul and sends then sizzling to the top of the mind for attention and amendment. Prayer therefore contributes enormously to perfection. Prayer clears the mind and dark clouds of imperfection are replaced by a flow of grace that enriches the life of a person.

Chapter Five

Big Eye

Liam well done. Your writing is sincere and improving all the time. I like your ideas and you are making good use of words. Don't mind the literary sharks that criticise your style. I like your dialogue with me. It's lovely. And it is great to find a soul on earth that has me the focus of his reason to live. I like your ideas. You have offered your mind to me. I'll turn it into good soil where my Word will grow in you. I have a batch of Golden Eggs to plant in your soul. I'm very impressed with you. I'm convinced you have eliminated everyone and everything so as to free yourself up to love me. Thank you very much.

Liam, I'm going to change your focus a little bit. Instead of looking up into the sky and calling me by Name or calling me Father I advise you to live as if you are in the scenes of the Gospel and focus particularly on my Son's crucifixion. House scenes should be of particular interest to you. I want you to think and feel as if you were there on the day of the scene. I solemnly tell you that is what St Thomas Aquinas understands by his advice to stay with Jesus. I'll give you an example in Luke's Gospel of the day a Pharisee invited Jesus to a meal in his house. As Jesus sat at table a woman with a bad name in the town entered the house and I want you to notice the treatment my Son received from both the Pharisee and the sinful woman. My Son was impressed with the tears of the sinful woman as she washed his feet with tears, dried them with her hair and covered his feet with kisses and anointed them. The bad woman's love was greater than the little love and inattention the Pharisee offered his guest. Liam think of yourself at the table with

Jesus on that day. What had you to offer? What amount of love could you give my Son?

Liam, love me. Liam you can find your way to me through the crucifix. It is never too late to bathe my Son's feet and dry them. It's never too late to cover them with kisses. It's never too late to weep for the hurt and pain caused to my Son through the nails that were driven through his feet. You see now what I mean by placing yourself in the scenes involving my Beloved Son. The Pharisee was worse and lower down in my estimation because of his hate and rejection of sinners represented by the woman who had a bad name in the town.

Liam, it is through the Body and Blood of my Son that the Way is shown and the Truth is found and the Life becomes a reality. Then savour my Son on the cross. Ignore him at your peril. The crucifix is stuck in the ground at Calvary for every human being of all ages to find salvation for his/her soul. You are saved by the love you show for my Son.

Liam, I didn't like sacrificing my Son. I didn't like the plan. It broke my heart. The thought of looking at my only Son humiliated was hard to take. I allowed it to happen for you, and for every human being living and for future generations of peoples on earth. I emphasise emphatically the importance of this love. I solemnly proclaim and advocate worship of Jesus Christ. The Catholic Church are custodians for the evangelisation of this love throughout the world. Priests celebrate this love every day at the altar by consecrating bread and wine. The mind and heart of each person at Mass recognises the Body and Blood of Christ in the breaking of bread and blessing of wine. It doesn't matter how many attend Mass. It's not a crowd game. It's about been stitched to Jesus Christ. Human life needs me. I grab souls for heaven through the Crucifixion.

Liam, I ask for renewal all the time. I call people to prayer. I want to refresh human minds with my love and crucifixion of my Son. People must understand the Eucharist. Children's faith must be nourished. Adults must believe in my Son's Presence in Holy Communion. There's a massive weakness in the Doctrine of Faith regarding the intake of my Son's Body and Blood. Priests must refresh the faithful and urge a holy reverence for my Son. There are two types of infiltration that can effect a mind. My preference is that each soul allows Christ through into the core of every cell in all human bodies. The trouble and danger for each soul is an infiltration of another sort – an unholy infiltration that weakens considerably loyalty to Christ, my Son.

Liam, Divine Blood was spilt to save you and mankind. I am your God. I'm your Father. And I gave the world a Son of Man - a Divine Person to save you. My Divinity was tangible. There are no excuses anymore. My Divine Son was seen and heard. And there are records of these events in the Gospel.

Liam, I outsmarted Satan. He laughed and thought I had gone crazy when I allowed men to beat and humiliate my only Son as they crucified him to a piece of wood. But that man on that piece of wood saved the world. I have thousands of holy men and women in heaven with me due to them following my Christ. The doors of heaven were opened to followers of Jesus Christ. Therefore, belief in him is the Way, the Truth and the Life. Nobody has a direct line to me. You have to find your Way through the crucifixion, through the Body and Blood of my Son.

Liam, refresh the minds of people in every city, town, village and isolated houses in the countryside that they must obey my commandments and love me. Otherwise consequences for those who have no cross in their homes or outside their homes will indicate to me that the light of Christ or the mark of a Christian isn't written in on their foreheads or emblazoned in their hearts. I wouldn't be happy to see bodies littering the streets or strewn around the hills due to their self-inflicted rejection of my love. I can't Father those who don't want me in their lives. I cannot force a single human being to worship because each person has a human will to make their own decisions.

Liam, if believers of me and my Son respect me they would feel the scourging of my Son as the Roman soldiers lashed his bare back and drew blood. Liam respect is huge in heaven. Compassion is too. I expect good people to feel the pain of my Son when brutal and cruel men made a crown with thorns and pressed it down on my Son's head. The mockery of Jesus highlights evil in men.

Liam, enter the scene of Calvary. My Beloved Son's suffering t doesn't end there. The soldiers forced him to carry a wooden cross up a steep hill so as to crucify him. I felt awfully sad for Jesus. He fell three times.

Liam, was I daft? I did this for you. I allowed it to happen for every human being. I wanted to save people from sin and corruption by showing how much I love you. Liam you must grasp the importance of my Son's suffering and death. Everyday feel the pain of the nails hammered into his hands and legs. A holy man would spend time at the foot of the cross praying and reflecting. And if he can't feel the pain of my Son he is heartless.

Liam, I'm like the sun. My light shines eternally on the whole world. My Big Eye sees all. I glance across the earth and see the movement of all human beings. My advice to each human person no matter who they are, or what religion they are, or whether they believe in anything is to concentrate on worshipping me through belief and love for my Son. I solemnly tell you that I have power over life and death. My Son dies on the cross. But I have power to resurrect. The Messiah that the whole world waited for rose again through my power. All of heaven adore him and he is a spiritual King for all who pray.

Liam, the whole world knows about my Son. His influence is everywhere. Pagans know about him. Muslims know about him. I as God your Father and Jesus as my Divine Son has given the world an example of Love that nobody can match. I recommend that you give him your full attention. You can do this by spending time before the Sacred Host. My Son's Body has been given up for you. Holy Communion is directly linked to Good Friday. Anyone who loves me should receive the Body and Blood of my Son – the same Body and Blood that hung on the cross.

Little Man

Father I love you. Big Eye I'm grateful. I'm delighted with insights revealed above. I concentrate now on love for the Cross in which your Son hung. I'm embarrassed mentioning it to you for fear it might hurt your feelings. It was a horrendous death for a Divine Person who did nothing wrong except side with the poor and sick. I love you Jesus. I meditate on the cross. You did nothing wrong. In fact, you are very courageous and brave. You fought evil in people. You discovered the wickedness that engulf the human being. Evil continues to exist this very day. Acts of despicable horror plague us. I'm shocked Father by depravity. It's a shame that we kill each other. I attach myself to you Father. I want to stay with Jesus. I live for his love. And I want to spread it. I have no hatred for anyone.

Father, thank you for pointing me to Jesus. I appreciate it. I'm inclined to pray to you a lot. I think of you in heaven and call you Father. I said to myself why not contact the boss directly. I used my imagination and travelled billions of miles into space in search of you Father in heaven. But you have redirected me to Christ. You made me realise that it's wrong to bypass the Son of God. I obey. Often my son Luke tells me that he loves me but I reply do what I tell you so. I tell you sincerely Holy Father that contact with a Divine Person is precious and a source of happiness. I'm crazy for heavenly friends. I relish Good News about you Almighty Father whether it comes from yourself or the Holy Spirit or a Saint. I also hold in high regard priests explaining scriptures in sermons. All Good News is welcome.

Father, a strong reason for my interest in you is Truth. I can't imagine a lie ever coming through you, my Trinity of Friends. I know where I stand with you. I receive straight answers from you. And I'm never tricked. I love that about you, my Trinity of Divine Friends. It's what attracts me too you. The opposite is true of people. People are a mixed bag of honesty and lies. I'm annoyed by deceitful people and broken promises. The experience brought a question of trust into my assessment of others. But I can't judge because everyone has a different level of honesty and dishonesty. I look for genuine people who have a good reputation. I like integrity, honesty and sincerity in a person.

Father, human relationships break my heart. It's another reason why I have such a strong love for you. I can't stick frustration, animosity, and defiance. I'm convinced without doubt that nothing bad comes from you. The rich ocean of love that you are Father flow powerfully into the soul that loves you. I can see it coming over mountains and valleys into my heart. It's Perfect Love. I receive no insults from this Love, nor do I receive disappointments. All is positive. All is genuine. That's why I want to cling to you. That's why Father I want you to hold my hand and pull me away when an evil shark swims around my senses. I don't want to be bitten by angry humans who violate my efforts to be peaceful, humble and quiet.

Father, people's experience of life differs. I'm happy in Ireland. I had good Catholic parents. And I have a reasonable amount of freedom to write to you and express my beliefs. I come from a rich tradition of Christian culture. But many died in the past to protect our Catholic faith. I don't like war. I don't like evil. I don't understand why humans kill each other. It's in-house fighting. It's insane. Human weaponry is not aimed at the Moon, or Pluto or anything away from earth. Atomic bombs are aimed at populated cities that are regarded as the enemy. I don't know Father. I can't see the sense in killing people. Maybe it has to do with paganism and irreligion. It might have to do with power and oil too.

Father, I love you. My strong reason for loving you is that you guarantee holiness and safety in heaven. I don't know what causes fighting within the human family. I've seen rows break out over something small like a hairbrush or a displaced cup. I've heard of people being murdered over silly arguments. I've seen families destroyed over land. I've known people to end their lives. I've witnessed alcohol and drug abuse. The reason I believe for all this sadness and evil in the world results from families that don't pray and have lost faith. My father and mother always prayed. And that was the greatest treasure my family handed on to me.

Father, you see all. You see the houses where there is love for you. You notice the houses where no prayer is uttered. I'm so glad my family prayed. I love my family and pray for them every day. Prayer is the greatest gift a father or mother can hand on to a child. Prayer makes a home. The family that prays together has the Spirit of God living with them.

Father, I learnt from my father and mother the importance of prayer. The rosary was recited each evening. All of us attended Church to hear the Word of God and receive the Eucharist. There was regular confession too. By this practise I believe you protected my family from tragedy and harm. For I saw other families who didn't pray ruin their lives with alcohol and had awful tragedy befall them.

Father, I increase my love for you. I have questions to ask you. And I wonder what's in it for me. I devote my time writing to you now. And I sort of know what I want. I'm not looking for the best seats in heaven like the two Apostles requested. All I want is to be loved by you. The world is buzzing with industrious workers going here, there, and everywhere while I sit still and think of you all day long. I like making myself available for you. I'm under the radar in human terms but hopefully you Father can pick up my signal of intent to adore and praise you. I've known for a long time that I've nothing to give unless it's given to me from you.

Father, it's a beautiful thing when a human being gives his life to you. It's the best vocation in the world. Imagine waking up in the morning and turning straightaway to you in prayer. Indeed, it is wonderful. I call you by Name. Straightaway I feel protected. And throughout the whole day I turn my mind to prayer. I call my Sweet Father. I call my delicious Lord. Life is so much better to have my Three Divine Friends beside me because I pray and love them.

Big Eye

Liam, that is mighty sweet of you. You are precious to me. I look out for you and for all who you pray for. I'm in touch with everyone on planet earth that raise their mind and heart to me. It may not be apparent to the individual. And sometimes their desire wane. But I love them and their prayers are invaluable.

Liam, the same applies for any person who is loyal to my Son Jesus. It's worth billions to me. Nothing pleases me more than to see a man or woman on earth on their knees praying to my Son. I encourage you through this writing to tell people that there is no place for hatred within my family. I never inspire anyone to kill. I teach love. And if anyone wants to be a man or woman after my heart they are obliged to love every single human being. I stand firm with a solid mind and rigid stance against evil. I love the poor killer and hope for them to relent from carrying out acts of evil.

Liam, I enjoy conversations with you. You are an interesting man. I could send messages to the world through what you do. It's a good form of communication. A writing dialogue may benefit every individual as well as National leaders throughout the world. I enjoy sincere conversations. I like your mind. It's beautiful watching you grow from nothing. It's beautiful noticing you coming to your senses. It's fascinating watching you figure out in your mind my importance to you. O Liam. I love it. I see all human minds as raw and in need of development. Your mind is beautiful now Liam. You have made it that way. It's because you have worked out a few things and moved to a higher level of performance.

Liam, the significant step you have taken is your rating of me. You regard me now as the Highest and Greatest of All. I Am that and more. I can teach you to respect me more if you enter the scenes of the Gospels where my Son Jesus is active. I'd like to see how you would get on.

Liam, I love you. Your sincerity is beautiful. Your search for me is beautiful. I could keep you waiting for hours and yet you would not lose patience and respect me. No one on earth has done what you have done. You have in some strange way blocked of everyone and everything in order to find me. That makes you different. Others want to enjoy living in the world. And most of them make progress by exploitation. The motto is less work and more money. The margins of profit are too high and unfair to the payee.

Liam, continue what you do. I'm fully aware of you raising your mind to the skies in search of me. I see you on the road pondering my importance. Others are immersed in the world. But your mind has changed. It has dumped the lumps of garbage that held you back. You've picked up all the weeds and stones and dispersed them. You are good soil now. I like it. My Word could grow in you now. But you are not perfect. There are areas that require growth especially right judgement – a gift of the Holy Spirit. I'm sorry to have burst your bubble. But a sense of reality wouldn't do any harm. You are no way near a level required for saintliness. Liam, you lack discipline. I watch your operational judgement regarding discernment. You should not be eating foods with lots of sugar in them. I see you, day after day caving in to this weakness. I've been trying for years to offer you the gift of discipline but you kept pushing it into a dark and dusty corner neutralising it's intellectual capacity in your mind.

Liam, you are making great strides towards holiness and you have improved immensely. But I want more. There is more work to be done on your problems. Your will power is all over the place. And at times I wonder if it working at all because nothing happens. It is like as if it is dormant. This faculty Liam has to be steelier and solid as it a force in the mind that determines what's desired as well as the quality of the desire. I don't like my human being sitting about idly and behaving as if they are dopes. I expect a return from the engine room of the mind that I created. So use it Liam. Determine what you want.

Liam, I offer you a great challenge that will bring you up to the standard of my Doctors in the Church. I love the deep thinking mind of St Thomas Aquinas. He was a member of the Order of Preachers that you loved. This holy man devoted his time to study. And he wrote extremely well.

Liam, listen to me. You write for me. You are not doing it for anyone else. You are not trying to make a name for yourself. You just want to love me. And I will accept your effort. I'm having a look at your lovely mind Liam and in that examination my main objective is to strengthen the functioning of your will power. This faculty can malfunction in people. It can also not function at all. The strength that I look for in you is to keep your mind fixed on me and don't let anyone or anything divert your determination from love of me.

Liam, a fickle and changeable personality is no good. These flirt all over the place with every whim that's going. They say that they love me but something attractive turns up and they are gone. In order to build up mental strength Liam I insert a spiritual steel beam inside you so as to keep your faith solid and strong. The steel beam will help you to resist the lure of pleasure. It will keep you strong to face forthcoming tribulations. This spiritual beam Liam wouldn't melt when faith is tested. Nothing shall break your spirit.

Liam, I love your mind. My intelligence can renew and nurture it's functional ability. With my fingers I caress you. I transmit rays of sparkling grace into the core of your soul. I have to tell you Liam that your mind is underperforming. I'm unhappy with your memory levels.

Liam, I don't mind if you forget quickly billions of words that flow from mouths every day. Words are equilivant to bags of rubbish if spoken without consideration. But my Word cannot be forgotten. So I ask for greater care of my Word Liam. I want you to remember what you hear and read about me. This memory weakness in human beings is on a large scale. My Golden Words should not be forgotten. My Gospel should be embedded in the hearts and minds of my sons and daughters on earth. A child that doesn't listen to his Father is in trouble.

Liam, it's because I love you that the tips of my finger remodel your intellect in such a way your will level will increase your commitment to me as well as increase what you remember from our conversations. I feel disappointed every time my Word is heard and after a short period of time whether it is a minute, an hour, a day, a month or a year is forgotten. It goes to show people are not taking me seriously. I'm happy to make you better. And don't doubt my creative ability. I made you. Therefore, I know every cell in your body. I can touch and heal anyone. If a mechanic can repair the engine of car and make it run better so can I repair the mind of a human being to function to its full potential.

Liam, there are huge increases already in your development to please me and become a proud child of mine. Your holiness levels have increased. That's progress. Your eye is cleaner. There's less filth allowed through the senses. And you have also made rapid progress in the way you react to difficult situations. There is room for more improvement though. There's to be no anger at all. Your voice must not be raised. I can't see you becoming a saint unless morals and virtues are growing. Patience with dry souls and the plight of every human being is part and parcel of the role I allotted to the Son of Man – my Christ. You will have to show the same concern as me and my Son Liam.

Liam, in regard to memory what will help you are my Golden Egg challenges. This activity will help you to focus on my Word that's in the Egg. I'm happy with that. I like the way you pick my Words from the

Office of Readings and cherish them. I expect a better return from my Word. And I'm glad you can remember the message about the Pharisee who showed little love to his guest Jesus whom he invited to his house for a meal.

Liam, pray to my Holy Spirit. The gift of understanding is an essential ingredient in coming to terms with my Word. This gift requires hard word. Once prayer and study are combined insights open up for the soul. I'm glad you comprehended the difference between the little love shown to Jesus by a man who thought he was an upright citizen and a female sinner who felt worthless but showed greater love for Jesus.

Liam, I'm happy to be involved in your book. You give me an opportunity to make you beautiful. And that I will do. You cannot have a better Doctor than me. I make you special. Through our dialogue others might follow me and future generations benefit. I welcome spiritual opportunities to shower grace on souls who turn to me for I am the creator of beautiful personalities and all beautiful things that grace earth and heaven.

Liam, I'm here for you. Don't be upset about anything. Climb up the ladder towards me. The higher you go the better. Each step is a rung closer to heaven. Shake off the mud from earth and rise higher towards clearer and purer air. Let pigs wallow in mud and pooh. You rise up to a high level of sanctity. I wash the dirt from your eyes and ears. My water is pure. My soap cleans inside the soul and all over the body. I don't like my faithful friends feeling dirty for I'm Pure Grace. My Love has the power to clean. I offer jars of sweets to my friends that contain sweet virtues that changes life. Pray Liam for those virtuous sweets. Taste the holy Body and Blood of Christ. Eat my Holy Word. Climb up to Me. I am Holy. I am Tasty. Closeness to me serves as a deterrent. I cull sour sweets from my jar of delicious favourites. I remove bad apples from my orchard of golden delicious. It's best Liam to be on the alert for contamination.

Liam, I have great resources in my Kingdom. Holy sweets are available to those who persist in prayer. I promise to assist every person that desires me. My requirement is crystal clear. Give me your mind and heart.

Little Man

Father, you wrote wonderful stuff. I chuckle with pride in my room. I promise to raise my level of sanctity. Don't worry. I'm delighted internally with your Sacred Touch. The effect of your fingertip close to my body has magnified my personality like a lamp shining brightly. I'm tremendously pleased. I'm humble enough to see myself as a dot. You are awesome Father. Rest assured Father that I'm more than willing to give you my heart and mind. And I'm thrilled to bits to receive Divine help. Good News is positive. I don't have to concentrate on reasons for snappy attitudes. The touch of Big Eye's fingers unhinges my ugly bits. Thanks Father. To be on your side is what I crave.

Father, I pray. Please give me more bread for today. I'm hungry. I'm on the crest of a wave in a flight away from evil. I hide nothing from you Father. You have permission to expose my small faults. I welcome assistance from the Holy Spirt. I embrace Saints assigned to help me through life. It's great that help is available. The greatest task for me is to act wisely in my treatment of others. I'd feel unhappy if anyone carried a grudge against me. I try my best to treat others with respect. I don't like arguing with anyone.

Father, help me. I pray sincerely to you. You may be surprised by my saintly choice for help. I picked a woman. It is St Monica. I like her patience with a temperamental husband and a wayward son, St Augustine. St Monica's care for her son's spiritual well-being and her worry that he could lose his soul struck a chord with me.

Chapter Six

Big Eye

Liam, I like your female choice for spiritual assistance. Some women are great with men. Life is better when someone has belief in you. And I saw this belief in Monica's prayers and tears for her son. Augustine developed his love for me late in life. And his mother died happy known that he had become a faithful Christian. He became a priest, bishop, Saint and Doctor of the Church.

Liam, you are on the right track. I too am very fond of women. They are endowed with affection for their loved ones. I saw Monica chase Augustine across the Mediterranean Sea to pray for his safety and encourage him to follow my Son Jesus. I saw her intense prayer for him. She approached St Ambrose crying her heart out so that her son would commit to Christ.

Liam, these are the mothers I desire on earth. I want mothers who will stay with their children growing up and pray for them. Mothers and fathers are the greatest teachers of faith in me. If all did what St Monica did I would have Saints all over the world. So pray to her Liam. You could not have a better woman in your life. You could not have a better mother Liam. St Monica, helped to make her son Augustine a Doctor of the Church. I urge her now to be your spiritual saint.

Liam, I'm very serious about this piece of dialogue with you. I desire young ladies to model themselves on St Monica. I want prayerful mothers in your country Liam. The art of prayer is dying among men and women across the globe. The future is bleak for the human being if the only space they will give me is on a piece of wood stuck in the ground with my Son hanging on it. So be it. I can't force girls to love me. I expect mothers to teach their children values and a way of life that include a love for me – the One True God.

Liam, St Monica is a gem. Many husbands beat their wives and treated them badly. Patricius her husband was a temperamental man prone to fits of rage. Yet Monica displayed patience with him and influenced him too become a committed Christian. So Liam you have one of the best to help you.

Liam, I will talk to her in a Sacred Room in heaven about her care for your soul. In fact, I'll assemble a spiritual team that includes St Anselm, St Patrick, St Dominic, St Monica, Fr William, St Augustine and Edward your father. All these are assigned to your care in promoting sanctity. It's a joy to have a little man craving and carving out friendship with me.

Little Man

Father, I enjoy you. Big Eye, I thank you! It's a marvellous opportunity. I have a spiritual team working from heaven to keep an eye on me. And I'm exceptionally pleased to have a woman in the calibre of St Monica on board to help me in the same way as she helped her own son to become a saint and Doctor of the Church. I can understand from the example of St Monica the value of a mother's prayer. And I pray now for girls all around the world and in particular for mothers to pray with their children as well as for their children every day. There is an old saying in Ireland that says a family that prays together stays together.

Father, I adore you. I'm very happy with the outcome of this writing. I have a team of saints caring for my soul. It is beautiful news for me. It is superbly reassuring. I not only have Big Eye caring for me now but I have five wonderful saints to guide me on to the path that leads to a holy way of life. I love Catholic Saints and all Popes who came after St Peter. Their lives teach us. Their lives and writings are a history of holiness. This is the beginning of an inner transformation and a growth in holiness.

St Monica is it too soon to call upon your assistance. Pray for me. You are the best mother a man could have. I can unite with your spirit at the altar of God where you wished to be remembered. It is a union and communion made in heaven. I pray for all the little girls who make their First Holy Communion. The Eucharist unites us all to your Son, Holy and Almighty Father. So let us start a crusade Monica to bring families back to the altar. Nothing hurts Jesus Christ as much as when his flock strays and fails to pray. Nothing would please me more as to see families coming out of their beds on Sunday mornings and walking through the doors of the Church to hear God's Word and receive the Body and Blood of Christ. St Monica I'm awfully worried about families. Sanctifying grace has dried up and spiritual poverty has tripled. That is why I love you Monica in the way you prayed for your wandering and wayward son Augustine and brought him back to the Church.

St Monica, I miss the love of Christ myself. I need someone to believe in me and someone holy to embrace me. That is why I choose you St Monica. You converted a temperamental husband and brought a sinful Augustine back to Christ. I need conversion too. I can't compete with your son though. He wrote a classic book called, "The Confession". I erred by leaving the priesthood. I should have stuck it out. The state of the Order should have been different from the love and honour of celebrating the Eucharist for the faithful. I loved the Eucharist. I don't know what came over me. Tell Jesus I love him. Tell him that I'm sorry. I would celebrate Mass again in the morning if allowed by Christ and his Church.

St Monica, I pray to you. I'd like you to mother me. God Our Father has assigned you to help me because of your diligent and persistent daily prayers that saved your own son. I know that by being mothered by you that you will have an eye on me everywhere I go, and not only that but you will be my spiritual director tackling all inklings of corruption whenever they appear in my mind and heart. I know that you will follow me everywhere in order to save me. love you St Monica. You are my new mother. I need a few lessons from you Monica. How are you going to burst my bubble? I'm full of myself. I'm arrogant. I believed in myself that prayer was my strongpoint only to realise at a later stage that my prayer was driven by pride.

St Monica, pray for me as my spiritual mother. Help me to dismantle my problem of pride. Even my natural mother knew of my arrogance. My error is that I think everything depends on me. I'd behave like the Apostle in the boat with Jesus asleep during a storm. I bucketed water out and wore myself out not wanting anyone to help. I work my socks off doing hundreds of little tasks. But I do it alone. I never ask for help. I never woke Jesus up and requested help until it was almost too late.

St Monica

Liam, I'm not a Doctor of the Church. My humble role as a mother was to keep close to the altar and pray for my children. My son Augustine could advice you. He is a Doctor of the Church. He wrote extensively and beautifully on the Words of Jesus in the Scriptures. I pray for you Liam. The story of your life so far has just been handed to me and it will take a little time to address your issues. I can see a black mark already though in relation to impatience.

Liam, I'm entitled now to mother you. And my first correction is to remain patient with people. Listen Liam! I'm a Saint. Be extremely kind and patient with every person that you encounter each day. It is only by being that way that you discover the beauty in each person. If you brush them aside, they will view you as arrogant. If you snap and lose your head it could end up in an ugly confrontation. I've always been sensitive to my husband and others. Antagonise no one. In regard to pride talk to Augustine. He's a bishop and has studied the operational effect pride has in a person

Little Man

St Monica, thank you. I'll do my best to be patient with everyone. Thank you for your prayers. I feel protected when someone prays for me. I switch my attention now to the theologian and Doctor of the Church St Augustine. I pray to you Augustine. It's my first time praying to you. How are you? I love your writings. Can you help me? I feel overworked and stressed out. Pressure is severe. I go from one task to another and sometimes three or four tasks are coming at me at the same time. Help!

St Augustine

Hi Liam! How are you? I'll gladly help. The answer to your problem is simple. You have more pride in you than humility. Your challenge Liam is to reverse those two opposites. The feeling of doing everything yourself originates in pride. I want you to allow me to pull it out. It's the most dogged of sins and if not controlled could resemble a driveway full of weeds. Pride keeps reappearing if not treated properly. I suggest that you bend the knee at the name of Jesus and pray from a lowly and humble disposition. You are not God Liam. Therefore, don't think that you have to do all the work. I have Jesus asleep but nobody asks for his help.

Liam, when dealing with deadly sins I'd like you to call Jesus Christ. Always call Jesus when you need help. I clicked with him late in life and immediately rave changes occurred. Don't be afraid. God has the power to extract whopper sins. God didn't send his Son to you so as to sleep in a boat. Wake him up. Tell the Lord that you need help. Nothing is too small for God. So turn to Jesus. It's the theme that's running through the whole of your book. My team in heaven will work with you. We are backed up by Our Almighty Father. The whole team are onto your problem of pride. And the lesson simply is don't depend on yourself. Work with others. If you need help call Jesus. Wake him up and don't be shy.

Little Man

St Augustine, thanks for your time. I appreciate your help. I'm honoured and embarrassed to have such a heavenly star communicating with me - a lightweight in the Church and unknown to mankind. I'll probably never sit at the same table as you and Thomas Aquinas in heaven.

St Augustine I see my error now. You have helped me. I relied on pride rather than Jesus. The Apostles made the same mistake. They relied on their own human strength. I know what to do now. I call Jesus for help. After all his portfolio as Son of Man is to help human beings overcome tragedy, natural disasters, wars, sickness and poverty.

St Augustine, I shrivel in awe before your greatness. I'm delighted to have your mother and yourself as holy friends linking with me during my time on earth. All that matters are heaven and eternal life. I long to join you in heaven.

Augustine I pray to you. Teach me to sit with your team and not be overawed. Fr William knows me. So does my father Edward. St Dominic knows me too. Tell Jesus I love him. I'll show him everything about me. I open up to him. Nothing is hidden. My physical, mental, emotional and intellectual concerns are laid bare. I carry all my baggage and problems to the inner room of our meetings. I'm ready for renovation. I'm willing to allow my holy team to spread a holy plaster around the walls of my body so that I become a new man captured for Christ.

Augustine, I place myself on a seat in a boat and tap the sleeping Jesus on the shoulder to wake him up and ask him to help me cope with the storms that threaten to smother my progress in pursuit of a holy life. I seek my Holy Father.

Augustine, your mother wasn't a fool. Neither are you. Your mother Monica kept Jesus awake. She was desperate. She kept after Jesus praying with tears for your conversion. Augustine make my conversion complete. Kill unspiritual desires. Defeat my daily struggles. Kill passions that are unrelated to the Holy Spirit, Jesus Christ and God my Father. I've no interest anymore in human achievements, great events or successful sports winners. I'm a fool if I don't give all to Christ.

Big Eye

O Liam! That's my little man. That's my boy. I agree. Give your all to Christ, my Son. I agree with you too on the danger of pride. I lose a thousand souls a day to pride. It's not a nice feeling when little men and women behave as if they are more important than me. Pride is a deep rooted vice. And unfortunately Liam there is a little bit of it in everyone. And straightaway that leads to confrontation with me. There is no pride in me. I'm perfect. I laugh when little men and women try to boss me. It's very funny. I see plenty of puffed up little men so full of themselves that they think they are governing the world.

Liam, sincere worship and prayer counteracts pride. I love the humble soul. I'm drawn to the humble. These don't offer me any resistance. I love repentant sinners. I'd pick the humble man any day before a pride driven man or woman. I need listeners in my Church and not people who tell me what to do. Also I don't like lifeless and heartless souls. These have no feelings for anyone. They are cold and poor at prayer.

Liam, I spoke to you before about staying with Jesus and spending time with him. I need you Liam in my Church. My tangible Presence is in the tabernacle. At Mass you receive the Body and Blood of my Son. Divine Life is there for you in tangible form.

Liam, your passport and entry in to heaven is through participation in my Son's Body and Blood. The Eucharist is the heartbeat of a Christian. As soon as worshippers stop receiving they die slowly. All grace, holiness and intimacy with me come through this union with my Christ at the altar of the Church.

Liam, there are a lot of dead wood in my Church. They kill the celebration of a wonderful meal. I need men and women who inspire devotion. I desire freshness, enthusiasm and love. What I get are elderly people chatting at the back of the Church with each other before Mass begins. They should be praying to me and respecting others who try to pray. I want fresh services Liam. No matter what age a worshipper is I desire a bit of passion in their responses. And I'd like the celebrant to shake of the lethargy that sets in from succumbing to religious repetition and burnt out enthusiasm from liturgical services.

Liam, you write for me. Tell the Bishops and priests to wake up. Tell them to enjoy leading the congregation in prayer. And above all tell them to pray before celebrating Mass and facing the people. I want dynamic priests. St Paul is the model I desire. He was a fearless preacher of my Word. I want the Doctrine of the Eucharist expounded for the assembly and passionate sermons preached in such a way that the hair on the head of each person would feel goose pimples.

Liam, worshippers departing from a Eucharistic celebration should be joyful. My Word just heard in sermons should sizzle in the ear as it makes its way into the inner ear for consideration and consequent action. And the Body and Blood of my Son Jesus Christ just received at

Mass should spark of a wild inner celebration of euphoric joy as Divine Life enters the human body.

Liam, shake up human life. There is an inner deadness. I'm concerned as a Father and God of the state of modern man and woman. Most of them have stopped praying and spirituality has nosedived into the abyss of darkness. People's interest has become money and every deception under the sun is used to rip off others.

Liam, my Son died for you. He loves you. He is still Present on the altar. His sacrifice was an eternal act of love. Something unique should occur during the reception of my Son's Body and Blood at Mass. I'm concerned about the tiniest of space that each person allots to welcoming a Divine Person. My Son's Body is unique. He deserves a strong response.

Liam, wake up. Priest wake up. People wake up. Church wake up. I take offence if my Son's Body and Blood isn't shaking up desire for me in Church. If you ignore me my Son Jesus Christ will not be known to present and future generations of men, women and children living in your country and everywhere on the globe. I tell you solemnly wake up Christian. I wouldn't be able to break the thick ice that form around your hearts if you grow cold towards me.

Little Man

Hello Father. Hello Big Eye. I'm sorry on behalf of mankind. I'm and frightened too. It's not a good sign if the world ignores your Son Jesus Christ. I'm worried about your tolerance levels Father. If it come from your mouth Father, I believe it to be true that spirituality worldwide has shrunk to a dangerously low level. I agree fully with you to admonish us all and plead for Bishops, priests and people to wake up. It's bad news that God has concerns. And what makes it worse is that I'm powerless. I don't belong to a group or committee in the Church to influence change. In fact, I expect very few to heed my message. Nobody will listen to my voice. I'm a single man living near the River Shannon.

Father, I pray to you. I take seriously your call to wake up. Father, encourage Jesus to throw a bucket of cold water over me. It's about time

I came to my senses. I call your name Jesus Christ. You are on the cross for us all to see. Yet the world has falling asleep and don't see you. They pass by in droves driving cars past houses of prayer and never think of dropping in for a little chat with the Lord. Father, they don't think. They don't realise that someday they will have to meet you.

Father, I wake up. I call you. I'm on your side and feel for lapsed worshippers. I don't know how to bring them back. I can't hear the voice of an outstanding Good Shepherd. I'd like the spirit of St Patrick to return. Catholicism has weakened in Ireland. St Paul pray for us. You said that the sum of all evils was to fall away from the love of Christ. I'm afraid that has happened. Ireland is different today than it was twenty years ago. The numbers worshipping in Church has dropped significantly.

Father, I'm proud of my strong faith and Catholic inheritance. The faith of the Irish has not only done Ireland proud but has influenced the whole world. We had a golden era in the past and were known abroad as a land of saints and scholars. And we fought strenuously against the English to defend our Catholic traditions when our neighbours changed God's Law in favour of divorce and remarriage.

Father, I live in a time when the Catholic Church has lost credibility and the media with politicians drive the agenda for a modern Ireland that is less friendly towards God and the Church. I'm disappointed with the spiritual state of modern day human beings. Many are bad and millions of more are following them. They have no soul. They have no light in their faces. And they have unfit bodies because they feed on filth.

Father I pray for them. I desire to work with the Son of Man. My objective is to restore the human being to a simple way of life. I want you God Our Father to remain at the centre of Irish life. I pray for pagan intellectuals that their influences are blocked from eroding further Catholic traditions that are more morally sound and safer for the future. For us as a beautiful Nation of people it would be a tragedy if this generation became less Catholic. I write in defence of our Catholic faith. Under the stewardship of recent Governments and the media I see an almost complete blackout on speaker time given to the hierarchy on television or radio. There is a quiet social revolution occurring that's favourable towards challenging Christ and the Church in regard to legislation allowing for immorality to be available because people want it. I will throw a stone at the Government if they promote immorality. I'll throw another at the media. I'll never condone the murder of a potential baby. Nor will I consent to same sex marriages because their bodies are a mismatch for each other. And I also feel irked by my Government and their Educational Ministers for their interference in the Catholic education of children. The family and schools are prominent social groups that form values in our children and promote a Christian way of life. I'm disgusted with pagan politicians who attack the fabric and gene of St Patrick that has survived for generations in families across the length and breadth of our country. It's a huge mistake to cut out or change children's Holy Communion and Confirmation celebrations from the Catholic school curriculum. I'm all for Christ remaining in our schools.

Father I pray for my country. I'll stand solid against beasts that rush at me for fighting for little children to learn more about Christ in schools. Remember God's Son is the greatest Master. And yet our Government want to cut Jesus Christ out because he might offend minority religions. That is an insult to the Divine Son of God. The modern attitude is to push Jesus out of the classroom. If any Christian is worth his salt, he would not accept the weakening of Christ in Christian schools.

Father, I love you. I recall Pope John Paul 11 receiving a rapturous applause in Limerick in nineteen-seventy-nine where he told the youth of Ireland that he loved them. It was a glorious acknowledgement of faith in young people. He told them that Jesus Christ loved them. I solemnly tell you that the same message applies today. Christ loves you. Please don't throw away his love. Please don't reject a great friend in Jesus. If you do rely on your own devises the likely outcome is that youth might prefer to swallow a drug than say a prayer.

Father, I retired from the drudgery of the fish counter so as to write my account of a hunger and thirst for you Big Eye and share my experience with those who pursue the same desire. I informed colleagues at the butchery counter many times that my plan on retirement was to write books and for Prayer Groups. I try to be a man of my word.

Big Eye

Liam dear! I don't envy you but at the same time I'm delighted with your honourable intention. Every attempt should be made to please me. I search the world every day for men like you. I look for virtuous men. I look for holy men. Liam you see the stars in the sky and admire their brightness. I look upon earth for bright lights but few are seen. All I see are blankets of thick weeds and in amongst them a few dimly lit or lukewarm souls that might commit to me.

Liam, I'm a strong Bright Light with a Big Eye. I enkindle the fire of love in prayerful souls. I light their lamps. I brighten up their appearance. I see my faithful and loyal people as stars on earth that beam in the midst of adversity. A lit candle is a holy sign. It reflects the light of my Son. For my Bright Light to shine in you I rely on you to shut out raging winds and stormy waters that quenches my flame due to a lack of concentration and prayer. Many who see the dark clouds form run for their lives because they don't want to fight for a place at my table. So Liam be open to my holy hand. No matter what trial comes your way my light must not go out. I'm in the eye of your intellect. Protect me with bags of prayer. Protect the laser beam of my Bright Light as it flickers delicately in your fragile and unpredictable intellect. Liam this is a challenge for you. I can't be responsible if you allow anyone or anything to switch off the light of my Son. The effect of an unlit soul has the same effect of a torch whose battery is dead. It can't give light. So I tell you solemnly Liam always recharge your battery with prayer so that my candle shines through the darkness.

Liam, I test you daily. You have a bit to go. My Bright Light flickered last night in your soul due to your inability to manage a massive storm. You allowed a moody demon to jump into and infect your mind and it knocked you for six. Instead of my Peace been available to you to deal with the confrontation you resorted to a pride driven counter attack. It's not my Way Liam. I don't want you to hit hard with punchy words. I don't want sparks flying. I want a gentle response Liam. My adversary enjoys arguments, aggression and disruption in families and communities.

Liam, I'm your Father. I have discussed this with you before. You are to call my Son for help when storms brew. If he is asleep wake him up. Tap him on the shoulder. My adversary is a powerful enemy who thrives on the success of evil.

Liam cling to the crucifix in times of trouble. Your faith and trust in my Son Jesus Christ will save you from been overwhelmed during bad moments and engulfed through fiery storms. Liam there is no escaping dangerous battles. My Son saved the world through suffering and death. Offer the wicked person no resistance.

Liam, if you require solace because your soul is in a bad state bury your head in my Son's lap. Jesus knows the human mind. He knows all. My adversary fights inside you. And my Son knows about the horrendous beatings he dishes out to those that declare for my Christ. So go to my Doctor for treatment. He will pamper you and heal the blows that bruised your soul black and blue. Time with my Son results in calming your soul and returning it to a peaceful state.

Liam, my advice is priceless. I'm your God. You would do well to obey me. My Words are nuggets. My Words Are Golden Eggs. I push my adversary out of your soul and build a nest in it for my Golden Eggs to produce holy results. I have the power to enwrap you in cotton wool and take you into my heart.

Liam, I'm keen to accept you beyond reasonable doubt because of the strength of your desire for me. You value what is above the belt. I want your heart and mind. I'm less interested in what goes on below the belt.

Little Man

Hello Father, I'm delighted that you may have use for this little man's heart and mind. They are yours anyway. And I think you could make better use of them than me. All though I do say that I'm more interested in the life of the heart and mind than what goes on below the belt. There's enough sexuality besides I adding to it. I grant full permission for you Holy Father to make use of my heart and to make use of my mind. All I ask in return is that the love that you put into my heart is compatible with Christ's love. And I also add that your Truth, your attributes, and your holy thoughts become part of my mind-set. It is of great importance to me that the same Godly substance of Father, Son and Holy Spirit filters into my soul, and that I'm one hundred percent open to what I call a holy infiltration.

Father, I've had a good day. I can't explain the reason. All I know is that I was sad. And now there is a turnaround. Earlier my stress levels bulged through my veins. I had multiple issues that appeared unfixable. Then I met a Bank Official that drew up a Personal Account for me to use instead of a Joint Account. The reason for this move is to keep tighter control of finances. The family budget was so much out of control that money was running from it quicker than water running from a tap. Financial spillages had to be plugged.

Father, I love you. Prayer solved this issue for me. I had money leakages on my mind for a long time and many times when I prayed this issue flew along in my prayer. My prayer was often intense before a crucifix and lit candle. A troubled soul should pray. I know Father of your quick response to the cries of troubled souls. There's lots of sorrow on earth. I found prayer gave me confidence. It also steadied up my internal grieve and troubles. Prayer can be used to find solutions. Of all human actions I find prayer surpasses them all. I'm pleased today. I thank the Bank Official and prayer for giving me hope. I was locked into a stalemate situation for years where there was no winner in how the family budget was managed.

Father, prayer is magnificent. The ability to reach you and Jesus Christ through prayer is something that sweetens my experience of life. I think there would be less trouble in the world if people prayed. I'm going to bring all my needs to Jesus and talk them through with him. It's truly magnificent. I can soar into heaven on wings of prayer. I feel secure Father under your care.

Chapter Seven

Big Eye!

Liam, I agree with you. Prayer is a great thing. I love it to see human beings going away to quiet places in order to be alone with me. I also love it to see crowds of people assemble together for Pilgrimages, Novenas and other religious services. No matter who you are I love to see the elderly and young, the healthy and infirm make their way to Church. The whole experience of life doesn't make sense unless prayers and faith ascends to me in heaven. I take every prayer on board.

Liam, I don't like money. It corrupts people because of their love for it. I'd advise you not to be mean but generous. I see a lot of angry souls lose their way because of a love for money. These are greedy Liam. They have no conscience. Don't follow them. I see them exploit poor people who have very little. Business people rip you off too. I speak the truth Liam. No lie falls from my mouth.

Liam, your journey towards me is full of trouble. I warn you against riches. It's difficult for the rich to enter heaven. My Son Jesus had no home. The only spot my Christ had was on a piece of wood fixed into the ground. So don't be anxious about bills, or clothes or food. I look after you. I give you all that you have.

Liam, you don't have to have anything to receive my affection. I cured seven lepers. I made a prostitute a saint. I called a good rich man down from a tree. I saved an adulterer from murder. I gave sight to a blind man. So Liam have a bit of faith in me. I love you. Stop complaining. You are nothing and yet I love you. I jump obstacles with you. Nothing is too great for me. I called you from plastering. I called you from retail. I called you from a Religious Institution.

Liam, you are mine. I have you for myself. I have helped you to isolate yourself so that nothing disturbs my Super Truth and Love from purring around your battered but loyal mind. I can't however turn you into a Super Saint free of sin while battles galore and nasty experiences blow your way on a regular basis while in the flesh on earth.

Liam, heavenly life is perfect. Those who make it are washed clean completely. There is no mixture of good and evil in those that make it to heaven. On earth my adversary does damage and influences human beings to defy me. For that reason, I classify all human beings as a mixed bag. There's a bit of everything in them. It's not all good. It's not all bad either. I'll help you to defeat the bad things that are in your bag. I can help to remove the bad eggs. I can shift through your mind and heart and pluck out sour sweets and all unpalatable thoughts, words and actions. While on earth the process towards heaven can be like a pendulum. You can move up towards heaven or sink down towards the pleasures and miseries offered by my adversary. The way forward Liam is to align your thoughts, words and actions with the lofty titles attributed to my Son Jesus Christ. These bear the great name of Christ my Son

Liam, listen to the motives behind conversations with you. Traces of evil are never far away in words expressed. Others promise the world but behind their sweet words are crafty cunning rogues who play deceitful tricks. Only trust those who are close to my Son.

Liam, my Son has been through everything human life has to offer. It was hell at times. But there were sweet moments. I don't need you to tell me the tragedies that befall people. But most suffering is due to human fault. \people don't want to belong to me. I made them and yet they reject me. When I cast my Big Eye across the globe and see herds of pagans swallowed up by Satan my tears fill with buckets of sorrow. I'm so sorry for humanity when people cut themselves of from me.

Liam, I can't foresee change. My Book the Bible is there for them. They don't want to read my Word. So I can't see your book making any difference. My Son's life written in the Gospels has a story to tell that none can match. Yet today the majority in the world live their lives independently from his teaching and message. I'm hurt by anyone who rejects my Son.

Liam, examine your thoughts, words and actions. I saw you down the road this morning on L0909 with your son Luke cycling. You prayed the rosary. I saw you trying your best. May I remind you Liam that my Son is a precious jewel. The Perfect Way is found in him. So ensure that your book praises him. I want my Holy Spirit to hop in and out of your soul without irritations or interruptions. No more holidays Liam. I desire a high level of devotion for Jesus Christ.

Liam, decency in life comes from thoughts which are inspired by Christ. So you need to know what my Son says. You need to remember my Son's Word. And don't let self-will get in the way. Perfection for you is to share in all the lofty titles used to describe my Son. I know Son of Man is amongst your favourite accolade. Pray to him. It's a phenomenal Divine title and after four thousand years of theological studies none has revealed the true nature of my Son of Man.

Liam, be aware of self-will. My Way is hard work. I instructed Jesus to employ idlers and give them work. The problem of self-will has to be tackled. This is a very defiant attitude that tells me to get lost and mind my own business. This is an attitude that demands selfish time for oneself. This is an attitude of doing what one wants. This is an attitude that blocks challenges. I'm attracted Liam to humble souls. They resemble meek and harmless lambs. These follow me without any resistance. They listen to my voice. So denounce your will and desires Liam. So no more screaming and shouting. I can't have you scaring my little beloved lambs.

Liam, the way forward is to change yourself and allow the Son of Man change the world. He has the power and authority. You are not on an equal par with me. And if you want my Son of Man to pick you it's best to withdraw into yourself and work on your spiritual revolution. Nobody who follows my Son Jesus fights with him. Nobody bosses him.

Liam, I love you. Don't worry about Empires in the world. Don't bother changing the world. Don't concern yourself with Super Nations. As I have told you that role is for the Son of Man. He guides the world and Nations every day, and deals with forces of evil that threaten mankind. Your battle is to give your heart and mind to me. Of course, it is not easy to turn a blind eye. You have no power over earth. You don't have power within your own home. You can't stop arguments. You can't stop evil. I know you want to have a say here. But just pray for them Liam. Pray for your wife and son. Pray for yourself. Keep the Divine lofty titles of my Son close to you. I admire your prayer to call me and to call my Son Jesus.

Liam, don't write about evil. It shames us in heaven. It also blackens your history. Man's inhumane treatment of each other is despicable. I'm opposed to every form of hatred whether it's through thoughts or actions. Liam, don't act as if you are God. I know about evil. You can't eliminate it. My Son Jesus point to the problem through his crucifixion. Roman, British or Chinese Empires mean nothing to me. I didn't agree to my Son's death for political motives. My kingdom is different. I never set out to rule the world.

Liam, I'm not aligned to Religious Hatred. I'm a Peaceful God. I'm not in support of any man, or any group, or any Nation that carries a bomb or a gun to kill. Liam, let dialogue about wickedness go. I don't highlight evil. I prefer to concentrate on all who love me and practise worship of me in the Eucharist every day.

Liam, life is tough. Irreligious souls point the finger at me for allowing atrocities to happen. I have a few million bad eggs in the world. When a man sets out to commit an act of evil do you want me to pluck him from the earth and throw him into hell? I encourage holiness Liam. But I can't reverse an evil will. It would be contrary to my intended involvement in the world. The effect of plucking evil doers from the world would make human beings puppets. Jesus dealt with and taught on this subject in the parable of the darnel. It's at death that the separation of good and evil occurs. Everyone at the end has to face Jesus Christ. And I'm sure you can judge for yourself that a jihad bomber has a different story than a Chernobyl charity worker. I'm sure most of us would choose a good person over an evil fiend.

Liam, I encourage you to tell every human being about my offer of salvation through Christ Jesus. Pin the name of Jesus Christ on your hearts. I have spoken of my First Commandment. It is to love me beyond anything else. I value friendship and loyalty. Can you love my Son Liam? Are you up for the call? I expect love and obedience from the whole of creation. Nobody can reach heaven without love.

Liam, you don't need knowledge. Sometimes you write as if the world, creation, the human being, sexual activity, life, death, evil, and other branches of knowledge are an encyclopaedia in your mind and that you know more than me. Liam come down of your horse. You know very little. And I don't want you to compete with me in having total and supreme knowledge. I ask you to do one thing. I'm your Father in heaven. A relationship with me is through prayer. My Son is Jesus Christ. A relationship with my Son is through his Word. My Divine Holy Spirit is the best Person of the Trinity to activate my Way, my Life and my Truth within you. I guarantee you Liam that it's the Holy Spirit that gives life to the Church. I want you therefore to befriend my Holy Spirit when you pray. My holy Spirit personalises me as Father and my Son Jesus Christ as Body and Blood within your intellect and heart – the two main centres of affection and understanding in each person.

Liam, my standards are high. By this I mean virtuous and moral standards. The rejection and disinterest in my Name has consequences. You don't need to know what goes on in the media. What benefit does it do your poor soul in finding out about a rape, a robbery, a suicide bombing, or any other inhuman act. I advise you not to view pornography or any form of immorality. Even a life in politics doesn't lead to me. All I ask of each person is concentrated prayer using words like, "Hallowed be thy Name". I give you my Word Liam. Concentrate on their meaning. My Words are tools in which you can work out who I Am. Also my Word is a gift.

Liam, my Word is sublime. Life is in them. A batch of my Words have power to change lives. You know who I Am through my Word. When I say, "Blessed are the clean of heart, for they shall see Me", is Truth itself. There is no deceit in my Word. I Am not a liar. So Liam clean your heart with the help of my Holy Spirit.

Liam, I concentrate on Good News. I'd like you to do the same. My world is beautiful. I provide for you every day giving you heat, light, water, air and food. So try and appreciate me. At the end of your road you admire a large cornfield. I provide every year. So don't worry. You are not Me. As Father of All Life I have authority to judge. You don't. And as I have told you know your own situation and prepare yourself for my Love. General problems about the world shouldn't concern you.

Liam, I have a mechanism in place to deal with practises that are opposed to my Commandments and Laws. I'm well aware of what is going on. So don't worry about sick and evil mentalities. I deal with morality. I never waver. The weapon I use to defeat every facet of evil is Truth. I fight corruption and immorality with Truth. Nobody can gain entry to heaven if they are corrupt or immoral. My Son and Me will judge the soul of every person. I'm well aware of groups pushing laws into legislation that differ from my Holy Law.

Liam, you don't really need to know about depravity, immorality, religious hatred etc. My Mind is Super and Pure. I want you to love me for those reasons. I want you to see how Great I Am. I want your mind thinking about Me and my Word. I bless your soul Liam every day if you keep it clean for me.

Little Man

Father, I take into my heart and mind your adorable words above. You are right. I'm not a judge or a solicitor. Studying evil should not be a theme in this book. My task is not to decide the moral levels of others. I refocus therefore on your Word. I know now that your Holy Spirit comes through your Word. I will do my best to clean my mind out for you and my body too. If beauty comes through your Word, I want to eat it and drink it all day. If juice comes from your Word, I want to fill my heart with it.

Father, thank you very much for making me aware as to how Great you are and how Small I am. I thank you sincerely. The slightest improvement in spiritual growth is welcome. It is one step at a time. Father, you have done that this evening. I'm to mind my own business about the world and focus on building a spiritual power within myself. I have a team from heaven to work with me.

Father, I aim to sit, listen and pray with my Saintly Committee. Demons are furious with me for choosing you, Lord. A bad mannered fiend struck and vexed my soul. The fiery little thing hoped that it would influence me to stay away from my Holy Committee team. But I'm not going to allow Lucifer's bully to prevent me from sitting among the Doctors of the Church. My team of Saints waited for me. They sat in a circle with one empty chair. It was for me.

Father, I'm delighted. It bothered none of the Holy Team that I had been battered a short time earlier. They saw it as a test. And immediately all at the meeting pointed to the image of Christ on the cross. And they want me to accept suffering.

Father, I'm sorry for my blindness. I fail to see Christ everyday hang on the cross. I don't see the blood dripping from the thorns in his head. Neither do I feel the pain of the nails in his hands and feet. I am required to show empathy and love for those who suffer. If I can't feel the pain my Crucified Lord went through than something cold exists in my emotions.

Father, I have to feel the pain of those thorns pressed into your flesh as if they were my thorns. For it is us sinners that mocked you and drove a crown of thorns into your skull. I'm sorry and apologise to you on behalf of humanity. Unfortunately Father the world of sinners continue to crucify your Son. But I for one commit to Christ, and hopefully others might too that want to be pure and good. For I am in love with your Word. It promises so much. I shall see you if I remain pure or clean. I long for the beatific vision. I pray as often as possible for a perception of you, Almighty Father. Your promise is great. I look forward so much to hearing the sweet voice of the Holy Spirit. For purity consists of unceasing happiness and a vision of the True Light.

Father, from another point of view and I have given a lot of consideration to this connotation that the crown of thorns signifies an insight of huge significance. After a lot of prayer and meditation I believe the impact of the thorns is to tell us of the importance of puncturing sins in the mind. The tip off each thorn when pressed into the skull punctures a whole in the skin and that in turn is a symbolism that bursts sin bubbles internally hidden and dangerous in the soul of each person. Father, it was very clever of you. Satan ran when he saw the way you tricked him. The evil one didn't like the thorns that were used to drive his demons out of the minds of human beings.

Father, I also believe that the scourging of your Son at the pillar symbolises an attack on the sins of the flesh. The lashes on Jesus's back repels pleasures of the flesh. And I believe from my prayers that the carrying of the cross is nothing other than Jesus hauling all our sins to the top of Calvary for exposition and execution. I see wonderful insights here. I see Jesus carrying my sins to the cross. I see Jesus' thorns puncture and kill the sins in my mind. I see the scourging of Christ as killing the desires of the flesh in my body.

Father, I love life now. I'm learning so much. Your Holy Team working on me must be pressing all the right buttons. I see significant progress. I must grasp completely the thorn theory. The nature of a thorn is to hurt. It prods pride in the mind. A thorn prod results in pride leakage and this in turn creates a more amicable atmosphere in the mind for Christ to make an entrance. So Father I'm in favour of receiving a crown of thorns.

Father, I'm unsure though that I could bear the pain. I lock myself away for fear of people. I don't like mixing with anyone. I had a man do work for me and he conned me. I see that as a thorn. I talk to a woman and she criticises me. I see that as a thorn. I don't know if I could cope with people that stick thorns into me. People like to prod others with their thorns because they don't want to suffer. And they see me – an idiot of a man – and stick their pain onto me for me to carry. I decline and reject sins in another person from prodding me. I'll sympathise. But I object to a person trespassing by pulling a thorn from their mind and placing into mine.

Father help me. I'm mixed up. Is the thorn a good or bad thing? There is ambiguity in my thinking. What is a thorn? I'm thinking that if it used to kill sin inside of me it is a good thing. But if it is the sin itself it is a bad thing. I wouldn't mind thorns stuck in me if it helped spiritual progress. But if thorns were sins that others use to pierce my flesh then I would be furious. And I probably would fight and resist the thorn thrower.

Father, I begin to struggle here on thorny issues. Thorns cause pain and draw blood. They are sore too. The thorns I symbolically refer to are sharp tongues and crunching bites from aggressive and arrogant people. If I'm to be like Jesus thorns are to be accepted with pain and humility. I bless myself in response to aggression and offer no resistance. If I argue or fight it's because I want to remove the thorn so as to avoid suffering for anyone.

Father, I'm sorry if I laboured and misunderstood the message behind the crown of thorns. I think though that an insightful reflection of Jesus crowned with thorns is classed as a mockery of his entitlement by branding him as nothing more than a King of Thorns or a King of Fools. It is indeed sad that a good man like the Son of God found no home on earth and that political and religious powers had no welcome for the greatest servant of humanity that ever existed.

Big Eye

Liam, I don't like the title King of Thorns or King of Fools but you have stumbled upon the Truth. My Son is the King of Suffering. He took everyone's pain and sin upon his own shoulders. I allowed my Son to suffer and die because of my great love for every human being in every Nation on earth. I appear foolish. In fact, I appear insane. I allowed my Divine Son to sacrifice his life so as to give hope to sinners, the sick and the poor. As God your Father I could not stand idly by as political and religious authorities ostracised the most vulnerable souls in society. The thorns in my Son's flesh symbolises corrupt political and religious establishments who abuse their power and make life intolerable for those they govern.

Liam, I expect you to feel the pain caused by thorns pressed into Jesus head. If you never felt a prod of a thorn it indicates that you are living a comfortable life and are unsuitable for friendship and priesthood with the King of Thorns. Any man worth his salt in following Jesus must feel the pain of people and their struggles to shake of sin. To accept Christ is to accept a Crown of Thorns. There is no other way to become an outstanding Christian. If a follower isn't willing to suffer for others he or she is a dud. My Way of Life Liam is not to focus on human achievements or success stories. My Way of Life Liam is to mocked, laughed at, and insulted by wearing a Crown of Thorns. This keeps you humble Liam. And every time someone prods a thorn into your flesh you instantly think of my Christ and pray for the poor soul. And any time you sin Liam think straight away that you have pressed the Crown of Thorns further into my Son's flesh.

Liam, I love you very much. Pay attention to Jesus. There are more insights to be revealed. I'd like you to consider the nailing of my Son's feet and hands to the cross. At the moment you don't understand. But during your walks on road L0909 think of the significance of the pain in Jesus's feet. And also think of the agony in his nailed outstretched hands. Both sets of nailed limbs carry insights not yet known to anyone. I want you to keep the pain of Jesus's scourging as well as the crowning with thorns, the nailing of his feet and nailing of his hands close to your thoughts and feelings in your heart every day. I can't emphasise enough the role of my Son Jesus Christ who is there for you all the time. So ensure that you are his friend. You live in an age that is smothered by a fog. The minds of people are almost closed in relation to memories of the Son of Man who is the centre of history.

Liam, trust me. There isn't a day to pass in your life without acknowledging my Name as Father and my Wonderful Son as Brother. Don't be afraid. Be affectionate with your Divine Brother. You can feel sorry for his pain on the Cross. But don't allow it to lower your level of love for Jesus. The Eternal Vision is cemented in your heart and mind by nurturing through prayer the tiny little seeds of Purity and Love. Therefore, Liam continue building a spiritual house of union with me and with your Holy Team of Saints. At the moment I care for the world and for human life with my Son of Man. I'm happy for you to concentrate on strengthening your love for me.

Little Man

Father, I feel fearful and frightened though. I don't trust military powers and the threat of a Third World War. I don't want my son to live in a world of disease and destruction. I feel uneasy about human beings lack of respect for each other. But I will obey you Father. I do what you tell me. I will love you more and more based on the capacity of my heart and mind to focus on my Brother Jesus and you God my Father. I have a right as an adopted son to call you Father. I wouldn't like anyone to find fault with my desire to love you.

Father, I express my love for you now. I feel very warm about this sweet desire. It's pure honey. I call you into my heart Jesus Christ. I welcome you Holy Spirit into my intellect. I'm surrounded by Divine Love. This is warm stuff Father. I'm more in love with you now then during my years in religious life.

Father, all I wanted from religious life was to study the Truth. I wanted an opportunity from the Order to combine prayer and study. That didn't come. The House of studies didn't rate my talent. I was a Third or Fourth Division player. My intellectual ability wasn't rated. For that reason, my life in the Order had to bypass what the Master General and Provincial had to offer. Therefore, Big Eye I choose liberty in order to approach you directly.

Father, I'll not knock Religious Life. I loved it. I met some fine priests and brothers. I loved Study. I loved preaching your Word. I loved celebrating the Eucharist. I enjoyed Community Life. I'm very grateful to the Order. My faith had two pillars to hold me up – my family and the Order of Preachers. I'll not forget Fr Paul who had faith in me and introduced me to the Order. Nor will I forget Fr William who guided me through a rough patch and assured me that I had a vocation. Nor will I forget my beloved father Edward who prayed with us when children. These men had faith in me. I honour them here and now. I'm glad to have a Team of Saints in charge of working on thoughts in my intellect and love in my heart. I'm absolutely thrilled Father. St Dominic, St Anselm, St Augustine, St Monica and St Patrick are on my Holy Team. It's Wonderful News.

Father, I'm slightly worried though that I did put my hand to the plough. I was in the vineyard. I was in a Religious Order. I stood at the alter and changed the bread and wine into the Body and Blood of your Son Jesus Christ. I prayed with brethren who were committed to your Son. Yet I came out of it for some strange reason or two. I'd like you to know Father that the reason had nothing to do with my love for your

Son Jesus Christ. That love is stronger now than ever. All I want to do in life is to clearly express my complete devotion to Jesus Christ. I could not tolerate within myself a shallow commitment. The shell that covers and protects my delicate intellect waits night and day for the love of my life Jesus Christ. I'm all for a reunion. The kick, the energy, the drive that's in me become dynamic once Jesus is either in me or near me.

Big Eye

Liam, stop now! I love you whether you are a priest or not. So don't mistrust me. I'm All-Powerful and an Almighty God. I can love a soul regardless of his or her status. You never fell out with my Son Jesus Christ. The Body and Blood of the Lord is there for you. I don't recall my love from anyone that desires me. And I'm always waiting for a sinner to repent. So rest assured we are connected silly goose. I'm always there for you. Have no doubt.

Liam, I'm like you with your son. You walk a good bit ahead of him on the forest walk but you don't forget him. He calls you when you go a bit too far ahead and you answer him. I'm like that with you. I'm ahead of you and you don't see me. But you know I'm there. So you call my Name, Father. I am there for you. Liam, there is no way that I as a Father of all human beings intend to give a heedless response to someone that declares their love for me.

Liam, I'm a Father for everyone. I love feeble and elderly people. They are adorable. I see them with their sticks and making their way to Church. These are very loyal around the altar and great at prayer. I love them. Nicodemus was in his seventies when he changed and committed to Christ. I welcome all on board the ship that sails to heaven. I call all lambs who listen to the voice of my Son Jesus. I call people of every age and background. My Love is Universal. I don't care if a person is a Jew, a Catholic, a Muslim, a Protestant, or any religion. I call people from every background. Nicodemus changed his mind-set. He accepted Jesus Christ, my Son even though he was a loyal Jew for seventy years.

Liam, don't doubt my power. I'm happy with you and love you. So stop hankering in your mind whether you are loved or not. I'm sharp eyed Liam. There's no doubt whatsoever that you love me. I'm a huge part of your book. I have no doubt that my Angelic Postman will deliver your book to my Office in heaven. And it will receive an imprimatur that your writing doesn't harm my Pope and the Catholic Church. Souls can be saved through your work. I keep to my Word. If you save one soul there's a place for you in heaven.

Little Man

Father, thank you for your confidence in me. Thank you very much. I'm inspired by your dialogue. It refreshes me. I'm delighted to learn that anything done in my past wouldn't be held against me once I love you now. That is reassuring. I feel within myself a holy joy because you respond to my pieces of writing. It really is sweet of you Father. It's an absolute pleasure that you have the time for a holy conversation with a little unknown man like me. You have a beautiful mind Father. I can see a liquid tube of sweet grace and juicy love running from heaven into my room and brightening up my little lost mind. Big Eye your proximity radiates everything around me as well as inside me. Your grace and love is more beautiful than sunlight. O my God. The feeling is similar to an eternal brightness or a beatific vision. I don't want this feeling to ever go away.

Father stop. I'm lit up. I feel as if my whole being beams. It's a beautiful and holy feeling. I think of St Stephen's face on the day Jews stoned him for been a Christian. It's a sensational feeling. I welcome you Father. Nobody knows about my lit up cell and bodily transformation. I'm privileged - one person out of seven billion people on road L0909 has a halo as bright as the moon lighting up my heart and soul.

Father, I'm a little scared. You are Pure Light and Pure Fire. I'm melting and exposed with your extraordinary and powerful Divine substance. Nevertheless, Father I'm not going to scare you away. I want the stuff or the Substance that transfigures old bodies, dead bodies, poor bodies and sick bodies. I want the Fire and the Light that heals broken limbs and cancerous bodies. I want to change the world with your Magnificence Lord. O foolish human beings, how dare you ignore the Greatest and Highest of All. Our God has the power to heal every broken leg, every broken arm, and open every blind eye, and deaf ear.

Wake up! Wake up! You are idiots if you reject your only hope for eternal life.

Father, you are Pure Fire and Pure Light. I can feel your heat burn inside and melt my nutty sins into nothing. I can feel the heat of your love penetrate through my veins and heal body parts that are infirm and painful. O this is exhilarating new life. The Pure Fire of Divine Love restores life to its original state. This is True. Have no fear. I know now that God can do anything.

Father, I think of you first thing in the morning. And I acknowledge my Brother Jesus. I can't forget the holy glow felt yesterday. It was like a visit from you Father. I felt your Presence shining through my window. My whole day brightened up. And the best thing of all Father was your Pure Fire that burnt the weeds of evil from my life. Last night I walked down my road a different man. I felt six foot tall and energised. I felt like a new man in a new body.

Father, I have found what I was looking for. I have found a Father that loves me and a brother that adores me. I am so happy about it that I can't express it with the right words. My friend Big Eye watches like a shepherd on a mountain his humble and lowly lambs. The question now is to listen to his voice.

Father, the thought of you as Pure Fire and Pure Light has sent a shudder through me. I'm not fearful though. In fact, I'm the opposite. I face the future with an Almighty Power that has the ability to quell my storms, my worries, my sadness, my irritations and impatience. Father this is the stuff of dreams. And I'm humbled by the Greatness of your Power. I pray in awe of your Greatness.

Father, everyone may feel they are more important than me. I don't care. I'm happy to be your little lamb. I'm not after high places and seats of honour. I lived in the House of Studies next to the dust room – a room that nobody wanted. It was better than a bed of straw or to be homeless as was my Brother Jesus. I'm happy to feel the love of my Lord and that is everything for me.

Big Eye

Liam, I love you. Your words delight me. What you say is true. I am God Most High. There's nothing greater than me. And to love me is everything. You are right to say that I prefer humble people. These are my little lambs. These type of humans have a better chance of a relationship with me. I had and still have that relationship with Jesus Christ my Son. He is the perfect Lamb of God. I gave him to the Church and through him my flock follow him through a narrow gate that leads to an inner sanctuary and a happy union with me.

Liam, what I have always liked about you is that you try to dig meaning out of my Word. You try to understand it. I like that. Most Nations and the majority of populations throughout the world are unbothered by My Voice and Word. I have recognised a huge change in you Liam. You come alive when you hear my Word. In recognition of your interest in my Word I aim to give you Golden Eggs to keep my Spirit warm in your mind. I keep my promises. If you love me, you will keep my Word. A Golden Egg if not meditated on indicates that a person has no thoughts about me.

Liam, there are times when you will feel dry, lonely and lost. You may question my existence. You will feel bewildered and frustrated. And I may mean nothing to you. That's your prompt Liam. It signifies that you have run out of fuel. You stopped praying. I'm there for you during those times. But I want you to do one thing. Don't suffer alone. I want you to call my Name. I'll meet you in your moment of pain if you call me. Your Brother Jesus called me. He cried out in pain and said, "My God, my God, why have you forsaken me". All who follow me will have similar experiences of abandonment, desertion, disownment and rejection. You may be called too suffer Liam.

Liam, I know you feel like screaming at me. And you feel I was cruel. You feel I'm crazy. You are right. No Father would put his Son through a crucifixion. I did it for a few powerful reasons. The first of these is that I Am God and my Almighty Power brought my Son Jesus Christ back to life, assisted him in his ascension to heaven, sat him at my right hand, and crowned him King of heaven and earth. Liam my

Christ is not dead. He is forever the Son of Man and he has authority and domination over all creation.

Liam, my second reason is that my Son's crucifixion is the Ultimate Sacrifice of Love. My Divine Son accepts death in order to enact an Eternal Sacrifice of Love that gives all human beings an opportunity to go through the narrow gate of the Eucharist. To this very day Liam and this is two thousand years after my Christ's crucifixion you have a close union with the Body and Blood of the Lord. If my Son did not set up a Way of Worship, then there would not be a Holy Team of Saints for you to find union with me. Liam, I honestly and truly adore what Jesus Christ did for the salvation of human souls. Liam, look around the world. I see Catholic Churches in every Nation. My doors are open. My priests celebrate the memorial of my Son's crucifixion. Liam, I tell you solemnly you and all believers in Christ are better off as a result of my houses of worship in cities, towns, villages and rural areas. It's wonderful Liam. Your King Jesus sits at my right hand in heaven. I'm forever grateful to him for bringing so many holy men and women into the kingdom of heaven. I admire beyond reason the hard work of my Son and the establishment of Worship Houses where people can unify their aspirations and worship me in Spirit and Truth. I Am the Father of All. I'm the One True God. So Liam relish your Church. It's the best Way to find me.

Liam, I like you. And I can use you for a good purpose. Tell my Church and its leaders that they are obliged to seek holiness in their line of work. I expect priests and religious to pursue sanctity and likewise politicians. I abhor religious and political corruption. I loathe exploitation and rogue dealers. I'm not a fan of any dishonest person. Nor am I a fan of work for self-gain. My motto for employers and individuals is to serve people in a dignified and honest way. It's unfair, unpleasant and dishonest for someone to trick or rip anyone off. I'm uneasy with rich people that exploit the less well-off.

Liam, continue to walk in the Way of Humility. It's a beautiful route and a desirable quality in a human being. I notice every little act of humility. I remember the day you didn't compete with other students for the best room, nor did you seek the best places at table. However sometimes you don't listen and you come across as arrogant.

Liam, I'm God. I'm Big Eye. I dislike intensely high levels of pride in people. The tendency for everyone is to aim for greatness. But that is not for you Liam. I'm happy for you to kneel at the foot of the Cross and pray. It will keep you humble. This activity too prevents you from quizzing me about rewards. This is a mentality that says, "What is in in it for us"?

Liam, it's not an easy task choosing disciples. I created a very ambitious and cute creature. On their way along the road Jesus had to deal with in-fighting and jockeying for positions. Ambitious mothers were involved requesting places beside Jesus in heaven. Ambition is a form of selfishness. I don't think you are like that Liam. I can't see you scrambling for a Bishops hat.

Liam, I often brought my disciples away to quiet places on hills and out into boats for rest and refreshments. Sometimes it is necessary to go away and be alone for some quiet reflection. It's good to get away from crowds and the noisy chatter of yapping. I have no problem with a soul looking for solitude. But I do expect loyalty for attendance at Church gatherings to listen to my Word. It's a far greater choice of activity than been packed into a stadium looking at a group of twenty-two men chasing a bag of wind and everyone shouting for their team.

Liam, I'm impressed with you. Most people go for rich cream. But you settle for sour cream. You don't care about success. You mind your own business. You prefer a quiet life. You seek me consistently. You hide nothing. I love that about you. The limelight doesn't suit you. In the quietness of your room you write to me. And that is good enough for me. Liam keep writing. I watch you at prayer and see the ball of your eye like a magnet drawing my Word into your soul. You love the Psalms Liam. These are inspiring personal prayers. Sing a few lines for me Liam. I hear birds sing around you. Why don't I hear you sing Psalms?

Little Man

Father, thank you. I like praise. What man doesn't? It's great to sing. I like Gregorian Chant. It must be sweet for you Father to hear a group of religious sing psalms in honour of you. It's beautiful when men pray sweetly. I'm sure you love all singing in praise of creation. Some birds are lovely singers. I'm not a great singer but I love chanting. Singing prayer is melodious. Father give me strength to practise chanting a Psalm every morning and night.

Father Big Eye, nothing hides from you. It is that factor that drives me towards you. Your gorgeous Big Eye knows every human sin. I cannot hide mine. All human action is seen. My little eye sees only a portion. But Big Eye has such powerful vision that he can view the whole world in one glance as well as focus on a ladybird sitting on a leaf. And if that gaze isn't powerful enough Big Eye also sees and knows what's going on in the head of each individual. From that point of view God knows the level of evil in each of us. God cannot be fooled. That's why I love him. It's a pity I didn't have such vision when I trusted a conman to do a tarmac job. I feel awful about being tricked. I wasted big money on a crap job.

Father, you have Great Vision. But not only have you vision. You have a Super Intellect. You have a Super Memory. You read a book in an instant. This enables you to view the history of each city, town, village, household and individual. With that fear Father I worry about the book that is my life. I find the story of my life frightening but fascinating. I'd prefer to hide some sins. But that is impossible. Big Eye scans through each page of my life. He sees my sins. The action of each day is in the pages of the book. I remember a very sinful period that blacken my record. I rely however on your mercy Father. I'm sorry.

Father, I look back on my life and think whether my talents were used. Nothing has survived. I can't remember any outstanding deeds. I plastered, worked in retail and administered the Eucharist. No Father. I can't agree with that judgement of myself. I broke the bread and gave it to the congregation. And I preached your Word. These were outstanding deeds. I have done good Father. And in writing this book I express my deep love for you Holy Father. I shouldn't be too hard on myself.

Father, I feel ground has to be made up. I haven't contributed anything in the world and did nothing to make life a better place for everyone. This is worrying. I move towards the latter stages of my existence. O I have just thought of something. I place an **arrow** in the book for everyone to follow. Forget about going to Mars or Saturn. I point my finger to Jesus Christ found in the Catholic Church. I address you seven billion people. I live two thousand years after John the Baptist. That's a long time. And I do now what he did. I point my finger towards the Lamb of God. May I also point my finger towards God the Father who is found in the Lord's Prayer. The sincere Christian should not let a day pass without praying the words of the Our Father. Words cannot express the importance of what I say to you – my seven billion friends living across the face of earth.

Father, enkindle me with your spark. Otherwise I can't ignite anybody with the fire of love. I can't inspire anyone. Give me Father a sack of holy seeds to plant in the ears and eyes of seven billion people. I'd like them all to be saved. I'd like sexual control too. I fear further multiplication of National populations might stretch resources leading to starvation and bulging borders.

Father, this book is my greatest sermon. I believe in what I write. I don't believe it is dead wood or a book lying on a dusty shelf. I think I'm fit to exist in every living room. This is my effort to do something for human beings. I have always wanted to preach to a wide audience. I spoke twenty-five years ago to my Provincial at the time of a desire to write. He thought I didn't have the ability and didn't encourage it. I never lost faith in you Father. Men may not rate my talent. But you do Father and that is all that matters.

Father, I am ill-mannered and impatient sometimes. You are a person of high rank. You are God Most High. You are higher than the leaders of the most powerful Nations on earth. My approach to you must be in order. I must address your Name with the highest respect and the dignity that you deserve. I pray with care in order to gratify you Father, and avoid offending you. I regard as vitally important what Jesus tells me to beg for. I think over what I pray for when saying, "Your kingdom come". I pray for awareness in my intellect as these holy and Divine Words are thrashed like corn in order to extract the sense from their meaning. O Father, I love your Divine Word. I walk tall on road L0909 reflecting and praying. Your holy Word deserves serious consideration.

Father I try my best despite my natural defects that often render me unfit to hallow, praise, glorify, magnify or extol your Holy Name. I desire piety Father. This virtue will enable me to approach you with good manners. I sit and think on the garden seat. I reflect on God's Kingdom and long to be a member. It would be so wonderful to be part of a kingdom with Jesus as my King. I pray so that I may belong to Jesus.

Father, I enjoy your protection. Your Big Eye is on me. Nothing escapes you. I'm thrilled with the quality of your observation. I can't go wrong once we remain connected. I ponder your Almighty Intelligence. I know you cannot be deceived. That's why I want to stick to you. I want nothing to do with liars and deceitful scum who make life miserable for decent people. I stick to Truth. I stick with Jesus. I love my heavenly Father. With Divine help I crush every sin found in my mind and treat it like a ball of dirt. And to ensure that the sin doesn't reappear I throw it into a fire for it to become nothing but ashes.

Chapter Eight

Big Eye

Liam, I admire your tenacity to ditch evil. The process though is complicated. Temptation and evil are like clouds. You have no control over them. They keep appearing and nobody can stop them. What I expect is that you be on guard. You can stop sin entering at source. I have millions of little angels ready to help you. If you are willing I can place a guardian angel in your eyes and ears. These act as a filtering system. Anything dirty is stopped from entering. Even sneaky sins and bits of crafty evil are prevented from entering the soul through your sense inlets.

Liam, another strong preventive measure for fighting sin and evil is by staying close to Divine Life. A simple prayer like the Sign of the Cross can do the trick. There is power in a Name. So call the Holy Spirit Liam. Call Jesus Christ Liam. And call me Liam. My goodness has begun to grow in you after a very rocky beginning. The effect of Me in you enables you to be sincere, virtuous and loveable. Therefore, I give you tools or virtues to use in the hope that you can attach yourself to me like the vine is to a branch.

Liam, I give you another image. I'm God the Horse. And you are Liam the Cart. You can't go anywhere without me. By prayer, love and faith you connect to me. It's only then that I can draw you to where I want you to go. I can draw you into the kingdom of heaven. I can hold you in the palm of my hand. I can shelter you under my wings. I'm the Horse that gallops faster than an express train and carries carts full of sincere souls to heaven.

Liam, I want to move on. The next idea that may be of some use to you and would definitely benefit me is to expand your awareness. I'd like you to know what's going on in the world. I have plans for you to work with my Son of Man who has authority to sow my Word and win souls for inclusion into belonging to the kingdom of heaven.

Liam, I'm your Doctor. This isn't funny. I created life. So I know each part of the mind and body. A dead, idle, inactive, dysfunctional or sick brain isn't capable of standing out as a bright light for the world to take notice. This issue of been the salt of the earth or a light to the world is of enormous importance to me. So allow me as your Doctor to examine you. Allow me to prepare, renew, touch, heal, repair your beautiful mind and body for the spiritual tasks ahead. Instead of your mind work operating at ten kilometres an hour I intend to speed up your intellectual usage to one hundred kilometres an hour. And the outstanding task at the moment is self-examination.

Liam, I'm God. I understand human life. I created the human mind. People think they are gods. I hear them talk and make suggestions to solve world problems. While at the same time they can't get their own lives right. I tell you solemnly Liam internal scrutiny is of vital importance to me. I create new life. I give you a complete make-over. I nurture bodily, emotional, intellectual, and spiritual growth. Every hair on your head is counted. And if you want to stand confidently before me I'll reform you now and make you a beautiful human being. If you allow me Liam to change everything about you I would regard you an earthly saint. My Spiritual formation of you and many more like you would change everything on earth and help to fight back the force of evil that's gripping the world.

Liam, I have my eye on you. You have a beautiful mind. And it is more beautiful because you practise what you say by wanting to obey my Will. Straightaway that indicates your intention to co-operate with Divine Life. As I said to you above I am your Doctor and a few spiritual issues have to be addressed. My Holy and hot Sacred Finger examines your external and internal body and mind. I intimately touch any damage parts that require healing. I cure defective senses and memory power. There is Liam a weakness in your memory capacity. It is no use to me if you hear my Word and five minutes later forget it. So I suggest praying to the Holy Spirit in order to remember all that I revealed to you. My Spirit will teach you everything. Your brain could work better. The fact that you are willing to trust and place all in my hands is the key that opens up Divine life for you.

Liam, focus on awareness of what's happening in your own mind. Practise being aware of yourself. Hear yourself talking. See yourself looking. Catch yourself thinking. Catch my Word in your memory. Feel your body. Liam, there are two ways you can come to me. You can come to me because you don't feel well and need help. Or you can come to me as good soil, or a branch that is healthy because joined to me. I'd like you to approach me because you are ready for my Word. And just to add I don't want a rogue either. I'd be a clown to reveal myself to a mind and heart that isn't well or taking me seriously. Also I couldn't adjoin myself to a person with a short memory or whose intellect functions sixty percent below its capacity. My operational Spiritual progress can't work in a bad head, a bad engine, or useless mind. I couldn't trust giving a secret to a clown or someone with amnesia. I couldn't give a talent to someone who has a lazy mind, or to someone whose mind is unable to think and work.

Liam, I repeat. Watch yourself. Notice yourself. Watch every minute of your life. Try to pile up and remember little things that happen throughout the day especially if they are relevant to you in forming a modern day Apostle. I want you to catch like a spider a fly in his web all the little things and words about me every day. I'm disillusioned with so many souls hearing about me and dropping what they hear as if my Word is a piece of ordinary chatter. To re-evangelise the world I need a new breed of Apostle.

Liam, no matter how busy you are, or no matter how much talk reddens your ear I require that you freshen up and shake off clutter in order to focus on me. I repeat Liam that I need a mind that ids fully compliant with my will. A good mind working hard could shake up the world.

Liam, think. Produce holy ideas. Cows take notice of you when walking on the road. Do you take notice of me? You are not an Aquinas.

Nor are you an Augustine. I know your mind is six decades old but that is no excuse. You have thinking ability. It's like turning a key in the car. You start the engine. You start the mind.

Liam, I order you to catch my thoughts in your head. You ensnare my Word. You delight in my Word like a spider is content with a fly caught in his web. I'm your Spider Liam. I caught you in my Son's web. I'm not going to eat you. I aim to adorn you with sacred armour and equip you with gifts of virtues so that you believe firmly in my Saint of saints, Jesus Christ.

Liam, I refer to an activity that's of vital importance to all. It's called capturing and discerning thoughts. In practical terms it's like fishermen coming in with a haul of fish. He sifts through the fish keeping the good ones and throw away anything that's of no use. The same applies with your catch of thoughts every day. I want you to dwell on the good ones and dispel anything inane. My main concern with you Liam at the moment is that you have no thoughts at all. In that case a question of being idle or lazy come into play. My Word is nor for layabouts, or for those who screw people for a gain, or for those who rip off anyone.

Liam, you are unaware of your thoughts every day. And you are a lazy Spider because you can't catch a fly or My Thoughts in your intellect. All My Thoughts that pass through your shabbily formed web escape. So I aim to correct this intellectual fault.

Liam the best way to tackle this issue is to pay close attention to everything that happens during the minutes of each experience. You hear a laugh. You listen to a conversation. You see cows in a field. You admire the large cornfield. You read the saints. You are conscious of sunlight in your room.

Liam, this is very important. Turn your mind to yourself and enter deep within yourself. Acknowledge your sin. If you want to be reconciled with me learn to act towards yourself. It's pathetic to worry about others sins while at the same be out of touch with sin within oneself. The first port of call is to check your thoughts and feelings. Awareness comes in here. I'd like you to register your thoughts, feelings and memories in your conscious mind. I'd like you to examine your motives. I'd like you to examine the way you speak to others. I'd like you to capture your actions each day. And in that process turn your actions and thoughts towards me.

Liam, your friend Augustine in a sermon has told you what I want. The sacrifice acceptable to me is a broken spirit and a contrite heart. What is acceptable to me is in your heart. You must tear it apart so that I can clean it and make it pure. My Word cannot lie beside filthy and impure minds and hearts. And Liam let me tell you solemnly the reason why my Word cannot settle comfortably within you. Your pride levels are too high.

Liam, in order to improve your task is to capture my Holy and Sacred Words and carry them into the core of your soul, let them grow strong there, and act on their meaning. The bulk of ungodly stuff beat into a corner. Flatten the rubbish, bless the space, and fill it with my Holy Word. And above all be loyal to this activity every day. You are old enough to know that Sacred Reading about the Saint of saints is of paramount importance if you are to find your Way towards me and heaven. I further warn that your Blessed Team assigned to your Personal Spiritual Progress are unwilling to stick around if you continue to allow your mind to drift away on long holidays or display inattention to your promises. I Am God remember. I don't wait around for disinterested souls or for those that keep me waiting.

Liam, don't let me die in your mind. Stop going away from me on ego trips. Remember why you retired. It is to write to me and tell me that you love me. So pray Liam. Spend time in quiet prayer with me. Continue meditation walks down the road. I want you to catch my Word like a spider a fly caught in his web. So cast out your net like a web and haul in my Words for each fine fish or fine Word deepens your spiritual prosperity and richness of my Way of Life.

Liam, self-reflection is good. It's like looking at yourself in a mirror. It's like stepping out of yourself and thinking of what is going on inside yourself. To hear my Word and forget five minutes later is no good. That's poor fishing. That's the mentality of a Lazy Spider. He catches nothing. Work Liam. Think Liam. Act Liam.

Liam, I saw you drive today. In the sky ahead of you there was a big black cloud and the sun shone through a hole in it. You thought of me giving light. And you thought of the black cloud as an image of dark problems that threaten the world and you personally. I liked the idea. It's an image of life Liam. There's darkness looming but don't allow it overwhelm you. What you must always do when threatened by danger is to trust in me and show faith in me as symbolised by the light shining through a hole in the darkness.

Liam, I'm your Father. I'm Big Eye. I'm aware of your unawareness of me. I'm not happy about that. I struggle to resurrect your unconscious state of mind especially in regard to my Presence. Come on Liam. I'm your Father. You have a duty to love me. I hear you tell Luke your son about three head levels – a head down is for sadness, a head straight is for the earth and all that it contains, and a head looking up aims for heaven. Your head is all over the place and rather dead. A dead head can't rejoice. Neither does a sick head feel like rejoicing. And I want my followers to be happy not because of the power I gave them to use my Name but because their names are written in heaven.

Liam, my Name must be on your lips and in your mouth. My Word is very near to you. You don't need anyone to bring it to you from heaven. You throw out the net Liam and haul in my Words. They are like beautiful fish or sweets Liam. Eat them and enjoy them. They have the power to change your life. You could change the world with them. You could teach my Peace and Truth. There should be no rending and tearing asunder the limbs of my Son. You all belong to the human race. You are brothers and sisters. Liam, tell them all in the world on my behalf not to kill but to love because you are all members of the same family.

Liam, use truthful imagination to make sense and give reasons for the existence of life on earth. There are billions of living things. There's a continuation of births and deaths every day. You are aware Liam that some relation of yours lived over two thousand years ago. You don't know what tribe you descended from. You know of other planets. And you don't know whether there is life somewhere else. You know about old age and how feeble limbs become with age. It's possible to make sense of me. It's possible too to find reasons for my Eternal and Divine Nature. But once again Liam I call upon you to focus on my Christ.

It's all fascinating. And I have the whole history of your ancestry in my Book of Human Beings. I know your gene. I know every person related to you in the same way as you know all your aunts and uncles that have passed away.

Liam, don't query me. Don't be nosy. I accept though truthful imagination where you think of me in heaven as an Almighty God and Most High Father. I accept your gleeful mind's eye picturing the Coronation of Mary Queen of heaven and earth. And I accept an imaginary long lens put on a camera to capture an image of my Son Jesus sitting beside me in heaven as King of the Universe. But other kinds of knowledge I prefer to protect you from. It simply best that you don't probe and rub your nose in wickedness as well as fearful dangers that threaten the world. What happens to the dead is my business? What happens to perpetrators of evil is my problem? None of you know what tomorrow holds. I'm God. I know everything. When the world ends nobody knows. I know you are anxious as to where your father is or where your friend who died of leukaemia is. You can send your mind of on a space odyssey if you like but the simple rule for finding facts and the Truth about your life and the afterlife is found in you belonging to my Son Jesus Christ. You find real life by going through my Son and by living a holy life. There is no other way.

Liam, thoughts are in your mouth. There are hundreds of them ready to come out through your lips. These originate from what you do every day, from who you interact with every day, from what your senses pick up, or from your memories. The greatest thought that you can have is of me. There is nothing greater. Your friend St Anselm from the thirteenth century told you that. I'm the greatest. No one is higher than Big Eye.

Liam, think of my Name. Always call me. I Am a Father to you. I Am God. Keep walking on road L0909 and continue telling me that you love me. Keep praying to me. I'm in your mouth and you didn't know it. I help you to form the sound of my Name. I hear your voice. Call me Liam. Call Jesus Christ, my Son. I love to hear the sound of my Name on the lips of sincere and humble souls who know how to pray. Liam, listen to your prayerful voice when you call Divine Names. My

Holy Name has power to go from your mouth up into your intellect and down into your heart. Think deeply about me Liam. If you love me, you would desire me all day long. Deepen the love Liam. Deepen the intensity. It's time to move up another level. I want you to come close to me. And every time you pray Our Father you move closer and closer to my Great Heart and Powerful Mind. The Pure Fire and Pure Love that I Am will drag you like a magnet into me. All I ask you in return is to approach me gently and effortlessly. I don't succumb to pressure. Instead I capitulate when I see people approach me like beautiful butterflies, gorgeous ladybirds, or gentle little lambs.

Liam, I've written a lot in this chapter. What's written should help you. Dialogue with you unites us. I have a Big Heart and I take yours into mine. I have a Super Mind and it will reflect into yours. I'm happy with your motives. In fact, I'm delighted. You want to tell others of my importance. That's honourable. You declare one simple message. I hear it. You want every person to make an effort to love me. That's good. You want every person to take Jesus Christ seriously. I do too Liam. Best of luck. I love you.

Little Man

Father, that was a long piece of writing. How am I going to remember it? I like it though. You are right. You are spot on regarding my motives. That's why I love you. You don't lead me astray. You understand what's in the mind of each person. You don't waffle. You hit the nail on the head and you're very direct. Father, the reality of your existence and my faith in you is pivotal. I don't want to bobble, hesitate, or waver when pagans attack me about your existence. Therefore, my confidence and strength must jump up a few levels. There can be no chances taken in our relationship. I seek unity in the same way as you are One with your Son Jesus Christ. I desire you Father and love you. I don't want any doubt appearing. I give you full access to do with me as you please. You are welcome. I invite you to lift me up and take me into your loving and tender care.

Father I give you full consent to enter the core of my being. I hide nothing from you. You have my full permission to cut out all my bad bits. Use a double edged sword to nip little bits of evil, ugly sores, nasty snakes, thistles and weeds that lay hidden in nooks and corners. I reject evil. It's best to cut out a bad eye, or a limb that is a threat to my soul. My only desire is to love you. I pray to you Father. I seek unity with my Sacred Love. The desired effect is to keep my body close to you Father through faith, prayer and love. I have the utmost confidence in you God. You can deliver me from evil. I allow your holy soldiers entry into my mind and heart so as to partake in running battles to drive out the enemy from every hidden trench within my soul. I choose Peace, Truth, Love, and Purity over war, lies, hatred, and immorality. Father I can't wait for the war to begin. I welcome the Holy Sword of my God to cut clean every type of sin that exists within me. Father, help me. Please burn the bins full of past sins. I don't want baggage from the past carried forward into my new Way of Life as a member of God's Holy Family. I want to please you with a virtuous body. I want to make you proud. I'd like you to see me as newly born little lamb crying for his Father's love and protection. I want Jesus as my Shepherd. I like his voice and I feel safe with his genuine care for my safety.

Father, once I have established a relationship with you I turn my attention to the welfare of my neighbour. I need to be sure of my love and unity with you Father, and with your Son Jesus Christ before any quality of care for others can come into play. I have been critical of people, of my religion, of women, and of people who harmed me. Life is a struggle at times. Showers of problems descend upon us. Situations frustrate us. And people can't help it when their dark moods infect others. And often miserable people can't help the way they behave. My true and beautiful Brother Jesus Christ calls me to love everyone and that includes my enemies. There are those who make us angry by carrying out acts of evil or by exploitation of poor people. I need to take care that evil doesn't affect me. It's rather easy for a mind to become infected by evil through the poisonous words of another. A venomous speech could infect thousands in seconds. I'm called to love enemies. I'm not to hate anyone. I build up the Body of Christ. I pray for all who suffer. I support the broken hearted.

Father, there's nobody like Jesus. He is the Greatest. He loved all and ignored faults. Jesus' love was outstanding. He saw a person rather than their imperfections. The greatest gift is to care for broken lives. Your Son, Big Eye cured lame bodies, blind and deaf people, a man with a withered hand, a woman with a brain haemorrhage, seven lepers, and a woman caught committing adultery. The focus for Jesus was not the healthy. He concentrated on helping the poor, the sinful and the sick. Jesus disliked the way political and religious authorities treated the weakest in society and the policy of ostracised polarisation of the vulnerable.

Father, I hear your message loud and clear. My neighbour has to be loved in the same way as you expect to be loved. I recall your gospel story about an invitation to a banquet. Influential people that were invited turned it down and made excuses not to go. So the poor were invited. And they accepted the invitation. I'm well aware of the consequences of neglect for neighbours. I have to have a concern and to help if possible all who suffer like the homeless, all who are handicapped, all the elderly, all who are exploited or deceived, all who have big crosses to carry, and every vulnerable soul in society. It's not good enough to pass on the other side of the road and fail to bandage the wounds of my neighbour. It's not fair to remain silent and have no feeling for brothers and sisters throughout the world who are afflicted by inhumane evil acts.

Father, I must love every person on earth regardless of their colour, religion and politics. I'm useless to you if I don't have this mentality or attitude. I cannot be a racist, or bigot, or snob. Your Commandment is quite clear. I must love my neighbour, and he or she is every person living in the world. I'm a member of the human race. I belong to the human race. Therefore, I cannot live in isolation or hibernation from what the journey that drives us forward each day.

Father, I'm worried though about today's human being. I walk along streets and only one out of ten might say hello. I'm sure if your Son walked along the streets of a big city today nobody would recognise him. We have all become strangers to each other. The odd one has a Christian smile for you. So I don't know what the best way is to evangelise modern man who has only the slightest space within for you Almighty God and Father of Our Lord Jesus Christ.

Father, I want to be like you and Jesus. I want to have an eye like yours to see pain in people and love them as they are. Let me see beyond heartache into the beauty of the person. Let me ignore faults and not judge anyone. Let me penetrate beyond the scars of hurt people. Let me show sympathy for those who suffer and hear their cries for help. To behave with love towards others is a great gift. I'd love to give hope and a home to those whose lives are shattered by bombs and war. It isn't easy to pick up broken bodies from the gutter and mend their pain

Father, I commit to you. I may be carried off from time to time in a storm. But I come back. My desire for you Big Eye is unbreakable. It is also unshakable. I'm a strong man and can take body blows as well as stand firm against gusts of wind. Faith has to be solid. I appeal to every human being on the planet to stand up and be counted. Active Christians are rather thin on the ground. I appreciate my faith handed on to me by my parents. I bless myself passing a Church. Faith is a beautiful thing. Baptism is beautiful too. I'm as proud as punch to have hung on to my faith giving to me by my mother and father's choice. It was their greatest gift to me. I love being a Catholic Christian. I clench my fist with confidence in Jesus Christ, my Super Hero. A man can have no better friend.

Father, too many have fallen asleep. Their religion is gone. Just the tiniest spark flickers. So with your support Father, I command an inner uprising in every person. I call them to rise up. I call myself too.

Father, I haven't fallen asleep. I rise up. I rise up and declare my love for you Big Eye. I hallow your holy Name. It's in my mouth. I wouldn't misuse it, overuse it, or abuse it. But I would like a little inner boost to trigger off inside me a sense of Awe in order to worship my Great God and give him the respect that's due to a Sacred and Divine Deity

Big Eye

Liam, you don't have to tell me what I Am. I know my strength. I'm powerful. Descriptions and words are sometimes remote from strong emotions. Poor little human beings. Very few on earth experience my Greatness. You are kept in the dark. Your eyes were opened to evil through disobedience. Seeds of evil were sown through this act. Knowledge of sex made you hide from me. Your potential to kill set you on an opposite course to me. And your deceit prevented a beautiful friendship with me.

Liam, I'm serious here. The complexity of evil mixed in with goodness complicates unity between us. I'm perfect and all belong to heaven are in a state of eternal bliss whereas imperfection crept human relationship due to original sin. So there will be frustration on your side in trying to rise to my Holy standards. Your complex and intricate intellect with evil mixed through it gives rise to conflicts, problems or many issues of misunderstanding between each other and me. Nobody escapes the flow of lies or corruption that seeps into the mind and heart of each individual unless they are already in heaven.

Liam, open your soul. I will come and make my home in you. I promise. Trust me. Throw open your inmost mind. By doing this you will see the riches of simplicity, the treasures of peace and the sweetness of grace. Liam, open your mind to me and open you heart too. I'm a bright light to enlighten you, and I advise you when to blink your eye to shut out anything other than me from approaching the door of your mind. My Christ knocks at your door Liam. My Christ enters through that door. My Word knocks insistently even at night to protect you from falling or be overwhelmed by distress.

Liam, I have to ask the question in regard to what you want from me. What are you looking for? I know you are desperate to connect. But what are you after? Why are you doing all this writing? I suspect you look for a privileged position. Are you looking for a direct line to me without going through the Catholic Church or any other religion? You are faithful. There is no doubt about that. And I admire your tenacity in linking yourself to me. I know you have asked to be spiritual by having an enlightened mind and body. But I don't know about seats in heaven. I don't know where you are going to fit in. My Son Jesus has pride of place. So to his Mother Holy Mary. And I have prophets, kings, saints and martyrs who contributed enormously to human history in spreading My Word. These holy men and women deserve their places in heaven because they influenced the world by their example and had the effect of keeping alive my Son's Presence in every person that believes in me.

Liam, come on. Very few people know you. The Catholic Church reveres Mary so much that she is referred to as the Mother of God. That is unique Liam. I have a beautiful woman as Queen of Heaven. This woman is full of grace. She is a Spiritual Model for every girl. The Mother of my Son Jesus is there for you too. Sometimes a man needs a good woman in his life too. Holy Mary is more than that good woman. She is the model of virtue and is well capable of helping men to respect women.

Liam, you wouldn't feel comfortable in among my Queen of Heaven and my Universal King. I can't see you mingling with my great Saints or Doctors of the Church. All through the ages there has been outstanding ministers of my Word. Liam be realistic. Get a grip. You are not above Popes, Cardinals and Bishops – the cream of the Church and most loyal servants of Jesus Christ. Liam, can you imagine yourself in the company of Elijah, Abraham, Moses, Isaiah, and David. The Apostles are the Chosen Twelve. So Liam forget places of privilege in heaven. I am loyal to my followers who keep my Word and preach it.

Liam, at the moment I can't give you a seat at my table. I can't even give you a stool in a quiet corner. I can sit you down within groups of fifty to eat my Body and Drink my Blood in the Eucharistic celebration of my Son. Only my Son can bring you through the narrow gate that leads to heaven. So stop right now. Liam stop fantasising about a place of privilege among Aquinas, Augustine, and Anselm and other saints who passed the test and made it to heaven.

Little Man

Father, I'm shy. I dislike the limelight and it suits me living on a quiet road. I have no one to bother me. I spend my time writing to you. Father, that is all I want from life. I seek no position of privilege, or greatness, or desire to outdo anyone in heaven. All I ask for is to be a member of the team.

Father, I'm a little bit jealous when I look at all the beautiful flowers that decorate your Church. They are sweet and colourful. I love their beauty. I love their intelligence. I love their contribution towards my sacred desire. I'd love to be a flower. But I'm afraid of being a weed. And I don't know how to change from being a weed to a flower. I'd settle for a daisy, or a daffodil, or a dandelion. I don't have to be a Doctor of the Church or classy saint. I want to be on the team with Fr William my spiritual director. I want to share in the life of St John who is the Apostle of Love. I want the spirit of Saint Patrick whose faith means a lot to me. I want St Anselm as a friend who taught me to treat you as the Greatest and Highest of All. I want St Dominic who preached the truth. These holy men delight my soul. They fill me with an odour sweeter than any food on earth. I desire to follow their example of love and obedience.

Father, what is going on? Protect my family. Somethings are going wrong. I love my wife. She's ill and suffering a bit. I love my mother who is ill too. I don't like to see her suffering. She's very devout. But she's ill now. I love my son Luke. He is an extension of ourselves and hopefully the boy will grow up to love your Son Jesus. I pray for him to have strong faith. I'd die happy knowing if my Son was a good Christian. St Monica felt the same about her son Augustine.

Father, I love your Word too and the Eucharist. I love people who have heavy crosses to carry. I feel sorry for all who suffer greatly. I support and love families with special needs children. Is that enough? I pray with love to you every day. Is that enough Big Eye? Does that qualify me to be part of your team?

Big Eye

Liam, I see deep into your interior life. All stirrings are known to me. Nothing escapes my attention. And I tell you solemnly that following me is a great challenge. There is a huge difference between word and action. The Pharisees thought they were the cream of the crop. They thought they were keeping the Law. They thought they were holy and perfect. They looked good on the outside, said their prayers, and preached the traditions of their fathers. But inside they were rotten.

In fact, they were sons of murderers. They killed prophets because they had far seeing eyes and exposed distortion and corruption.

Liam, I warn you to be careful. There's a huge difference between helping the poor and preaching about being good to the poor. There is a huge difference between visiting an elderly sick neighbour and writing a line about him in a book. Never turn down an opportunity to help. For the person could die and you would regret been helpful. So be careful that the hypocrisy of the Pharisees isn't in you.

Liam, I warn you again. I want workers in the vineyard. The world needs another uncompromising preacher like St Paul. He went around towns and villages fearlessly preaching about Me, and about my Son Jesus Christ, and about the Holy Spirit. He preached with conviction.

Liam, people need good priests and good people. These are people who love their neighbour before themselves. Some priests and religious are not happy because their relationship with me isn't right. I see it in their faces on the altar saying Mass. They have not prayed enough until it hurts. They have not prayed enough to receive the mantle of being salt to the earth and light to the world. I want my Word to dwell in holy bodies. I want men and women to love me more than anything else. And I don't trust those who go away on holidays from me, or those whose minds forget me for long periods throughout each day because they held back little luxuries and pleasures for themselves.

Liam listen to me. My sharp eye, or my Big Eye see through hypocrites in an instant. A tiny glance from my Big Eye exposes corrupt groups or individuals. I spot the state of an individual soul in a jiffy or as quick as clicking my finger. Nobody escapes my Truth. Many fall from grace through crafty legislation. The drive is to become rich. The method is to rip-off people by overcharging people with an unfair fee for poor services. The drive of the greedy rich disappoints me. Your friend St Augustine wrote extensively on the subject. He saw shepherds were more interested in feedings themselves than the people they serve. Greed is a fatal flaw. I feel sorry for those who placed love of money before me. The wonderful love of Jesus Christ has vanished in these souls and in its place are wads full of €500 notes. My Big Eye sees into all Green Eyed souls – all those who live for money, luxury, power and pleasure.

next

Chapter Nine

Little Man

Dear Father, I'm frightened. It scares me to think I'll be scolded by Jesus. I'm proud and that makes me arrogant. Pride is an infestation of selfish desires. I try to love you Father directly. But by doing this I ignore the plight of others. I avoid been caught up in people's problems. And I don't share the burden of caring for vulnerable and sick people. I have nothing but praise for those that help with mentally and physically disabled people. They are the real saints and deserve a place in Jesus' heart.

Father, I do sincerely want to love you. If Jesus needs to whip me into shape I'll allow him to beat my sins into a holy submission. I want to be one in mind and heart with you Jesus and with you Father. I dread making a mistake. I commit to loving you Father. I know you watch me. And I'm not immune to those that suffer. I'll judge no one or condemn no one. I'm not to have any hatred feelings for anyone. I call upon everyone to love Muslims and Catholics and see them as brothers and sisters. I beg for forgiveness for those sucked into committing acts of evil. Smother evil. Smother acts of war with love. By my message of peace, I care for every Nation. There is no need to fight each other. Instead serve each other. Big Eye I love you first. Then I love my neighbour and he or she is every person on earth.

Heavenly Father, I feel like a prophet. I'm called to preach on the decline of religion in my country. I don't belong to any religious group. But I'm a member of the Catholic Church. I love my faith. I adore it. But I'm excluded from leadership roles and positions of influence.

I'm blocked from ministry. But that doesn't stop me from preaching through this book. I beg priests to preach good sermons and freshen the congregation with vigour. I beg for a resurrection of prayer in each soul. I want Christians to wake up. Think man! Wake up man! Jesus Christ is dying a slow death every day because hearts and minds are intoxicated with lethargy.

Father, I find a sweetness in your Name. I have tasted you. And I desire to drink and eat more. I never have enough of you Father, nor do I have enough of your Son Jesus Christ. I do find it frustrating though that bishops and priests are unaware of my deep faith. Over the years my best efforts were shot down. Intellectuals who had less faith controlled power. I wanted inspiration, change and enthusiasm. But the hierarchy in both religious life and priestly life hung onto the status quo. Comfort was preferred to hard work. Liturgical life dominated over pastoral care.

Heavenly Father, I needed this time to work out my vocation. I would celebrate Mass again if permitted. I'd preach again if permitted. I would challenge every person in Church to discard bad habits. I'd like to have authority like Jesus and wake up sleepy minds and stir up a proper response in each soul to worship in spirit and truth. I'd love to speak Truth and declare it solemnly. I'd love to touch the eyes and ears of each person in the congregation with solemn statements to take seriously and carry Golden Egg Words home within their hearts.

Father, I have beautiful sermons and fabulous ideas in me. I have shared them with prayer groups and close friends but nobody takes me seriously. I have a super family event in mind based on Ezra's story of Scripture Reading after a long sojourn from worship in the Temple. Nobody supports my plan. I'd invite willing families to participate in Scripture Reading. It would be aimed at families who haven't been inside the Church door for a number of years. Each family would read followed by a long quiet pause. Confession and the Eucharist could be included. And afterwards the parish could provide refreshments for all.

Father, I'm alone with my suggested endeavour. A good shepherd should visit and encourage lost sheep to return to Church. A good shepherd works day and night to save souls. A good priest should care for families. If people don't go to Church the priest should go to the people. New ideas to bring Jesus Christ back into Parishes and Communities ought to be viewed by parish committees. The whole purpose of Christ coming into the world is to save souls. Only the zealous pastor would go the extra mile, put in the hard work and extra work to convert a soul and bring him/her back to Church. There are not enough of St Monica's around today. Please pray with your children. Please bring them to Church.

Holy Father, I pray for priests. There is a priestly crisis emerging. Very few are available to cover services. And with the way family life has gone I can't see emerging disciples coming from a weak faith and prayer less background. Also I dislike rabbit priests who celebrate Mass and disappear for the day.

Father, my heart was often breaking when my good ideas were never supported. I'd make recommendations for sensible changes at meetings and one by one my brilliant thoughts died one after another.

Father, I'm struck by Jesus' criticism of religious hypocrisy. God Almighty I hope my inner state of being isn't rotten. I hide nothing and expose rotten bits. Every day I must check myself and examine my conscience. I'd feel horrible about myself if Jesus classed me among those he referred to as a brood of vipers.

Big Eye

Liam, you are on the right path. I like you're thinking. You attempt to identify your inner thoughts and feelings. I like that. You can change. I watch out for men like Simon Peter. He fell at the feet of my Son Jesus and declared his unworthiness after recognising Divine Power at work in Jesus.

Liam, I'm pleased for you that you are honest. I'll deal with your bad bits once you follow Divine Power found in Jesus my Son. Nothing on earth is greater than to love my Christ. I want you to be one with the Church Liam. Your bishop, your clergy and your deacons are special friends. Allow nothing to cause divisions.

Liam, always beware of hypocrisy and deceit. I can see the rotten parts inside the soul of each person. I am Truth. Nothing lies hidden from me. So expose yourself to me. I want to see all. Hide nothing. I continuously ask my special friends on earth to deal with their inner life. A daily examination of conscience is recommended. For I would not like to send a priest or lay person out on a mission if he hid something that was rotten inside. The faithful would spot the demon. Then you are ruined. My credibility is affected by a bad example.

Liam, check deeply into your subconscious mind. There is the possibility that a nest of imps could grow and thrive undetected in an alcove within your mind. With your love for me I can help to pluck maggots, worms, weeds, or any unwanted thing from secretly sabotaging your desire to give all to me.

Liam, the Holy Way of Life is a battle for your heart and mind. I want you. But so does my adversary. And he is a cunning and powerful imposter of goodness who delights in destroying unguarded souls. Satan spawns' evil eggs inside your mind and they have terrible consequences when you try to be good. These little sharp imps cut, chop, slice and disturb every good thought you try to manufacture inside yourself. These bad things in the heart and mind can be defeated through prayer and close proximity to me.

Liam, try and align yourself to me as much as possible. It's a deterrent against a fox, or a rat, or a mouse from running in through your holes, the senses. I Am Truth. And I have the power to clean up your mind and heart. Your inner life is dear to me. My Son referred to it as the good soil. I can build up a sanctuary within you. I have the power to remove from your inner nest faulty, bad, unclean or evil eggs. I can chase them in your soul until they have nowhere to go. Think of them as a nest of ants. I pull them out one by one until they are all gone. The only thing I want in your soul is my Word and your love for me.

Liam, do you understand what I am doing? I'm cleaning up your soul. I'm training you to fight yourself by uprooting mortal and venial sins with my help. For I cannot have on my side a man who has no knowledge of his spiritual state.

Liam, I do love you. It's a good sign that you desire to do the right thing and ask for help. Even though it is a little bit vague I see that you recognise I Am Absolute Truth. Liam, keep doing what you are doing. Invite me into your home. Invite me into your heart and mind. All you have to say regularly is, "Come Lord Jesus". Or, "Come Holy Father". Or again, "Come Holy Spirit". Once invited I Am inside you in a jiffy. It is then that you will reap the benefits of a relationship with me. It is your invitation Liam that enables us to be friends.

Liam, I'm more than interested in you. I love my Little Man. I'm Almighty and Majestic with power over the whole of creation and yet I have time to relate to one single little man living on my planet. You are different Liam. You invite me into your life. You allow me to do anything to you. You trust me. You co-operate with me. You open up to me and hide nothing. I like that. I like a man to bare his soul.

Liam, the vast majority of people don't live for me. The prayer effort of each person is poor. With you I have noticed a consistency in your quality of prayer to find me, and speak sincerely to me. I Am your heavenly Father. Those who obey me find me. Those who respect me have a chance of a loving friendship. I cast my Big Eye across the world and I see millions upon millions of people living as if I don't exist. They are busy going here and there and they forget that they will die someday and face me. It's a mistake for every person to live as if the world is there lot. I see the way they comfort one another but have no faith in me. I Am Real. I exist in a Spiritual Place. Your Way to Me is inscribed in the Lord's Prayer. Very few realise that the Lord's Prayer is a pot of gold. You do. Your heart burns for it.

Liam, I can tell you solemnly comprehension of the Lord's Prayer cannot be priced. It is an immeasurable source of enlightenment. It's a bridge between your mind and mine. A person who unites with me through my Christ's Holy Words strengthens a sacred bond between us. The effect of this holy bonding scares away all mice, rats, foxes, or slippery eels from the edge of the soul. A clean house can't be dirty. Nothing evil hides in a holy soul.

Liam, holy and meaningful prayer has the effect of a roadblock in the mind. Prayer generates sanctity. And anything unsavoury or unwanted that arrives at the roadblock fails to get through for two reasons. One is that their wickedness is exposed by Christ. The snakes, the spiders, the rats, the fox, the vicious dog come to the roadblock but can't go further because germination occurred between the soul at prayer and Jesus Christ. All temptation is conquered through prayer. The person constantly seeking me can't go wrong.

Liam, I solemnly warn you to be on guard. Be aware of every person. Damage can be done in a split second. That is extraordinarily fast. Test the spirit of each person before you trust them. A slippery eel could gush in through the ear in a jiffy. The unwanted trespasser races into your mind undisguised through a child, a man or a woman. I try my best to warn you. I'm not responsible if a lapse in concentration results in you finding niggly and irritating sprats from swimming inside your head. And you know yourself once they are in you can't catch and kill them without a struggle. It's best to keep them out at source. I don't want to find an infestation of ants or cancerous maggots in your soul when I check in on your spiritual condition.

Liam, your soul is like a seabed with rocks, pebbles, plants, leaves, seaweed, and small nooks. If you are not alert horrible little evil sprats will hide in your mind. And for you to chase them out is extremely difficult because they dart from one hideout to another quicker than your mind can think. They hide under a stone. And you are lost. Only I can catch them one by one and throw them out of your mind. But that depends once again on the quality of your prayer to me.

Liam, little demons in you are like pests. They lurk for opportunities to smash your confidence, drive you insane, make you unhappy, and cause you to feel miserable about life. These little dark creatures shoot down good intentions. They create an abundance of uncertainty and make you deaf and blind to my Presence. Your demons destroy true friendships.

Liam, I Am your Protector. But I can't prop you up all day if you drop in and out of consciousness. My Power doesn't work when you sleep while you are awake. You are vulnerable when your conscience is somewhere else. I require one hundred percent concentration on me your Father, on me Big Eye, on me your God. I'd like you to comprehend that truth Liam. I'm your Sacred and Divine Lover. It's only proper that you walk a straight path towards me.

Liam, I Am Holiness itself. I Am Pure Holy. I Am ready to pump grace into you. I have the stuff that makes you fit for heaven. All I ask for is better concentration. I Am like a Petrol Station filling up those that come to me for grace. I pump up your heart and mind with grace.

Liam, I Am the stuff that makes men and women holy. I make Saints. I am so Hot that proximity to Me cause changes to occur within your whole body – externally and internally, emotionally and intellectually. I Am the stuff that make your mind beautiful. My sanctifying grace and holy oil trickles through every vein in your body. My Well Liam is eternal. You can drink all you want if you love me. My Divine and True Love is beautiful. The most beautiful woman in the world is nothing in comparison to Me.

Liam, I'm outside your window. I'm testing your loyalty and love. I place wealth before your eyes. I put before you a rich and a beautiful woman. Would these tempt you to forget me? O Liam, I love you. You have found the Holy Well. It is refreshing to drink from my Heart and Mind. I have been trying to tell you for the last number of years to break the obscure mirror that keeps us apart. My Holy Water will keep you alive longer. All other drinks and foods will kill you quicker. Discipline is very important to me Liam. Eat from Me. Drink from Me.

Liam, can you feel anything bubbling up inside of you? That's my grace. That's my Love. I touch every bone in your body. I relief your pain and stress. I create you at birth and recreate you now from a battle scarred body and mind so as to make you a beautiful new man. Your levels of holiness surge high. Your glowing face is like a bright light for the world to see. My Sacredness and Sanctity have the power to change the evillest of human beings provided a little kink of remorse is detected in the sinner.

Liam, the indisputable experiences of Jesus Christ, My Divine Son must stick deep inside of you. You are to be unshakeably convinced of Divine Truths revealed through my Christ. The most notable of these are his birth, passion and resurrection. But think of all his spoken holy gems too like, "You are the light of the world". All Christians and Muslims who connect sincerely to me through prayer are like little lamps in the world. My brightness is in them. When you pray Our Father that light is switched on. I'm very happy Liam. I shine brightly through you. The imps have run from your soul because through me you are a new man. You are on my team. I assign you a Guardian Angel and welcome onto the official path that leads to the kingdom of heaven.

Little Man

Hello Father! Hi Holy God! Good day. Thank you so much! I'm delighted. Your writing is brilliant. It is brilliant news for me. It makes me happy. It makes me super happy. I'm a part of God's team. Let the journey begin right now Big Eye.

I say, Yes! Yes! Yes, to you Father. It's wonderful news!

Father, I'm well aware of the battle in front of me. But being on your side is over half the battle. I couldn't defeat temptations and evil on my own. It's through you Father that I overcome wave after wave of Satan's tests. My prayer to you Father will defeat evil.

Father, I have found new friends. I work with God. I walk with God. My new family includes God the Father, Son, Holy Mary and Holy Spirit. I'm among the flowers of the Church. My goal now is to urge loyalty and unity with All Saints, Bishops, clergy and godly minded deacons as well as faithful women who pray daily in the Church. For I would not like to be a weed among flowers, or a goat among lambs.

Big Eye

Liam, you have acted in haste. Get a grip! You are not in heaven yet. It takes more than an instant to transform a human. Change doesn't come about with the click of a finger. A period of transition occurs. And the journey to me is full of hurdles and setbacks. Spiritual surgery hasn't begun. You saw that for yourself when you ate ice cream and sweets today. Those luxuries replace me. Yet you acted as if I supplied you with an abundance of sanctifying grace. Did it work? It didn't Liam because you caved in to tests. You could not say no to the ice cream.

Liam there is work to be done. You have to go through a process. You achieved nothing yet. There is an agreement to unite. There is a willingness from you to
start living like a disciple. You announced your intention.

Liam, there are appointments forthcoming. I can't allow mad men, perverts, duds, or human heads that can't look me straight in the eye work in my vineyard. So you are checked into Heaven's Hospital for Doctors of the Church to discern if you are sound in mind and your intentions to love me are honourable. St Thomas Aquinas, St Catherine of Siena and St Augustine are your Church Doctors. Also you might require surgery to repair cracked ideas and unstable consciousness so I refer you to St Anselm, Fr William, and St Dominic. Liam, don't question my professionalism. Co-operate with the team. My Saints are holistically the best in the business. So allow them to do their work. Liam, I have to ensure that you are healthy psychologically, emotionally and bodily. For I can't risk seeing you collapse under pressure at the first hurdle when called upon to be a witness for Christ against the forces of evil around the world. My Doctors are your friends. They are your consultants. I will liaise with them and decide whether operations are necessary.

Liam, pray to your Holy Team and count yourself lucky to have them. I'd like you to sit with your team and explain what troubles you. Liam, they will help you. I can see that you prefer Me. In fact, I see you run to Me. But it looks like you run from a Trinity of Women and I don't blame you. Your ears are red from listening to them. My Church Doctors will refresh you. I Am Big Eye. I'm excited. I carry you Liam to my Sacred and Holy Surgeons. They are the best in the business. Just relax Liam. St Augustine will check your heart to see if your levels of love are high or low for Me. St Thomas Aquinas will thrill your intellect with rational composure and methods to study your life in Christ and focus on what is important.

Liam, the first symptom my Holy Team has reported for consideration is the state of your mind. It has to be sound Liam. Yours's is battered black and blue. Satan has lashed out at you. You have taken a heavy beaten. Straightaway Church Doctors saw the marks and scars in your brain. It looked as if you were under siege from a long drawn out storm that rarely abated.

Liam, my spiritual advice for you is to gain back your life by giving yourself plenty of time while you listen to your inner murmurings. You can do this by going for walks and taking time to be alone. Also plan your day to suit you. Take time to recuperate. What you have gone through is on the severe scale of things.

Liam, don't blame anyone. Don't be hard on the Trinity of Women. Neither be hard on yourself. My healing is Peaceful. I can calm all that goes on in you. And you will more than enjoy my Holy Team of Church Doctors whom you love to bits anyway. With the help of my Christ and all the Saints there is no need for you to worry. Pray for the Trinity of Females. For I would never command anyone to hold a grudge or despise another human being. My Son Jesus was victim and victor. So offer no resistance. People don't know what they are doing.

Liam, I carry you and take care of you. Trust in Me alone. I'm involved in your Spiritual Service. I want your mind as Peaceful as mine. Once you are in my care I ease those pains that hurt you and restore your mind, memory, and emotional state to a brand new or original condition. I Am an Almighty Power. I have Authority to heal the sick. I can heal cancer. If you are damaged by wordy storms call me. If parts of your body are cancerous I can heal you. All I require is faith, prayer and trust.

Liam, preaching my Word requires healthy bodies and sharp minds. My trainee disciples must be able to stick the course. I can't have them running away with fear at the bark of a dog. Only men and women made of steel should follow me. I don't want crook priests. I don't want immoral priests. I don't want clergy to give up when black clouds of evil descend on the Church. Just like my Son Jesus Christ I expect loyalty from Bishops, clergy and people.

Liam, just like medical checks I carry out spiritual checks on populations in cities, towns and individuals. I watch to see if people pray. I watch to see what people prioritise in their lives. For some it is sex. For others it is money. The fact that you are frank with me and desire me makes it possible for us to cement a true friendship. But it is necessary to check you spiritually. A big and evil rat could be hidden inside. As God and Father it is my duty to catch vermin and remove it from tormenting you or anyone who vouchsafe to love me.

Liam, I have you back. You can bare your soul to me. I wouldn't hurt you. You can tell me everything. In fact, I love you Liam because you allow me to see you as you are. You hide nothing. Whereas trust in people is dangerous. A close friend could disclose secrets. Also betrayal could occur. Confidentiality is often broken. But for Me you can trust. I admire those who confide in me. So Liam allow my Holy Team to dig deep in search of vermin. We don't want ten or twelve mice having a field day playing games inside your head. Vermin playing would hold you back from union with me. Confess your sinfulness to me. Don't be ashamed. Sometimes great sinners show more love to me. I hold very high those who bend their knees in respect of Who I AM. Millions of people around the world are spiritually sick because they have no respect for Me or each other.

Liam, on first inspection pride and anger are strongly showing up in your test. These two vices do awful damage. Pride places you first. Humility places Me first. Pride has the same effect as cancer. It kills spirituality. Cancer kills bodies. Your results show a higher level of pride than humility. Liam, it can't go unchecked.

Liam, I saw anger in you too. Many times you are enraged. The vice usually erupts through differences of opinion, or when someone disagrees with you. Anger is aggressive and is like a mad dog. The vice manifests itself through angry outbursts of temper caused often by small things like a paper, a brush, or a seat. I don't like anger in you Liam. Pride and anger definitely repels those who aspire to holiness. I don't allow noisy, disruptive and aggressive souls entry into heaven.

Liam, on further inspection I found other faults too. There is a bit of lust. But you have made great strides in subduing carnal knowledge and desires towards sexual gratification. Lust is not a problem in you. However, sex is a problem for many. Some are affected by pornography. Liam, keep an eye on your desires. it. Keep your eyes pure.

Liam. My Eye is Big. I see all. You are a diabetic. Yet, you eat biscuits, sweets, and ice cream. What is wrong? I regard discipline as serious. Work on the virtues. To fast is better than to over overeat. Say no to temptation is better than saying yes to gluttony. I work better with people who fast for Me. Life isn't the best for unhealthy blobs who feed on high levels of sugary foods and drinks. I love fasting Liam. I encourage you to drink water, eat vegetables, and bread. You will feel better and live longer if you do what I tell you. You also follow in the footsteps of the Great St John the Baptist. So Liam continue to pray and monitor your diet. I would appreciate more and more of fasting.

Liam, a spade is a spade. Use a spade to remove sin lodged in your soul. Dig it out. Fill buckets with weeds. Burn them. Snip ugly night bugs. Smash oncoming vermin. The fight in your journey towards Me is disheartening due to its toughness. But you can succeed. You are on the right path. Examine your conscience so as to amend failures and correct faults. The pilgrimage way is tough. There are times when you will feel like giving up. That is the time to work harder.

Little Man

Father, thank you. I appreciate help from you. But is your writing a little bit farfetched. I can't see my sins nor have I power to eliminate them. I can't catch pride. I can't fight anger. I can't control gluttony. I can't root out lust. I can't prevent sloth. It is not within my power to compete with the evil of Satan. It is not a physical fight either one on one. It's more mysterious, sophisticated and impersonal. I don't know if seven deadly sins exist nowadays.

Father, there is a better way. It is the way of contact. I believe contact with you has power to dissolve sin and cure sickness. Contact with Jesus healed the haemorrhage woman. To touch Divine Power heals. She touched Jesus' hem as he walked through a crowd. Her bleeding stop. She was made well again.

Father, how can I follow the example of the haemorrhage woman? How can I touch Jesus?

Father, I want to touch your Son Jesus like that woman. But Jesus physical stay on earth in the body is out of reach. There must be a different way to touch Jesus. I can be touched by the power of his Word. Or I can receive the Lord through Holy Communion? Or I could tap Jesus on the shoulder in the boat while he lay asleep during a storm. I could throw myself at the feet of Jesus like St Peter in recognition of his own unworthiness before a Divine Power.

Father, you tell me that faith can move mountains. I have faith. I clench my fist and tell you so. I believe. I pray. It is through the medium of those words that contact is credible with the Son of Man. Even though Jesus doesn't walk around physically in Ireland today I can imagine myself with him through scenes in the gospels. I have great faith in you Jesus. I love you. I approach the throne of grace. I experience contact with Jesus. I sit at his feet and listen to my Lord. I walk with Jesus going from place to place.

Father, I plead on my knees for you to save me. To lose contact with you would kill me. I'm fully confident that the closer I am to you Father the greater are the chances of vices and sickness melting away. Proximity to you God is everything. I believe this truth because of your Sacred Nature Father. So hold me tight Big Eye. Don't allow me to wander. I love you. Proximity to you Almighty God is the best way to defeat evil. It's like melting jelly in hot water.

Father, I'm worried that people might regard my writing as crap. I keep writing to you as my Father. But nobody knows you as Our Father, nor do they realise the Sacredness of your Holy Name. It hurts Father when pagans and intellectuals bypass Power that is in your Holy Name. I want simple faith like that of mere children mentioned in the gospel. I don't class myself as a philosopher or theologian. I pity those who are so intelligent and successful and yet can't find the Lord in a very simple Way of Life. All is necessary is faith and prayer in a Word called Abba.

Father, there is no quick fix. There is no permanent solution in solving sin found buried within each one of us. Our nature is as such that we are prone to evil as well as good. What your Son Jesus offers us is a gift of love. We are to lead in love. The love that we have for each other weaken the effect of sin. The leader in society is the one who burns with love for the welfare of everyone else. Love is a glowing virtue. It stretches hearts wide open.

Father, help me. The struggle with sin and poor judgement strangles me. I can't defeat my vices. The slippery little evil imps appear regularly on the edge of my soul. And if I'm not on guard they run into brain cells and impregnate my decisions advising me to reject right choices. I see it happening with food. I'm thirty years fighting selfish and unnecessary comfort eating. I'm a diabetic now and even the threat of losing an eye or a leg doesn't stop me from indulging in an ice cream, a jam doughnut or a bar of chocolate.

Father, I can't expect you to intervene and take sweets off me. The simple truth is that I ignore the Spirit's promptings to stop. I disobey the Trinity that tells my inner voice to stop. This is reality religion. There's more to it than attending the Christian community for prayer and the blessing of bread and wine. Religion is about listening to your voice Father in everything that is done and said. My heavenly Father cares. If my child is obese I must try and stop his supply of sugary foods. There are great Christian lessons to be learnt from fasting, self-control and discipline. My Father does not like to see a child of his harming his body and soul in any way. So I have to destroy the imp that prevents me from choosing between water and fizzy drinks, or ice cream to an apple.

Chapter Ten

Big Eye

Liam, I love you. The extension of my love expands your heart. Liam, feel it. My love is the only sweet that you need. You can Eat and Drink my love. But be careful about consciousness. By this I mean chewing and munching my Sweets or my Love without any acknowledgement of Me. I observe people. I Am Big Eye. I notice gluttons take me for granted. They eat and drink but never say thanks.

Liam, you are right to highlight that proximity to Me is up there as the best method in accomplishing unity and perfection in me. My Perfect Love oozes from my heart into those that come close to me. True friendship with me is a treasure. It's where love meets. And nothing is greater than love. I urge you Liam to love me during every minute of the day. A little lapse allows Satan to swiftly jump in and trigger a storm.

Liam, a lack of love or lapses in love result in major blow ups between individuals, families, communities or Nations on earth. To avoid war and storms, arguments and hatred each person must turn to Me, the God of Peace. So love me always. You will make mistakes. You will have arguments. You will misunderstand words and fight against each other.

Liam, I repeat, love me. I Am your Father. My Presence and protection is enough to unsettle imps that attempt to nest and rest in your soul. Imps do not come near your house if you have Me in your home. They keep their distance because they do not like me. The odd time though a demonic attack occurs. These ones are vicious and dangerous and it takes longer to remove them. From your point of view

Liam turn to me and love me. But watch out for the nice demons too especially the one called charm. That's the one tempting you to eat chocolate and seek pleasure. During everything that happens Liam I highlight the importance of seeking approval from your Father and pray with love before giving in to discussions and events.

Liam I saw you were attracted to Isaiah's purification experience. You read of a seraph with a hot piece of coal touching his lips. That happened before my Son's entry. Isaiah's writing is true. He prophesied about the coming of my Son – the suffering Messiah. I burnt his sins. I purged his demons. Isaiah unfolded my plan for the future.

Liam, I could do to you what I did to Isaiah. My red hot piece of coal on your lips would create a wonderful mouth of pure and holy words. I kill crap talk. I silence your tongue and place my Word in your mouth for the world to hear. My red hot piece of coal burns to a cinder sick bodily parts, and sinful bits. At the sight of my burning fire everything unwanted like weeds and vermin run for their lives. My Fire is a great source of purification.

Liam, listen to me. All you need to worry about is your love for me. You don't have to have knowledge. You don't have to worry. Peter was a fisherman. You were a plasterer. Isaiah was in a wretched state. You don't have to be at the top in your profession. I'm attracted to ordinary people.

Liam, don't forget who you are in dialogue with. I made the world a long time ago. I have a Big Eye. Nothing escapes my attention. I see all. I am very good. I thought of everything. My creation is beautiful. Liam, enjoy your stay on earth. I created each person a self-contained unit. You can work independently for me. Don't blame others if you err. I gave you a body, mind and heart to find me. I gave you intelligence. So don't be a baby. Think like a man using the gifts I gave you. Work hard to find Jesus Christ while you have the chance. I cannot hold your hand and forget the rest of creation.

Liam, I have high standards. I see your secret emotions. I know every plot that originates in your mind. You can't fool me. Remember I Am Truth itself. I like integrity in a man. So Liam always tell the truth, always be honest and reliable. I like dignity in a man too. Your self-respect and desire to be holy and confident is important to me. And above all I like a man to be sincere with me. It's not easy for a rogue to make progress with me.

Liam, I'm happy with your attempts to love me. In fact, it is beautiful. I have not forgotten your prayer attempts while walking on road L0909. You were very sincere every time you call me Father. I hear you. You don't think I do. But I revere every attempt to Hallow my Holy Name. I solemnly tell you Liam that you have chosen the better part. The younger generation think of me as an idea. I acknowledge your adoration of me. I value your faith. I appreciate your dedication. You have chosen me above everything else. My Little Man in Limerick thank you. I bring you now up a couple of levels and nearer to my holy mountain. The climb is tough. But I'm pleased that you have left behind desires for sexual pleasure and luxurious living. I Am your wealth and you want nothing more. That ticks all the boxes for inclusion into my academy to learn more and more from Jesus Christ, my only and Divine Son. I solemnly add that every step up that mountain to me is far more valuable to you than lazing about everyday doing nothing.

Little Man

Father, I'm overjoyed. Your advice is thrilling. I'm running over with joy. I make room for you in my heart. You are a magnificent Father. I'm proud to have you. Your glory fills me with joy. I've never seen you but I feel you. I can't believe my luck. I've found you hidden behind a few special words. My only problem now is concentration. I hallow your Name Father as an adopted and loving son. My plan is to increase awareness of your magnificent Divinity. I can't fall asleep. I call you Father all day long. I thirst and hunger for you.

Father, my time for prayer is not in the morning or evening. It is every minute of the day. I turn to you Father. If I drift off into a dream or wander into the unknown, or stray by distractions tap me on the shoulder to wake me up again and again so that I can return to praise the greatness and holiness of my Father. I'm his adopted son. I'm not out of line calling God my Father. He is Father to everyone that obey him.

Father, life is wonderful with you. There is no annoyance in you. There's no evil in you. You wouldn't hand me a stone if I asked for bread. You wouldn't hand me a snake if I asked for a fish. Nor would you hand me a scorpion if I asked for an egg. You are a Father that doesn't fool anyone. That's why I love you. I meet enough snakes and scorpions every day. You give me Real Bread. You give me Golden Eggs. You give me delicious Fish. For this I love you more and more. You provide for me even though I worry about not having enough. I love you Father. You give me good things. I'm am never wronged by you, my Beautiful Father. My only concern sometimes is my inability to feel you hidden behind the words 'Father', and 'Hallow.'

Father, I learn fast. I turn to and trust in your Son Jesus. He is more graphic than you. He lived with us in a human body. I call Jesus. I beseech the Son of Man. I received cruel mental beatings because the Holy Name of Jesus wasn't invoked. I relied on self and fought storms. Waves of troubles lashed on top of me. I never thought of wakening Jesus to ask for help. All my troubles, all attacks on my life, all my drowning experiences could have been avoided if I woke Jesus up and asked for help. A gentle prayerful tap on Jesus shoulder asking for help brings Divine Life into dangerous and wicked experiences. I have learnt not to fight my enemy alone anymore. Instead I align myself to Jesus Christ. This point is hugely significant. And if not grasped you may never know Jesus or his Father.

Father, I love your Son Jesus Christ. I truly do. I'm amazed by Jesus' cool personality. He slept in a small fishing boat during a storm. I love this boat scene. Jesus changed terrified disciples into faithful friends on that night he saved them from drowning. Jesus wanted his disciples to trust in Divine Power The wind and the sea obeyed him. He calmed the force of nature and the minds of his friends. I wouldn't let Jesus sleep now. I'll knock at his door. I beg for Jesus' help during all my stormy experiences whether they are small or large.

Father, I'm pleased with this insight and discovery. I'd be the kind of person that wouldn't disturb Jesus. I'd let him sleep before. But now I would wake him up. I believe now that I can win the toughest fights of my life with Jesus on board. I have found a graphic way through a boat scene of praying to a sleeping Jesus and waking him up to help in a crisis situation. Indeed, it is wonderful news.

Father, I'd like more graphic scenes to think about. Gospel scenes bring me into the life of Jesus. It's great news. Reflection is great. Imagination brings Jesus alive. I'm at the well listening. Jesus talks to a Syrian woman. Both met there because of the need for water. Jesus treated her with respect and had time to talk to her. I don't know all the words that were spoken. But I do know that the experience of talking to Jesus changed her life. A greater kind of water welled up inside of her. The Syrian woman became so enthralled with the Jew Jesus that she excitedly told everyone about him. I'd love her experience Father. It was the day that anyone anywhere in the world learnt that worship of you Father is possible outside established religions. She had a beautiful conversation with Jesus. The Spirit of Jesus and the Truth about how to worship welled up inside of her in such a way that she became a true friend and disciple of Jesus. I'd love that to happen to me Father. I'd love some of that water that she received. I'd love it to bubble up inside of it. It was an offer of great magnitude. It was an offer of eternal life. I'd love friendship with Jesus. I pray and beg for holy water, for a holy friendship, and for holy conversations with Jesus. I'm going to search for that well. I going to search for that Syrian woman. I want the Holy Water that she received. I want in me a bit of the same joy that made her proclaim and praise Jesus among her Syrian neighbourhood. I pray to the Syrian women. The war-torn people of Syria need her this very day. All of you need to drop your weapons and walk to the holy well and meet Jesus. It is because you have all lost contact with the greatest prophet and greatest leader of mankind that disaster has struck. You stopped listening to the woman that could save Syria. You ditched friendship with Jesus Christ. You dumped the very Person that knows everything about you. I'll walk with you to the holy well and act on behalf of Jesus with a fresh message of hope that refills empty vessels with the Spirit of God our Father.

Next

Big Eye

Liam, thank you caring for Syria. And thank you for encouraging friendship with my Son Jesus. Your message needs to be brought to the whole world again. I'm awfully disappointed that there isn't enough people throughout the world drinking from the Holy Water offered to mankind by my Son Jesus Christ. My Son is Divine. You need to tell other religions this Truth. My Son told you to worship me in Spirit and Truth. It hasn't happened. Tell Catholics this Truth. Tell Christians this Truth. Tell Muslims this Truth. The message of the well is about true worshippers. My Son has that Truth. Listen to him. I solemnly send this message through you Liam to the ends of the earth. In a nutshell my advice is to make friends with Jesus.

Liam, my Little Man I'm delighted for you. You are happy inside because you drink from my Son's Word. You feel good about being my friend. By this love you have for me you are my Son's friend too. I appreciate your commitment. Of all seven billion people living on earth I admire your dedication and persistence in singling me out as the Greatest and Highest of All. I love you Liam for your relentless pursuit of me. You're one living thing among billions. Yet you are magnificent in your appreciation of me. I pick you up from the ground. I hold you between my fingers and kiss you like any father that is proud of his child. My Holiness is Red Hot Liam. Grace runs through my fingers into your beautiful little body. I caress you and love you. I see the smile of joy on your face. Intimacy is lovely Liam. You can purr and enjoy my gentle touch. I'm a Great Father. Keep coming close to me.

Liam, I mean this. Thank you very much again. You are one in a million. But don't tell anyone. I want you for myself. A merciless army of begrudging and jealous driven proud enemies of mine would stampede down your road and kill you if they thought I favoured you and loved you. So keep everything as it is. Tell them nothing until the time is right for us to print the book or near the time of your death when I take you to heaven.

Liam, my Office of Saints and Departments of Virtues are happy with your choice. All in heaven clap their hands in rapturous applause when a human being decides to give all to me. There's great dancing and singing. My Angels and Saints know how to celebrate. You have climbed three great steps. You have risen above the underworld of wickedness. You have climbed above the world of humans. You have moved into the spiritual realm. This is a super stage Liam. This is where Satan is kept down. Holy Mary and my Power of Holiness keeps a foot on that fella's head – the father of lies - once you remain close to me and Jesus.

Liam, continuing a spiritual walk towards me isn't easy. And when it comes to climbing Calvary with a heavy cross many give in and run back down the hill. These are people who seek an easy way of life. They don't want to search for my Son. They don't want to suffer for my Son. Yet it is only through my Son that Eternal Life is attained. Liam, he is the Porter. He has an Obedience Key. Those who obey me and my Son Christ Jesus has the door unlocked for them. Those who disobey me or don't know me are locked out. They are trapped in the world and will never step off unless they find the Key of Obedience. Believe me Liam there is no chance for the vast majority of seven billion inhabitants of finding this key because they don't accept my humble Porter, the Son of Man. It is the Messiah that unlocks the door for you. Jesus has the Key. Obedience to Me unlocks the door. It's the difference between Eternal Life and perishing. I urge you Liam to do everything possible to find my Porter and convince him that you are obedient to me and my Son. I don't want you ever again running down the hill and away from hard work of preaching the Gospel.

Liam I appreciate your love. But it can't remain fruitless. I desire to save souls. I desire Obedience. I'm hoping your book will convince others to love me. I urge you to tell each European to stand up and clench their fist in a show of strength for my Christ and Saviour. I can't tolerate seven billion people living on the planet as if I don't exist. And I can't open the doors of heaven to non-believers and for those who think their religion is above my Lamb and Porter.

Liam, I try to tell you that your neighbour is important to me. Your country is of enormous importance to me. I'm deeply concerned these last few years with the drop off in obedience to Me. I see the father of lies shift a multitude of Irish people. Catholics in their droves fell like flies over scandals. And the tempter in chief laughed his head off after causing havoc in the Church by dragging weak priests down into the pit of the most despicable and dirtiest of sins.

Liam, pray for families. Pray for your people. Pray for youth in your country. The new generation don't know about my sweet Christ. The pitiful outcome of life without prayer is similar to the difference between a bright person and a dull soul who lacks grace and holy love. I desire committed and strong Catholics. I prefer a Catholic world. My Son Jesus Christ is Commander-in-Chief. He is my Divine Son. Like St John the Baptist I point to the Lamb of God. You are lucky Liam. You belong to my Christ. I encourage every soul to walk on a pilgrimage towards me. Climb Croagh Patrick every year. I Am the Holiest of Holies. Walk towards me. I expect reverential fear because I Am God and Eternal Father. I Am above All Creation and I Am Sacred.

Liam, there has been a dramatic drop in worship of my Son in your country. My Sacred Committee for the Faith in Ireland see the decline in worship as a worrying trend. A large chunk of the current generation of Irish people have rejected me. The situation is dangerous for if people cut themselves of from me they die. Remember the Porter Jesus has the Key of Life. And this current generation of Irish people are lost because they don't get out of their beds on a Sunday morning anymore and go to Church to hear about my Son and receive the Body and Blood of my Church leader, Jesus Christ. The Porter will never meet them. The Church door is open. But people have cut themselves off. The connection has broken. I'd like you to warn them Liam. Tell them that if they close the door to me I can't see them ever finding their way to heaven.

Liam, very few are sincere like you. You have gone to great lengths to love me. You treasure more than anything a relationship with me. I'll not turn you away. I refused the rich young man. He lacked commitment. I'll not turn you away because you keep telling me that you love me. You love me more than riches. You love me more than a beautiful woman. That's good enough for me. You have access to the door. Jesus turns the key and opens the door for you. Come in Liam. I Am your True Friend. Call me if you need me.

Chapter Eleven

Little Man

Father, of course I love you. I long for you all day every day. I'm grateful for this opportunity to write to you. And I'm overjoyed with your correspondence in this dialogue. This activity makes me feel good.

Father, there's restlessness in my life. I realised that the earth has nothing to offer. Nothing earthly pleases me. The ability to pray is the only thing. It pleases me immensely because it is my way of expressing my love for Jesus Christ. I'm desperate for the Lord's love. I worry a bit though. My fellow priests need me. And I can't return to ministry because I have a woman and child.

Father, I'm sorry if I ran down the hill of Calvary instead of climbing up and assisting Jesus in his great work to save souls. I blessed the Bread and Wine and preached your Holy Word. I loved it. I can't explain what happened to me. Maybe I took an easy option. I'm sorry Father. Please don't think less of me now. I haven't lost my love for you Father. In fact, it is stronger than ever. I'll all for peace. I don't want to harbour an evil thought in my heart. I appeal like Pope Francis to every person on earth to reject hatred.

Father, I prefer the Way of Jesus than the Way of Wickedness. I want nothing to do with lies and evil. Big Eye, help. Show me the way back. I don't want to disappoint you ever again. I want to make up. I didn't turn my back on your Son. I just couldn't cope with scandals that engulfed the Church. St Dominic I love you. I pray to you. Please help. I desire full reconciliation with the Order of Preachers. I loved the kindness shown to me by the brethren. I'm proud of the Order.

The ideals of St Dominic are a beautiful way of life. But the Master General and Provincials should constantly be renewing and refreshing itself. Staleness and bad habits should be weeded out. The option for security should be addressed. And using Religious Life as a cosy, snug, comfortable and easy way of life should be reversed. Like St Dominic zeal and enthusiasm should be in the heart and mind of each Dominican. The Church needs Dominicans to preach the Truth and reinvigorate the beliefs of the Catholic faith. Instead there is silence. The hound of God has died. The torch has dimmed. The voice is silent. I hear nothing to contribute to Truth. I hear of atrocity after atrocity around the world but the voice of Truth to condemn wickedness is silent.

Father, I'm sorry. I have no right to admonish others. I failed to stay the course. For that reason, I beg and pray for reconciliation with Jesus Christ. I'm sorry for every sin committed. I join my hands and pray. I will obey you now Jesus. I repent fully for every sin committed against you and for all offences committed against others. Father, have mercy on me. I fail miserably to maintain a high standard of virtuous living.

Father, I loved the priesthood. Please forgive me. I failed to control my thoughts and actions. For that reason, I'm wretched. I bow before the cross of Jesus Christ. I bury my hands and cover my face. I'm ashamed of my efforts to remain a true friend with my Lord and God. I can't reconcile my soft living with the cruel crucifixion. Father, please don't hold my bad decision against me. I should have stuck it out. I was a fool. I fully acknowledge only a fool would turn his back on such a great love. The Body and Blood of Christ is everything. The Word of God is Pure Truth. I cherish it in my heart and yet I can't stand behind the altar and perform the greatest act of love ever witnessed in the history of human life.

Father, I do my best without the support of the Church and Religious Order. I haven't turned my back on you. I love you more and more through my writing. I focus on Christ and beg for forgiveness. I long for an image of the crucifix. The image refreshes me as I attempt to pray and feel the pain he went through for love of me.

Father, I dread losing my soul. The world is a big dark lonely place. I hear strong winds and heavy rain. I hear of the plight of human beings across the world. Big Eye I worry so much. Are you watching at all? Powerful Nations are a worry with large armies, warplanes and nuclear weapons. There is the threat of war every day. There is the threat of diseases, sickness, cancer and bad health around us. And worst of all wicked men full of hatred commit crimes that have become so common that words of condemnation has no effect anymore. If we committed the same offences against cats or dogs, there would be an uproar. It just goes to show how cheap human life has become. I wonder are we worth less than ten cents now. And that amount of money would buy nothing.

Father, I know what the world needs. The whole human family must respect you. You are not two gods. Allah and God is One. So Muslims and Christians should love one another. There is no place for hatred or terrorism in a true worshipper. From my angle and religious perspective, I point to Christ crucified. The killing of people by evil people makes the world a sad place. But hope springs eternal. I recommend Nations and Governments to adopt Christ as their inspirational leader because he taught every one of us that service is at the heart of authority. Christ crucified has the Key of Life. There is no other door. There is no other entry. Unless you go through Christ you will all die and perish. And there is only one little spot on earth where that Key can be found. It's a small spot in comparison to the vast abyss and terrain of a wild and sometimes crazy world. It's the Door of Life. It's the crucifix stuck in the ground. The man on that crucifix is Divine. He is Jesus Christ. He is the Son of God. I want to speak well of him because you Father take into account every thought and word that falls from my lips. Listen fools on earth. Listen you who live as if there is no Father to care for us. I offer you a chance to change. Please accept my warning. Go on fool! Reject Christ. Neglect Christ. Enjoy your life. But don't blame me for not warning you.

Father, on my knees I beg for a second chance. I deeply love your Son Jesus Christ. I bring my life before you and hide nothing. It means everything to me for your Son Jesus Christ to turn the Key and allow me access into your heart and mind as a true friend belonging to God's kingdom.

Holy Mary, I pray to you too. I know how you dislike proud and arrogant men. And you are so humble. I'm sorry Mary. I'm sorry about all my condescending attitudes towards women during my life and forgive me for it. Please mother me Holy Mary. I'm awfully sorry if I hurt you or any woman that crossed my path in life.

I pray to you St Dominic. I enjoyed so much the brethren. I'm sorry Dominic for opting out. Please Dominic, forgive me. I love the Order. I love you St Dominic. It was the right Order for me. But I lost my way in it and couldn't pursue Truth. I was afraid of being lost and smothered in liturgy.

Every day I ask you Dominic to pray for my family. I pray to you every day. I'd very much like to be part of the Dominican family in spirit and truth. I think of all the brethren who died. Please include me Dominic among your followers when I die.

My best friend in the Order was Fr William. He was inspirational. I had lots of chats with him about the importance of study and prayer. And I'll never forget his postcard that said, "Give yourself to Jesus Christ". He was a holy man.

Father I've reflected deeply about life. I have an appetite for chewing on the lives of the Saints. I praise them for renewing my love for you. I find holy men fantastic, brilliant and incredible. They're the best. I love St Augustine, St Anselm, St Catherine, St Patrick and St Dominic. I love all the Saints.

I love St Augustine immensely. I read his confessions and admired his bluntness about his search for meaning in life. This holy man confessed his sins and wrote beautifully about you Big Eye. He had an amazing mind and way with words.

Big Eye

Liam, your offer of repentance is accepted. I forgive you. I wouldn't hold your departure from the priesthood against you. I Am a Father full of mercy and compassion. You had nothing against my Son. You were a good priest and harmed nobody. By the way it's very good news too that you enjoy reading the lives of Saints! That's great news! I recommend communion with all holy men and women. Saints are your companions on your spiritual journey. They made it to heaven by living exemplary lives during their experiences on earth. All had one underlying principle - their love for Jesus Christ and the Church. These beautiful men and men were loyal to the Eucharist and treasured my Word. Liam you must do the same. Continue Sacred Reading. It unifies those who desire me with my Son Jesus Christ and every believer in me. My Word must never be taken lightly.

Liam, I notice that you are an admirer of my Church Doctors too. These wrote brilliantly about me. Pray to them. St Thomas Aquinas wrote a library of Catholic Doctrine. He had a super thinking mind. Can you learn from him? He stopped writing at a young age because he saw my Greatness as more important that his Summary of Theology.

Liam, don't get lost. Don't lose the run of yourself. You are not among the big boys. My Church Doctors wrote well. They helped the Church to understand the mysteries of faith in Jesus Christ, my beloved Son. I have no written tasks at the moment for a new Doctor. There's no need for further interpretations. You are not an Aquinas, nor an Augustine.

Liam, I can make your soul happy though. I encourage prayer and reflection on my Word. My juicy delicious thoughts are joyous. Eat them Liam. It's better to think about my Golden Word than to have nothing worthwhile at all in your head. By dwelling on my Holy Word real spiritual entertainment is dished up. You will dance. You will sing. You will love life. My Word is delicious. Nothing is greater than the effect of listening to Jesus. If you are serious about me reflect on the scenes in the Gospel. Put yourself in the shoes of Mary choosing to listen to Jesus rather than fuss about the house worrying about trifling things. Think deeply about my Holy Word. Keep it warm in your mind and memory. It's like hatching an egg.

Liam, I repeat. My Word matters. If you have a short memory capabilities try and embed Golden Egg Words in your mind. Listen to the prayer of the psalmist, "O God, you are my God for you I long". That's valuable Liam. Carry my Word in your mind all day. It may make you hungry for more and more of Me.

Liam absorb images from scenes in the Gospel about ordinary and simple things in life to discover more about Me. I know you like the water well experience. Water is an ordinary element. Both Jesus and the Syrian woman were thirsty. Jesus though used water to symbolically refer to his Holy Spirit welling up inside the lady just by talking to Jesus. You see Liam how important it is to talk to Jesus. You have never done that properly have you? The lady was thrilled talking to Jesus. She became excited spiritually. It was like drinking grace. It was like drinking Holy Water. It was a meeting with Me. The lady went into town and told everybody about the wonderful Jew that she met at the well. The conversation changed her life.

Liam, as you well know I'm a Father for every human being. My love is universal and with open arms I welcome everyone that desires my friendship. I exclude no Country from my care. I include females in my ministry of love. I'm the Father of the whole world. My love extends to the care of seven billion people.

Liam I advise you to eat and drink the Body and Blood of my Son. That is Divine Food. That is Divine Drink. That is Spiritual Delight. Think Liam. That is Divine Nourishment. That is Divine Water. That is the Spirit of Jesus in you. So spend time with Jesus at the well. Find a quiet place. Sit down and wait. Jesus will meet you. Once Mary runs in to the village to tell everyone about her meeting the Messiah your turn will come. Be ready. I want you fresh rather than run down and ragged by the worries of life. My Son searches for disciples around the world. He isn't interested in unhealthy and broken souls from the point of view of requiring hounds to carry the Light of Christ around the world and spread my Gospel of Truth to save souls.

Liam, I happy for you. You are not a Scripture Scholar or theologian. But you love me and that is what matters. You love my holy saints too. These shining lights lived throughout the centuries and you have benefitted from them. At the end of the day Liam I'm attracted to every soul that praise and adore me. True worship delights my heart.

Chapter Twelve

Little Man

Hello Father. I love to call you Father. But I love to think of you as Big Eye too. Your Big Eye reassures me. You look from afar. You gaze into my room. I love you. You are a wonderful Father. I feel your care for me. Thank you. I'm happier having you as my Father. I can't err by having God as my Father. I love your advice. It's beautiful. It's sound. It's full of wisdom. My face smiles because of you Father. My lips feel delicious. Something lovely is reaching me from you Father. My inner demeanour is electrifying. I'm burning with a feeling of something very nice happening to me.

Father I look for Holy Bread. I look for the Blood of the Lamb. I desire a Holy Word. Doctors help. You are precious. I find your explanation of Holy Scripture and your expounding of Holy Truth like a running stream of grace racing into my mind and heart.

Father, St Chrysostom is a favourite. I pray to him. Holy Church remembers him as the preacher with the Golden Mouth. His mother taught him piety. She sent him to the best schools in Antioch. His words are Golden Eggs. I'm charmed by his words. They are precious eggs. I welcome them into my mind.

Father, St Chrysostom said that there is nothing more worthwhile than to pray. I agree fully. My Golden Mouth added that prayer unites us with you. If prayer unites me more to you Father than I want to pray all day.

Father, I love you. St Chrysostom, my friend wrote about contemplation. This prayer is deep quiet thinking about you Almighty

God. I love contemplation. I quieten everything inside and sit still calling upon you, my Father. I love it. By doing this my holy Doctor of the Church and precious saint wrote that contemplation results in illumination of the soul. I want to contemplate straightaway. Father, I would love enlightenment. The higher the level of prayer the greater is the level of illumination that lights up the house that is inside my head. I'm deeply attracted to this form of prayer. I always walk away from it with my body and soul beaming. It's a holy light inside my head. It's Christ inside. It's the Light of Christ spreading around inside my head sending grace through the whole of my body. It's like a plant in bud form but opens out into a gorgeous flower. The effect of successful periods of long contemplation sends grace through every nerve in the body. In particular, the holy stuff emanating from the Father, Son and Holy Spirit flows forth into the mind and sends a holy glow streaming onto the surface of the face making it wonderfully joyful. It is the stuff of dreams. I want more Father. You give me something nice and I want more of it. I want the brightness of Christ shining through me.

Father, my writing makes me happy. I'm inspired by my writing. I praise St Chrysostom. He wrote too that prayer is not confined to a timetable. It is a state that endures day and night. I like that too. I don't have to wait for evening to come to spend time with my Father. Nor do I have to wait until morning. I can pray or talk to my Father at any time during day or night. That's a nice one. Morning and Evening Prayers are important. But I can stay with and pray to my Father outside set times. This holy writer St Chrysostom utters a Golden Egg with every few words. He preaches that we should season our actions with a desire for you, Almighty God and Father. I take my hat off to you my holy friend. I utterly respect you. Season actions with a desire for God. St Chrysostom adds as well that we should season our actions by remembrance of you my God and Father. It's like spreading a bit of salt to season the words, 'Desire for God', and 'Remembrance of God'. Act on these words and Eternal Life is yours.

Father, what about concerns, worries, cares, problems, and setbacks? I couldn't contemplate when bogged down with stress. I can't go over to my prayer shed for a few hours if I have to care for a sick person. Time would be split. There are always concerns. Things go wrong from time to time. I could be busy in some other way. There is so much to be done. So what do I do in that case Father?

Father, St Chrysostom is a gem. He has the answer. I salt my concerns with your love Father. I pour your love on the sickness, on the worry and on the problems. I'm not to worry. I spray the salt of love on the sores and broken minds. In that way my life and work becomes a sweet dish for you, my Lord and God. O this is lovely stuff. A sweet dish for the Lord. I must make my life a sweet dish for my Father to relish and ravage me.

Father, I pray to you. I love St Anselm too. He is another Church Doctor. This holy man is dear to me. Anselm, pray for me. I feel a holy communion with you. Your spirit is in me. And this is a reality after fifteen hundred years. My birthday is on the day that the Church celebrates Anselm's memory and holy life. Father, I seek you in the same way as Anselm did. I loved his mind and spirituality. What stands out most of all are his word about you Father. He said that you are, "The Highest of All and that nothing greater can be thought". The words are pure beauty. I love them. I agree fully too. It is Super truth. Father, you are the Highest of All. There isn't a greater thought that can exist in the mind than the one mentioned.

Father, I love this man St Anselm. Imagine having a friend and learning from him even though he lived hundreds of years ago. I feel very close to Anselm. His spirit has not died. I love Anselm's cheeky way of encouraging me to contemplate. Anselm's tells me to wake up from sleep. He tells me to arouse my mind in such a way as to contemplate God, the Highest and Greatest of All.

Father, I obey Anselm. I will not err if I follow his words written above. It was through Anselm that I came across the idea of myself being a Little Man. He tells us all to this very day, "Wake up, Little Man". I try every day to wake up. I shake my mind up. I check my ears are awake. I open my eyes to creation. My whole being searches for God. My beautiful friend cares for my soul. Anselm exhorts me to wake up from my lethargy, from my lazy mind mentality, and from my easy going attitude to life. I have to go to quiet places and away from tumultuous crowds and families. This is for the purpose of freeing up time so as to contemplate the Holy of Holies. It is train my eye to look at Big Eye, and for Big Eye to look at what is occupying my eyes. I love this wakening up call. Thank you Anselm. I'm grateful. Your ideas are lovely. I can see you praying. You think like me.

Father, I like Anselm's twin approach of coming to know you through the use of reason and faith. Most human minds are asleep. Our knowledge is taught and conditioned by culture and education. I have never come across a mind that thinks differently to the norm. I saw Anselm struggling to understand his faith. In his prayers he wanted to know why you wouldn't show your face Father. I try to use reason to find you Father. I try to see you in Nature and Creation. I try to see for myself. And I try to grasp the difference between an idea and reality.

Father, St Anselm refers to you as a Supreme and Inaccessible Light. You are that Father. You are Supreme. You are an Inaccessible Light. I can't see you in heaven. But you can see me. You view me at my desk writing. You see me all the time on road L0909. You must have a terrific Big Eye, Father. I'm lucky. So is the whole world to have an Eye that is so powerful to see the whole world as well as penetrate deep into the mind and heart of every human. Father, I want that Supreme Eye with so powerful a beam to light up my life. You have other ways Father to enlighten me without having to show your face. No Father would allow his creatures to crawl around in darkness. So I have every faith through the recommendations of St Anselm that Light Inaccessible illuminate's contemplatives who shut out all lights of the world. Even though the eyes are closed and the body still God the Father switches on a holy light in the centre of the contemplative's soul. It's a peaceful light. It's a bright light. It's a holy light. It needs the spark of prayer to ignite the light that gives the most wonderful transfiguration or transformation that any man or woman can experience throughout their lives. But there may be a period of dryness. There may be a period of frustration. To deal with a lack of progress just persist with prayer.

Father, I cherish another true great in the list of Church Doctors. He is the great St Augustine. He graced the history of the Catholic Church with his great mind and prolific writing. He poured his heart and soul out to you Father. He was frank in telling you everything about his life in the Confessions book. I love his fluent ideas and honesty. He tells us about his misdeeds and his struggle with the Catholic faith. I love his writing.

Father, what I like about St Augustine is his caring mother St Monica. This holy mother is definitely my model for all mothers. She had great faith in her son. She stood by him through his years of doubt and exploration into all known philosophies at that time in the fifth century. She made huge sacrifices. Her tears for him to be a Christian and Catholic priest didn't go amiss. St Monica died happy knowing that her son had committed himself to the Father of Christ Jesus. Her motherly tears and persistent prayers were answered.

Father, I love Augustine's book. He told me of his mother's sad end on a boat from Italy to North Africa. She was dying and Monica told her son that she didn't care where she was buried once she was remembered at the altar of God. Beautiful Father! I love it. What a mother! What a wonderful woman! Augustine's mother has helped me. I like her reference for remembrance at the altar. Yes, indeed St Monica found the Porter Jesus at the altar of God. I can see Jesus turning the key and welcoming the greatest mother ever known into his kingdom through the sacrifice of the Mass. St Monica lay at the altar of God in the same way as Mary Magdalene and Martha's sister Mary sat at Jesus' feet and loved him.

Father, I have discovered True Love. You are the Father of Christ Jesus. O my God! O Big Eye! St Monica has helped to realise the Sacredness of the Altar. All Christians of every age are remembered every day at the altar. I want all my clan going back two thousand years, and even before the time of Christ to be remembered like St Monica at the altar of God. The altar is the gateway to heaven. There we are inebriated in the life of Christ by the holy Eucharist. I'm bubbling up with happiness. I lost sight of the Eucharist. St Monica refocused me. Her powerful words have Eternal Value. I call back Christians to the altar. Come on! Life is short. Don't die a stranger to the Father of Christ Jesus.

Father, I love you. Tell me about modern man. Where is his focus? It seems to me a great number of people have taken their eyes of the ball. Or it seems to me that people prefer to play with a different ball. O foolish human being. You have rejected Christ. I don't see you at the altar with the Christian community on Sunday mornings anymore. Farewell so. Goodbye! I can't force you to come back to the altar.

Father, I adore your Sacred Altar. It's very precious. It's valuable beyond measure. The Divine Son of God meets us there. He is in the bread and wine after consecration. Fool! You allowed your faith to die. There's no substitute for Divine Life. And don't be casual at the altar. I strongly recommend preparation before the Body of Christ is received. It is similar to nonattendance if the mind doesn't prepare and welcome warmly the Body and Blood of Christ into the very fabric of your self-awareness. Otherwise you take the Sacred Sweet for granted. It's like eating a sweet without thinking or acknowledging its delicious taste.

Father, St Monica is a rare thing of beauty. She knew where to find Jesus. She found the entry point. She found Eternal Life. She had patience and waited for Christ Jesus at the altar. Well done Monica. You brought your precious son Augustine and husband Patricius with you to the altar. O what a genius of a mother. You found the table where Divine Life feeds us. You ate from the table of the Lord. You rested at the foot of the altar. You knew of the place where Jesus meets his faithful. Your spirit was at the gate for Christ Jesus to pick you up and carry you to heaven. Your task was done.

Father, St Monica's words have given me a hunger and thirst for the Altar. I want to go to Church now. I should be at the altar. I can meet Christ Jesus there in the form of bread and wine. This realisation that the Body and Blood of Christ is present on the altar has blown my mind apart in recognition of this Magnificent Truth. My trust in Jesus' Word tells me the Truth. Wake up idiot. Wake up fool. By receiving Holy Communion I'm connected to the Body and Blood of Our Lord and Saviour Jesus Christ.

Father, help me. Father, shake me. Father wake me up. My unconscious state is a problem. I lack a permanent awareness of a Scared Truth. I focus on myself and order myself to burst out of my lethargic state. I want a fresh mind and body to acknowledge a Magnificent Truth that you Father Are One with the Body of Christ that I eat. The problem for most Christians is that this Sacred Food isn't illuminating the receivers mind. The reception of the Body of Christ isn't having an effect because the human brain is rather dead. It takes real belief, real truth, real love, and real awareness in the heart and mind of each person to benefit from such a Magnificent Moment when the tongue receives a Divine and Sacred Host. Little man, think. Little woman, think. Unless you wake up to the Way of Light your drowsy, sleepy or unconscious living experience will be rocky, confused, and frustrated. There will be no improvement or increase in the way that you experience the Lord. You remain dead like a stone.

Father, I'm no different. I struggle every day. I bang my head in frustration at the thought of you being God and I a buried worm in the clay somewhere lost in a cold world. I can't grasp the Greatness of You. I can't grasp the fact that You Are One with Jesus Christ, and One with the Holy Spirt and all Three of you come into my life in Holy Communion without me being fully aware of it. I can't find that something in my mind to acknowledge that fact. I'm looking for the Xfactor that should occur when Divinity is received in the Holy Eucharist. I don't experience a sense of awe. I search my mind and body for an answer.

Father, you are God. You are Big Eye. Surely I would know if something of you was shared with me. Surely I would know if a connection was made. The only other possibility is that there is something not functioning properly in me. Or it could be that you Father, and your Son Jesus Christ have never introduced yourself properly to me. Or I haven't made enough of an effort to meet you. It could very well be that I have not settled in life or made any effort to sit at the table of the Lord at the Last Supper. I may not be one of his inner friends.

Father, I'm afraid now. I pray to St Monica. I'm in urgent need to run to the altar. I want to be there at the table with Jesus when he takes bread, blesses it, breaks it, and shares it with his special group of loyal disciples as a sign of unity and love between God and man until the end of days. I should be at the altar. It's my fault Jesus. It's my fault Big Eye. I'm not at the Last Supper everyday through my own fault.

Big Eye

Hello Liam! I love you. Your thinking will make people sit up and take notice. I'm overjoyed that in your writing you emphasised the role of a mother. You picked a gem. St Monica is a perfect Christian mother. I need more like her. Her persistence and prayers created a giant in the Church. Her tears of love for her son not only helped to establish herself as a great saint but also led to Augustine becoming a Doctor of the Church. This mother Liam made me cry seeing the magnitude of love she displayed for Augustine. She died happy knowing that her prayers were answered. Monica didn't want to die until Augustine committed to me and my Christ Jesus. I granted Monica's request because Augustine had a fine mind. He became a priest and bishop and wrote extensively on Christian faith

Liam, I'd love more mothers like St Monica. She chased her son across the Mediterranean Sea to ensure he committed to my Christ. Pray Liam for Christian mothers. I Am God. I bless mothers. I need their help. I depend on them to tell their children about me, the Father of Life. I depend on them to pass on faith about me and Jesus Christ to their babies. My Son loves children. He wouldn't allow his disciples to drive them away. He called them and blessed them. I Am Big Eye. I crown St Monica the Patron Saint of Mothers. I haven't come across a passion as great as Monica's. It was this great mother that inspired Augustine to convert to Christ and become a Great Light for the Catholic Church. Liam, I would like you to have the same passion to convert lapsed Catholics and all human beings across the planet. I don't see your tears for humanity Liam. I don't see you crying for the world. I don't see your hand held out for broken lives. There are forces in the world and dark clouds approaching who want to wipe away every trace of the crucifix. And it will happen unless men like you stand up and shout from the rooftops to repent and belief in the Gospel.

Liam, St Monica is with me. I told her of your warm praise. She is delighted. Both of us take you on board ship. I'm your Father. St

Monica is your Christian Mother. Together we will Father and Mother you with whatever virtues you need. It's great news for you Liam. Monica will pray for all members of your family. Their names will be mentioned in heaven. Do your best for your son.

Liam, I return to your queries above regarding contact with me. You have many options. One is that I call you every day. You hear my Word. I Am your Father, come to me. I offer you rest. Why labour in pain? Come into my Church. Pray to me. I Am on the altar in the Eucharist. If you are overburdened come. In my house there is Peace. I calm every tired muscle in your body and every trace of stress in your mind.

Liam, the Way of Light has several offshoots. The basic criteria are to put your whole heart into it. It's called passion. You can come to me through the Eucharist, or through the lives of the Saints, or through the Holy Word, or pray directly to me, or through praying together. Passionate prayer is beautiful. I love it. I'm like a magnet drawn to a sincere soul at prayer. You can opt to contact me through all possibilities mentioned above. All you have to do Liam is call me. It is enough to say come Father, or come Jesus, or come Holy Spirit.

Liam, I'm a long, long distance away in heaven. I'm not easily contacted unless you can find the holy key that opens the secrets buried in each part of the Lord's Prayer. All authority on earth has been given to the Son of Man. He is the Good Shepherd. He is the Porter that has the key. He is a Saviour. I tell you solemnly go through him. Christ will feed you. Christ will lead you to the Way of Life. As God your Father I look after my Son Jesus Christ who in turn calls his sheep and they listen to him. The door of my Church is open. Christ calls you. All little lambs shelter in the Church. I'd advise you to turn pride into humility and put on the tag of one of those little lambs. These beautiful little children of mine listen to the voice of Christ Jesus. My Christ is a True Shepherd who cares for and feeds his flock every day.

Liam, I love you. You are my little man, my secret weapon. You work quietly on road L0909 and the whole world is oblivious of your existence. My Big Eye zooms on you. You don't know I watch you. I intend to be big in your life. I touch your heart and remove cold pebbles that harm your feelings for me. I desire love Liam. So I am in your heart cleaning it and making it new. Love me Liam. Welcome me into the home of your mind. Keep me in the home of your memory. Keep a desire for me burning inside every minute. I can give you a dignity that is lacking among Governments, Presidents and Kings throughout the world today.

Liam, I know of your circumstances and responsibilities towards your family and household. And I know of your battles with finances and females, and children. But you are doing fine. I provide. Don't worry. My Sacred Touch heals. The Tip of My Finger on your skin is enough to transform you. I touch my creature. I love my little man especially the one who desires me through the test of many years of searching. Do not be afraid. My Holy Touch will generate wonderful changes in your life.

Little Man

O God, my Father. I found you at last. I believe you too. Thank you for cleaning my heart. Thank you for my new heart. Thank you for removing my heart of stone. Thank you for loving me. I'm honoured. I love you too. My mixed bag of finite substance mingles with Divine Purity. Wow! I'm thrilled. Father, this wedding means a lot to me.

Father, I'm joyful this morning. My dialogue with you enhances my aliveness. I find my mind sharper. My memory has richer and more sublime spiritual thoughts. I'm longing for Jesus Christ now. Whereas before there were long blackout periods when images of the Divine Son of God crucified didn't stick in the memory. I'm brighter in myself too. My mood is positive. My family can't understand what has got into me. They can't understand what has made me happy.

Father, is St Augustine with you now? Holy Church celebrates the memory of his mother today. Tell him I found peace in my life just as he did through the prayers of his mother and after a long restless struggle with faith. I attribute my great joy to the prayers of Monica and Augustine. I send you greetings in heaven from road L0909 this morning. Thank you very much. I hope to join you someday. I'm delighted. Your Sacred Touch Father has sent shivers of renewal through my entire body from head to toe. It has had a mesmerising effect on my aliveness.

Father, am I greedy though? Am I selfish? I want a bit of You; a bit of Jesus; a bit of Saints; a bit of Eucharist; insights into your Holy Word and revelations from Golden Egg meditations. I'm not selfish. My intentions are honourable. I desire friendship with you Father and I make no apology to all seven billion people on earth if I'm successful in achieving such a unique and holy union. Also I can't influence one single soul with something I haven't got. I'm not a dud. I'm not a fake. I'm in a race to find God my Father and Jesus Christ his Son and I will beat you all and leave you all behind through my stronger desire. Sorry human race. I have chosen the better part. It will not be taken from me. I place God My Father at the summit of all things. My God is above people and above the most treasured commodities on earth.

Father, I'm not selfish for your friendship because it is a good thing. I'll take every scrap that falls from the Master's table. I accept every Word in the Gospel. I'll chew it, and chew it until I'm filled with Divine thoughts. I have a batch of Holy Eggs to meditate on. Every sacred experience is welcome. Every bit of sacred reading is welcome. Grasp grace now. Never put it off. Grace flows through all forms of heavenly links. Feel Divine grace emanating from the corridors of heaven, from the rooms full of Saints and Angels. Feel the flow of a beautiful odour descending straight from the Godhead of Father, Son, Holy Spirit and Holy Mary straight into your nostrils. The odour of heaven is unimaginable. Its scent is pure bliss. I'm tracing a smell that transcends the whole way to heaven.

Father, do I deserve a connection with heaven? I'm unimportant. Why am I able to taste the beauty of Paradise? Why am I receiving a glimpse of Eternal Life? I'm a small dot. The Church doesn't know me. Muslims don't know me. I'm not a King, or President, or a Rich Man. I'm not a Government Minister, or a Chief Executive Officer, or a Business Owner. I'm not a Cardinal, or an Imam or a Jewish Rabbi. I'm not successful at all. My only claim to fame is to have a little bit of faith that my father Edward and my mother Mary gave me. The growth of that holy seed was further enhanced during my time in religious life where I searched for Truth. I live now a short distance from the River Shannon glorifying in the maturation of that seed into a full blown commitment to you Father, my Lord and God. I'm happy to have given up everything to find the one treasure that matters – that is the friendship and love of Jesus Christ. I have work to do. I'm not a perfect man.

Father, I'm a happy little man. Your light beams through into my room. Light inspires me. I'm working on the mind. Each day I carve slices off the rough goat in me. I pressurise my inner self to be less stubborn. I dig up the weeds. I beat my demons with a hammer. I know what you like Father. You want good soil. You want another lamb. You don't want evil words and holy words coming out of the same mouth. Unfortunately, multiple temperaments can be at work within. I hope through the grace of God that my temperament doesn't fluctuate between a goat and a sheep. I don't want to be annoying to you Father sometimes and nice other times.

Chapter Thirteen

Big Eye

Liam, my little creature in Limerick, I like your thoughts. You're coming around to My Way. You are doing the right thing. If it takes two hundred pages of dialogue to work out your relationship with me do so. Your intensity has a good work rate. I particularly like your mirror reflection of your own state of mind. That's the important part Liam. That's the intellectual centre of your aliveness. I'm all for prudent use of the mind in pursuing self-knowledge that may help spiritual progress. The above reference to a goat is significant.

Liam, I have something to say to you about that. The characteristics of animals can be in people. Goats are stubborn. People are stubborn. A goat is not a good follower. Goat people are those who live independently from me. They wouldn't go where I want them to go. I try to lead them to Church but they end up in a pub, or some other ungodly place. Goat people are divisive too Liam and this mentality is stuck in a lot of people. It's the cause of millions of disagreements between people every day. I tell you solemnly goats are not the best of company for Christians because their attributes are evil due to their disobedient mentality. Look Liam! There's a bit of the goat in everyone.

Liam, wake up to reality. With my help I can suppress the goat in you. I can move you forward. By prayer and co-operation, I impress the characteristics of sheep in you. Sheep are harmless Liam. Sheep people are harmless too. Their mentality is mild and gentle. I pick sheep-like people to follow my Way of Life. I like their defenceless nature and willingness to follow the voice of my Good Shepherd, Jesus Christ.

Liam, pray so as to behave like a lamb. Goats don't make it to heaven. I couldn't have them challenging me or refusing to comply with my Will. Judgement will come to all. I separate goats from sheep at death. If I were you I would pray to be a lamb. My Jesus loves childlike souls. Let him bless you Liam. Follow my Jesus everywhere. I urge you to pray Liam. Break down the unpredictability of the goat. Break down your independence. You can't find my Jesus on your own, nor can you do what you like. The Master calls. The gentle soul hears him. Picture the simple call Liam. I Am the Good Shepherd. My sheep follow me. Do you want to stay behind with the goats? Your independence could cost you your life.

Liam, I have no time for contrary and devious individuals posing as lambs in among my flock. If an effort is made to repent and be sorry situations change. But in general troublemakers are not good news in Christian congregations. My lambs in whom I feed thrive in an atmosphere of unity, peace, security and love. I solemnly tell you Liam to follow Christ Jesus by becoming his quiet and obedient little man or lamb. It's a tumbling and humbling experience for you to withdraw your aggression and independence. I don't want even as much as an angry glance from you.

Liam, I have fine bishops that care for priests and people. I'd like you to acknowledge them. These are new Apostles. I send them to preach the Gospel, celebrate the Eucharist and administer the Sacraments. I ask you to remind them of their calling to spread faith in me and evangelise the world. Liam, a good bishop leads by love. Love is the one thing that breaks down barriers. Liam lead by love. My Trinity of Father, Son and Holy Spirit is at work in you by participation. I Am in you. And you are in Me. Your participation in prayerful and holy ceremonies guarantees the same thing - a union of love.

Liam, pray for Church leaders. Don't be afraid to stand up for Christ Jesus. I Am God and I prefer my Son's Way, my Son's Truth, and my Son's Life. I preach Peace, Liam. I discourage fighting. And don't forget to tell everyone including Muslims that Christ Jesus is Divine. Faith in him alone guarantees Eternal Life. I give you full permission to take up your cross Liam. I think you are a little bit afraid to offend

Muslims. Don't be. I encourage Muslims and Christians to follow the route of the gentle Lamb of God. Believe me there is no other escape route from earth to heaven. Salvation and Eternal Life is wrapped up in knowing and loving the Divine Son of God, my One and only Son, the Lord Jesus Christ. I know you love my Divine Son and are grateful to be born into the Catholic faith. But don't forget Liam. I'm not divisive. I love Muslims. I love all human beings. I am a Father to all. It's regrettable that my Name has been used as a reason to kill Christians, or Shiite Muslims, or Sunni Muslims. I have a strict Commandment on this matter, "Thou shalt not kill". I authorise no one to kill human beings.

Little Man

Hello Father, can I help to bring peace upon earth? I'm sure you are sick of killing. I'm appalled with the level of hatred and evil. Why is it happening? Is there anyone listening to Jesus Christ anymore? He's a Peacemaker but there is no peace. I don't want to say anything that might offend. The tongue is a fatal snare as remarks often start trouble rather than bring about peace.

Father, help me change myself first. Help me practise peace in my own home. Help me demolish the goat within me. Help me cope with the goat in others. For if those living with me can't see a nice and friendly person then there isn't a hope in the world that the wider community would see better unless I am a house devil and street angel. I think Father that it is an impossible task to keep Peace in the world. The forces of evil are too great.

Father, I'm struggling. I don't know how to bring about a union of love between different religions, different cultures or different ethnic groups that hate each other. I'm a human being. I can't stop evil. Your Son didn't stop evil. Neither did you Father. Your Son Jesus tried but look what political powers and religious powers did to him. Those forces who were meant to represent us gave Jesus Christ an awful beating and hung him on a piece of wood.

Father, I'm stuck. I'm thinking maybe that it would be best for me to stay away from religious and political powers by being like a goat on an island of goats. My goat-like independence would prevent my crucifixion. For death is what would happen if I took up my cross and followed Christ Jesus. I wouldn't hold back. And if you Father wasn't supporting me I would be engulfed by evil forces. I'm well aware that it would be easier to climb the toughest mountain in the world like K2 or Mount Everest than tackle evil. Perfect Peace between human beings is impossible.

Father, I'm frightened by what threatens the world and for me my desire is to aspire towards being your Little Lamb. I feel safe with you Father. I lost sight of you this evening and something worse than a goat ran into my mind and deeply unsettled me. I'm sorry Father. Whatever the thing was it was nasty. It caused me to snap and curse a few times. Father, touch me. Please pull that nasty thing out of me. Please drag that goat mentality out of me. I don't like what I find in myself at times. Please help. You are my Father. Pick me up and cuddle me. Bring me to Jesus. I'll be safe with him. Open the narrow gate and push me through into the field with all your Lambs who graze on the goodness, virtues, and holiness of the Great Shepherd, Our Lord and Saviour Jesus Christ.

Father, I'm sorry. What you want is love. Instead a shower of venom spat out of my mouth. I'm very sorry. I don't know where it came from. I think the snappy manner is in me all the time. Or the venomous snake mentality could shoot into my soul when off guard. I'm devastated to be found of guard. I spotted my nasty streak. I'm unworthy to be in a field with lambs. I probably should be on an island with goats, or in a bed of snakes hiding around a hillside of a rocky terrain.

Father, what does it matter anyway? I live on a small island as far West as man can travel along the Atlantic Way. Most Asians don't know about my beautiful little country. Russians don't know. Brazilians don't know. Africans don't know. Chinese don't know. Iranians don't know. What a little man writes on a small island will never reach the ears of millions of people. My book could be blocked from entering big Nations because I glorify the name of Jesus Christ. The whole world should be able to glorify the Name of Jesus Christ through the Church. My small Country is open-minded towards multi denominational groups. But some large Countries forbid Christian evangelisation. Is that fair?

Father, help me. I'm too hard on myself and serious. I'm like the son in the gospel that never had a party. I labour and work all day in my efforts to please you Father. Life for me is drudgery and pain. Yet my sinful brother returns from partying with women and squandering his inheritance has a party thrown for him. Father, I pray for light-heartedness. I want to be jolly. I want to laugh. I want to accept people as they are. No more do I want to correct anyone. I accept their sinfulness and efforts of failure. For I sometimes come across as judge and executioner of everyone that hasn't set standards for themselves. I'm sorry for this too Father.

Father, I pray for a prudent spiritual makeover. I kneel before you a broken man. My personality is a problem for me. I have no help or mechanism in place to prevent myself from sliding downhill into dirty pits of devilish attitudes and actions. I don't like myself at times. I don't like my bad bits. So Father I kneel before you ashamed of myself. Even now the bad spirit in me tells me that I'm good. This nasty thing doesn't want me apologising to You for fear of You dispelling him from my soul.

Father, you are God. I trust you. I sign in for treatment on my soul. Place me in an ambulance and drive me to Church Doctors. I require spiritual treatment. Doctors from heaven can treat this wicked thing that appears in my mind. I've every faith in St Augustine, St Catherine, and St Anselm. These are top Spiritual Doctors. I trust them. Their Church teaching is excellent.

Father, thank you. I'm in good care. Big Eye, thank you for overseeing my trip to Heaven's Hospital. My father Edward and Fr William were there at the ambulance when I was shifted from a trolley to a glorious and beautiful bed for examination. I'm very grateful Father. You are made of Hot Stuff. The sight of Catherine, Augustine and Anselm at my bed has filled me with joy. I'm vulnerable lying on my back as they test the depth of my stubbornness.

Father, I'm delighted with Holy Hospital Services. I couldn't have asked for better. I'm completely relaxed as holy Doctors of the Church lay their consecrated hands around my head to calm my mind and bring peace to my soul. I'm delighted Father. I lay still on the lovely white bed as my body and soul is x-rayed for Satan's clumps of rotten cancerous lumps of evil matter. My sense inlets are checked for breaches of security against unwanted guests. I personally thank you Father for your Holy Team of Doctors. I feel better now.

Father, thank St Catherine for me. Father thank the Great Surgeon St Augustine for me. Father thank my beloved friend St Anselm for me. I feel better and lighter. Their Sacred Hands has calmed the storms inside my head. I feel too that lumps of cancerous evils like stubbornness, impatience, pride and other undesirable clumps of dark growths are removed. Once again Father I'm sorry for my prayer deficiencies that weakened our friendship. I'm indebted to your Sacred Doctors who gave their lives to Jesus Christ. I feel better about you Father. The operation was a success. I'm cured. I return to you Father a humble man and in complete gratitude for taking care of my external and internal well-being. I'm aware that only one out of seven cured of leprosy expressed their appreciation. I'm sure the same applies today. Only one human being out of seven make an effort to praise you. No wonder people are not cured due to the disease of disloyalty.

Father, thank you for guiding me. I follow Jesus now like a lamb. I want to follow him. And I love you, my Father. I've gone the extra mile. I climbed the tree to see Jesus coming down the road. Jesus stopped and called me down from the tree and told me that he was calling to my house. Wow! I'm a Little Man like Zacchaeus. This is a Golden Egg nest. I can become Zacchaeus. I welcome Jesus to my house. I look at him. He looks at me. We can chat Jesus. I'll own up to all the wrongdoings in my life and offer to repay with kindness anyone that was at the wrong end of my actions or words.

Father, I'm happy. My new motto is to be nice to everyone. Big Eye, thank you. Your helpful observation from heaven has had an inestimable change in my mentality towards everyone. I can say now with clarity that I have the same mentality as you Father and that of your Son Jesus Christ in attempting to love and care for all seven billion people on earth no matter what their religion or tribal affiliation.

Big Eye

Liam, you write beautifully for me and learn all the time. You are great. I like your ideal to love every person but the reality is different. No man on earth is capable of loving seven billion people twenty-four seven. Yet nothing is impossible for me. I am God. I have power to create and make things happen.

Liam, I can reveal things to you. I can fill you with love. And I could include you in a top security meeting on Mount Tabor to discuss a future plan for the human race. I had a meeting there before with Moses, Elijah, Jesus, Peter, James and John. An image of future glory was on display there. But there was much more. I finalised on that day a plan for the Salvation of Mankind through the Life, Suffering, Crucifixion, Resurrection and Ascension of my Son Jesus Christ.

Liam, the whole story of Salvation moves on and moves on every day. It's unfolding all the time. I always kept in touch with my creature especially those who give me an open ear. I'm in the whole of your history. I worked through rough times with great men like Abraham, Moses, Elijah, my Christ, Prophets, Kings, David, Apostles, Popes and All Saints up to this very day. I'm grateful to all.

Liam, the story continues even as I write. My Christ is the centre of it all. My Messiah is the One the world waited for. My Christ is there to save until the end of each life and until the end of time. He has the tiniest of space. He is visible on a height. He can't move. Wicked men stuck him on a cross. Nobody from East to West, or from North to South has an excuse for bypassing or rejecting my Son. My Christ is real religion. My Christ is visible for all. I draw all men and women to myself. Unfortunately, only one billion out of seven appreciate my Call of Love and Offer of Salvation.

Liam, I pick good seed from a choice of seven billion. The harvest is rich but labourers are few. I pick those who are willing to work. Weed seeds are no good to me. These make a nuisance of themselves and are generally unwanted. They are aggressive in growth spreading fast and everywhere. I don't like them. They thwart spiritual growth. You are a good seed Liam. I pick you because you love me. I hear you pray to me, your Father every day. You are on the side of the Church. You love my Christ. And this belief is consistent over a long period of time.

Liam, I pluck you from a small country of five million people near the Atlantic Ocean, west of Europe. I call you Liam from millions upon millions of people to serve me. Don't be fruitless. Every potato sown in the ground sprouts and produce fruit. So I expect the same from you. I expect converts. I expect a catch of fish. Your writing and reverence for my Word should net you a great haul of fine fish. Your vocation is to win souls for my Christ. It will not be easy because you are up against Nations whose politics and religion are intertwined. You would be seen as a threat if you had a different belief than the religion of a Muslim State. Yet you must tell them the Truth. I am their God too. I want Peace. Christ holds the Key to heaven. You must tell Muslims salvation comes through Jesus Christ. So convert them to Jesus Christ who is my Divine Son. I am Allah. I am God. Wake up the whole world. I am the Master. My Son is equal to me. So refresh lethargic Christians everywhere in the world. I call you Liam to send this message everywhere throughout the world.

Liam, I draw you a picture. Photograph it in your mind. Link in with heaven. I'll give you a picture that may help to break down barriers. I want you to preach a sermon of a vision for the world as seen with my Big Eye. You will view the world and every Nation on earth from the viewpoint of my Son of Man who has Authority, Domination and Power over all. My plan will be known to you. My Truth will be communicated to you.

Liam, my world is beautiful. My Big Eye view the magnificence of oceans, rivers, mountains, valleys, arable lands, trees, vegetation, air, heat, rain and an abundance of living things. My sun, moon and stars brightens up earth. My creature the human being has used his intelligence quite well. I gave resources for the building of cities, towns, villages, and rural houses. My creature has multiplied and filled the earth. Kings, Presidents, Dynasties, Governments, Dictatorships and Prime Ministers keep law and order over millions upon millions of human beings.

Liam, after seventy years of reasonable peace census growth has multiplied. I am a Father now for seven billion people. My Son Jesus Christ whom I call the Son of Man has authority for Earth and every Nation under his care. There is a concern over census growth, restlessness, senselessness and volatile situations between Nations whose populations are bulging at the borders. I'm afraid my people are wandering aimlessly from the point of view that they have lost sight of me, their God.

Liam, the vision I have for you to preach to Nations has a two pronged International Emergency Proclamation. This message is as important as the Sermon on the Mount when my Son Jesus proclaimed characteristics he regarded as making every human being happy and blessed. You Liam were a member of an Order that valued study of Sacred Scripture and Truth. This Order of St Dominic which is a beautiful branch of the Catholic Church also had in its founder a devotion to win souls for Christ.

Liam, I command all seven billion people living on earth to turn their eyes to me their Father. I have enough of complaining and wandering. I have enough of bitterness towards each other. I have enough of fighting. I have enough of evil. You either love me or lose your lives. I'm sick of pooh talk and lazing about. I solemnly proclaim and ask that fourteen billion human eyes kneel before me and turn their eyes in prayer to me, Big Eye in heaven. I give you this last opportunity.

Liam secondly, I mentioned St Dominic's key motto for his disciples. It is study of the Truth. I don't advocate abortion or war to curb populations. Nor do I send plagues or sickness to wipe out Nations. Yet there is a lot of conflict in my creature. So I advocate study in Universities, Colleges and schools to map out a better future for human beings. I preach unity, love and peace Liam. But there is a terrible animosity in the minds and hearts of people towards each other. The abuse of each other is frightening. I'm not a happy God at all. The enemies of good are increasing. Many have become friends of evil. I solemnly proclaim Liam and this is my second International Emergency Proclamation that all seven billion human beings Love Each Other. I'm hugely concerned about the lack of interest and respect people have for each other. I advocate a School of Study to teach the mind and heart that we all have seven billion friends on earth. We should not live as strangers or enemies. We should not live selfishly. Neither should we use, abuse, or exploit. I am God. I am Father. I am Big Eye. I insist on the world to change and build a better future for everyone. What I do not want is a Third World War that plunges the world into suffering, chaos, disaster and death. But if greedy Nations persist and irreligion deepens then devastation isn't far away.

Liam, I love my people. I love Israel but the more I called the further they went from me. I sent prophets to call them back and pleaded with them to denounce wickedness. But they wouldn't listen. The sword will appear again. Cities will be wiped out. Towns will be destroyed. The thirst and hunger in humans for power and domination is always an appetite. Rivalry will always exist. But don't worry. I save those who commit to Me. I care for those who obey my voice. I am a Father to those who love me. And I have Great Power. But I cannot force any Nation or individual to love me. The choice of free will to live independently of me or for me is a prerogative of the conscience of each man and woman. I can roar like a lion calling. I can bring the horse to the water. But I can't make a man or woman do anything.

Liam, if fifty thousand pagans reject my Son but there is one believer among them I'll save that one. If Nations reject my Son Jesus Christ and live as if he doesn't exist than the gap between heaven and earth widens for them. I call Governments to accept the religion of my Son Jesus Christ. My Son is the Messiah and his nature is Divine.

Liam, I'm sorry for diverting and advising you to preach about a new World Plan for the human race by encouraging all eyes to be raised towards me and that a study be done to improve love for one another. You can talk more about my Plan in Zacchaeus home. Jesus likes him and will visit. Distance doesn't matter anyway. Neither does time. Jesus could turn up any time in your room. Have you time to talk to him?

O Liam, my Little man from Co Limerick, you have seen nothing yet. Nor do you understand very much. My thoughts are very different from world knowledge and your educational structures. During formation years Educational Departments pump volumes of information into two little ears of each child. This conditioning squashes everything into an ear drum and allows very little room for internal personalised thinking. I'd like that to change. I like my children to think about their world for themselves and figure out ways to adore me their One True God. Knowledge and skills don't teach you how to love me.

Liam, I see you are animated and happy at the thought of a visit from Jesus. This visit will brighten up your beautiful mind. Keep a chair ready for him. If you want something more adventurous walk up a mountain and experience my Son Jesus' moment of transfiguration. Bring seaside chairs with you, sit down and talk. My three favourite Apostles were mesmerised with that they saw. So will you. And you will be a participant in the history and future of mankind.

Liam, use your imagination and bridge the gap of over two thousand years by allowing Popes and Saints from that period to spiritualise your personality. My Son Christ Jesus and the Apostles have been kept alive by the Church. So walk today with my Son on his journeys. Be one of the disciples on the road to Emmaus. Walk alone the coast road with Jesus. On your own little road there is grass in the middle. Think of yourself at one side. And my Jesus will walk at the other side if you invite him. All you have to do is pick up the phone and call him.

Liam, you know I love you. I truly love you. Out of seven billion people I picked you up from the earth in the same way as you allow a ladybird lodge on your finger. I'm that beautiful and glorious butterfly that you had the privilege to glimpse on while walking this morning. You thought I was beautiful. I can transform you into a butterfly or ladybird. You can be my new Saint.

Little Man

Father, I love it. Your speech to me is wonderfully positive. I can't wait to speak to the world on your behalf. I know of your desire. You want me to warn Governments. You want me to address citizens of all Nations. You want me to preach a Universal Love that's available from you Father. Your mind Father, and the mind of your Son Jesus Christ has bent backwards to win the love of people. I aim to advance your holy offer. I pray for solidarity between countries to overcome conflicts and regional problems. I pray to rebuild ties so as together racism, and all forms of evil infestations of hatred are driven from hearts and minds everywhere in the world. I preach a Universal Love.

Father, my prayer is to rise above divisions in religions, divisions among Nations, divisions among peoples. It doesn't matter if you are a Muslim, a Christian, a Buddhist, or a Protestant. My Father's Love is Universal. So cop on everyone. Come to your senses. I detest hatred buried in hearts. My Father has a Big Eye. He sees around the planet. He responds to those who accepts this message. It doesn't matter if you are Russian, Chinese, Iranian, Egyptian, Irish, Finnish, or Nigerian. It doesn't matter if you are a liturgical priest, or a banker, or a doctor, or a plasterer, or a technician. All that matters is that hearts and minds are raised in prayer to Almighty God.

Father, I jump with glee. Your last piece of writing has me in a state of joyful jitters. I can't contain my excitement. Are you promising to make me a Saint? It would be the happiest day of my life if you Father thought of making a saint out of me. Imagine me a Saint. I'll probably be called Saint Liam. But what have I achieved? I'm an unknown writer. I haven't directly cared for the elderly, or the sick or the poor. Pope St Leo said that if a man shows love to anyone in any sort of misery he himself is blessed. The virtue of charity is linked with serving others. It's a characteristic of sainthood. It guarantees a seat in heaven. It's the greatest service of all.

Father, what are you doing to me? A few minutes ago I was a goat and now I'm carried away thinking of the possibility of being a Saint. I imagine what it would be like to be a Saint. I think of myself having new skills; being a problem solver; manage situations more wisely; exposing wickedness in myself; having strength to be firm against evil; being loaded with virtues; to help the broken-hearted; and point to the Lamb of God.

Father, I look forward to unity with you. I want nothing else. I'm sick of lies, deceit and roguery everywhere. I don't trust anyone. I want Truth only. I want friendship with Christ. I'd like to be like St Dominic having a desire to win souls for you Father. Dominic had a joyous heart, was very affable and had a firm mind. I'd like to be joyous, friendly and full of ardour too Father. I have great reverence for your Word. Sacred scripture means everything to me. It's because Truth is in your Word. I hate been conned, cheated or lied too.

Father, I accept you wholeheartedly. For the moment I don't care about the world. I push aside seven billion people so that I can have a pure view of you Father, nothing but stress, pressure and problems emerge from interaction with human beings. So I turn from the world at the moment and gaze into your home Father. Please take me into your arms and console me. I'm coming to you like a battered ram. I run a hundred miles an hour from what's after me. I need to escape from encircling sharks that snip at my feeble mind and body. I'm scared Father. Please allow me jump into your arms for safety. A storm of pollution chases me. Help me find refuge in the Church.

Father, I close my door and windows. I shut myself away in my room. I seal the keyhole and edges of the door, and windows so that Satan's dirty tricks and filthy pollution doesn't seep into my sanctuary. I'll block sinful men and women too that my carry the disease of Satan into my holy place. I'll block phones, internet and television. I just want to be alone with you Father. I wouldn't expect you to come and make your home with me - a dishevelled mind and cluttered room.

Father, I accept your offer. I'd like to be a Saint. But I need to be a bull against evil and a lamb before you. I accept my fate Father. From now on I approach situations like a lamb. I stand alert and discern quickly the spirit of a person so as to be on guard against a restless soul that enjoy hassling me.

Father I'm a sandwich at the moment. One slice of bread was hassle and it left an unpleasant taste in my mouth. It deeply distressed me. In the middle was Holy Mass. It was delicious and it brought peace and calm to my mind and body. I loved it. On the other side of the sandwich was more hassle. How do I cope with that? The nicest part of the sandwich was Mass. I enjoyed the Body and Blood of Christ. I enjoyed the Gospel. It brought peace and calm. The slices of bread symbolising two incidents before and after Mass deeply upset me. Both had a spirit similar to an aggressive wasp. I don't know how to defend against aggressive adults or kids. They are inside stinging before I am aware of what's happening.

Father, a Saint is holy. I am not. I'm not able to cope with badness, arrogance, and boldness found in adults and children. I can't cope with defiance. My mind sizzles when met with challenging children, and disobedient children. It is fantasy thinking that I can be a light to the world and salt of the earth. I can't cope with what I'm finding in people. The evil vibes inundate me with frustration. The bad emotions that flow from others into me drown and kill the Lamb that I would like to be. I can't prevent the flow of badness flowing into my soul. I'm like a sitting duck. The Trinity of Females and the Defiance of Children have shot me down. I'm struck with multiple dart wounds that have obliterated my home where I expected Christ to visit and make me his friend.

Father, I pray to you. I can see clearly the value of celibacy in the Church. There can't be cross-contamination. There can't be a mixed bag. Christ is Divine. Friendship with Christ deserves all our love and attention. A wife and children reduces that commitment to love Christ and save souls. So maybe I should return to religious life. I'm ravaged on my own. I have no protection.

Father, I pray for help. I need salt and light. I wouldn't want anyone to see me in my present state. I'm riddled with stress and tension. Please Jesus don't shine a light on me. My weaknesses would be seen. I wouldn't be attractive at the moment. Yet I pray Father for that light. I'm dark at the moment. There is no light in me. My oil has burnt out with worry. I have nothing to inspire and brighten up the life of my son, the life of my wife, the life of the girls, or the life of my neighbours. In fact, I feel wretched rather than a holy Saint.

Father, I pray for right judgement. I don't think you would want me on your Holy Team because my prayer training is start/stop every few days. I don't know why I mismanage time. Self-control is difficult due to acute stress. So what good would I be standing at the altar in this state. What good would I be helping a stressed person when I'm worn out by the same problem. A blind man cannot lead a blind man.

Father, I pray again. What am I going to do? You have tested me enough. I'm no use to you worn out. Throw me into a Sacred Bath full of Holy Oil. For I cannot appear at someone's door wretched, stressed and tired. Christ wash me. Church Doctors heal me. I'm sick, tired and tormented. I've lost my battle to be friendly and affable. Father, I'm not happy with my body and soul right now.

Father, throw me into a Sacred Bath with Holy Oil. Hopefully I'll come up out of it a clean man, a new man, a refreshed man, a lit up man, a salty man. Oh no! I lost sight of Christ. I took my eye off him again. And that is why my Lamp flickered and died. I have to find my way back to Christ. He is the Light of the World. The Light comes from Jesus Christ. There is no other Light.

Father, I pray for your Holy Brightness. I pray for the Divine Bulb. I pray for the Light of Christ. This is not hypocrisy Father. I want my soul lit up. For I can't knock at the doors of families with a grim face, or a dark face, or a wrecked face. People want to see a holy man. They want to see a man that is in love with you Jesus. After all the purpose of visits are to care for souls and bless in your name Father, Son and Holy Spirit.

Father, if you want me to be a true disciple embed in me that Holy Light and that Sacred Salt. With you in me Jesus I could face any kind of man. I'd be afraid of nothing. Bring me away from the crowd Father. I need rest and a Sacred Bath. And I'm not going out to evangelise the world without Holy Salt and Sacred Light. It would be madness Father for me to turn up at doors and pray with people without the sprinkling and taste of Christ's Salt in me and around me. The people must find my Christian love. If people made me welcome, I'd sprinkle the whole house and every individual in it with a delicious Holy Salt that seasons all present with the wonderful food of the Body and Blood of Jesus Christ. The Christian must have flavour. He must be happy. He must be attractive. Otherwise you are talking about dead lumps of meat. They lack the flavour that comes from being properly inebriated into the heart and life of Jesus Christ. O happy Church, cheer up. Allow Christ to sprinkle Sacred Salt into your experience of Holy Communion. If salted you will be happy. If not your Sacred Food and Sacred Word will be tasteless.

Father, I pray sincerely now. Give me some Holy Salt. Give me a bag of it. I want to be flavoured all over with Jesus Christ. And I want to flavour the world with Jesus Christ. I call all citizens in China. I call all

Ecuadorians. I call all Brazilians. I call all Iranians. I call all Irish. I call every human being. I solemnly proclaim that Jesus Christ has a Sacred Taste of Divinity that every believer and non-believer should know.

Father, I'm thrilled with your Word. My heart burns for Sacred Scripture. I'm salted by Christ. My character changed already. The child and adult irritations lifted. Christ's Sacred Salt contributed to a more affable flavour setting in. I'm confident in my ability once again because Christ's love is trickling through into places that were filled with irritations.

Father, I now turn to Sacred Light. I want to understand your Word. You told your Apostles that they were lights to the world. What is this Sacred Light? I'm sure you are not talking about light coming from sun, moon, stars, bulbs or candles. Yet they all have a common purpose – the same function - to shine out. But how can St John, St Peter or St Paul brighten up the world? What is it that generates the Light of Christ? Do they have a coal miners torch strapped on their foreheads?

Father, I thought your Words, "Lights of the World", would be easy to explain. I can't find this Sacred Light. I can't find Christ. I just want to hide and let no one see me. There's nothing enlightening or illuminating shining forth from me. I'm dark. I can't light up my own house and there I was thinking my book might light up the world. I had better pray to Jesus and knock at his door. I seek answers as to why I am deprived of Sacred Light.

Father, I bear the Name Christian. I received Sacraments of Baptism, Confession, Holy Communion, Confirmation, Ordination and Marriage. Should I not be enrolled as belonging to you Father? I'm your child. Surely you wouldn't deprive me of Sacred Light? Father, I demand a meeting with your Son Jesus Christ. I want to know why my Christian batteries are dead for I have no energy or light to inspire anyone.

Father I pray about this. An unspiritual tiredness set in. My lights went out through exhaustion. I'm burnt out from my Trinity of Women with issues a minute and over fifteen phone calls a day. I'm also burnt out from child defiance and boldness. I'm worn out issuing warnings and corrections. I gave way to anger over these hostile events. It was like thunder and lightning knocking Christ completely out of my mind and heart. I'm in the dark.

Father, summon me to an urgent meeting with Jesus. I'm blind. I can't see. Anger has made me blind. I couldn't cross a busy road in this state. So how can I ever be a Light to the World? A blind man couldn't evangelise the world. The first Muslim I meet would throw me down an empty well.

Father, I see the importance of your Holy Word. I'm attracted to the idea of being a Christian Light for people. And for you Father to beam through me into the hearts of Muslims and into the hearts of seven billion people a super Sacred Light must be at work. There's no point in carrying a little candle for the tiniest of breezes would quench it. Then my Light dies. My mission would have failed.

Father, I seek an appointment with your Son Jesus. I knock at his Office Door. Can I walk in? I know what has to be done. I have to restore friendship with Christ. Light is a Golden Egg. Understanding the Light of Christ requires much prayer. Christ is a dynamo of Sacred Light. I have a prayer meeting with Jesus to discuss the breakdown that occurred over my anger. I lost contact completely over a weakness that allowed a weasel to chew light wires that kept Christ alive in me. I'm expected to spend time on long meditations to restore and reconnect my life with Christ. For I have nothing to give to the world unless I am called by Christ and energised through some form of illumination, transformation and enlightenment.

Father, I'm sick of poor torch performances. I'm a flickering candle. My Light isn't enough to brighten up a shed not to mention the world. I'm fairly sure that for me to shine like a beacon one thing has to be done. I have to die to self and embed myself in Christ. The more I walk in the direction of Christ the brighter my Lamp shines.

Father, the answer is clear now – less of me is more of Christ. I can see Jesus walk the earth in search for homes that welcome him. My door is open. I sit and wait. I have an empty chair in front of me. It's for Jesus. I need to look into his face and eye for reassurance. I can have knowledge of Christ in my mouth. And I would have the lingo of a Christian. But in the head, in the mind there is no trace of him. The same applies to the heart. The Light of Christ isn't breaking into my inner chambers. My interiority is cluttered with old stories. Nothing is new.

Father, I call you. You are the Father of Jesus Christ. I write for enlightenment in the middle of the night. No rays of virtues come my way. I took vows of chastity, poverty and obedience. Yet nothing shifted me. Nothing made me smile. Nothing stitched us together. There isn't enough awareness in me to unify my life with the Body and Blood of your Son.

Father of Sacred Truth, Sacred Salt and Sacred Light come to me. I'm your child. I can't go around the world without essentials. No Christian would travel without the Light of Christ to brighten up the intellect and inflame the heart with Pure Love and rays of glorious virtues pouring in the soul. I cannot face the enemy unarmed. At the moment I'm not equipped to Light up the world.

Father, the chair is empty. The door is open. I sit and wait for Jesus. I wait. I wait. I wait. I persist. I persist. I persist. Come Jesus. Come Jesus. Come to my house tonight. I have a chair waiting for you. I want to meet you. I want to test myself in your Presence. I want to mirror my thoughts and emotions as we look at each other. I want to understand your Word. I want to ask you for the Sacred Light that shines forever.

Father, I think I see Jesus coming. He is two thousand and sixteen years away. That is a long time ago. And he is a long distance away too. But he travels faster than a jet. He comes through stars, planets, oceans, mountains and valleys in an instant. Christ is Eternal and bridges time and distance. In a jiffy the Holy Spirit could descend from heaven and land on my head. I would be instantly electrified with Sacred Light. And Christ could come forward over two thousand years and sit on my chair anytime for spiritual conversations about plans for me and plans for years to come.

Father, you know I could not spread your Holy Word nor sell Golden Eggs unless there were meetings with your Divine Team and the Sacred Congregation of the Faith. I'm glad the Holy Spirit came. And I'm glad scenes from the Gospel are vivid in my memory especially ones relevant to meetings about spreading the Scared Light of your Son to all Nations.

Father, I am now in contact. I feel it. The Holy Spirit has come. The resurrection experience has come. Christ stood in the room and said Peace be with you. A Sacred Light was infused into the Apostles. It came down on their heads like tongues of fire. I'm looking for that same experience Father. I want to be lit up and be on fire with your Word. Holy Spirit, give me courage and strength.

Father, personal holiness is important to me. It's lovely thinking I'm close to you. It's lovely feeling that I am attached to you. But I'm not fooled. I don't know if I am a Pharisee rotten on the inside but impressive in appearance. I don't know if I'll gain any credit for cutting myself off from everyone because I can't tolerate a rip-off culture that prevails nowadays. I have never seen such greed in all my life as that which exists now.

Father, maybe I'll turn on the Sacred Light of Christ in my country first and expose the rotten culture of fat cats prevalent in Irish society nowadays. I see these creeps everywhere. I'm sick of the way they changed Laws to make themselves rich. I'm sick of Businesses, Politicians, Consultants, Companies, Banks and CEO's receiving more than generous pensions and salaries over quarter of a million per annum. And I'm sick of politicians setting up enquiries to investigate their own mismanagement and corruption. And I'm doubly critical of Public Servants stretching inflation by constantly looking for wage increases over and above what the economy can afford. I also criticise the wastage of Public Funds and Exorbitant Pensions. It's right and just for the country to protest against failures to modernise and refresh cities, towns and villages around the Nation.

Father, I'm sorry. I lost the run of myself. My mind forgets to remain in the room and wait for further instruction from the Holy Spirit and Jesus Christ. I sounded like a prophet and condemned corruption. It is true though. I will not hold back. I condemn greedy fat cats who exploit the poor, or those who inflate the price of services that result in struggling families to pay the bills and feed their children.

Father, I'm sorry again. I'm back in the room with Jesus. Thank you for been gentle with me when I allowed my imagination run riot by preaching. I'm back Holy Spirit. I tell you what I seek. Or I will tell you what I lack. I do my best to revere you Father, and to revere you Jesus Christ, and to revere you Holy Spirit. First of all, I seek friendship with my Trinity of Divine Friends. I want to meet you regularly so as to embed myself into an Eternal friendship that's steady, loyal and loving. I'm ready to pray, to listen and to learn before doing anything. And above all Father I beg for a lasting blessing for protection so as to carry out my intentions to hold onto your Holy Friendship no matter what tribulations or trials attempt to sabotage my choice for you.

Father, I beg your pardon. I gave you no gift when we met. I invited you to my home and my greeting of you lacked reverence and excitement. I gave you no kiss. I didn't bow down humbly before you Father, my God Most High. I know you don't expect gifts of calves, or rams, or oil, or anything else. Instead you prefer the gift of myself to act justly and love tenderly. I try Father to walk humbly with you if you will have me.

Father, I have a proposal to make. I change my mind about a commitment of Holy Friendship. I want to remarry you. Can't you see how deep my love is for you? On my knees I ask you to marry me. I'll do my best to be loyal this time. I have the flesh of a man Lord. And nothing would please me more than to be married to my Divine Trinity of Friends. I want to marry Jesus Christ under the influence of the Holy Spirit.

Father, I'm excited about my proposal. Will you have me? I'm not a perfect partner Lord but I'll do my best to please you. I want this Father? Can I marry your Son Jesus Christ again? My reason is clear Father. It's to do with my desire to be holy and saintly. It's to do with what makes me happy. It's to do with becoming pregnant with a heavenly seed. I know what I want. I want the stuff that's in Jesus Christ. It's only through him that a Sacred Light can light up in me and shine out for the world. It is only through him that the heavenly seed can be inserted into my substance. It is only through him that I want to live.

Father, I can't marry you. Nor can I marry your Mother Mary. You are my spiritual parents. You care for me an adopted son. You also care for your Divine Son Jesus Christ. I ask God our Father and Mary the Mother of God for permission to remarry Jesus Christ. I promised vows before and broke them. But I never stopped loving you, my Lord and God. I have always loved you since the days of my childhood. With such a Powerful and Divine Assembly, I'll never go wrong again. I'll have the strength and support to remain firm in my commitment.

Father, I feel wonderful about the news of a remarriage. I'm delighted. I call upon the Holy Spirit to marry us. I solemnly profess my love for Jesus Christ. My love is cemented. It is bonded. Nothing will rattle it anymore. I'll not change no matter what savage and persistent floggings torture me because of my love for Jesus Christ. Nothing will subdue my love. The difference now is that I'm not alone anymore. I fight Satan with a power that Satan can't corrupt or beat. My Holy Friend and Wonderful Love will not stand by idle when I'm flogged for opposing fraudulent liars and for throwing light on transactional deceivers.

Father, I'm sorry for writing such a lengthy piece. I' just can't hide my excitement. It's Good News all the way. I'm with Jesus your Son and I hope you don't mind. Big Eye, there is a sparkle in your eye. You are happy for me. And I'm sure preaching your Word through writing is an acceptable form of hard work. I'll help to refresh the world of your importance.

Father, I pray to you for courage. I'm afraid evil might return and destroy me. The force of an evil battle is worse than a tsunami. I scamper up a hill and run for my life when I see tons of water and debris chase me with powerful force. I'm forced to doubt when confronted with frightening storms and bombs of hatred. In these circumstances my Sacred Light dims considerably. The real test is to cope under pressure. The genuine response is to trust Jesus. Doubting allows the enemy in. And he will pour pooh over the Sacred Light and laugh if you hesitate.

Under pressure Christians must tap Jesus on the shoulder and ask for help. I'm an idiot. I stood like a dope and allowed evil to overwhelm me.

Father, I'll not make a public declaration of my marriage vows. I do it silently with you. Everyone don't have to know my business. I declare privately to you Father and to Jesus in prayer that nothing in life matters as much as my union with my Precious Lamb of God. Also I want to work out with you Father my mission. I hope that it is to spread the Word through pen and paper.

Father, I'm iffy, iffy about my participation in the Assembly of Heaven due to the possibility I may be asked to die like Christ and experience the fate of the martyrs. Jesus help me! Why am I thinking like this? I'm not sure if I would accept martyrdom. There is no doubt in the world that evil forces will attack me for belonging to Christ. I wouldn't mind dying for my son, or my wife, or for Christ. But to die for those who make life miserable for everyone else would make me rethink

Father, let be realistic here. I can help seven billion people by working quietly and unnoticed, or working under the radar by writing. I don't have to die. My book could help future generations. My book is for the future. The spoken word is often lost. I don't like speaking to people. It is due to the fact that words uttered are running against time like sperm going through a fallopian tube. Sperm has a short life except for the one that is lucky enough to stick to an egg. The same applies to words. Words spoken in the morning are dead by evening.

Father, I admit though that a Holy Word uttered with aplomb might make it through into an ear and connect with our intellectual system. Holy Words are like fragile seed. If they reach good soil they might grow and bear fruit. Also a book can travel everywhere around the world and into every home. That would be impossible for me in the flesh. My intention is to support Nations to do the right thing. I pray for Chairpersons and Presidents to serve tenderly and act justly with all. I preach Jesus Christ. Sorry Muslim. I prefer my Catholic Church. O happy Church. I love my Catholic Church. I love you Muslims too. We are all one family. We ought to care for each other. I would never want to fight with you. I hope my book is allowed into Muslim countries and that converts are not suppressed. The West doesn't suppress your beliefs. My friend Bishop William believed in Christ and was exiled. I pray for the conversion of everyone to Jesus Christ. If one child in Iran wants to become Catholic, the authorities are wrong to stop him. In five million Iranians want to switch to Christ the Government should accommodate it. I don't believe in religious suppression. But I insist on Peace and Love. There is no need to fight and kill. In the last fifteen years we have more Muslims in Limerick than ever before and no one suppresses their right to worship. In fact, the Government supports multi-cultural minorities. My book is designed to save souls. And I'm all for inclusion and a sharing of faiths. I'm happy for Muslims to convert to Christianity. I'm also happy if a Christian becomes a Muslim. It's individual choice. But I urge individuals to focus on Jesus Christ. I have found love in him and it means more to me than life. Jews, Christians and Muslims believe in One God. Yahweh is the same person as God. Allah is the same person as God. And God is God. I have the experience of two thousand and sixteen years of spiritual history that Jesus Christ is the Son of God. I love him, and I tell you Jews, and Muslims that you miss out on having a brother like Jesus to walk with you and help you through the arduous journey of living a human life.

Father, my book could serve as a warning against war. Is the human brain more intelligent now than at the time of the First and Second World Wars? If it is why display military aggression? It is why go down the route of Syria's civil war? The displacement of people, the destruction of buildings, the splattered blood of children and the family grief for lost ones is enough to stop any war. Listen Korea! Listen Ukraine! Listen Muslims!

Father, I bring to the United Nations a message of Peace and Love. I bring a Sacred Light and a Salty Heart to the table for discussion. I flavour the world with the Peace of Christ. Please world! Lift your hands in prayer. Muslims you can pray. Christians you can pray. Don't succumb to the evil of war. I don't want the effect of Hiroshima to ever happen again. Korea change direction. It's better to pray and love than have dead bodies lying everywhere in cities, towns, villages and in fields.

Father, I warn against the consequences of unspiritual living. The Son of Man regards rejection of his Church and the lack of prayer as the worst death of all. A devout person dies and go to heaven. But a pagan or an unspiritual soul is cut off. I see a lot cut off. I know by the appearance of the body and face that a soul is dry. These are not praying. It's another form of death. Unspiritual people are unhappy in themselves. They look depressed and stressed. Without you Father we are worse of then animals. They are happy doing what is expected of them by grazing grass and drinking water. People who neglect prayer are blobs of unhealthy matter. They rejected God and are no good to God.

Father, my book is a prayer. It is the story of my love for my Father. It is the story of a Big Eye looking out for me. It is the story of my Father, God Almighty and my Mother, Holy Mary offering me a Holy Friendship and sacred marriage with their Son, Jesus Christ. This book originated from two words on the Lord's Prayer – Our Father. My Brother Jesus and Sacred Friend saved my life. In his Triumphal Procession he took my faults to Calvary. He used evil men to drag my sin of anger out of my intellect and nail it [anger] into his hands on the wood of the cross.

Father, call me like you called Isiah. Send a seraph to me with a burning tongs and touch my mouth. Burn the crap talk and my faults. Make me clean so that I can preach ardently and teach serious Doctrine. I ask for strength to face the wrath of the world and the evil condition that has to be fought. If I am not ready for battle my call is in vain. And if I am ready the abuse will do me no harm. For life is a struggle against evil.

Father, I know what has to be done. I have to work in close proximity with my Sacred Salt, my Sacred Light, my Sacred Friend, the Son of Man. The Preacher lit up with the Light of Christ and Spiritual Salt has to carry the Word to the ends of the earth. The whole world needs to hear again the Sacred Word of God. A Spiritual Salt needs to be sprinkled on the whole earth so as to prevent human beings from rotting through the evil condition of sinful decomposition, religious division and political corruption.

Father, I support fully the Son of Man in his work through the Church to spiritualise families everywhere throughout the world in local gatherings of faithful followers. I also beg and plead for Political Powers to adhere to and submit to Divine Power in their Constitutions, and to do nothing that would harm the moral well-being of each person under their rule. Father, I believe Divine Anger would bellow harshly against State Leaders if they suppressed the will and freedom of its citizens to opt for worshipping the Lord, my God. Trouble beckons for a power that rejects their Father who happens to be God.

Father, my book is a way of communicating with every person that read in the world. A book outlives the writer. If I were to visit and speak to groups around the world, it would take years. A book could conquer the world as has the Bible.

Father, my motive is Truth. I picture a planet full of human beings and other living things. The origins are a mystery, and life is a mystery, and continuation of human life is as fascinating as the human mind. I dislike though intellectual paganism. This group of people use knowledge and arguments to take Christ out of politics, out of education, and out of society. They don't believe in you Father. They think we are on our own. But I don't. I believe in you. I love you. And I will not standby and allow intellectual wolves weaken little children's faith. I know that your little lambs receive solace and dignity by praying as a group of believers every day in the local Church. The faith of the remaining few believers has to be protected from a rapidly changing society whose game plan is to weaken the power of the Catholic Church.

Father, I fully commit to the Powers of Heaven. I'm ready to fight evil. And I do this by my powerful belief and thirst for friendship with my Divine Mother, my Divine Father, my Divine Brother Jesus, and my Divine Friend the Holy Spirit. I look for God and I've found him in all Five Divine Friends. Nothing is as High as these. Nothing is as Great as these. I have proclaimed my faith. And I have no hesitation whatsoever in condemning falsehoods or attacks on Catholic Doctrine. I condemn ambiguity. I have cleared my mind of pooh. My belief is crystal clear. I urge every single person on earth to give a little bit of their time to prayer. By all means enjoy life but don't allow your mind to run out of grace. The Prayer Station is the Church. Drop in and refill.

Father, I love you. I have never loved you as much as I do now. I feel this joy running through me. And I know it is coming from my Five

Glorious Friends. The joy also comes from Great Church Doctors and Great Fathers of the Church. I love them too because a Gift was given to them and they shared it with me. The Saints are absolutely wonderful. I love them to bits.

Father, I pray to you. I always address my writing to you. I'm a child writing to my Father. You are the same Father as Allah. So your children should never hate each other. My plan is to encourage people to fight evil. My metaphor to bring lucidity to this invisible fight is water. I see the flow of dirty water invading souls by the minute right across the world. Evil forces gather pace and floods threaten to engulf the heart and mind of each human being. Dirty water represents the push by Satan to engulf the world in horrible evil, corruption, murder and crime. On the other hand, is pure clean water that's becoming scarcer by the day. But this is beautiful stuff. This is God's Stuff. This is the solid Christian. But it's defences has weakened. Dirty water infiltrated and leaked into the Church. And it is taking a long time to wash clean with pure and holy water the stains of evil. The wash must start from source – from the Source of Holiness. What has to be done is for Jesus Christ to pour tons and tons of Holy Water into the Church to flood out and clean out contamination. In other words, a push is required by Bishops, clergy and the faithful to resurrect the Holy Well. We all need to be washed clean and that should pave the wave for fresher, and more enthusiastic celebrations of the Eucharist. The thing is we can't wash others unless we wash ourselves first. Therefore, once each of us become a clean tap of running water we can wash the dirt that appears before us.

Father, I have another metaphor too. I equip each Christian with a hammer. In fact, better still I supply every person on earth with an invisible mallet. I encourage the use of a hammer. Each person must examine his/her conscience. Every time a sin crops up bang it on the head like a hammer with a nail. Psychologically therefore you drive a nail through your sins. You can nail sins. That is what my Divine Brother Jesus Christ did with all of our sins. The thorns punctured them. The nails in his feet and hands killed sin. Satan does not like pain or for anyone to nail his evil little eggs at work in the soul.

Father, you are Big Eye. You see everything done in secret. The Catholic Church have been subject to hammer blow after hammer blow by political atheists and irreligious media members in recent years. You Father, don't matter to them. These people preyed on a wounded Church. These people have no conscience. These people have dirtied and changed society. These people have taken over the moral high ground from the Church and in doing that they slapped you Father in the face by introducing Laws that oppose your Word and Will. I don't like it. I suggest that the Church fight back on the grounds of Truth and Goodness. I suggest taking the hammers of the pagans and hammering their bad anti-God policies before they ruin the country of our proud traditions except for the scandals. I would keep the biggest hammer for paedophiles and pin them to prison cells for a long, long time. I make no excuse for a corrupt man or corrupt priest. But I would forgive and show mercy if the paedophile relented from evil acts. Mercy is the great hope a sinner has.

Father, I'm clear in mind on the task in hand. The Christian, the aspirant towards virtuous growth has a holy hammer to nail each sin as soon as its ugly head pops up in the mind to tempt the sinner. This must be done consistently so that the root of the sin becomes frustrated and dies with a lack of progress.

Father, I have to walk with you carefully here. I don't want a scenario where someone might say about me that I come across as arrogant with an attitude of being better than thou. I want to be sure that I deal with my own faults first an argue with no one. I remember Christ Jesus teaching on criticism of others. My Divine Brother Jesus Christ spoke of a person who was hyper critical of others. I love your teaching. Wow! Look at the plank in your own eye before you try and take out the splinter in others. See your own big faults before you correct the small faults in others. If you are wise learn this lifelong lesson.

Father, I' m grateful for that lesson above. I'll stop being critical of others and try instead to correct myself by being nice and humble at home towards my family members. But I must be careful not to lie down and be trampled underfoot by sinful judgemental goats or aggressive bulls who harm the Church and scatter the lambs. I have to stand firm like a Good shepherd. I must protect what is precious to me. And nothing is more precious than my Five Divine Friends who have grave concerns about empty Churches, a shortage of good clergy and the effect scandals had on the scattering of the faithful.

Father, I pray for people. I'm upset with the loss of so many people from practising their belief in the Church. I'm concerned about the zero amount of time people have now for prayer. I advise people everywhere in the world to return to their Heavenly Father. Please return to prayer. Shallow prayer though is no good. My Father likes an active mind and passionate heart in prayer.

Chapter Fourteen

Big Eye

Greetings Liam. I nearly fell asleep waiting for you to finish the last chapter. It's very long. You took off. How are you? I see you take life seriously and you intend to speak for me without my permission. For the moment I command you to take it easy. I haven't worked out a role for you so don't preach using my Name. I may never call you to preach. You had your chance in the Order of Preachers. I search the world for potential carriers of my Word. Sound Catholic doctrine must be heard. For you I'm not in favour of a return to preaching. I'd prefer to use the option of the written Word. For I look forward to engaging with you in conversational pieces of writing.

Liam, I am with you all the way in combating modern evils. I am in complete unity with my Divine Son. He has the title of Son of Man. That implies Supreme Lord over Man on Planet Earth. The Son of Man is above all Titles of Human Power. His devout followers over the last two thousand years are Doctors and Fathers of the Church. These are Saints. These cast the darts of my Doctrine. These darts are hurled at my foe in a fierce battle to repel evil from spreading and destroying the beauty that each soul should depict.

Liam, I love you. I'm glad you intend to work with my Son. The future of man is safe with good men and women dedicated to me. I'm impressed with you. I admire your focus on me, your Father. I wish there were a few hundred men and women in every country that had faith and dedication to work on behalf of families and neighbours in their relations with me. I'm happy though with you. I have one beautiful mind that penetrates deeply my Divine Nature and submits humbly to my Magnificent Splendour and Power.

Liam, I can't take my Big Eye off you. I'm attracted to you. It took you sixty years to finally fall in love with me. I watch you every morning on road L0909 as you raise your voice to the skies and call me Father. You are like a bee Liam extracting pollen from a flower. You extract juice from my Name. You stumbled upon a method to suck life from me your Father. You done this by concentrating on the meaning of the Word Father. Well done! Only a deeply spiritual man grasps the sense of my Word. There's power in my Flower. I Am Beautiful. Suck from my Flower Liam. Suck from my Name. Suck from your Father. Beautiful Gifts are found in there. Suck from my Mind Liam. Suck from my Heart Liam. The Sweetest Stuff or a whole ray of virtues that decorate the earth come from the Father of Flowers or from the Beauty of Butterflies. Tell my bees to suck deeply. Tell my people to breathe the odour that emanates from my Sacred Name.

Liam,

Liam, I'm more than delighted with you writing in my Name. It's a work that you enjoy. And it is a work that bonds us together. I remember your gene Liam. I know all your ancestors going back four thousand years. I have seen them struggle near the Holy Land and across in to Europe. I saw them land in Ireland. I saw them land in boats, and I saw them accepting Catholic faith. Your people struggled to survive during wars and poverty. Liam, you have to be grateful for your ancestors. All their hard work paid off when you like a bee found me – the Highest and Greatest Flower of All. There's never a doubt in my mind about the welfare of your relations, friends and neighbours once a man like you remembers them in prayers.

Liam. shout from the rooftops. Preach Truth. I don't like a silent Church. Where are my darts of Doctrine? Who sets my Word on fire? Sting the congregation. My Word is sharp. It should sting the Christian into action. The celebrant fails to set the congregation on fire. I like vibrant and enthusiastic services. Dead hearts are no good to me. Neither are dazed heads. Wake up Church. Wake up priests. You were not called to hide like rabbits in a burrow. You are not mice called to sneak around undetected. I called you to roar like a lion and preach my Word. Or maybe no one will listen to you Liam. So I might ask you to write instead to all the Churches in the world as well as those who don't practise anymore. For I like your Universal Love approach that nobody is excluded from me. I am Big Eye and all are part of the human family.

Liam, fight for me. Roar out powerful sermons. Shout from the roof top. I want everyone to have a chance to change, repent and return to me. On my behalf tell them that I love them especially the poor, sick, elderly, lonely, broken-hearted and victims of exploitation. Liam, tell them again. I'm their Father. Tell everyone that I care. I particularly want to touch broken hearts who struggle to overcome bereavement, accidental death, and families coming to terms with suicide. Liam, tell sinners I love them but they have to repent and change.

Liam, I am weary with my people. I patch one puncture for them when I hear them moan about another. They are never satisfied. That's why I rely on your sermon. Hit them with sound Doctrine. Hit them with darts of Catholic Teaching like a dart player hitting triple twenty in succession. Keep hitting their hearts and heads with my Word. Tell them not to be lazy and to work for a living. Tell them of the dangers of storing up riches for themselves. Tell them to go back to Jesus Christ. Tell them to put people before profit. Tell them to put me first in their lives. Tell them that competition for My Love is better than competition for a sports medal. Tell them that My Friendship surpasses all human friendships including the intimacy and friendship of sexual unions. Liam, shout from the roof top. I am to have priority of place in every humans' life. I Am the Greatest of All and Highest of All. I'm above family relationships and the love of romantic couples. I ask you across the earth to reconsider your lethargic and dismissive attitude towards my Son Jesus Christ. I became Man for you. So listen dope. Listen before it is too late. I wouldn't like anyone to die on bad terms with my Son. You have to go through Jesus to arrive at heaven. My Son has the Key. Your book, your life, your spoken words, your actions, your work, your treatment of others are available to me. I have a better media system than Facebook, Instagram and Messenger. So I warn you that rejection of me is rejection of heaven. And no matter how bad you are now you have a chance to change and commit to my Christ.

Little Man

Father, you frighten me. I don't know if I do enough to save my soul or whether my words and actions please you. And why call me dope? It isn't my fault if I am hard of hearing. I admit there is a bit of deafness in me. And I long to be free from it. I'm dull of hearing. It prevents me from capturing the sense of Holy and Sacred Words. Deafness harms comprehension. I would settle at this stage of my life for full comprehension into the significance and beauty of your Name Father.

Father, I apologise on behalf of the Church. The Gospels shouldn't be silent on scandals. I accept your criticism of priests who fell foul to the power of the evildoer. And I accept criticism of those who enter religious life for security, peace, and repose. Scandals affect us all. I pray Father for the Church. I pray for Pope Francis, Cardinals, Bishops and Priests that they wash themselves clean by neutralising and removing bad apples found within their ranks.

Father, good priests and those who carry on found themselves tarnished by bad apples. I speak using a metaphor. A bad apple is a rotten priest who succumbed to horrendous evils by abusing children sexually. The actions of bad apples were a paradox between a Sacred Act and an Evil Act occurring side by side by the perpetrator. I pray for Bishops to take greater care of the spiritual welfare of priests by setting up supports, retreats and parish visits. A priest needs a caring pastor. A priest needs his bishop to listen to him.

Father, I'm so sorry to hear of this evil in the Church. Paedophilia rocked the Church. Satan grabbed the weakest part of a priest's nature, his celibacy, his virginity, his chastity, and his sexuality. The devil broke through a priests weak defences. He paralysed their minds by offering sick and lonely priests an abominable pleasurable temptation on the weakest and most vulnerable members of society our innocent children.

Father, I pray for victims of child abuse. The scars of this evil never go away. The sexual predator remains in the memory. The dirty sexual need is hard to wash away. Forgiveness is hard. For the victim have to live with the paws of a paedophile smearing a child's innocent body forever.

Father, I pray to for those affected by clerical scandals. I pray for good and holy priests to survive this suffering, this distress and this tribulation. I regard it has unfair to tarnish every priest with the same brush. It's unjust to destroy all apples just because a few were rotten.

Father, I pray for the Church to clean itself up. Clerical paedophiles scandalised the faithful. Therefore, I am sad. My heart goes out to those who don't practise their religion anymore. I see them in their houses on Sunday mornings lying in bed and saying no prayers. I'm so sorry Father that bad priests drove people away from the Church. I call them hypocrites doing a good act on the altar and an evil act away from it. These betrayed Jesus.

Father, I solemnly advise Catholics not to allow a bad apple to cause decay in their relationship with God. It is an immature decision. By staying in bed on a Sunday morning or placing sport before Christ you started your own process of decay from belonging to God's family. You are foolish to allow scandalous behaviour to cause you to fall. The Church needs the whole community praying together. The best way to display faith in Christ is to gather together for worship. It would give everyone a lift if members from each household return to Church.

Father, I feel strongly about the spiritual death of so many over scandals. I see them dying in their homes. Nobody calls to them. They don't trust anyone anymore. They may not even open the door to a pastor. It's rather sad. At least fifty percent dropped off from worshipping in Church. I don't know how to save them. Big Eye help.

Father, are we to forgive paedophiles after they caused so much trouble by ruining the lives of innocent children and corrupting the faithful by their evil deeds. I know of your teaching on unlimited forgiveness and unconditional mercy for sinners. But you also implied Father that it would be better to put a millstone around your neck and fling yourself into the ocean if you caused scandal by corrupting little children.

Father, I can't judge. It is your decision. I cannot comment on the fate of a paedophile. All I can say is that the sin is worse than the woman caught committing adultery and the woman who had a relationship with seven men. You forgave them both Father. Who am I to throw a stone at a sinner? The Gospel is not silent about scandals. It never should be. Nobody should hide a paedophile. I thank you Father that Child Protection Policies are in place. The Church is much safer. Priests are removed from ministry immediately once an allegation occurs. Also police are informed.

Big Eye

Hello Liam. Please let it go. I don't want dialogue about evil acts. We don't want to give Satan a platform. Stay clear from highlighting his damage. I'm about Good News Liam. My Son is too. Concentrate on the Highest Virtue. Suck Love from my Sacred Heart. I Am your Father. I urge prayer for Bishops and Priests in their tough work in fighting nettles, thistles and thorns growing among the remnant of my loyal flowers that continue to pray around my altar and receive the Gift of my Whole Presence in the humble reception of my Son's Body and Blood. Pray for good priests. These men have to be open to my Heart of Love. These men have to possess a Sacred Connection. Otherwise they are extremely vulnerable. The Highest Virtue is my Love and its attributes are mercy, purity, poverty, peace, humility and a hunger and thirst for what is right and just. My priests should have these qualities. So should you.

Liam, move away from horror stories. There's enough damage done. There is enough said about it. Pray for priests to love my Son. I concentrate on the formation of priests by preparing them for hard work and the cleansing of sin from within and without the Church. I desire a return to former glory where Churches are full and the priest generates the Gift of my Love present on the altar and shared with delightful and happy Christians. Don't dwell on evil. If a member displays symptoms of evil smother it with Love, with the way you care for each other.

Liam, there is one more thing. I'd like you to know this. My Sacred Team care for children. Their welfare is of the utmost importance. Buckets of tears were shed in heaven over a priest or any man collaborating with my adversary. My Divine Committee are strong on crimes and sins of that nature. No perverts are in heaven. No criminals are in heaven. No evil is in heaven. I would urge you to tell everyone on earth to shake of their sins before it is too late. The procedures are in place through my Son Jesus Christ who is a Redeemer for each wilful soul to repent and turn their backs on evil.

Liam, rescuing boys and girls who are in mortal danger is important to me. My Divine Mother Mary is there for them. Tell all children, teenagers and young adults to pray to their Holy and Pure Mother. If their natural mothers are errant remind them that my Divine Mother is there for them. Holy Mary is beautiful and gentle. She is the epitome of grace. She is a Model Lady. Liam tell the children to love her. Tell them to pray to her. She is a Holy Mother for adults too. You Liam have me as your Divine Father. But you have a Divine Mother too. The love of your Divine Mother enriches your spirituality. So pray to her and love her. She's the Mother of my Son.

Liam, the Holy Game is simple, so simple that intelligent and selfish people don't want to play it. You either play and pray or you don't. It's a you in Me, and I in you game. Jesus Christ is Player One. And the Human Being is Player Two. The challenge of this Holy Game Liam is for you to take into yourself as much as you can the true nature of your Lord Jesus Christ. In other words, just in case you are not clear his spirit, his heart, his body, his soul, and all his faculties are to be used by you as if they were your own. That is a lifelong challenge Liam. You are never finished playing and praying the Holy Game.

Liam, there are further beneficial additions to my Holy Game for you. The successful player integrates Jesus into his own body by having the same spirit, soul, life, will, intention and heart. So Liam accept into your body all these features named above from Jesus. The Holy game could become so enjoyable that you would fall completely in love with a One True Friend. You would want to praise him, love him and glorify him all the time. Imagine the effect Liam of having Jesus Christ in you. His spirit would be in your spirit and his heart in your heart. All the powers of Christ' soul would be in your soul. Liam this is a good game for you. Pray it! Play it! At the end of the Holy Game you should be able to say, "I glorify and carry God in my body".

Liam, most people cannot play this Holy Game because they have no image of the First Player, Jesus Christ. So I recommend selecting a favourite scene from Jesus' life and bringing it forward to this present day in such a way that you see him look at you and you look at him. The Holy Game begins with two players sitting on a chair facing each other. One is Jesus and the other is you. And the task is not what you can give to Jesus. The task is for you to take from a Divine Life all that is in Jesus's mind and heart. Do you want to play?

Little Man

Father, of course I want to play. I think it is a great game. I didn't think Father that you would favour playing games. I thought you were very serious. I'd love to play a Holy Game with your Son Jesus Christ. I sit in the Human Seat. And Jesus sits in the Divine Seat. I could spend the whole day looking at Jesus. It's a very attractive and exciting Holy Game. The first few times the game is played could end up frustrating, unprofitable, and disheartening. This mentality is due to the Blank Chair syndrome. The Human Player can't figure out a way to imagine Jesus Christ walking towards his home, knocking at his door, entering his house and sits on a chair in front of his guest. The Holy Game can never occur unless the host believes there is a Real Presence of a Divine Person on the chair. The Holy Game can be varied too. A Great Doctor of the Church could sit on the chair. Imagine the joy of it. Imagine a chat with St Augustine. Imagine a chat with St Thomas Aquinas. Imagine the joy of it. I propose an invitation to the Risen Christ. Come Lord Jesus. Sit with me.

Father, I like your Holy Game. It is best played in a quiet place. I'm going to play it now. I sit on my chair in awe of Jesus Christ. I look at him. I continue to look at him. I look for thirty minutes. Nothing happens. I look for an hour at Jesus and there is only slight improvement. I can't communicate with my Lord. I don't know what to say. I see God in human form. The Risen Christ is magnificent. I see a Beautiful Mind. It is frightfully Divine. I don't think he will want to settle in my mind. It is hopelessly dull. But I play and win the Holy Game by allowing Christ gaze at me. I win by shutting down my defences, by buttoning my lips, and by listening to no one except Jesus Christ in front of me on the chair. I receive an abundant of beautiful gifts if I satisfy my Lord by dropping my head and offering no resistance to the Master.

Father, as I sit before Christ Jesus I melt away in complete nakedness and embarrassment as the Man before me knows every pain and weakness in my soul and body. I'm on the chair wilfully inviting Christ to dress me with Truth, Love, Mercy, Peace, and Humility so that I can be like him. Once the flow of Divine Beauty in the form of a multitude of gorgeous virtues flow from the Body of Christ into my muddied soul and lukewarm heart the Holy Game is won. The Trump Card in this game is True Unity where the Human Player becomes like another Christ.

Father, do you mind if I use this chair to ask Jesus questions. When Jesus was twelve years old he displayed amazing knowledge in the Temple talking to High Priests. His questions and answers were awesome. I'd like to ask a few questions. The disciples asked it too. My first question has to do with salvation. I'd like to know who can be saved.

Father, am I doing enough for you? I haven't laid down my life or took up my cross. But I do try and teach my son and lead by good example. I do pray and attend Mass. I write to you every day Father. And in my book I declare my love for you. I also know you are a Father with a kind heart for sinners. I'm aware in the Psalms and Gospels that you are forgiving, merciful and compassionate towards sinners. That gives me hope. And that should give everyone hope.

Father, you taught your disciples to forgive trespassers. You taught us to forgive an unlimited amount of times. That definitely applies to those who reoffend. So I would be inclined to believe that you would welcome sinners like paedophiles, idlers, rapists, perverts, murderers, fraudsters, robbers, pornographers, and rogues provided they repent. You showed that mentality when you didn't condemn the adulteress, and when you welcomed home the prodigal son. Anyway Father, I'm not to judge. And the lesson for me here is not to condemn anyone. My duty is to Love people that hate most. My duty is to Love the whole of humanity and hate no one. It is none of my business if aggressive goats, or unwanted weeds, or evil doers make up with Christ in the same way as Mary Magdalene did when crying her little heart out with tears pouring on the Lord's feet.

Father, your Mercy is a great gift. All human beings are tainted with sin. We depend on your Mercy to turn things around. My soul has been dirtied so I should judge no one. In fact, I rely on your Mercy as well as everyone else. I'm far from the state of perfection. I rely on you Father to make me New. You can wash me with the gifts of Truth, Life, Justice, Holiness, Grace, Love, Mercy and Peace.

Father, I pray for evil doers and sinners that they may come to their senses and change. It is our duty to develop on earth the values of human dignity, brotherhood and freedom. I personally find it sad to hear of a murder, or to discover a greedy fraudster, or to hear of the promotion of conflict and division. All bad actions are a stain on human dignity. If anything goes wrong in my life, I find it is a time to reflect on my conscience.

Father, I pray for sinners including myself. It seems to me that the conversion of horrible sinners like murderers, rapists, perverts, paedophiles, exploiters, and pornographers require high amounts of grace to bring about a repentant transformation. St Paul persecuted Christians before becoming one of them.

Father, I pray for sinners in Ireland and the whole world. I pray for evil doers to change. It's highly important that bad people understand that hatred brings nothing but misery into family life, community life, Irish life and world life. I propose that individual battles to overcome evil are done by nailing Steel Plates of Virtues over rotten parts in the body. The number one Steel Plate to pin is Love. Pin it around the vice of anger. This virtue should help to fight hatred. A number two is Purity. Staple this Steel Plate of Holy Virtue over immorality. This should help to cure a body that lives for pornography, sexual gratification and bodily pleasure. So hammer the Virtue of Purity over the vice Impurity. Another Steel Plate is the Holy Virtue of Kindness or Generosity. This will curb fat cats and the desire for money. Pin this Steel Plate over greed. And there is one more Steel Plate of Virtue that

I desire to nail on every heart and mind in the world. That is Holy Faith in Jesus Christ. This will plaster over the vice of irreligion and indifference. I want to prepare and guide human beings everywhere in the world towards the narrow door of faith in Jesus Christ. I do my best to save souls so that when they try to enter the Kingdom of God they are not turned away and referred to as wicked men.

Father, I love you. I love you because you train me. I love you because in the Book of the Hebrews you treat us as sons. I want to be your son. I love you to correct me. And I love the unity between you Father, and your Divine Son Jesus. I'm very sorry if I overstepped the mark and tried to comment and write about matters that are your prerogative alone. Also I plead for mercy for myself. For I apply the Steel Plates of Holy Virtues to be nailed into my bad parts too. I hate sin and evil Father. I'll do my best to love sinners but hate the sin. It is a new start.

Big Eye!

Hi Liam! You got anxious there. But you are right. Don't judge anyone. Be level headed and sensitive. A lot of people are sick. They can't help it. They had bad experiences growing up and you have to weigh up everyone's circumstances. So be careful in your judgement.

Liam, I like your thoughts written above. It's good stuff. But be careful. Don't mix up Divine thoughts. I am God. I am Big Eye. I am Father to all. And I know what's happening. I can sweep away everything on the face of the earth. I can send the wicked staggering and wipe man away from the face of the earth. I have sent great prophets, John the Baptist and my Beloved Son Jesus Christ to warn men and women to change. So why should I give another warning through you? It is regrettable to corrupt children. It is regrettable to use a child as a suicide bomber. Every evil act committed is regrettable. But I urge you Liam to concentrate on your thoughts above especially the Steel Plates of Virtue that may be inserted over every heart and mind that's rotten with hatred, and rotten with every form of evil at work in a human or in millions of people across the globe. Liam I'll train you for this mission directly. I'll help you to evangelise the world.

Liam, I like your Steel Plate of Virtues spirituality. But don't forget that my Holy Spirit inspires you. Because it is a new idea I'd like people to think that this is a Holy Operation. The Steel Plate refers to the strength of a Holy Virtue that counteracts and fights against its opposite vice. You see Liam Holy Virtues has to have power and steel to survive in a bad soul. The Dirty Vices will kick up a stink by displays of angry tantrums and horrible bouts of bad humour when crucified by a Steel Plate of Virtue. I like it Liam. Well done.

Liam, I love your new idea. I'm beginning to think it could be a new way of spiritual fighting throughout the world. I could ask all my Cardinals, Bishops, Priests, and followers of my Way, my Truth and My Life to carry Steel Plates of Holy Virtues everywhere with them throughout the world. Liam you are a genius. I'm going to use your idea. I see potential in them. In fact, I could supply millions of Spiritual Plates for my faithful and zealous disciples. Every Holy Saint that desires me carries Steel Plates of Holy Virtue to crucify bad hearts and bad minds with my Love. Wonderful News.

Liam, it will be difficult for the demon or the wicked vice to survive the heat of the Steel Plate. I'll heat the Steel Plate and burn out wickedness in a soul. You can also inscribe the name of the Virtue on each plate to fight its opposite vice. Once nailed to the heart or to the mind the vice should die. I can see the sizzling stuff of my Sacred Virtues purifying every soul. Liam I love you. I see the death of Satan if millions of Muslims, Jews and Christians sign up to the acceptance of Steel Plate Virtues embedded in the battlefield of every mind and heart alive in the world today. All that is necessary for the Holy Operation is simply a willingness to reject hatred, and every form of evil that troubles the internal evil condition inside each person.

Liam, that is more like the writing that pleases my heart. Instead of naming evil acts you have provided a remedy or a cure to heal sinners. I can see millions accept your spiritual remedy. I'm delighted Liam. So is my Son Jesus Christ. Together as a Heavenly Spiritual Team we can pluck out those who wish to be healed from hatred and evil and gently lay them down in the field that leads towards the narrow gate where my Son Jesus Christ welcomes them among his saved lambs. It will take time though for the Steel Plate of Holy Virtue to penetrate through bad parts at work and make them clean, new and holy. Liam, keep up the writing. I am God. I like your new and refreshing effort to save souls. It will be a welcome addition to a Church that has stagnated over Satan breaking through my walls and into the core of Trust and Truth that my Church should be for loyal followers of my Way.

Little Man

Father, thank you for praising me. I love you. I insert and nail a Holy Steel Plate of Virtue onto my own sins and faults. I might need about ten of them to prevent bad parts from functioning again. I'm pleased to nail a virtue over a vice. The first relevant Steel Plate for me is to pin a Virtue of Calmness into the vice of worry and impatience so as to smother the life out of the evil vice.

Father, I'm sorry for attempting to judge sinners. Most High Judge I humbly apologise for thinking that I am on an equal par with you. You are the Father of seven billion people. I don't have a leg to stand on in comparison to who you are and what I am. I am nothing Father. Big Eye sees a little dot when he looks at me. Yet I had the audacity or boldness to try and judge my brothers and sisters around the world. Muslims and Christians are One Brotherhood and One Sisterhood. The belief in Allah for Muslims, the belief in Abba for Jews, and belief in Father for Christians suggests One God for All. So stick together and show that we are all one Brotherhood, or One Family. I suggest Father a Universal Prayer Moment to highlight solidarity between Nations and the Brotherhood of Man. This could be planned for next year, or the year after in order to give time to Leaders of Nations to drop everything for one hour and pray for unity and peace. This Universal Moment of Solidarity could be used by the most powerful leaders in the world religious and political to pray together for hostilities to end and acts of evil are shunned. Can you imagine that Father? Can you imagine all seven billion people praying together on their knees for one hour?

Father, I return to my apology for acting as if I am God. You are the Highest Judge. I err terribly by judging sinners. Many make that mistake. Preachers around the world sometimes speak as if they were

God. These fit God into their mind set and think they own him. They park him where they please too. It is awfully important to kneel humbly before Almighty God. I'm nothing in comparison to my Holy Father. I'm not fit to undo the straps of his sandals. So I tread cautiously to be with him. And I think proximity depends on the state of the soul. I want to love but it is not always easy. My Father keeps his distance in accordance to the levels of stress my mind endures. I walk towards God but I will never catch up with him until I act like his son and allow him to Father me. There will be no experiences of radiant joy until my approach is that of a humble and loving child.

Father, I consider my approach to you. Do I drive to the Church? Do I turn my eyes to the sky when walking on the road? Do I call you Father? These questions are relevant. O Jesus. Do I have to do an examination of conscience in order to find you? For I believe that there are things wrong in my life that prevents me from being close to you.

Father, what has gone wrong? Something has happened. My lights have gone out. I took a beaten from a demon. The evil thing battered my head and body black and blue. I'm lost and dazed at the moment. Where are you father? Why didn't you save me? Why didn't you warn me? I'm disgusted with a demon's tantrum that attacked through the personality of a child. I saw a banner in the Church this morning that read come to me if you need rest. I'm beyond rest at the moment. The damage done by a mad demon beat you Father out of my system. It knocked you out of my senses and mind. I struggle to cope with it. My confidence has gone. It hurts to approach you in a badly wounded state. Send me to a Spiritual Hospital. I need comforting.

Big Eye

Liam, calm down. Don't lose focus. I agree with you that something has gone wrong. It looks like a spiritual blackout. You have had one. This happens when a soul loses consciousness of me altogether. It is scary. It's similar to a child not seeing his father or mother for eight to ten hours. A blackout causes great distress. But look Liam refocus. I am here for you. Just call me Father. Don't worry about your wounds. I can soothe them quickly.

Liam, focus on my Divine status. If you desire a few days in my Spiritual Hospital go to the Good Shepherd at the Mystery Door. Christ is the Porter at the Door. Tell him that you are my friend. Christ will let you in to rest for a few days. The side of the door that you see is earth. When you go through the door you will see heaven at the other side. My Good Shepherd will take care of you. He holds the key to allow you entry. You can have all the rest you want in a Holy Bed. I'll inform your Holy Team. They will sit at your bedside and nurse your wounds. I'm sure you will recover quickly if St Anselm, St Augustine and St Thomas Aquinas sat at your bedside and doctor you to full health again.

Liam, I'm going to give you a few ideas regarding ways to approach me. Think of the Throne of Grace. Think of the Throne of the Lamb. Think of my Throne. Think of your Father's Throne. Think of who I Am. I sit on this Throne. I am God Most High. I am All Powerful. I'm Head of the Church. I am Head of Nations. My Son of Man who is Supreme Governor of the human race sits beside me. And my Divine Mother sits at my left. The image of these words must be imprinted in your mind. It's helpful when you pray to have an image. It is one way to approach me.

Liam, my Church rely on Sacred Scripture to worship me. I like to hear Christians sing psalms, hymns and canticles. I like lips that are clean singing to me from the heart. It's lovely Liam. Don't be afraid to shout for joy. Think of my Immense Majesty. Think of my Infinite Perfections. Think of my Inexpressible Holiness. Do you not think I'm worthy of praise? So sing to me Liam. St Augustine wept at the beauty of hymns. He was powerfully moved. It's lovely Liam hearing sweet sounds of songs coming from the Church in praise of me. Sing to me. So Liam that is another way to approach me. Sing psalms. I accept delightfully Church singing. I accept singing Christians. I doubly accept a sincere Tribute of Lips. The Divine Office and Sacred Liturgy is precious to me.

Liam, praise me. Stop being sad and miserable. I really enjoyed King David despite his faults and sins. I loved his harp playing, dancing and singing. He was a delightful man full of fun and a good sense of humour. So cheer up Little Man. I tell you about David because I'd love you to be jolly and happy instead of behaving like the hard working depressive son who couldn't welcome his prodigal brother home.

Liam, I provide everything. I created life. So praise creation. Everything created is blessed. So be glad of your life. I have a system in place and it has worked for billions of years. I gave you earth, water, heat and air. So be grateful. I know you love plant life and the ocean. So you can approach me by praising my creation like the Atlantic Ocean that you love, and the majestic high trees in the forest, and the fantastic flock of crows flying in unison. You can praise me for all that my hand made Liam. Don't worry about your life. I value it. You are precious.

next

Liam, I finish this chapter on a positive note. I know now that when you fall you get up again and seek me. There are times when you wouldn't feel close to me. My Son Jesus had similar feelings of abandonment. In a disciple's life there is no grace without suffering. So I expect you Liam to travel along the penitential road so as to heal your wounds and receive my precious grace. There are five little roads to walk on. There will be no repentance unless you walk these little steps on the road day by day.

Liam, the first thing to do is acknowledge your sins. Secondly forgive others their offences against you. I urge you strongly to forget wrongs done to you. And this second little penitential step may help you to control your temper. The third little road for you to walk every day is fervent and diligent prayer. The fourth is almsgiving and the fifth is humility. Do not be idle then Liam but day by day set out along those paths.

Liam, I help you. I challenge you to work hard on cultivating the five roads of repentance. It's a work in progress. It's not finished until the day you die. I expect confession of sins. I like to hear my sincere admirers to say sorry. And I expect more than anything else for you to forgive others that walk on your toes and offend you no matter what insult, what suffering, or what evil they slap you in the face with. I expect you to forgive trespassers. Otherwise you don't die to me. You are too busy shouting, roaring and complaining by protesting about the disturbance of the intruder into your mind with the wrong done to you.

Liam, I tell you too that diligent prayer cleans up the mess in your soul. Sins fall off you if you travel through the prayer road every day. The practise of prayer to me Liam removes clumps of hard rock sins. Prayer scoops up unwanted weed sins. Prayer prepares you to cope with muscular trespassers and aggressive Rottweilers that are never far away and ready to bite you. Almsgiving too is a very effective road that draws you closer to me. I love to see generosity. I am always closer to the kind person. To walk on the benevolent road Liam melts away a multitude of sins. The gap between my Throne of Grace and the Almsgiver is narrowed considerably by alms giving. So Liam ensure that you look closely at you your steps on this road as you are a bit stingy. You don't give much time to others. Nor do you support charities.

Liam, next comes the road of humility. I expect modest and gentle behaviour from you. Humility annihilates sin as drastically as all the other methods. There is no doubt that I am attracted to humble souls. I love them. There is no doubt too that the gap between my Immense Majesty and the Humble Soul is almost perfect. My Virgin Mother's humility surpassed all others. If I were you Liam, I'd stay on that fifth method. Humility leads to Perfect Unity with me.

Liam, don't worry. I have given you a Way to Love me. I don't want you to stray from the method. So confess more, forgive more, pray more, give more and be humbler. Do this and you will see a Throne of Grace sitting high above in a roundabout where the ends of the five roads converge. I will flow grace into your soul from there Liam. The measure might be a drop, or a trickle, or a stream, or a large river. The effort you make each day determines the flow level pumped into your body and soul.

Liam, before I go from my Penitential Plan for you I want to teach you a lesson about loving me under severe adversity. You know Liam that the Highest Virtue is Love. The Highest Commandment is Love. I gave my Divine Son in exchange for your Love. Redemption is offered to you. So stop worrying. Stop feeling miserable for yourself. Stop complaining. I can see the strain and pressure on your face. You don't have the strength required to override, outbox, or outfox adversaries. I wish to do something for you. I wish to help you. I have a gift for you.

You see Liam I'm not heartless. I see you attempting to climb up to the Throne of Grace and the Lamb. You want to be confident. You want to be strong. But you are stuck in earths mud. I help you now. Come on. I have tested you a lot to see how genuine you are in finding me. I have tossed ideas around in your head to see what level of commitment you have at this moment in time. And I see the level of battering you are willing to suffer for my Name.

Therefore, Liam I lift you up. I raise you up. Your love for me is all that matters. And I know you Love me. So I give you a gift. I give you an experience of me. You wouldn't see me but you may feel my Presence. Sit still Liam. I touch you. My Holy Finger heals. It is red hot with Love. I touch and heal your body pains. I burn sin out of you. I soothe your stressful mind and body with my Holy Hand. I dress you Liam with Holy Virtues. You need New Life. I help you to throw away your tattered and battered body with my Red Hot Love. The things that annoy you run when they see me coming. Can you stand before me Liam? I'm Big Eye. My Majesty is immense. Come to me, your Father. Allow me lift you up. Rest in my arms a little while. My Holiness sizzles through you once in my Sacred Arms. Even though you are a man you are still my child. You are not too big for me to embrace you, hug you, kiss you and love you.

Liam, don't run away. Don't be embarrassed. I want to spend time with you. Rest and cry on my shoulder. Lay your head on my shoulder and tell me all that troubles you. Tell me what is going wrong. Listen Liam. I love you. I am your Father. Don't be ashamed of me. My Love is there for you. Don't walk away anymore. You are long enough fighting to befriend me. I aim to take this matter of your relationship with me seriously. I know what is wrong. You don't have the luxury of solitude due to family responsibilities. The wars you are fighting and losing at times come from adults and children. They give you no rest as they constantly make demands on you.

Liam, I love you. And I know you love me. But your circumstances drag you down. External influences constantly flood your good soil with stress, pressure, demands, and unsavoury issues. This kills your focus for me. I will address that. With your permission I take to the battlefield. While you rest in my Love and sleep I intend to use my Red Hot Holy Fingers to dig deep into your mind and pluck the roots from the stuff that troubles you. Also I give you better techniques to deal with external influences.

Liam, you can see from different styles of living that religious life is most suitable for building up unity with me, your Father, and Jesus Christ my Son, and the Holy Spirit. Remember the lovely solitude and times spent with me in the Blessed Sacrament Chapel in the House of Studies. By giving up everything you can give those hours to me. You could spend hours loving me. I'll have to see ways of restoring that in the future. For I know that is what you long for. But I think you could turn your lovely and peaceful shed into a Prayer Place. It's away from the house and distractions.

Liam anyway I hope you benefit from your sleep in my arms. Come to me anytime you need rest. You are my precious little creature. I'm delighted by the way you have used your mind in the last few days by consciously choosing to humble yourself. Keep going and don't forget to get onto the Five Roads quickly and walk the Five Penitential routes that may transform you into one of my Little Lambs that has access to my Good Shepherd Jesus Christ at the Throne of Grace.

Liam, embrace my Son Jesus Christ. He loves little lambs. He loves little newly born lambs. If a lamb goes astray he gently brings him back. My Good shepherd protects his little ones with his own life. Jesus is with me to help you. I can see him carry you away from the threats of evil. Enough is enough. I intend to protect you from the sources of unnecessary suffering. This can be done by your love for Jesus Christ and by cherishing his Word. Above all Liam do not be a Stubborn Goat. Allow us to carry you. Allow us wash your feet. Allow us to lead you to the Narrow Gate. Allow us to mind you. I can tell you solemnly that much of your suffering was self-inflicted by going it alone without the love of your Four Great Friends and Church Doctors.

Chapter Fifteen

Little Man

Father, your words in the last chapter are lovely and reassuring. I intend to comply with your advice. I'm a big child and not too big to cry. You are right. What you say Father is really nice. I feel good knowing you watch me. I feel your Big and Holy Eye looking at me through the light of my window. I'm willing to be led by you and your advice is invaluable. I appreciate your sacred promptings and reminder to focus on you.

Father, how is Saint Anselm? I love that holy man. Even though he lived in the eleventh century I feel his spirit alive in me. I regard him as my Spiritual Director and Holy Friend. Anselm advises me to set time aside for you. I comply with his words. Anselm gives me encouragement and hope. His advises me to focus on what is important. I have to set time aside. I have to do this. I can't ignore my Holy Friend. I walk along my little narrow and quiet road meditating. I pray in my little shed too. And I visit the Church for a holy hour. I adore my Holy Friend's spiritual nous. The thoughts in his mind are like mine. I love his perception that you God my Father is the Highest of All. He saw eight hundred years ago that you were Above Everything. O Father of Creation I adore you. I'm in a state of awe thinking of You. You are High above me. I would be mesmerised if you took me high into the sky and away on a safari through unknown galaxies and near the gates of heaven. It would be a frightening experience. But I trust you Father. I'd feel safe with you God Most High.

God our Father, there is another part of St Anselm's spiritual insight that attracts me immensely. It tickles my mind with excitement. Anselm said that you are that in which nothing greater can be thought. O my God! What a terrific spiritual insight. Oh! I could meditate on those words for the rest of my life. Most Holy Father thoughts about you are the greatest of all. This Holy Insight boggles the mind. I'm in a state of bliss. I'm flabbergasted that an old idea whether it is two thousand years old or eight hundred years old can be so much alive this very minute.

Almighty Father, you are the Greatest of All. But how many of seven billion people across the globe acknowledge Anselm's Insight. How many treat you as the Greatest? And why do you create so many ungrateful people? They are incapable of thinking about you. And others even though they are intelligent don't think you exist. I really need to tell the world about this Great Thought. Father, I grasp the magnitude of this mind boggling sensational thought. I grasp the magnitude of my Holy Friend's intellectual formation of a Spiritual Golden Egg. I love it. And if the rest of humanity fail to cogitate the Greatest Thought of All than there is a serious problem worldwide. The world is full of bold brats if they fail to hear, or to see, or to think about their Holy Father, you my Lord and God.

God our Father, I love you. I'm at work internally making space for this wonderful Big Thought that you are the Greatest to rest permanently in my mind. I'll make space for you. I'll squeeze everything out to make room for you. Thank you Anselm. You are a True Friend. Thank you for giving me a Golden Thought that is heavy, big and powerful enough to squash and kill every silly idea that tries to take root in my mind. The entire usage or non-usage of my will be affected by this. Nothing is as Great as you Father. You Big Eye are the Summit of All both in the mind and in reality.

Father, you are the Greatest of All. Nothing greater can be thought. Thank you Anselm for those beautiful words. It's the Pearl of Great Price. I demote everything else, or reduce everything for the nucleus of a Great Pearl. You are that Pearl Father. You and your Son Jesus Christ. You and your Divine Mother.

Father, I buy the Great Pearl. It has great spiritual value. I want my Divine Friends more than anything else. Everything else is cheap in comparison to you. All I want is the Great Pearl that you are Jesus Christ, Son of the living God. I'm very happy this day. The insertion of the Greatest Thought that can be thought in my mind has giving rise to a wonderfully new and refreshing feeling this day. And the growth of this Great Thought has given rise to a feeling that all junk thoughts have been dumped into a skip.

Father, if pushed I would give up everything for you. I'd give away my money. I'd decline a house worth a million. There is no desire in me to own a Mercedes. Winning the lotto wouldn't buy me heaven. My spiritual welfare comes first. And my neighbours welfare follow a close second. A life of luxury doesn't appeal to me. My priority is to get off this earth and find my true home with God in heaven. And I would wilfully help others to do the same. I don't care what religion you are once you have an open mind to allow the Greatest Thought of All to take root in the core of your intellect.

Father, I feel a shower of grace has just fallen on me as a result of my decision to buy the Pearl of Great Price. I haven't felt this way for weeks. Thanks Father. I appreciate your care for me. I'm willing at sixty to change and love you more and more. Most people don't raise their minds towards you Father. They are conditioned to live and behave in accordance with cultural habits. Very few human minds are fully active from a reality point of view. Most brains don't work. They are dead. They follow a system. They follow habits learnt from others. They have knowledge slapped sloppily into their heads. It's rather sad that people don't think for themselves. A mind that doesn't think is useless.

Father, I must be aware though. For before this day is over another one or two afflictions might come my way. A high magnitude earthquake could buckle my composure and break up the Straight Road that leads to the Good Shepherd and Throne of Grace. I want to run away into the desert for I can't take anymore ferocious attacks from the Bastard Vine. I was hit by an earthquake in the head. My peace and happiness came tumbling down and a deep distress ensued. And what's more an aftershock occurred to compound my misery. I want to run away.

Degenerate plants are everywhere. Pernicious thoughts are everywhere. The least little thing causes an eruption of great magnitude. I want to run for the desert Father and be alone. For I am powerless to stop evil attacks.

Father, I'm sorry. I couldn't prevent the earthquake from demolishing my composure. I'm on trial again. I'm wounded once more. Lord, I accept my tribulation. I repent Big Eye. I'll prove to you that my repentance is genuine and that it comes from a sincere heart. I'll fast on Wednesdays and Friday and return to the Holy Traditions of the Church. For I know the Truth. You are able to detect the stain of my guilt. You know when I am disloyal and playing games with strangers.

Father, I hunger and thirst for the return of the Greatest Thought of All. The earthquake shook it, moved it, broke it, and cracked it from its dominant position in the core of my intellect. I'm glad about my recovery. And I'm glad you haven't gone away. You are the Greatest Father. You are my All, my Life, my Light, my Salvation, my Food and my God. Inspire my thoughts to cherish you, my Great Pearl. You are the pinnacle of my life.

Father, I'm reflecting on the failures of my intellect. The earthquake could have been prevented if I acted differently. Impatience was one factor. I saw it tumbling down the hill and into my soul. It triggered off a strong reaction because what happened affected my composure, my peace and time with you. The affliction diverted me from writing. It demoted the enjoyment of my Greatest Thought by having to deal with realities other than you Father.

Father, I'm sorry again. If you send me tribulation, I should endure it. It is for my good. I say thanks to you Father. I may have deserved it. Now Little Man, get back to work. Study St Anselm's concept. Nothing is Greater than yourself. Help me to know the thing I love. Come on Liam. Think! Think! Think! What thing in me tells me that you exist. For there is a difference between the word earth and the fact that there is an earth. There is Life. Who made it? There is a difference between the word Father and the fact that there is a Father. Okay! I think of God as Father and Creator. There can't be any doubt that God exists. I tell you why. I sit on a chair on a piece of ground near the Atlantic

Ocean writing. I am sure by this fact that there is life. It is certain. I see it. I know it. And it is absolutely fascinating figuring out the origin of substances like my body and the stuff that makes up a planet. I don't agree with evolution because of the mind boggling fact that something can't come from nothing. I need to go back to basics. The truth is found from basic facts. Think of intellectual realisations. Forget about language. Forget about words. Shut the mouth. Say nothing. Stand still for a long, long time. Forget education. Forget senseless motion. Think! Think! Think! Is there a God? Bypass all previous history and all knowledge in order to draw a few conclusions about the origin of existence. Someone causes the sun to shine. Someone sustains the placement of the sun and the work it does in maintaining life. Someone filled the oceans with water. Someone created living things. Someone created raw resources and seeds to grow. Substances exist. There is life.

Father, I believe in you. You made the world. But who made you? I lack comprehension here. I'm interested in my aliveness. And I'm interested in your aliveness Father. And I want to experiences this aliveness. I don't want four thousand years of history, knowledge and libraries full of philosophy and theology. I want to stand in a field and reflect on what is my aliveness and figure out my reason, or your reason Father for me been here.

Father, I urge within myself intellectual activity instead of having mouthfuls and mouthfuls of words flowing freely from my lips unto paper. I want to search deeper into the recesses of the mind for answers. I want Divine answers from you Father. I want to know why I live. I want to go deeper and beyond where no man has ever gone before. I crave for spiritual illumination and for Divine Gospel insights. Father will you tell me? Please enlighten me. I beg for Truth. I'm angry Father with the lack of consciousness, discernment, and comprehension in me. I'm not much better intelligently wise than the curious look of a cow wondering what a man is. I'm unaware of no original thoughts alive in me, nor can I find a deep experience of you Father.

Father, maybe I am not meant to know. You chose and sent out twelve unlettered men to preach the name of a Crucified Son of Man or Son of God to the whole world. And they were instrumental in handing on a Masterpiece for future generations of people in the Divine Gospel that tells the Truth about you. There should be enough revelation in the Divine Gospel for me to munch over in my brain.

Almighty Father, I am sorry for stepping out of line. I tried to steal a step or two on everyone else but chasing knowledge and insights about earth, existence, living substances and mysteries about things that are beyond the mind of man. But I want to know Father from the point of view of human intelligence. I want to think deeply using my intellect to work things out in such a way that might help me to praise you more. I want to have a deeper understanding of eternal life, about the things that no eye has seen or ear heard, or things that never enter the hearts of most people. I love you Father. I love your Son Jesus Christ. I love the Catholic Church. And all I ask for is an experience of your aliveness. And I ask for an experience of my own aliveness by observing intellectual progress. For I want to build a hierarchical structure of ideas that places you Father above everything else that I could think of. In order to achieve that I need to embed idea with reality. That's why I desire an experience of you. I know you are Truth Father. Don't play a game with me. Don't hide behind a bush. The world needs to see you. People are falling away from you every day as they become more sinful. So show yourself. It would make a huge difference. You have slept for over two thousand years except for the work of the Holy Spirit at work in the minds and hearts of loyal servants in the Catholic Church and other branches of religion that worship with a true heart.

Father, you know my desire. You know my Aliveness is ready for you. I completely accept you. Work in my mind. Work in my heart. Work in my behaviour. Work in my actions. Work in my attitudes. Work on my love for others. You want a golden heart. So change me and I'll teach proper religion. I comply and accept fully Christ's teaching on the importance of almsgiving. Christ is no fool. He had great perception. He advised Christians that it would be a greater honour for us to dress the poor found frozen outside the Church than to honour him by wearing silk vestments inside the Church.

Father, I'm really taken aback by your profound teaching. It's wonderful. So instead of looking for a sensational realisation or a miraculous experience maybe I should look closer at the Divine Gospel. It is through the Gospel that you Father could train and test me. I didn't take seriously before the importance of almsgiving. I can't love you properly Father without giving to the poor. Almsgiving is one of the Five Roads towards Spiritual Renewal. A kind heart is pure benevolence.

Father, I have lost the run of myself. My thoughts are everywhere like spilt paint that has made a great mess. I pursue one Great Thought about you Father but circumstances diluted the effort. However, I'm back on track. I block knowledge of you Father. Instead I close my eyes and pray. I join my hands. In there in the quietness of my mind I call you. Come Lord Jesus. Come Holy Father. The interior life is the best. Fr William told me so. St Anselm told me too. I believe my true friends. I have closed the doors of my external senses and opened up my internal faculties in search of you Father, in search of you Jesus, and in search of a connection with you Holy Spirit. I block out everything now. I pick up loose unwanted pebble like thoughts and dismiss them into the dump. There is a war on against godless thoughts. I pray for a long, long time cleaning up my interior self in preparation for my Holy Visitors. Everything is subordinate to Big Eye. His gaze will break through and light up my soul if I am patient and humble in prayer.

Father, the warmth of your proximity is worth the wait. I feel grace bubbling up everywhere inside of me. It's a marvellous feeling. What I want from life is friendship with you Father. Others have a different mentality. They are happy once they have money to pay bills, own a home, drive a car, and enjoy holidays. The wold is fine. The future is good. There are no shortages of beautiful future mothers and beautiful future fathers growing up under the supervision of shrewd parents. There's huge talent and progress in the world. My fear though is that they are poor in spirit. They have dropped you Father. They have squeezed you out of their lives. Spectacular human shows keep them going like music and sports events everywhere around the world.

Father, you are my music. You are my sport. You are my work. You are the Highest of All. Nothing Greater can be thought. I stick with this. Success for me is True Friendship with you. I pray and hope that you will accept me. I cuddle into you Father in such a way that relief and healing might ease my diabetes, prostrate, and arthritis concerns. I cuddle into you too in such a way that I might find a surge of love to care for the spiritual and physical welfare of my son and wife, and all those connected to my gene everywhere throughout the world.

Most High Father, even though you don't walk about on earth you are still my first love because your Divine Son made you known to me. You connect to me through all Four Sacred Friends – your Divine Mother, your Divine Son, your Divine Holy Spirit, and your Divine Gospel. I am in love with you. I recognise your Power. My faith is strong. I believe that you can heal sick bodies and broken lives. I believe in the resurrection and that there is a glorious future for those who believe in you.

My Holy Big Eye, Sensational Sacred realisations are coming through my unity with you. O Father, you are the best. Your Word delights me. Your Saints thrill me. I have found the Source of Life. I'm happy about it. I see a conveyor belt of Golden Eggs or Sacred Thoughts flowing into my soul continuously from such a rich array of Sacred Friends in heaven. I have found a spiritual goldmine. St Chrysostom pray for me. St Monica pray for me. St Anselm pray for me. I thank you so much. You have helped me to consider Eternal Thoughts and you helped me to consider almsgiving by caring for poverty stricken people. And I have the Greatest Thought of All fluttering like a butterfly in the core of my intellect when I think of your name Father. Thanks Anselm. Nothing compares to you Father. You have supernatural status and yet you stoop to look at a little dot on the planet near the River Shannon with your Big Eye. Marvellous. I solemnly declare a proclamation of contemplation for all to block out external senses and go searching deep inside the eye of the intellect for their Father – the God of all life. Nothing is more beautiful in life than to see a person find his or her way home to their Father. The beginning of this wonderful journey starts by praying the first two words of the Lord's Prayer at every possible opportunity. The struggle for every living person is about breaking free from the entrapment of evil. Life is about shaking off the shackles of sin. And the only way out of hells prison is by desperately latching on to the hands of Jesus Christ trying to save us. Sinners must come

LIAM WALSH

to their senses and return to their Father. So start of now Catholic
Christian. Christ calls you to Church. Get up out of bed. Go and pray.
The Christian community needs you.

Big Eye

Liam, good evening. Thanks Liam for encouraging Christians to
rise from their beds and return to me. I agree fully with you. And I'll
even go the extra mile. Wake up Europe. Wake up America. Wake up
all Christians everywhere in the world. You are all dying fast due to your
neglect of the Son of Man. The fine big Churches around the world are
almost empty. Nothing is more beautiful than seeing a mother bringing
her children to Church. And it is a triple joy when fathers accompany
wife and children in worship and praise of me through the Church.
I am annoyed with sleepy Catholics. I put my mark on you for Jesus
Christ at Baptism. I gave you the Eucharist – the Body and Blood of
my only Son Jesus Christ. I gave you Confirmation to strengthen you
with my Holy Spirit. So why are lying idle across Europe and across the
world by living as if you don't know me. And ye have made a mess of
the Sacrament of Marriage by ignoring it. Very well so human being.
Go on and reject me. Go on reject me. You will have the same result as
before – a world of orphans and a world of unhappy children because
they live without a Father. They don't want to know the Father that
created them. I advise strongly mothers, fathers and children to return
to Church before it is too late. Prayer-less families are sad and more and
more are joining the godless every day.

Liam, I have no doubt about you. You love me. You are persistent
too. I have to listen to you even though you bore me and seek attention
quite a lot. Some of my children are annoying too. But I have to put
up with them. It is impossible to please everyone and you are a bit
like that. You seek unity with me but your doggedness, nervousness,
and annoying mentality mars face to face communication between us.
You want to live in my pocket without any responsibilities. You want
to love me without working at it. You want a Divine connection to a
mind that's in a shambles with wires crossing everywhere and are all
mixed up. Liam, I know your thoughts. You can't fool me your Father.

I have the power to sort you out. Don't despair. Don't lose courage. I am your Eternal Electrician. Allow me to install the most beautiful light imaginable in the depth of your soul. It will be an Eternal Light. It will be an Unchangeable Light. It will shine in your mind.

Liam, you have all the words but you know very little. Your mind doesn't know what eternal life is. Your mind doesn't know what resurrection is. Your mind doesn't know what heaven is. You know the words and their definition from the dictionary. But you have no experience of my Light, my Love, my Peace, or me Big Eye. I try to help you. But I can see you are confused. You don't know how to experience me. You are troubled by a Trinity of Women called Sweet Pea, Crazy Pea and Wise Pea. You can see by your experiences that it's best for men dedicated to me to remain celibate. When you are married and have children you are never free to go away and spend long periods of time with me. I want you for myself.

Liam, I care for the world. And I care more for those that love me. You are in that category. But you have to face me in quiet prayer. You have to concentrate on my Name. You need to look at me. I want you to experience me. Therefore, fight for quality time with me. The whole of your book is about whether you as a married man, with a child, and responsibilities can give Sacred Time to me. You know that is what makes you happy. You know prayer is the only way for us to work hand in hand.

Liam, never forget that I am the Father of seven billion people, a Father to the whole of creation. The whole world is mine. You have my Name. Dwell on it as often as possible. My Son Jesus Christ taught you to call me Father. So call now. Call me in five minutes from now. Call me when you walk. Call me from your intellect. Keep calling me always. You are my spiritual child so respect me, please me, and obey me. Once you are lamb-like my Spirit will descend upon you. I claim you for myself before the evil one has a sniff. I have access to your heart. I have great love for the simplicity of children. Don't be serious so Liam. Liam, pray to me. Learn from Jesus Christ. I heard his prayer always. You know the way people dismiss each other's talk as bulls pooh. Well, a lot of it is. Prayerful communication with me is a great skill. If you are not sincere you waste your time and mine too. My Christ faced big decisions. He sought me his Father when in need of support. I helped him to choose twelve unlettered me. I helped him to face suffering, death and resurrection. My poor Son was in agony in the Garden of Gethsemane sweating intense prayer at what was expected of him to die for love of you and every person born.

Liam, follow Jesus. Do the same. Pray to me about every decision whether small or big. Pray to me about problems facing you. Pray to me because I am your Father. Theologians and Scripture Scholars don't understand that there is a little nuance in the word, Father that allows you to feel that you are my children. Therefore, you have the right to say My Father instead of Our Father when praying privately.

Liam, follow Jesus. Go to quiet places to pray like him at every opportunity. Learn from him. Pray like him. Don't complicate things. You have the recipe for success. My Son's legacy is available to you. Concentrate on Big Truths like Suffering, Crucifixion, Resurrection, Eucharist, and Holy Spirit. Pray to me Liam. I can give you insights into the resurrection that no one has ever received before. The same applies to every concept of Doctrine. Prayerful preachers should excite the minds of their congregations with deep sincere explanations of Doctrine as well as Scripture. My Son Jesus explained the Scriptures at twelve years of age when he read Isaiah's scroll in the Synagogue. He won the approval of all. People were astonished by his gracious words. When were you last inspired by gracious words or a devout preacher? People should be excited to hear you preach. They should look forward to sermons.

Liam, questions are good. The disciples saw Jesus at prayer. So they wanted to copy him. So they approached Jesus and asked to be taught. I gave them a Masterpiece. Pray to me by saying Our Father in heaven, hallowed be your Name. The question, how to pray, is very relevant. Magnificent insights lie in this prayer. You try very hard to reach me. You give it your best shot. The reason why your prayer effort is not successful is because your mind is troubled. An agitated mind takes a long time to calm down. Distress also prevents good connections with me. Some of you come to me carrying the world on your back. Shake it off little man.

Little Man

Father. I desire you Eternal Father. I look forward to dying and being with you. What you have to offer is greater than any show on earth. You should know that by now. I love the prayer of your Son. I call you every morning. After closing the door of my home and walk towards the road my first words are Good Morning Father in heaven. As I continue the walk I pray each petition sincerely. And I try to regard them as Golden Eggs. I pray these words to improve my relationship with you Big Eye.

I love the Our Father. It's powerful. It's full of wisdom. I try my best to unravel each petition and apply my mind to full comprehension of the task in hand. For when I use the words hallow your Holy Name Big Eye I try to muster up within my mind and heart a sense of the awesomeness of your Sacred Beauty and Powerful Sanctity.

I have a little taste of your Sweetness in me at the moment Big Eye. It is for that reason I never want to let go of my love for you. The most glorious moments so far in my life are in relation to the sweetness I feel in me because of my links with you Holy Father.

Holy Father I'm never going to reside in the Vatican or be in the blessed company of Cardinals and Bishops. I'm just a little Man living at the ends of the earth on road L0909. It's on that road that I foster my love for you each day. I'd prefer to be a St John or St Anselm who prefer to love your Son Jesus rather than be caught up in administration of the Church.

When your servant St Pope John Paul 11 visited my country I was among seminarians. There was rapturous applause as St Pope John Paul passed by. There was no tree for me to climb and hope he might greet me personally. I'm never in the limelight when big celebrations occur. I prefer to contemplate you Holy Father in the quietness of my room, or on my walks through your beautiful countryside. I couldn't be listening to people who disturb my peace of mind. I could be jockeying for positions by ambitious young clerics who shove their rivals into bouts of low self-esteem and frustration.

So when the Pope passed by a large number of seminarians on that day there was no eye to eye contact, no hand shake, or face to face greeting. I'm a small fish in the ocean. But I have glorious moments with you Father of All. And I know your Big Eye has a sharpness to spot one tiny human being in a house near the Shannon River by the Atlantic Ocean.

And what's more you know Holy Father about the passion and desire in me to love you. I'm delighted to have that glorious prayer the Our Father. And I thank your Son Jesus Christ from the depths of my heart for teaching the disciples how to pray and subsequently every Christian since the days they walked on the earth. I'm grateful to Jesus for it. On the road walking every morning my first words are Our Father.

next

Chapter Sixteen

Big Eye

Liam I can zone in on one individual on earth. Or I can look through planets, stars, and comets to view earth as an entity. I'm the Creator of everything. The world of humans is self-sufficient. Human beings are busy using the world to make a living. I give each person a life. I give each creature senses and a mind. And very, very few of them use those senses and mind to figure out my nature and existence. In other words, hardly anybody knows me.

I'm indescribable. Liam, think of all the names under the sun. None of them express my identity. The most common name used by my creature is God. All seven billion minds in the world don't know about my creation of galaxies, my creation of the sun, my eternal nature, and the destiny of living things.

The bulk of human beings want work for money, sex between the sheets, ambition to be the best and fun. Most are happy with that but not you Liam. You think differently. You are not fooled. People use my Name. It's on their lips. They have no image of me. I'm not an old man with a beard. Nobody knows me. The religious depth in each person is shallow. You don't know me either. Liam I dislike shallow believers. These use my Name a lot and pass themselves off as a personal friend. But their real ministry is to promote self.

Liam there is only one way to find out the essence of my Nature. There is only one person who knew me perfectly and he was my Beloved Son Jesus Christ. I repeat Liam. I repeat dope. The Way to the Father is through the Son.

On that day to Calvary my Son Jesus carried a heavy load. It was a big heavy wooden cross. This heavy load represented all the sins of the world. Christ tried in the past, during his own time, and up to this very day to carry everyone's' sin on his shoulders and crucify them on the cross. Liam this is what religion is about. It's about conquering temptation and moving into a position to gain eternal life through the way of the Cross.

Liam that is what you should pursue. It doesn't matter if heaven is a billion kilometres at the other side of the sun, or a luxurious ten-star hotel in paradise. What matters is your struggle in life to fight for my Son and pass through the narrow gate hidden in the Body and Blood of my Son's crucifixion.

And at the moment Liam I'm aware of your failure to stand firm against temptation. You are still eating sweets, biscuits and bars. It's an easy one to overcome. But you keep giving in to it. You are very easy to tempt, and you have little resistance to it.

However, Liam through my Son Jesus you know many of my attributes and this in turn depicts my character. The number one revelation is that I Am a Father to you all on earth. I'm a Father of love, peace, compassion, mercy and truth.

Little Man

Hello Big Eye. Thank you for your passage of writing. It's very inspiring. I'm happy with it Father. Your response is out of this world. I love it. I'll take note of Jesus' masterful revelations that describe your attributes Father. I want some of that love, peace, compassion, mercy and truth in my character too. It's an attractive package. I'd take it any time. You are the Highest of all.

I knock at your heart Jesus. Nowhere can I find perfection similar to Big Eye's. Your Son Jesus told us what you were like. Christ has the same qualities. It's simply pure perfection. I'm more desperate than ever. I want a chunk of that peace. I want to drink this perfect love. I want a dose of Christ's patience. You're my best friend. You're my only friend.

I love you my Christ. I adore you Big Eye. I can't buy these qualities. I can't earn these qualities. They are gifts from you Father. These super virtues and top human qualities may be attained through another source too. I'm sure to benefit if I befriend you Big Eye and your Son Jesus. I beg for your company Jesus. Can I be a close friend? Already even at the thought of it I feel shivers of bliss run through my spine.

Big Eye, this is a scant substitute for not seeing you face to face. My friend St Anselm touched on that issue of seeing your face too. The Psalms touch on it too. I can't put a face on you, Father. I could paint one though by showing a face that's depicts love, peace and joy. Look it doesn't matter Father. It's none of my business. You have your reasons. The absence of a face though gives rise to atheists arguing that there is no God. Anyway I'm happy once Jesus' super qualities reflect in my life.

Big Eye, on another note you revealed yourself as eternal. You survived billions of years and you were never created. I'm told by Catholic Doctrine and Gospel references that you always existed. I'm thinking to myself here. It's a mystery and incomprehensible. I wonder though have you changed at all? Has your face changed? Some artists depict you as an old man with a beard.

Big Eye

Liam, stop now! I'm not telling you why nobody has seen my face. And be careful about being pertinent and disrespectful towards me. I don't like your question about my face. But I will answer you. It's in excellent shape. It's in a permanent state of illumination, splendour and holiness. Millions of years don't matter to me. I live for eternity and never age. I always was and always will be. I am infinite and will never pass away. Does that reassure you?

Little Man

It does Father. I find life fascinating and mind boggling. I'm on the road every morning reflecting on the origin of everything as well as the things I hear and see. I observe the sky and the skilful flight of birds and their tweets. I watch the horses and cows in the fields at both sides of the road. The horses stand still while the cows stare curiously at me.

I allow my mind to imagine the enormity of space by pondering what might be millions of kilometres away. I'd hate to think humans are stuck here and that the death of each one of us is the end. Is there life elsewhere?

Big Eye, your Word is the only consolation and hope for each one of us. I believe. I have faith. I confess that Jesus is Lord. I believe Big Eye raised him from the dead. St Paul says that's enough faith for a person to be saved. I proclaim your Name Big Eye in this book and long for a place in your kingdom.

However Big Eye, what about me? What about finite life? I age and die and the thought of death isn't nice. On the roads over the years I've seen numerous foxes, hedgehogs, hares, and badgers killed. Fast car drivers at night kill them.

It's reassuring though that I have a Father to watch me. I very much believe that individuals who pray are protected by Big Eye. My own family are proof of the pudding. My father prayed the rosary every evening. We have had over fifty years of protection except for one tragic loss.

Big Eye life is funny. Death could be a happy occasion. Christian martyrs looked forward to dying. Those who are left seem to think it's a great thing to reach a ripe old age. But would it not be better to die and go to heaven where the standard of heavenly life is pure joy in comparison to the drudgery and misery in this vale of tears.

Big Eye I'm looking at this death/resurrection experience of your Son Jesus and the possibility of a life after death for each one of us. It's an extraordinary plan but many believe in the world that death is the end. Whatever our fate it's in your hands. All I would say is that if there is life after death and heaven is the reward for living a good and holy life I for one would rush for it to happen. I recall many disciples and Saints looking forward to death as it was seen as going to sleep for a little while only to wake up in the company of Jesus Christ.

Big Eye the classic story for all of us on earth in relation to death/resurrection centre on your Son's experience as well as the Lazarus and Little Girl stories in the gospel. The idea of a resurrection is fascinating. It gives us all hope.

In the liturgical cycle Easter is the greatest of all celebrations in the Catholic Church. It's the time of the year when Christians all over the world celebrate the passion, death and resurrection of your Son. For the Devil it was a sting in the tail. Your power Big Eye tricked Satan. Your Almighty Power Father brought your suffering Lamb back to life. And you brought your Beloved Son home to heaven. And you left an image on earth to fight Satan and temptations for the rest of eternity. In that sense your Son Big Eye conquered the world. And I want to help in that respect. I want to conquer my own temptations. This is indeed Good News.

Big Eye, the story of the Resurrection is the greatest story on earth. Who would have thought that Satan could be tricked? The Jewish religious leaders thought that Christ's death was the end. The Roman soldiers thought the crucifixion ended the influence of God's Son on earth. And the Devil grinned in glee thinking Christ was stopped from influencing the world by choosing holiness rather than devilment. These two together represented the political and religious powers at the time of our Lord.

Big Eye, thank you so much! I see in your Son's life an offer of hope. I want a share in the resurrection. I'd like my body to be carried to heaven. But I hope it's not like an MRI scan on my brain. I couldn't stick that experience going through a noisy tunnel with a helmet strapped around my head. I hope death isn't the same. I'd hate to be trapped with no future and no bright passage way from earth to heaven. I'm totally relying on you Big Eye and Father of every human being. It's the sole reason why I isolate every distraction that obstructs my vision of you. I could come across as a selfish man because I place you as the Highest and Greatest of All. I place you Holy Father ahead of everything. I place you as more important than any woman. I love my wife and my son Luke. But I know Big Eye that only you can save us all. I don't care about money and a place to live. Your Son Big Eye had no home throughout his life. Your Son had nowhere to lay his head.

Big Eye, your Son's life was really a true and amazing story. I love the notion that he was alive after dying. I love the Power that you have my Lord and God to resurrect a body from death and decay. And I love

213

the ascension of the Lord into heaven. There must have been great cheer and applause on that day in heaven when he arrived to sit at your right hand beside you Big Eye. I can well imagine Christ's arrival in heaven as the greatest triumphal celebration of all.

Big Eye I know the story of your Master Plan to save the world from darkness and sin didn't end either at Christ's departure. The Apostles were frightened and felt abandoned. But in comes a third part of the Divine Trinity – the Holy Spirit.

Big Eye, I take my hat off to you. O my God. Whatever happened on that day when the Holy Spirit descended on the Apostles had the effect of changing the world forever? It breathed new life into those men who were sent out to the whole world to preach a new religion that would improve love of one another and unite us to the Son of Man. Christ's chosen Apostles had no more fear of anything even death as the courage and strength received from the Holy Spirit gave them a power to bring the message of eternal life to the ends of the earth.

Big Eye I don't want to come across as a doubting Thomas. I have a question. I hope you don't mind. How can every man, woman and child born on earth rise and fit into heaven? I'm not a fool. Neither are philosophers and theologians. There are billions of people involved here. Man's mind is capable of working on profound truths such as each human life that came to be in the course of creation from the start. Where have they all gone? In fact, it seems that we may be lucky that there is death. If death didn't occur the world would be overcrowded.

Big Eye, are we like snails, frogs, flies and so on? Are we like animals, fish and birds? Every living thing has its own innate ability to recreate its own type of species through some kind of sexual ability. And we all live of other living things. The snail is a meal for a bird. The cow is beef for a human.

Big Eye, I see wild animals lying dead on roads. Fast cars ended their lives. Even humans are hit and killed on roads. Snails are flattened by the wheels of cars.

The species of everything continues though. The death of a few flies, or a few frogs, or a few animals, or a few humans doesn't mean the death of the species.

Therefore, Big Eye I think all living things are there for a purpose and frighteningly one aspect of it is that something's are created to feed other things. And I also think that birth and death was designed in such a way as for one thing to replace another through the action of sexual love.

Big Eye, I return therefore to your Son's promise of eternal life for all who believe. But where are we going to fit? I see eight thousand fans at a sport event. I see one million people at a Papal Mass. I see twenty thousand Israelites in the desert. I see fifty thousand at a Pop Concert. I see populations of millions of people in each Nation. I see from Adam, the first man to every man living on the face of the earth today. Do millions upon millions of people rise from the dead?

Big Eye, am I missing something? Maybe it is none of my business. But can heaven contain billions of people? Is there a beautiful place in the distance where billions of people sit on fresh green pastures and are happy? Or are there only a few saved? Unfortunately, I have to admit that I don't know. All I do know is that there are words to tell me that there is a place called heaven, hell and purgatory. This knowledge isn't available in detail to us on earth.

Big Eye

O Little Man, what will I do with you? I watch your mind working. There is no harm in exploring and probing matters that are deep and known to me alone. I admire though your efforts.

However, Liam you would be better off concentrating on loving me. Greek philosophers who had brilliant minds in the likes of Aristotle and Plato probed into everything possible regarding the origins of gods and life. The greatest of all though was King Solomon, son of King David. I'm present in his wisdom.

Liam you ask big questions that are way beyond your remit. All I want from you is a continuous effort to love me.

Liam I have enough on my plate besides entering into conversation with you about matters outside your control. Instead do your best to help Nations to concentrate on loving me and loving each other. The threat of wars and fighting in the world are the same as in the time of my Son. It's to do with human power and snug religious security through a comfortable life style.

Liam I'll not allow my ears to be blocked by unhappy, grumpy and mumbling human souls. And I'll deflect away from my kingdom people who blame me for evil in the world. I can't block the force of man who has free will. I can't wipe clean the evil temptations that arise in the heart and mind of man. If I scraped out all the dirt in the soul of every life it would reappear quickly again. I can't shoot dead a demented human being from carrying a gun with the intent to kill others.

Liam I have set out my stall. It's there in the world for everyone to see. It's the best that's available from among all the religions in the world. These stalls are available to everyone in the world. These are my Son's Churches. In those holy places my Word is read and the Body and Blood of my Son is consecrated and given to all believers in me.

Liam, the only snag is that human choice is decisive. A man or woman can opt out of Church worship and ignore my Son. And many have chosen that route. And adults opting out usually result in children doing likewise.

Also I'd like to tell you Liam that those who choose me are not on a rollercoaster fun ride. The Christian way of life is a narrow and tough road. It's a road where obstacles or hurdles are in the way every minute of your time on earth. It's a road where thorns and lashes of the whip are constantly flogging your flesh and prodding your brain. But the reward is great. If you pursue me above every other friendship my Son and I will make our home in you. My Way, my Truth and my Life will be in you.

Once this unity between us occur your mind and heart will see what menaces the world and a great fear will prevail in the seriousness of the task in hand to save souls especially those of your own flesh and blood. I want you to tell the Irish people to return to me. I want you to warn the whole world to turn to me. Mass goers too need some soul searching. Just because you sit at the back of the Church doesn't mean that you are doing enough to save yourselves.

Liam the Son of Man in which you regard as a Golden Egg later in this book is in the forefront to help make the world a better place. My Son is Chief Operator in the spiritual field of man in the world. I want you to unite yourself closely with his work. I can rely on your mind. In working together, I can unblock webs of evil that Satan has used to trap and paralyse weak souls in making decisions for me.

Liam, take heed. If my Commandments, my Way of Life, my Doctrine and my Teaching are dismissed by Nations, Governments and all individuals then the outcome is bleak for the rejectionists. It simply implies that they don't want Big Eye telling them how to live and what to do. And if humans are left to their own devices all sorts of dodgy and immoral legislation could be passed into Law. When irreligious atheists influence and tamper with My Law it tears holes in the fabric of morals and the love of my Son's Catholic Church. I have always loved your country but the seeds of corruption have been sown and it will affect future generations in a once proud land known to many as an island of saints and scholars.

Liam I am a proud God. I would be heartbroken to lose the soul of your people. A Nation without me would die a slow and painful death. I don't know what can be done to stop the slide into a black and dirty abyss. You know what I refer too. I'm talking about a lack of interest in the sacraments of my Son's Church. I'm talking about the Government playing cards with my Son's work. I'm talking about the decline in moral principles. I'm talking about people rejecting me and doing what they like. I'm talking about irreligious attacks on Catholic teaching, Catholic schools, and Catholic morals.

Little Man

Hi Big Eye. I'm frightened for my country. I have a young son called after the writer St Luke. I worry for his future in a country where the State has interfered with religious practises and encouraged an anti-God mentality.

However Big Eye I'll not waver. I might be the last man standing for the traditions of the past. I will not buckle under pressure. I love my Church.

I'll follow your way Holy Father because I love you. It's what I want. I write my love story. I enjoyed so much my upbringing in the Catholic

Church where Mass, Sacraments and Confession played a major part in my formation as a child brought up to know you Big Eye.

Nowadays adults and children don't care. Nobody stands up for the Catholic faith. We are bereft of leaders and teachers with faith to instruct the faithful.

Big Eye, I promise to follow you. This morning I went to Mass. It was the feast of St Augustine - a great saint like St Patrick. Both came to love you late in life.

I'm late too Father. It was the search for Truth that attracted me to you Father. I'm searching for you all my life. Only the Catholic Church could satisfy me. Three priests concelebrated Mass. They were happy around the altar. I admired their faith. These men are not to be criticised. They love the Eucharist. It is their life. Nothing like Mass occurs in Islam.

I recall St Monica's wish to be remembered at the altar of God. O what a mother! This led me to reassess my value of the Eucharist. My mind worked on the action taking place on the table of Christ. O my God. It has dawned on me. This is the table where Christ's Body and Blood are shared with believers.

But I'm sad now. I can't preside over it. The Church wouldn't allow me back due to a celibacy rule. I feel holy and priestly. I know in my heart and soul that I could bless bread and wine again. My love for Christ is intense.

I do admire women too. A good woman is very precious and beautiful. Women have qualities that men don't have. They are more affectionate. Also women have a more innate affinity with children. There natural feminine side differs from their masculine counterparts.

Women can be fun too and great company for a man. But I'd like women to be virtuous, good living, educated and holy. Also life with a woman is commitment. It's a relationship of unity and close proximity. The intimacy between a man and woman differs from a relationship with you Big Eye. That's why I'm not in favour of married clergy.

I' don't support the spread of gay life. In fact, I disagree with gay marriages due to the fact that their biological bodies are incompatible. I do admit though that it's possible for gays to love each other but there is an abnormality in the sense that same sex couples have similar private parts and can't produce babies.

Chapter Seventeen

Big Eye

O Liam, you have done it again. I can't hold you back. You switched from writing about the Eucharist to priests and from priests to women and from women to gays. What are you up to? Do you think you are all knowledgeable and a prolific writer?

Liam I should be preaching to you. I know of the beauty of my Son's altar tables, and my creation of beautiful females, as well as the emergence of rights for disorientated sexual choices.

Liam, how many times have I told you that it is enough for us at the moment to establish a beautiful relationship? I want you to concentrate on knowing me and loving me. The application of your mind and heart in prayer to me is the challenges I place before you. I want to hear your cry of love.

Liam, I watch you and test you. I know what's in your heart. You're from Kilkenny – the home of hurling. I'm aware of your team's achievements. And I often notice that you drop interest in me when Kilkenny play. So don't cheat on me. I'll not be pushed aside for hurling. If that game fills your heart after declaring your love for me than I have question marks hanging over your complete dedication for me. I might ask you to pray the next time a big match is on. I will test you Liam.

Little Man

O Father. That's my relaxation time. I have nothing else left. Are you that possessive Father? My love for food and my desire for big hurling matches cause a crack in loyalty between us Big Eye. You have hit me with a thunderbolt. Am I not able to enjoy anything on earth? I struggle with your severe test Big Eye. Isn't everything that happens around the world part of our living experiences? Why isolate me from everyone and everything?

I walked down the road and thought of your words Big Eye. You have asked me to sacrifice something enjoyable

O Father you ruffled my feathers. It's time for reflection. I recall your Word in Scripture Big Eye where it says that evil intentions emerge in men's hearts. Viewing hurling isn't an evil intention. But its enjoyment fills my heart. I'm an intense viewer. I don't like talk or movement in the television room during big matches. The same applies to football and rugby. What am I going to do?

Holy Father you have really hit my emotions on this issue. I'm patriotic and Irish success thrills me. The love of games has to do with National pride. An Irish success lifts the Nation. It makes us proud of our talent and people. I yell with joy when Ireland win.

The same fervour applies to my black and amber friends who wear with pride Kilkenny jerseys that bring success and excitement to hurling fans. In fact, over the last decade hurling enthusiasts have seen the greatest team of all. I'm proud of parishes and families in Kilkenny by doing so much work in giving children a great skill.

Big Eye

Liam, I'm not asleep. I watch everything. I can see the whole world and every individual living on the surface of the earth. And not only that Liam, I see what's in hearts and minds. Liam, you promised your love and commitment. And at the same time you intend to ditch me for a few hours of entertainment.

Come on Liam! I'm not a fool. During the time you give to sport I'm squeezed out of your heart. You have two kinds of love. Prayer fills your heart with my love. Sport fills your heart with another thing that shoves me aside.

Liam I'm God. I'm the Highest and Greatest of All. Am I not enough for you? There is nothing greater. So why do you shut me out over a ball? I want your eye on me all the time. There are no

221

holidays from me. All the time your heart and mind must be set on me. Unfortunately, you haven't tasted my Greatness yet. If you had you wouldn't place entertainment above me. I desire total focus from you. I want an excellent relationship.

Liam dear, there is no question of equality when it comes to hurling and me. If it is hurling that you prefer than I search for someone more loyal.

Liam I am sorry to point out this weakness. I don't aim to divide your heart. But I'm certain it's games and other attractions that obscure people from finding me. However, take your time with your decision. Don't worry Liam. I'm sure you are intelligent enough to choose what pleases your heart the most. My interest here is that you work on your on/off love desire for me

Little Man

Big Eye, allow me to reflect. I'll go for a walk down the road and reflect. The countryside is beautiful. It's quiet but a bit windy. The cornfield is ready for reaping. The cows graze away and the horses stand still. The birds tweet in the trees.

My life is different now after retiring from the fish counter at Superquinn. This is the life. For years I wanted to write to you Big Eye and make sense of life. I wanted to be a writer. I called my son after St Luke who wrote excellently a Gospel account of your Holy and Divine Word and Work among us.

Father I may come across as obsessive if I cut out everything except you in my life. There's a case for level-headedness and balance. I'm sure you wouldn't want me tagging along after you every minute of the day. Space is important. What would you say if I was in your face all day? What would you think if I wanted to be in your pocket as a little pet?

Father the viewing of a match wouldn't harm our relationship. It is not that I love you less. You can sit beside me on the sofa and relax while the match is on. How many times did your son bring his disciples away from the crowd for a rest? The hurling match is my time for chilling out and relaxing my mind.

Father I'm not viewing anything evil. I'm not reducing your love in my heart. All I'm doing Big Eye is viewing skilful Kilkenny hurlers battling it out on the field with rivals in our unique National sport. The guys playing this sport are healthy. These men have integrity and character. They are models in society who have great influence on children to follow a healthy lifestyle.

Big Eye, you know my views. I always felt in the Catholic Church that too much religion could smother our hearts and minds. That's why I argue for walks on beaches, for walks on mountains, and for cycling, swimming and sports in general. Our physical bodies are made for activities. In your Son's time there weren't cars, trains, planes and buses when people were healthier. Father you are involved in all human activities except evil acts. I do no harm watching a game. Can I enjoy the match?

Big Eye

Well Liam you can. But I watch activities throughout the whole world and a large percentage of humans play sport. It would be okay Liam if there was a bit of sport mixed with a bit of prayer. But I'm afraid many sporting social events exclude me.

Also Liam you heard colleagues at work slag each other about their Premiership Football teams. There is no talk about faith and love for me. Their hearts are passionate about the teams they support. And this is a Football League in another country.

Liam sport is a huge distraction. At the end of the day there's massive fuss stirred up over a ball. I'm the real God. A ball is empty air. The amount of human time consumed through sport outweighs time devoted to me. That balance isn't right. It's so hurtful to me and my Son within this generation that parents wouldn't bring their children to Church.

I admire you Liam for bringing your son to Mass every Sunday morning, and I recall your decision of two years ago that you preferred my altar than a rugby ball. But you still bring your son to karate, golf and hurling. That's fine.

Finally, on this matter see all the men and women of leisure playing golf. They enjoy the walk, the company and the striking of a little white ball. Where is their prayer commitment? And I hear a lot of curses of the white little god when it doesn't travel in the direction intended. So Liam I prod your conscience here.

Little Man

Come on Holy Father! What would we do every day if we had no fun, no work, no competition, no events or activities? Is it not amusing for you? Surely you approve of family day outs. Surely you notice support for teams. Surely you observe local communities coming together for good causes. You watch the movements of people gathering together in stadiums for big matches. We can't be all on our knees praying every day. There's a sense of pride in local communities in their work with people whether it be sport, or dance, or music or other activities for vulnerable members of the parish. I have no doubt blessings in abundance like showers descend on a caring community. There are multiple activities for everyone in the neighbourhood. Father, you can't expect religious dedication twenty-four seven.

Big Eye

Liam, listen to me. I had important meetings in the past about the future of the world. One of those meetings involved Moses, Elijah and my Son. My Holy Presence was on that mountain with those three glorious giants of Holiness. My Son brought three men up the mountain with him. They were Peter, James and John. On that day I told those three men to listen to Jesus.

Liam, please understand that the same applies today. Peter didn't understand at the time. He wanted to pitch three tents – one for each of the magnificent religious leaders of all time. But I rectified the situation by ordering my Son's three friends to listen to him.

I tell you solemnly, Liam that my command speaking through a dark cloud on that mountain on that day to listen to Jesus is paramount in helping the world to refocus. My message is very simple. Anybody that doesn't listen to my Son is out of focus.

My dear Liam I'm sorry to alert you in having to pass on a worrying trend that sweeps across the lands of the earth in recent years. It is very serious. In the past on Mount Sinai I gave Moses Ten Commandments for his people to live by. When Moses came down from the mountain in a state of glory he found his people partying and engaging in all sorts of immoral practises.

The worrying trend that I refer to has to do with a social revolution that rejects the Church of my Son in favour of political and people driven agendas to change the morals of a Nation. In the last number of years, you have had a weak political leader who gave power to the people to change Laws that in the long run have serious consequences for your future.

Liam, I'm worried. The focus is not on my Son Jesus anymore. The eyes and ears of man are elsewhere. They have become very individualistic. Morale is low. I don't like it. The emphasis is definitely not on me. I'm so sad to see your once beautiful and Catholic culture as well as holy traditions abandoned. And I don't think they are going to listen to me. That is why I solemnly command you Liam to listen to my Son Jesus.

I sent my Son to earth so as to personally call all who labour and are overburdened. He wants to refresh you Liam. And he wants to refresh the whole of creation. Jesus, my Beloved son received those who listened to his voice with open arms. Their sins were forgiven. Those who were common and profane my Son Jesus made them sacred and holy through my Word.

Liam, my Lamb is a symbol of supernatural qualities. All the virtues are in him. And like St Patrick hearing the voice of the Irish calling him I want you to call upon every person in your country to return to Church so that they can hear the voice of my Son Jesus again. It's about time the Irish stood up for their faith, for their beliefs, for the way of life and values that my Son taught you.

Liam, the Eucharist is pivotal. It's of huge benefit to the local community if men, women and children pray together. I command everyone to listen to my Son. My Word has survived two thousand years. Many souls continue to hear it. But millions die in ignorance with practically no trace of my influence in them.

Liam, tell all the sleepy men and sleepy women to wake up. I want every person to have a chance. If they prefer television and the internet so be it. If they don't want to worship me so be it. If they prefer a pint of a beer and feel gloomy about their future so be it. Liam you can't do anymore. Once you warn people to turn to me your back is covered.

Liam, I'm unhappy with politicians tampering with my Commandments and teaching. Some Natural Law legislation has become Corrupt Law. I solemnly declare this Truth because the changes are not good for the moral fabric of people. I refer to interferences in marriage, abortion, and religious education. But also I refer to neglect in primary care for the sick, the poor, and homelessness. I'm also disappointed in a culture of selfishness where the rich exploit the poor. I see politicians and public representatives carving out a fat cat retirement policy that triples an ordinary worker's salary for a whole year.

Liam, warn them. If they don't return from their erring ways nothing can be done. They are lost. The blindness of greed and power can't be undone.

Chapter Eighteen

Little Man

Hello Big Eye. I hear you loud and clear. I will listen to your Son Jesus. I'll seek occasions to be in his company through the scenes in the gospel and take heed of his voice. But I'm struggling internally to discipline my desire for food and sport. It's like a wrestling match between enjoyment of life and spiritual focus. The demand from you to give all breaks my heart. I've feelings of been dull and boring. But I've no doubt in my heart that you Big Eye are the better part. You do something for me that gives me an inner joyful feeling of content that nothing else does. I'd prefer a good Word in my ear than a sugary sweet in my mouth.

Father I smile on this one. I really struggle on this one. The imps tempt me to enjoy sweets, enjoy matches, and relax. But if I go for a walk and pray or sit in a meditation shed, or read a spiritual book, or write my mind keeps going back to who might be winning the matches. That's my mentality at the time a big game is played.

Big Eye, you have won me over. I direct my attention to you alone. Please give me the strength to squeeze the life out of temptations that beset me. The lure of pleasure and leisure drag my will in the opposite direction to you Big Eye. The internal pull of two powers fighting for control of my heart hurts. A decision favouring you Big Eye is huge and life changing. My Sacred Love wants total dedication. I give my intellect to him and my heart too.

Big Eye I'm excited at the realisation that I have the ability to turn everything that I am into a daily offering in service of your Sacred

Love. I give that commitment. It's not a part time commitment where I pray only while at Sunday Mass. I'm available to love God at every opportunity. I suspect most worshippers give a slot to God per week and the rest of it is free to self-indulge.

Big Eye if I practise awareness of your Presence each hour of the day would that is classed as an obsession. I believe everyone has obsessions. These are things that preoccupy us most of our time. A person could give his life to a football club, or to running marathons, or mountain walking, or managing a crèche. Obsessions take up a lot of time and energy. So am I becoming obsessed with you Big Eye?

O dear Big Eye. A bad stirring of anger has just erupted in my heart. I don't like it. Father, quench it. I don't like these mini eruptions of anger inside me. Please, Big Eye, pour a bottle of grace over it. This will stem its spread.

I'm certain an angry outburst and clashes of words with others is the same as an offence with you. It would be erroneous of me to clash with Christ. I would expect to be dumped from his team if I displayed disrespect. I wouldn't be deserving of finding peace and solace in Christ's heart if I bark, yell or shout at anyone.

Big Eye

Liam, what you say is true. I would expect eviction from a unified group of believers if an unsettled goat began to disrupt lambs chosen to work by preaching my Word. I'm cool and frosty with temperamental characters that flare up due to impatience over little things. Also I find unsuitable for ministry those who react to criticism and can't tolerate troublesome and irritating souls.

Liam you should know by now the kind of standard I expect from a man or woman. Saints are meek, gentle and humble. I wouldn't want an aggressive sleeping giant in my ranks. No follower of mine should fly into a rage. It's not the Way of my Son's teaching.

Liam, I oppose all forms of evil. I intensely dislike anger, impurity, lies and deceit. It's always the best policy to tell the Truth. Lies breeds more lies. Impurity dirties the soul. Anger batters' peace. I'll watch you

Liam. I'm aware that you pray not to be led into temptation. If we are to love each other stirrings of evil has to be dealt with.

Little Man

Father is life a question of hoping for the best and putting up with badness? There's no perfect man or woman alive on earth. All have their shortcomings. And some people endure horrible physical and emotional abuse. I'm not sure if married couples should remain together if a spouse causes unacceptable and unbearable cruelty. Why should a woman put up with abuse by a thug or alcoholic? Why should a man suffer under an uncooperative and unreasonable woman?

I'd like clarification on relationships Father. Bad marriages don't serve any purpose. A bad marriage is soul destroying. Abuse flung like cow's dirt at another or nasty words pelted like lumps of mud scars the integrity of a person for life. Any mistreatment endured by a person is like having bullets hit you in the heart, mind and body. Pain rips people apart. The hurt caused to a good person persistently from a tyrant is the same as slowly killing and tearing the gut out. Intolerable abuse results in poor health.

Big Eye

Liam, you are hard hitting again. You preach again. Why do you do it? Why are you challenging me? Why are you asking tough questions? I keep telling you to concentrate on love not problems. I suppose Liam you are concerned. I have no qualms about that.

Look Liam! Man/woman relationships are unpredictable especially when couples no longer value marriage as a sacrament. Good Catholic marriages are based on commitment to my Son. These couples practise their faith and have more respect for each other. I'd prefer pure white dressed virgins walking up the aisle for marriage to a good living man.

Liam marriage practise today is messy. Many couples live together and have children. It could be a social welfare benefit factor that causes this trend. Others use civil marriage ceremonies. And mostly people who use those options are non-practising Catholics. Then there are mixed marriages.

However, Liam you know my preference. And I delighted that you accept my preference. I'm all for one man and one woman walking up the aisle of my Son's Church and tying the knot by becoming husband and wife. Anything else is not blessed and supported by me. My Son Jesus follows my marriage rule strictly. For the sake of natural families, it's best to have both parents working together for the good of rearing their children. I am Scared Love. I support the beautiful and intimate love between a man and a woman. I made both male and female and I approve without question the unified love of both. No one has the right to break up a marriage.

Liam, why does this concern you? Family and marriage concerns are too big for you to study and write about in this book. This book is about our love for each other. It's about our marriage to each other. I don't want you writing as if you are a modern day philosopher and theologian. Our love is a simple love. All I expect from this book is the establishment of a Sacred Love that embeds you into holiness and virtuous attributes. Liam I'm certainly not catapulting you into the role of a Doctor of the Church or University lecturer. So down you go boy! My picture of you is an image of an ordinary little man that has an extraordinary desire to love me. I'm happy with that Liam.

So Liam, stop worrying. The attraction of sex will draw men and women to each other anyway regardless of whether they belief in any religion, or the Christian faith, or Muslim traditions. Males and females will fall in love. What I say to you now is that I'll manage that department

I'm Big Eye and I'm wide awake. My Eye scans the earth. And I'm aware of you writing at your desk near the Atlantic Ocean. It's so beautiful Liam to find a little soul that's in love with me. I'm proud of you. My focus is sharp. I'm slowly connecting my antennae's of Peace, Love, Truth and Patience to your body and soul.

Once I touch your life Liam a new burning sensation will erupt in side of you for me. And it will have the effect of dissolving your sins and faults. I can make you the most desirable and beautiful man on earth.

This is attainable through My Sacred Love touching your human body. Just the tip of my finger could make you glow like the sun.

Liam I'm involved in your formation. The package I require for aspirants doing ministry stems from the beatitude of those who are meek. This kind of a person I can reform into a new man, a bright man, an intelligent man, a loving man, a visionary man, a peaceful man, a holy man, and a virtuous man. Divine virtues originate from my Scared Love. The infusion of virtues usually transfigures the body and soul of a person so much that a glorious light shines forth in the world. A lit up person is a saint and a light for the world.

Little Man

O Father, I stand in awe before you. Fr William was right. Late in life I might become a saint. This is exciting news for me and my family and everyone living on the face of the earth. I welcome your intervention Big Eye. O Sacred Love, plug your life into me. I pray for a share in Divine Life and Power. I'm aware of the task in hand with the Son of Man at the helm. Father, drive me forward.

O Big Eye, you are like an electric power station. You light up cities, you light up homes and you light up lives. I'm so happy inside because you lit up my life. It's like as if surges of Sacred Love run through my body like an electric current. This love lights up my life and makes my face bright and it energises me.

Big Eye I think of your Son's appearance changing in order to prevent your disciples from feeling scandalised by the cross. Please Father, reveal your glory. Please connect to me your Little Man on earth. I desire very much to be tuned into your Sacred Love.

Big Eye, am I delusional? How can I be a saint? I don't feel holy now. I have ten things to do at the same time and this feeling causes havoc on my mental condition. I feel good at times but now I'm miserable. How can I feel good when things go wrong? There's sickness in the family. And I can't cure them.

Big Eye, I'm unsure of the quality of our relationship. You're there: you're not there. I'm good some days and then a few days could pass where I struggle to maintain the slightest spark in my mind to connect me to your Sacred Mind.

There are many doubts. I said to a bright UL athlete recently who called for fish at my counter that my mind has been preoccupied for many years with finding the Truth about God. The young man replied saying that God might not be there. I thought about his reply and felt foolish. The student caught me. St Dominic would have been disappointed with me.

Dominic argued with non-believers and persuaded many to return to God. But how can I do this today? How can I win? The bright students are well versed in philosophy and theology. How armed am I to cope with pagans? Could I defend the Catholic faith? Clever students might make mincemeat of my naive defence of the Doctrine of Faith

Big Eye

Liam, stop it! I want you to stop. I'm browned off with you. You look at life in the wrong way. Your queries are about impossible matters. Also you are very hard on yourself. Stop it Liam! I'll not open the door to you if you try to speak louder than me. I'm not tricked by you.

The reason why writing has stalled is due to tiredness. You are going through a tough time. Many turbulent emotions are coming into play. And it seems that multiple issues about endless little tasks are tying your mind up in knots. Liam let them go. The demands of others are challenging and sometimes these demands pin you down and irk you. I say to you that if you are constantly pressurised by unhappy souls and spirits just throw them over the head.

Liam, don't allow anything bog you down. I know how you feel. I can see you are weighed down with unbearable worries and burdens. The weight is like a heavy lead ball inside your mind. Liam your head at the moment is like a huge concrete block.

But you are not alone. The whole world is heavy at the moment. There's enormous pressure on human beings. But it is self-inflicted. These bouts of heaviness found in souls often result from a breakup of friendship with me. My advice to you Liam is to stop questioning, stop doubting and stop being downcast. It doesn't matter whether you are cremated. All that matters are trust in my Son.

So come on Little Man. Snap out of it! What makes you sweet? What makes you smile? Everything has gone well for you. You've been very lucky. There's being very little suffering or tragedy within your family circle. And I know who you credit for that protection. It was your father and mother's prayers and their example while growing up in the South East of your country.

Liam prayer is very important. Your parents taught you the basics. It was great in those days when schools and families worked in unison with each other to promote faith in My Son through the Catholic Church. I loved your Dad. He led by example. The importance of Mass, Confession and religious devotions meant a lot to him. It's a delight for us in heaven viewing parents praying with their children. Your parents did that with you.

Liam your father knew what was important. It's prayer Liam. What is it Liam? It's prayer. Your mother and father prayed with you. Families that pray together stay together. Prayer is massive for those desiring to do my Will.

Liam, your father had his heart in the right place. He obeyed my command to pray. By the way your father Edward made it to heaven. He spirit was accepted on the day he passed from earth so many years ago. I passed his entry into heaven on three counts for being a good religious man, a good family man, and a good working man who provided for his children.

Chapter Nineteen

Little Man

Big Eye, thank you very much. I'm delighted my father made it into heaven. He laid the foundations for us to build on. Hopefully his faith shall live on in us. But Father I rationalise sometimes about how you could be Present when we pray. I'm inclined to think that you sleep sometimes. My prayer sometimes feels dry. My mind feels there's no power. So I wonder if I should be aware and have an image of you Big Eye in heaven. Or when I pray should it be on my knees before a crucifix. Or should I call the Holy Spirit? I become very disillusioned when a spark isn't ignited every time I make an effort to unite with the Trinity of Persons. That's why I wonder if you sleep sometimes Father. Your Big Eye can't remain aware all the time.

Big Eye, a realisation has just come over me. The Three of you are involved in my personal prayer. The Power comes from you Big Eye, through your Son Jesus Christ and into me through the Holy Spirit. I know now what St Augustine understood when he said that he found what he was looking for. He declared that you Big Eye were around him and in him all the time and he didn't know it.

It clicked. The penny dropped. Father, you are above me, around me and in me. This Truth gives off a lovely feeling. It's an odorous sweet sensation. I like it Father that you could be around me and in me.

Big Eye

Liam, I created all, therefore I know everything. I made the first fish to live in the ocean. I made the first bird to fly in the sky. I formed all sorts of things and gave them life. I made the first man in the image of myself. I breathe life into everything that exists. You don't know me Liam as well as I know you. But by proper use of the intellect you could know more about me.

Liam, I saw you earlier walking and you praised my creation. You loved the blue sky and frosty morning. The sun shone in the east. I'm awake, Liam. You thought of your small mind and compared it to my Sacred Mind. I tell you now Liam that you're thought is significant. I would expect you to use your intellect. And if you could become more conscious of your brain and how it functions you might discover unimaginable revelations. I've had tremendous experiences from the very beginning to this very day with exceptional men and woman. I notice you Liam don't think very much of Patriarchs and Prophets before my Son's time. It's because you don't understand their value.

Liam, I loved Moses. His meekness attracted me to him. He was meeker than all the men on the face of the earth. I chose him to lead my people out of Egypt. Moses was their guide and leader. He led them out of Egypt and into a desert. Many moaned, grumbled and complained. As a result of disbelief and rebellion bodies littered the desert.

Liam the same applies today. All individuals need to know this. Bodies will litter the whole world if people don't repent and turn to me. Moses was a great leader who ploughed against all the odds in the desert until he found the Promised Land. All those who rebelled against him were left dead in the desert. At that time Moses was my man on earth. I worked through him and gave him Ten Commandments for people to abide by so as to stop more souls from going astray.

Liam, look! I have leaders all over the bible for you to follow. We are all one family. Abraham is your father. St Peter is your father. St Anselm is your father. Elijah is your prophet. Just because they lived before my Son's coming doesn't matter. Old Testament prophets and patriarchs with New Testament Saints are brothers and sisters in heaven. All contributed to my Word on earth.

I sent Mary, my Queen of Heaven to Knock in your country to plead for prayers for pagans and irreligious. To this very day the rosary is recited in Churches. The elderly in particular are loyal and they pray for the rest of you. I hear them in the mornings addressing in prayer my glorious and Sacred Queen.

Liam. I sent my Son to you. He meant everything to me. But wicked men crucified him. All my Son wants from you is prayer and commitment. And he is available for Holy Communion every day in the Church. Only a few meek people like Moses avail of my sacred offer to follow the right Way of life.

So Liam, don't ask me anymore about where you can find me. Remember the rich man Lazarus. He ignored a poor man outside his palace gate. This man had nothing. His clothes were ragged and he had no food to eat. Lazarus on the other hand had roast beef, turkey and ham regularly. I brought the poor man straight to heaven. Lazarus didn't make it. His offence to me was that he neglected his neighbour.

The negligent Lazarus didn't share his riches and care for the poor faced me at his death. He was intelligent enough to want permission from me to warn his brothers about Hades if they didn't serve the poor. But I turned him down on the grounds of their rich lifestyle and their refusal to believe in my Son Jesus who was clear in his teaching about care for each other. Lazarus brothers would not change even if I appeared as a beggar on their door steps. These people like their comfort and would send me away for fear I prick their conscience about less well-off people around the world.

Little Man

Big Eye, I love you this morning. The sun shines but it is frosty. Are you peeping through my window writing at my desk? Father you are right. I don't have any excuse for not following the gospel. The Master's message is clear. I'm to love everyone. If you pick up this book and read a few lines in fifty years' time I solemnly tell you that greatness is in serving others. And the Master tells us to go the extra mile and love enemies.

Big Eye I love you deeply. But you know the way you met Moses through the burning bush or on Mount Sinai I wonder if I could have a similar type experience. Father could you visit my room? Could you sit on a chair? I'd love to meet you. I'd like you to hold my head and look me in the eye and make a lasting impression on me. I would love more than anything an experience of a Divine and Sacred Presence. I'd love a chat with Jesus.

Big Eye

Liam I have just told you that care for your neighbour and others are the way to capture sentiments from my heart. If there was an old man down the road from you and dying of cancer would you prefer to write a book or visit him. If your wife was very ill and needing attention would you spend a lot of time writing or caring for your wife? I tell you solemnly once more that the sick, poor, disabled, and immigrants are dear to me. I'm on the side of those who suffer Liam. So I want you to know care for people is a priority with me. If I did visit your room I might give you a good telling off.

Little Man

Big Eye, I need to establish a connection before a flow of grace and love can run through me for the benefit of others. I begin to think positively about you. Your Sacred Presence is nearby. It makes me feel good. But I can't see you. I think your Presence is in your Word. Your Spirit and your Life are in your Word. So I may find you so Big Eye in your Word. We are not all as fortunate as St Paul. He was converted on the road to Damascus. I'm not expecting a revelation like St Paul on the road to Damascus.

However, Father if you have a solemn pronouncement to reveal I'm your man. I will deliver. I always wanted a chance to speak on television. It's the best way to preach for it has a wider audience. But I've no opportunities. I'd love to speak to the nation as a prophet. I'd love it Big Eye.

Big Eye

Liam, relax. What do you want to be on television for? You are a Little Man. Nobody knows you. My love is enough for you. You don't have to talk. You don't have to appear on television. Think of yourself as a little lamb or child. All I ask of you is to follow and listen to my Son Jesus. I'm you're heavenly Father. I know what you need. My Love keeps you warm. My Love keeps you beautiful. There's no need for you to go on television. Liam, you don't have to do anything. I watch you. You are my little lamb living on road L0909.

Liam I have to remind you though that there is an eruptive side in you for you came across as a bit nasty today. I've just called you my little lamb which is contradictory to a raging bull type of character. Liam, sort it out. I don't keep raging bulls with meek little lambs. Pray and pull out that vice. It is closely linked to one of the seven deadly sins. I dislike anger. It's an evil emotion. It's not the first time that it has cropped up with you. I'm the Most High and I can tell you that it would be better for you to work on eradicating anger than wanting to be a prophet.

Liam I have a spokesperson on earth to speak for me. Pope Francis speaks for me from the Chair of St Peter in Rome. I also have Bishops in every country to speak on behalf of me and my Son. So get it out of your head that you are going to preach as a prophet on television. You said yourself Liam that writing has a better survival rate than mouthy use of words. There are enough of Bible speakers everywhere. I don't need any more.

Little Man

Father I'm very sorry for desiring a platform to prophesy and for displaying anger with a child golfer. You have a Big Eye. You see everything. I repent for my impatience and expectations of a child. I blew my top over his laid back attitude and for him not to try his best. Luke played as if nothing mattered. I have high expectations for those I care about.

Big Eye I make no excuses. I was wrong for shouting and for being competitive. I like sharpness, energy and determination. But I hate laziness. I like people to be sharp and energetic. It's important to try and win. But if sloth is stuck in a child or in anyone it's frustrating for those who want to get up and do things.

Big Eye

Liam, I forgive you. I know your mind-set. You would like your child to be competitive. That's okay. The question most coaches would like to ask regarding anyone participating in a sport or in employment is whether he/she has talent.

Liam, I'm a spiritual Father. All I'm saying to you is that every activity has its price. St. Anselm, a friend of yours pointed out to you my Sacred Greatness. I'm Awesome Liam. I'm interested in your spiritual welfare. It doesn't matter how perfect you can hit a little white golf ball.

Liam can you grasp my precious point. Nothing greater exists than me. I'm Powerful. I'm an Almighty Father. I'm God Most High. I'm Father to all. I'm the Father of Jesus Christ. And I'm the Father of all whose lives are broken.

Liam, you would miss out if other things are placed before me. I'm not on a par with golf, or anything else in life. Remember the word in the Lord's Prayer that you struggle with – 'Hallowed'. Tease out its meaning Little Man. Look it up! Study it! Pray it! It's expected of you. It has to be understood in order to enhance your friendship with me.

Little man

Hallowed is to make holy! It is to be sacred. It's a religious term. It's to sanctify the Holy Name. It requires personal application. It is to make my heart and life conform to God. It's to think Big Eye in Sacred and Consecrated. The word, 'Hallowed', sets God apart! God is not an ordinary man. He is a consecrated person. He is separated from all other forms of life.

I feel happiness in my heart Holy Father. I'm delighted. I've looked up the word, 'Hallow'. I've always struggled with its origin. But I know how to use it now. I pray to you with great respect. I revere your Holy Name.

I now practise the application of those beautiful words, "Hallowed be thy Name" into my thought system. Whenever I use them it alerts me to something wonderful – the full comprehension of the Sacredness of God. This practise has to be paramount. The adoration of God is paramount.

Big Eye

Well done Little Man. You wrote well there now. Comprehension is a big word. Do you know its meaning? People use words they don't understand. I'll help you. Your comprehension of my sanctity will come alive. It's easy to use my Name without feeling. It's used callously. It's used commonly. It's used for self-interest. It's used for popularity. It's abused too.

So I want you Little Man for the rest of your life to respect and speak of me as the epitome of Divinity, Sacredness and Holiness. When you hear or use my Name I want you to grasp mentally that **I am who I am** is above everything.

Chapter Twenty

Little Man

Father, how can I experience this Awesome Hotness? Big Eye is red hot. I'm beginning to feel the heat. Indeed, you are overwhelming Big Eye. What is this Awesome Eternal Being? It's the Presence of God the Most High. It's pure ignorance on our part to walk on Sacred Ground without knowing it.

The Sanctuary and Altar of God is Sacred. Only priests should open the tabernacle. Only outstanding faithful Church members should distribute Holy Communion. Once it was only the priest that could touch the Sacred Host. The sanctuary which is the abode of Christ is sacred. Anywhere near God's Presence is Sacred.

Where does devotion start? Place God higher than anything. If I love Jesus, I love God. The two are Divine. How many times did Jesus say, "The Father and I are one"? Therefore, think about how Sacred Jesus is.

Father, I have to think this through. Yes! Yes! Think Little Man! Think! Big Eye is Unique. What's my image of Jesus' Father? I'm sure you have more to do than sit on a majestic throne surrounded by angels and saints? I'd love a glimpse of heaven. Are there lighted candles and beautiful flowers around you Big Eye?

Big Eye, do you have a body? Do you wear jeans and get muddy and dirty from hard work? I'm sure you are not idle and live a life of luxury. O red alert! Error! Big Eye differs from us. O dear! It has struck me. Big Eye is beauty itself. He has an eternal body that doesn't decay.

Big Eye holds the Secret of Life. His image is unbelievable. His glory is indescribable.

Big Eye is incredibly Sacred. He is the epitome of Holiness. I think of the beautiful Catholic Churches built throughout the world. Some of these are magnificent Churches. I think therefore of your abode in heaven Big Eye. Heaven must be superior to any Church dedicated to your Son Jesus Christ. Heaven must be more beautiful than anything we can make.

Big Eye I believe in your Word spoken through your Son. No eye has seen what is in store for any person that loves you. No ear has heard either of any magnificent places prepared for those who are loyal throughout their lives to you. I find great hope in those words. No eye has seen or ear heard indicates for me a big surprise. There are many mansions. Definitely those holy words are worth working your socks off for an insight. These words are in the category of Golden Egg territory that requires deep contemplation.

Big Eye

Liam, well done! I like you're thinking. At last my Little Man has worked out a Divine Truth. Well done again. I'm Great and Sacred. It's one thing for your human mind to grasp this Truth. But it is something different for you to experience my Magnificence. The tiniest little contact with me would send shivers of holiness through your body and it would be life changing. You see Liam I have the stuff that never dies.

Liam it would be well worth your while to remain loyal to me. This is a start between us. I'm the connection, friendship, union, communion, and alliance that every person craves. You are going to receive help from my Throne of Grace. It will change you. You will be a new and better man. You will have qualities to cope with every situation.

Little Man

Father, you have made me smile. I join my hands in prayer. Thank you, Father. I feel new already. I hallow your Holy Name. I adore you above everything. You are greater than the most beautiful woman on earth. You have Super Strength that defends me from the grip of demons. I adore you Father.

Big Eye, you see everything. I like my image of you. I hope you don't mind. I hope the Church doesn't mind. I do believe you are a Big Eye watching us on earth, and everywhere else in eternity. I know your eye sees things in detail. Nothing passes unnoticed. It gives me confidence knowing that you care especially for those that seek you. I feel you are a Father watching over me.

Big Eye I'm not perfect. I'm not a spiritual powerhouse yet. There are only a few scattered blocks and even those are disjointed. I pray for spiritual help that includes a few blocks of virtue. Father I'm helpless. I can't build my own holiness. I might build them on air with no foundation. And every time a storm comes I collapse. That would be embarrassing for me. I've got to stand solid and endure the pain

Big Eye, I must start with a solid foundation before building spiritual blocks. I must be fixed firmly in the ground like the crucifix that Jesus hung on. In fact, my foundation is the cross. I remain humbly rooted at the foot of the cross. I'm praying at the feet of the Master. I cling to the Lord's feet as Christ helps me to kick the grip of demons that constantly drags me into the mire and dirt of the world. I beg from this position for Christ to forgive me and have mercy on me.

Big Eye, once my foundation is secure I can begin to build spiritual blocks. I lay each one carefully and each one raises higher and higher into the heart and mind of Christ, my true Master. With your help Big Eye, I name each beautiful block with a holy inscription. At the moment I am on the first layer and this one has the inscription of humility. It's a lowly position at the foot of the cross. Here I learn to be humble. I'm not important. I cling to the feet of Jesus. It's like been born again. I crawl from the gutter of sin and cling to the feet of Jesus. I'm happy to receive help from my Lord and God. The spiritual life begins from this base.

Big Eye, I accept the block and spiritual gift of humility to begin with. In it I realise how holy and wonderful you are in comparison to me being nothing. By this gift of humility, I am able to see for the first time your greatness Lord Jesus. There were thick layers of pride blocking this vision.

Father, build me up. I desire more holy blocks to move up to your Son's heart. I need another layer. Pull me up to the Body and Blood of your Son. I can't live on humility alone.

Big Eye, I seek ways to increase closeness between us. I aim to do it through prayer and faith. I choose the Golden Egg technique. I hallow your Holy Name. At the foot of the cross I pray those words with more intensity. The Holy Name is Sacred. It's the secret that unlocks entry into God's heart. I don't know how to generate passion. But I'm aware of a lack of it. Contemplation and meditation on the Master's Word should generate sincere prayer.

Big Eye, I call you Father. The penny has dropped. If I pray to you as Father this implies strongly that I am a son. I'm probably an adopted spiritual son. I'll settle for that Father. So can I call you my Father in heaven? I perceive you to be Sacred, Holy and Beautiful. So my Father is outstanding in character. Nothing but goodness will come from this Father. I love it. This is focus. This is brilliant. This is Power in God's Name. There is life in his Name. I adore my Father now. Holy! Holy! Holy is his Name! Think Liam.

Big Eye, I'm a dot. You are Almighty. You see the bee, the ant, and the fly – tiny little things. I'm like that in your scale of things - a small dot on road L0909. And for you Big Eye to love me – a small little man among millions drives me crazy with excitement. I'm more determined than ever to silence the mouth and calm the mind in the hope that your deep secrets may break into the faculty of the soul so that I can treasure you forever. I pray for significant realisations that the true meanings of the word <u>hallow</u> are permanently applied through my mind every time I hear or use the Name Big Eye. There can't be any slip up. Big Eye is Sacred. I'm obliged to worship.

Chapter Twenty-One

Big Eye

Liam, I am the Father of all. I'm your Father in heaven. I access the whole world and see everything. I admire magnificent cities throughout the world. I observe towns, villages and houses in rural areas. I see all activities. Humans can't hide. I see sky life. I see road life. Automobiles! People working! Children at school!

I see Churches dedicated to my Son. I notice all who attend Mass. I see cars parked at sports events. I see those in bed. I see sinners too. I witness evil acts. Remember Little Man I see everything. I see a frog underneath a stone. I see a snail crossing the road. I see foxes and hares hit by cars. I know everything. You don't have to have a library of knowledge. There is only one thing that I desire you to know – and that is Me. Love me and life is yours.

Little Man

I love you Big Eye. I really do. All I want is you. There are huge improvements in my life. I'm happier and it's because of you, Most High. I'm in love with you. I practise this love now starting with family. For if I can't love those beside me, the chances are that I'm not on the right side of Big Eye.

Big Eye I had a beautiful morning. I promised myself to be good to my son. We went to Mass but as usual he didn't listen to a word. But I was still nice. I've come to the conclusion that I love you by loving my family. The world of human life is all about loving each other. I love every person on earth and that includes enemies. I love my wife and son and mother most all. These are my special three.

Big Eye you are love. You are unique, warm and beautiful. My love for you is paramount to anything else. I have no doubt whatsoever that it is you Big Eye that enlightens my soul and brightens my face. I've passed that belief onto my son. I encourage him to love Jesus.

After Mass we went for a long walk in the nearby forest. It was great and healthy. I advised my little boy to greet everyone warmly and positively. He accepted my message. In the new De Vere Cafe Shop we had refreshments. I advised my boy to look people in the eye during conversations. I looked my boy in the eye. It was a glorious morning. I was happy walking and talking with my son. I loved it. I love life. I see clearly now. I love God by loving my boy.

Big Eye

Liam, I'm glad you begin to see with my eyes. A holy vision of life is valuable. You can't see me if you're blind to the person on a wheel chair. You must love people Liam. People suffer. You must love Syrian migrants. You must love widows Liam. You must love those who trespass against you. You must love all. You must love the broken-hearted. You must love those who abuse you. You must love those who laugh at you. You must be a slave for all. You must be a servant for all. That is the true test of love. I'll test your genuineness. I'll test your holiness.

Liam, I caution you. There's a weakness in your prayer. The results cause frostiness between us. It also allows problems to overwhelm you. You are beaten if that happens. It happens due to your weak mind losing concentration on me. You must be strong and confident. You can't stand by and allow worms eat you. These annoying creatures come in the form of a worrying mind and a mind with insurmountable problems. These worms suck the life out of you.

Liam, pray to me always. Pray for discernment. You must know the name of the spirit that's at work in you. If a person snaps at you hold firm. If a person contradicts you keep calm. If a person is wasteful remain prudent. If a person is depressed stay bright. Liam, transcend situations. Don't allow yourself to be dragged into messy arguments and dissension.

Liam, I have advised you on building your house on a solid foundation. You have already enwrapped yourself in one layer of blocks and that is to have the mentality of a meek man. And the next layer of blocks that sits nicely on meekness is peace. I love a soul that desires peace. Nothing should disturb a peaceful man's mind. You could throw boulders at him and he wouldn't budge. You could torment him with wave upon wave of irritating problems and it wouldn't cause him to waver. Nothing shall erode my gift of Peace. The force of evil spirits could charge like raging bulls and my Man of Peace would still remain standing. Liam I tell you solemnly that my Gift of Peace could withhold ferocious attacks and storms. I love the peaceful man.

However, Liam, watch carefully. I don't want you capitulating under pressure from external disturbances. In the course of a single day numerous attacks will occur to upset your peaceful disposition. And the funny thing about this is that nobody knows the suddenness of when a sharp attack may occur. Watch carefully. A hot potato is hard to handle. Unbearable pressure maybe more than you could handle. The kitchen sink could be thrown at you. There are a lot of wicked people and evil demons at work in the world.

Liam dear, what's important through all the onslaughts against you is that you keep your eye on me. It's vital that you hold on to the feet of my Son at the base of the cross. My power travels through my Son. With me you can win. No force of nature can rock my Peace.

Liam unspiritual souls erupt easily. The slightest little remark could start a massive row. People are on edge and very volatile. They blow a fuse over nothing. I've seen it Liam. It could be a remote control, or a hairbrush, or a sneaky glance, or a shirt, or money, or food. People blow a fuse over silly things.

Liam, people are unhappy and depressed morally. Everything seems fine socially and economically. But there is a moral crisis. People's spiritual and mental state has descended into an epidemic. Liam, believe me. I have never seen the morale of people to drop so low. It's very, very dangerous because it pinpoints for me that the light of my Son in each soul has more or less quenched. And that is a sad state for the world to be in.

Liam I desire balance in each person. They can have a bit of fun, share in the economy and pray a bit too. But to abandon me and my Son is a worrying trend.

Liam, I could send a man of peace among them. But the forces of evil and dark irreligious souls have no conscience. I could see wicked men bark, snap, shout, and bite at my beloved man of peace and tear him to pieces over nothing. So I recommend patience and a few more virtuous blocks to be built before facing evil forces.

Little Man

Big Eye, I thank you for warning me. I'm more determined than even to cling to you and hold firm at the foot of the cross. I want to climb up from the gutter. I want to move up higher and higher from the underworld and the world of human life. I desire to crawl upwards from the foot of the cross and climb high into sublime areas of Divine Life through complete union with your Body and Blood.

Most Sacred Father, I have tasted Divine life and I like it. More than anything else Holiness of Life attracts me. I don't glory in wisdom. Neither do I glory in my strength. Nor do I glory in richness. Nor do I glory in beautiful women. I only want to glory in you Big Eye. Herein is the greatness of man. I truly know what is great. I cling to it. I only seek glory in Big Eye. I seek friendship and love from you, my Most Sacred Father.

Big Eye it is not easy. I know what it is like to struggle in the gutter. I know what it is like to be unpopular. I have been there. I remember a time I didn't want to go to Mass or mix with anyone. It was like a dark night of the soul. I really sank into a depression. I felt no one cared for me or loved me. I stayed in bed and felt sick. I skipped Morning Prayer with the brethren. In my isolation and desolation, I accepted been a loner and it bordered on expulsion from religious life. But during that time I did something that saved my life. I wrote my feelings into a hardback book every day. I addressed my feelings to you Big Eye. I updated Jesus every day and recorded all my irritations. I was like a child spilling everything that was in my mind to Jesus, my brother and that saved my life.

Chapter Twenty-Two

Big Eye

Liam, my friend I value you your love and friendship. I have noticed how sincere you are in that quiet room near the Atlantic Ocean. I'm glad there is a scholar left in the world to fight for the traditions and conservation of a small but great nation. I'm glad you are not in favour of a social revolution. I'm delighted that you long for the traditions of your forefathers like St Patrick, St Columba, and all who stood up for my Son in your country through persecution and turbulent times.

Liam, I have serious issues to discuss with you. Try and not be distracted by little things. There's too much importance attached to small fry. All these unimportant little things take away from commitment and devotion to me. In saying that though Liam, I regard attention to detail very important. I ask you to monitor what is swimming around in your head. It's possible to use a tweezers to pinch the flies, or to pluck the small fry from what floats around in your mind. All modern human minds require cleansing.

Liam in carrying out my order I pave the way for great love. You see Liam I'm not a rat. This animal would rummage through a dirty compost bin for food. I dislike rummaging through a dirty mind for love. If you can turn to me Liam and love me I have something special in reward for you. I like your warmth Liam. From heaven I transmit rays of love into your heart and mind. It bonds us together. It's like a covenant. It's a relationship. My Son and I will make our home in you.

Liam, I think you know although you don't articulate it very well is that success for a human life is based entirely on his/her love for me. I gave your life. I know your parents. They are good. I saw you as a baby. I saw your family home by the river Suir. I saw you grow up. I watched you growing. And I know what's in your heart and mind. I will also be there when you grow old and die. I am in charge of life. There are births and deaths every day.

Liam, I see you knocking at my door and I want so much to respond to you. There's a huge divide between Divine and human life. I'm Big Eye. You are a Little Man. I have responsibility for heaven and earth, and all galaxies in existence. You have responsibility for nothing. I don't know how I'm going to relate to you. Nor do I know what you truly want.

It's one thing to hear you use the word desire but it is something else to feel its vibrancy in action. Desire for me is honourable. But I know a temper explosion could blow the blocks of humility and peace sky high. Where am I then in relation to a tempestuous Little Man?

Liam, I know one factor that is coming into play between us and it's important. You have given me permission to touch your life. I see it as funny because the difference between the size of me and you are enormous. Liam, think of a butterfly or a ladybird. The size of them to you is enormous. I'm like that with my creatures.

Liam, you could sit on my finger. I could hold you in my hand. I could tickle your mind. I can touch you externally and internally. Are you put off by my size? It is extraordinary for me to pick up a tiny little man and caress him. It's lovely watching your little movements of feet, hands, head and eyes. I want to rub the stress out of your head by stroking you. Liam, I want my life in you. I'm a jolly God. I want to play and laugh with my creature. So I am all on for the best relationship possible with a human soul.

But don't forget Liam I am perfect. The complications in relationships with humans arise from the day when Adam and Eve ate of the forbidden fruit and their eyes were opened. The first man and woman disobeyed me. They hid from me and didn't want me.

Little Man

Big Eye, I'm delighted with what I'm learning through conversations with you. And I'm extra careful to heed what you say rather than compete with you as an equal. Big Eye, can you see the sweetness in my life that comes from you? I'm over the moon with joy that comes through a sixth sense that you are Present and love from you emanates into the fabric of my being.

I see my book as a preparation for death. I want all human beings to know that I'm not departing the world without saying goodbye to my brothers and sisters who have to live on and struggle. I also want everyone to know that I did my best to be Big Eye's friend. And I add that I do love the poor and sick. I feel for everyone with poor health and misfortune. I'm aware of those in hospital. I'm aware of sinners and prisoners. Big Eye, I love them and pray for them. I love the Catholic Church.

Holy Father, changes occur in my life every day. Your way is perfect. I'm willing to change. I offer my soul to you Father. I do my best to understand you. I do my best to satisfy you. You are awesome. Your love is breath-taking. I express it in this book.

I stole a yard on every other person but I don't care. I make no apology for finding love with God our Father. People wouldn't know anyway. They are too busy with their own lives. They don't need to know. I wouldn't tell them.

Holy Father, my beautiful prayer reaches your ears. I send a sweet prayer of love to you. I love your Sacred Name. I feel contrite and humble. I'm at your Son's feet feeling afflicted for all who are suffering terribly throughout the world. The pain of others is everyone's pain. I pray for a future generation of great men and women who would devote their lives to the welfare of the sick, sinners and poor. I cannot feel justified loving you Holy Father if I don't practise what I write by loving my sick family members and neighbours, and all who suffer terribly through injustices, war, and poverty.

Big Eye, I kneel in awe before your great gaze. I block my lips and remain still. I have nothing to say except to enjoy you. I'm overawed by your Majestic and Splendid Sacredness. I'm still before you as I attempt to quieten my mind.

Big Eye, what value has a human brain and what should we use them for? What ideas are in the minds of men and women? What's the quality of each person's prayer life? Does language condition us? I'd love to concentrate on you with the naked eye and naked ear to discover your Presence and beauty.

Big Eye I dislike pressure and the bombardment of the brain by happenings in the world, and local news and nationwide events. I desire to gaze upon you with a pure mind and clear heart. I think of all seven billion people on the face of the earth and wonder about what's in their heads. How many genuinely seek you Holy Father and God of All? At what level is our intelligence? What person on earth today has a beautiful and magnificent mind? Is there anyone using their mind to make that vital connection with you, Big Eye?

Holy Father, I attend your Son's Church on Sunday mornings and before Mass begins I hear a clattering of noises. It's not people praying. They are talking to each other loudly. Why are they not praying? What are they thinking about? I thought the Church was a Sacred Place. Maybe they don't understand. At least they attend Church. Their faith is simple. They are inside God's house. Who am I to judge anyway? I must concentrate on my own efforts to pray and teach my son Luke to do the same.

Big Eye

Liam I love you. I don't want to call you Little Man anymore. I want to call you by name. You are an important human being. You are great. It's because you have the right attitude towards me and humanity. A person is more important than religion. You are precious. You place people before religion. The value of a person is greater upholding a system of beliefs.

But I do insist Liam on reverence for Saints. I include greats of the past like Abraham, Moses, Elijah, Isaiah, and David. I also insist on respect for the Apostles and all holy men and women who showed outstanding courage and holiness throughout their lives. All these prepared their hearts to love me, cleansed their flesh, weeded out vices and sowed virtues. I sprinkled these souls with showers of grace.

Liam I desire a similar route for you. Don't mind the men talking at the back of the Church. I ask you like St John the Apostle and St John the Baptist to love my Son Jesus Christ. Jesus is a Sacred Person. I tell you to respect and love him. St John saw a beautiful mind in Christ, and he felt the love my Messiah had for every person. John was close to my Son and his gospel more than any other writer depicts a unity of love that can never be matched. By St John's writings a human soul can now unite in a unique way with us - a Trinity of Divine Beings. This is Super Golden Egg territory. Insights are within grasp here. I recommend contemplative prayer action on the Word made Flesh. I solemnly recommend becoming a friend of St John, Liam. His love for me was rich and he was the closest to my Son, Jesus Christ. I want you to experience that rich source of love.

Liam, John the Baptist pointed to my Son too. He lost his life for opposing a wrongdoing. This St John put up with no nonsense. And he spoke the truth. But I want to point out to you the respect he had for my Son Jesus. This is an area that you require brushing up on. John felt he wasn't worthy enough to undo the straps of Jesus' sandals. Liam, think about it. My Son is Sacred. I'm not sure if you grasp that or not.

There isn't any point in going any further if you can't show reverence for my Son's Name. Liam you mentioned above in your writing that you were at the feet of my Son. Do you really believe that? You sometimes act as if you are his equal. You have got to have the mentality of the Baptist. There has to be an increase in my Son's influence in your life. And puncture your pride.

Remember those who did kneel at my Son's feet crying for help as well as humbling themselves before him because they realised there was something special about him. I know you love the cross Liam. It connects you to my Son. I'm grateful for that. Do spend time kneeling and praying at the foot of the Cross. It is through my Son that you will find the Way, the Truth and the Life.

Liam, respect is a leading contender in the formation of a Saint. Remember the woman I choose from all the women on earth to be the Mother of my Son. What was said about her? She's blessed among women. She's beautiful Liam, very holy and humble. She's full of grace. I intend Liam to clean you up and make you holy and pure. I say this to you because you have for a long period of time shown commitment to me. I'm taking you on board. You served a long apprenticeship.

Liam respect is the key word. I have that from you. It doesn't matter about famous religious people. I look for someone today and you fit that description Liam. You have become very religious. My eye is on you.

Chapter Twenty-Three

Little Man

Heavenly Father, I'm honoured to converse with you. I love the things that you say about me. But I'm still vulnerable to aggressive outbursts. Nobody knows the place or minute for these mental volcanic outbursts to occur. Something definitely triggers it off. I'm worried about them.

Father, I don't deserve a call from you for that reason alone. It was my downfall in the past. And it's there to this very day. Father, you have some great priests in the Church. There are marvellous lay people who work for charitable organisations. These groups help the poor and underprivileged in society? My friend became a bishop? Pope Francis, Cardinals, and bishops follow your Son faithfully. These are the cream of the Church and much loved by you. Father I'm unworthy of a place at your table. Nobody has heard of me. I've achieved nothing.

Big Eye, I admire outstanding National Leaders throughout the world. They have unbearable responsibility. Son of Man, how do they keep law and order in their countries? How do they feed large populations? How do they care for their sick? How do they educate and employ large multitudes of people? There are more people in the world now then there were in your Son's time. What role is mapped for me to play in the world?

Nobody has heard of me. I'm not even a cog in the wheel of these big countries. I can't change the world. I've no responsibility. I'm powerless. I couldn't stop Russia, or China, or Korea, or America from fighting a war. I'm powerless Son of Man. I couldn't stop great human powers from fighting. I have no influence. I couldn't influence a thirteen-year-old child to go to Mass. But I would love to influence the world by being a peacemaker. I'd like to offer an alternative to war and spread a gospel of peace to every soul on earth.

Big Eye

Liam, you have a short memory. I call you because you have declared your love for me. I respond to a sincere and upright heart. Your love is very sweet. I recognise your attempts to be spiritually washed every morning on your walks down the road. I'm aware of your efforts to hallow [sanctify] my Name. You have a sense of awe towards my magnificence. And you are humble enough not to seek the highest places at banquets. You are humble and sincere.

Liam, we must bond. We must cement unity. We must be of one mind, one heart and one spirit. I wouldn't tolerate disparity. Remember I'm God. I'm perfect. There is no flaw in me. You're not. You depend on me. You are vulnerable to change and your levels of goodness is like a seesaw – going from bad to good and good to bad.

Liam, there are always snakes in the grass that can slip through every brain cell and destroy every good intention you have. There are also worms everywhere that if you are not on guard would eat you. These are all the little worrying things in life that eat away at your every attempt to love me. Liam you must go after these creatures and destroy them. The snakes and worms drag at your resolve to remain loyal and erode your strength to hold onto my Son at the foot of the cross. Shake them off. Have a spiritual wash every morning.

Liam I warn you to be on the alert for rampaging demons. These angry beasts rampage and attack suddenly. These hate peaceful and humble souls. Their teeth stick out and they snarl at you. Their point of attack is when you are off guard.

Liam, also watch for demons in others. These are bad spirits. Unexpectedly they jump from a bad soul into an unprotected soul in an instant. Watch carefully! How many times do you lose your temper? Who causes it? It's a bad spirit in another person jumping into your mind. And this causes a backlash resulting in a temperamental response. And because you lose your temper you are to blame.

But you know what to do. Liam, keep my Son's Word close to your heart. Pray to me. Pray to me. My Son taught you. Pray for protection from temptation. Pray for deliverance from evil. Those two petitions are safeguards. Pray them Liam. They are huge in your fight against evil and immensely important for spiritual progress.

Little Man

Holy Father! I love you deeply. Holy God! I'm sorry for my sins. Thank you very much for your good counsel in teaching me to be on guard against worms, snakes and wicked imps. I intend to do my best to keep calm when stirred up by a prowling demon.

Big Eye, I'm grateful for this chance to write to you every day. I love it. I retired from the drudgery of supermarket work to concentrate on been your friend. Big Eye I don't want to be a source of begrudging and jealousy if I have stolen a step or two to outsmart everyone else in Ireland and around the world by finding a new way to love you. I'm entitled to love you in every way possible.

I'm going to do my very best after many years trying to take the sugar out of my body by drinking water at every opportunity possible. The intake of sweet foods has prevented spiritual progress for years. This is a Friday – a traditional fast day and it is also Lent. I drink water only today.

Big Eye, could I hurt others if I moved up from the foot of the cross into the love of your heart. Would it be a source of jealousy for others? Wait a minute! Check. I'm not greater than anyone else. And greatness is not about moving up the ladder to Christ's heart and mind. It's about going back down the ladder and helping in the Church and assisting all who suffer. It's in helping others that greatness is achieved. I couldn't proceed in a race where there are losers. I can't accept that. Is it a joke?

I don't want to be greater than my wife, my son, my mother, my father, my brothers and my sisters. I'm not on a par with bishops, cardinals and Saints. I'm an ordinary little man and low in the order of importance. I'm nothing. Nor do I have anything.

But there is only one thing I desire. It's you Big Eye. It's you Sacred Truth. I love my God more than anything else. My heart is like a sponge that absorbs a beautiful feeling of love. It saturates my whole being with a joyous feeling. I chase my God of Truth and know that I'll never be deceived. I want permanent Love. I want a lasting relationship.

I believe my personal love for Big Eye can happen. The question though is can I achieve my desire outside the Church? Do I have to belong to a religion? Do I need a Buddha, or a Mohammad, or a Christ? I'm drawn to the words in the Scriptures where Christ encouraged believers to worship in spirit and truth. I think worship can occur through both avenues – the walk down the road and the drive to Church. Sometimes people praying together help more. It's also a question of internal disposition. The Church worshipper might rely too much on the ministerial leader and as a result fail to prod their own hearts and minds into sincere efforts to pray.

Big Eye

Liam. I have my eye on everyone. Every human being is my concern. I'm above divisions in all religions. I'm definitely not a sectarian God. I seek sincere worshippers all over the earth. I'm neither the Allah of Islam nor the God of Christians. I'm the Father of the Son of Man who cares for every person on earth. It doesn't matter if you are Catholic or Protestant. It doesn't matter if you are a Shiite or Sunni. I'm the God of everyone

Liam, I love all Nations. There should be no fighting. My Name is Peace. But war occurs when human beings lose the spark that connects them to me. People become raw animals when they don't have my Spirit in them. I command nobody to kill in my Name. That's not religion. That's a lie. That's hatred. It's evil. It's rather inhuman butchering people because they are Muslim or Christian or some other ethnic group.

Liam, I have an eye for everyone and my preference is for sincere and humble souls. I can find such souls anywhere around the world. I look for two things in prayer. One is a sincere effort to worship me in spirit and truth. Your prayer has to be passionate. I want an unquenchable desire and a strong love from my worshippers. I'm not on good terms with lukewarm love.

Liam, do you understand my Word. I accept everyone. I loved the Jews and for hundreds of years they were my chosen people. But their mentality became divisive and corrupt in the sense that they were favourites and all others were pagans who knew nothing about me. My Son had a different mentality and he found a true religion where sinners, the poor, the oppressed and the sick were a priority.

Liam, I accept every one. Nationality doesn't matter. My Son Jesus didn't care who you were and he gave every person an opportunity to love me. In my eyes you are a man or woman first. I never excluded or divided people from my plan. Ethnic division was manmade. Non-Jews felt the blunt of segregation. I did favour Israel as my chosen people but not to the extent of ostracising anyone who desired to worship me.

Liam, I'm all for inclusion. I love my creation. I see no difference between poor and rich. All are one family and belong to a world made by me. I care for everyone. In fact, I lean more towards the poor and sick rather than the healthy and rich.

Little Man

Father, I love Divine Life. It's perfect. I find human relationships tough. It's because of what's stuck in the mind and heart of every human being. People defy me when I try to do so much for them. People are ungrateful. People boss and use me. It's why I love solitude. Human relationships are imperfect.

Big Eye I can't change people. I haven't the power and skills to convert levels of badness into the path of virtue. The stubborn and defiant will even in small children is beyond repair. You see Father the cheek and ingratitude in people. I don't know how you maintain any level of patience with the human race.

God our Father, what would you like me to do? A virtuous seismic change is impossible. In fact, if you ask me Big Eye for the truth I would tell you that there has been in recent years a massive decline in respecting and doing what you want.

Two men can marry now. They pay a large sum of money for a surrogate mother. These children are deprived of a relationship with their natural mother. A male can never substitute for a female.

Politicians have become gods. They have changed your ways Heavenly Father. I'm deeply worried for the future of our people. I dislike new legislations in recent years that fly in the face of you Big Eye. The men that died a century ago to win freedom for our country were deeply spiritual men. They fought for our Christian values and our way of life only for a century later to find their successors dismantle bit by bit our once great Christian heritage. It's really sad.

Father I couldn't influence a child to go to Mass so what chance have I to convert the world to adopt the religion your Son found. Islam has a longer history than Christianity and they don't accept that your Son was Divine. I can't change that. Even if I tried I would be expelled, imprisoned or martyred. My late friend Bishop William was expelled from a Muslim country due to his influence as a Christian witness. When the Government of a country is the same as the religion of a country conversion is impossible.

God our father, how is Fr William? After he was expelled for his religious beliefs in a Muslim country he returned to our House of Studies in Dublin where he became my spiritual director during my formation years. Fr William was deeply spiritual. He turned my life around as I fought loneliness through a dark period. It was during a time when I was run down, depressed and unsure of myself. I wasn't sure if I was good enough to be a priest. This holy man influenced me. He reassured me that I had a vocation. He pointed to the importance of Christ, your Son. He thought me how to contemplate and be aware of the inner life. Fr William, thank you my holy friend. I'll remember you to the very last breath of my life.

Big Eye

Liam, you are preaching again on a scale that is louder than my Word. I'm well aware of religious differences and the power of Muslims.

My Son has dealt with it. And please allow Doctors of the Church to study and write about the amalgamation of my Truth by every worshipper whatever their religion.

Liam, I all for the Catholic faith because its founder is both Divine as well as being my Son. I'd prefer the whole world to accept the Way of Life mapped out for you by my Son's gospel. My Son is a Divine Messiah. My Son of Man has given every one of you a chance to be saved. The simple choice is there for you to reject or accept. I'll not force anyone to love me.

Liam, my Son sits at my right hand in heaven. I have made him King and his cross is stuck in the ground for all seven billion human beings to see. There are no excuses for those that reject my Son.

Liam, you know your stuff. There's no division in me. Division is manmade and buttressed by demons I expelled from heaven millions of years ago. They are still active and scavenging the earth for weak and vulnerable souls.

Liam, follow my Son. He is the Way, the Truth and the Life. If you love me follow my Son. Liam, you must break the chains that impede you from following me. The words Way, Truth and Life Are Golden Eggs. There can be no let-up in striving for the Way. It will bring you to Truth and Life. This is a tremendous promise. It is hard work. So I warn lazy men to rise up before it is too late.

Liam, my Son has authority over man. No one has understood his Divine title; Son of Man. This Man has authority and great power. He made the blind see and the deaf hear. He welcomes sinners and shows compassion towards all. He calms storms.

Look Liam, let's return to basics. You can't compete with me on world issues. All I ask of you is your love. Work on that Liam. I've told you this before. You are a dot lost in the world. You are not a god. The way forward for you is to follow the Way, the Truth and the Life. In other words, follow my Son Jesus Christ. World affairs are out of your depth. I tell you solemnly those three words are a minefield of treasures. You would do well to spend months pondering over their meaning.

Chapter Twenty-Four

Little Man

Big Eye, I'm sorry for trying to explore and discover things outside of my remit. And I'm sorry for grumbling and criticizing. I'm sorry for been mean with anyone and for been ambiguous in my dealings with people. I'm sorry for displaying irritability with those that don't follow my good advice. I have no right to judge anyone. In fact, by judging others I kill any little bit of grace that is within me. The way to deal with irritations no matter how big or small is to proceed with compassion and patience. If my son doesn't wash his teeth, I gently remind him of it.

I'm sorry Father. Mercy is high on the list of Beatitudes. I beg for your mercy every day. I find discipline tough. Prayer conquers you, Big Eye. I allow you Father to spiritually wash me. I'm dirty with sins. They are hidden in closets going back five decades or more. Father, wash me.

Big Eye, I know what you like. You treasure obedience from little men and women around the world. I'm called to honour my father and mother. It's about time I came to my senses. I'm commanded to honour you Father.

Big Eye, I obey. I smashed Satan in the nose when he interfered with my good intentions to obey you. I beat him back. Satan is telling me to disobey you. I'm like the prodigal son who was lost and dead. I return home to my Father and say I'm sorry with a contrite heart. I must not lose patience with anyone or try and change people. Satan likes me to fight and attack. This wryly snake has the ability to wrap my good intentions in knots. He loves to frustrate me. The devil deflates my confidence. I feel upset but it's my fault because I want to change people who are weeds into flowers, and when they don't change it results in feelings of disappointment. And it's hard to love you Holy Father when upset.

Big Eye

Liam, I understand your impatience with yourself and your frustrations in relationships with others. In other to proceed calmly you require confidence and emotional skills to grapple what's rampaging through your mind. You handle situations badly. Always move prudently and peacefully and avoid using force or shouting.

Liam, follow through with your advice and ensure the corrective action is adhered to. Otherwise loopholes will result and more than likely bad habits replace good intentions. I'd like you to put into practise good habits like going for a walk instead of lazing about watching television.

Liam, set aside time every day for praying and writing. If events overtake you and you can't manage your time you fail in your love for me. It tells me that your mind isn't strong enough to curb intrusions. There isn't any point in telling me that you love me if your soul is weak and timid.

Liam my Doctrine is clear. You can only love me if you love one another. I hear words Liam down the road every morning that you love me. But your mind and heart is disconnected. It's because your head is stuffed with worry. It's because you are not finding a quiet spot every day for prayer to me. I'm not attracted to a soul that allows a woman to occupy the inner place that ought to be reserved for me.

Liam, you are tired at the moment and busy with family commitments. You feel you are given the run-around. This scenario affects your quality of love for me. It restricts the examination of your mind and you can't subject your inmost thoughts to a true scrutiny. To receive Liam a guest such as me you must have a clear mind. It is love Liam that covers a multitude of sins and love too is the sum of all virtues.

Liam. I'm waiting. I want an outburst of passionate love from you. I'm put off by words that are disconnected from your mind and heart.

I saw you at Mass this morning and I didn't hear one passionate word from your mouth. I hope my message is clear. What I want is your love. I want to hear your heartfelt voice every day. Even your walks and prayers down the road are running dry of emotion for me.

Little Man

Hello Father! I'm struggling. I can't unite myself to you by the affection of my love. I'm not a saint. I'm nowhere near been a holy man. I don't understand key concepts taught by your son. I'm struggling with your benevolence towards scumbags, thugs, perverts, murderer, suicide bombers, prisoners, rapists, drunks and violent robbers. Big Eye, are you asking us to show mercy to unrepentant sinners? I'm not happy at all. I'd be afraid bad people would reoffend. It has happened. I suppose a Programme of Mercy could be put in place for sinners to make a contrite and complete conversion before releasing them from prison. Isn't that what happened with the woman caught committing adultery? Nobody condemned her but she was told to go and sin no more.

Father, I'm stressed out by many things. I see myself in the character of Martha at the time your Son Jesus visited her home. I'm concerned with my workload. Often I find myself doing one thing while at the same time three other tasks are knocking at the door of my mind seeking attention too. I want so much to sit down and Jesus' feet and listen to him. But I have to collect children and cook the dinner, and bring them to activities.

What's happening to me? The sun shines. The water flows. The birds sing. But my head is in a mess. I'm no saint while in this condition. Father, how do I multi task? I want so much to love you and dedicate my time to you. My wife is sick and it has trebled my workload. I've hundreds of little tasks to do and can't do the thing I want to do. I want to wrap my hands around you and love you, Big Eye.

My Father in heaven I call you. Help me to refocus and make up. How on earth could I possibly believe that there is the potential within me to be saintly? What' gone wrong? Have you abandoned me? I don't feel your Presence. There is nothing to put a smile on my face.

Big Eye, where have you gone? Maybe you were called to an emergency meeting. I have to wait. I don't feel your loving Presence Father. I feel more like your Mother Mary on that dark day when your Son dragged that heavy cross up to Calvary.

O Big Eye, you are my God. I long for your touch. I'm a lost son pining for my Father. I long for your loving touch Father. I presume you are busy. Anyway why should a Powerful God bother with one single little man?

If you are busy Father tell me. I can wait. I could spend time reading about your Son. He is Divine too. The complete Truth is in the Son. I'll befriend you. I switch to Jesus. After all Jesus is the Way, Truth and Life. And if Jesus hasn't time I switch to a Doctor of the Church. I long for contact with someone from heaven for I need spiritual help.

Big Eye

Liam, I dislike you switching to someone else when you have difficulty with me your Father. So stop it Liam! I have no time for unfaithfulness. I want you to wait and you failed the test. So stop the clock. Stop time and take stock of where you are with me. It's a lack of respect not to wait for me. And anyway if you prayed properly that feeling of coldness towards me wouldn't occur.

Liam you can't crumble as soon as I attend another budding saint. This experience shows how feeble your confidence and love is towards me. As soon as I step outside the door you fall apart. Come on Liam! It's not the end of the world. You will receive knocks in life. Your brain will struggle to cope at times. It's not the time for a panic attack. I like my disciples to stand up and be strong when I'm at a task in another place around the globe. All faith, all hope and all love shouldn't quench or die once I focus on a challenge from a major enemy. I'm busy Liam and can't stay with you always.

So Liam I ask you to calm down. I'm not far away. My finger nudges you. It will calm you and heal you. My holy touch will restore your love. In fact, my Presence in proximity with your spot on earth is more than enough to burn away all anxieties and worries that you have. My Holiness is a fire that burns everything that's wicked in your heart and mind.

Therefore, Liam you should feel better now. My Sacred Touch heals. Unless impatience is buried there can be little progress up the spiritual ladder. I know you mean well. I know correcting faults is a good thing. But you are wrong in the manner in which it is done. You don't correct calmly. You react and it causes anxious tension in yourself and in the recipient of the correction. I intend to do some mind work with you from the point of view of helping you to cope with losing control in contentious situations.

Little Man

Hi Big Eye. I feel better already. You can do whatever you like with me. You have free access to my mind. I fully welcome you to influence my free will. I'm open to you Father. I hide nothing for I trust you. Therefore, sift through all the chambers of my intellect. You know what's inside. You created me. You know of the rusty and unused cells that require repair.

Father, take your time. Take as long as you want. I welcome any help available. I welcome spiritual builders. I welcome Doctors of the Church. I welcome most of all the Son of Man. Holiness comes from allowing holy work to commence on building a sacred inner mansion.

Big Eye, I'll all in favour of a truthful renovation. I've no problem with a tough saint or angel sent to hack any dirt stuck in the eye. I'd like to bury all past sins. I know plenty went in through the eye. I also allow holy saints to stand guard at my ears and remove all the garbage accumulate over the years that blocks clear opportunities to hear the Word made flesh.

Big Eye, I'm all for the removal of obstacles and mud stuck in the ear and eye. These are bad bits of mortar stuck in the soul for years. St Anselm, my friend, drill them out. I fully consent to you to drive a spiritual bulldozer through the channels of my eyes and ears to rip away hidden sins or anything nasty that prevents spiritual progress.

I'm delighted with you St Anselm. I saw you crush impatience and every other bit of solid vermin stuck on the walls that pass through to the inner ear and eye. I welcome on my knees help from heaven.

Big Eye holy sentries are needed at the entrance to the eyes and ears. I'm all for rooting out badness and plucking out black, bad weeds. O Jesus! I'm shocked with the state of my soul. I can't believe the massive task your team had Big Eye is pulling up dogged roots of pride, sloth and anger. I didn't think my soul was that dirty and wicked? I'm ashamed Father. I'm embarrassed with what your saints and angels discovered. I thought I was a good man.

Big Eye, help me to change. I'm very reliant on your eye and it's my only hope. I'll all for renovation. In all walks of life, it's good to change. The same applies to old buildings. The splatters of sin must go. The musty and damp walls require fresh plaster. The creaking doors need oil. All rooms need a new look. Big Eye, I'm up for the task. You can turn me upside down and inside out in order to create a new body and soul. I'm sure you wouldn't want an old derelict house to make your home in.

Big Eye, I don't care how long the renovation of my soul takes once holy souls like St Anselm are working on the interior of my spiritual life. I want a lot of rooms inside my head and each one named to replace vices. I can think of two new interior designs to begin with. I want to close the door of my old room of impatience and move into my new room sweet with the virtue of patience. I also visualise closing the door from an old room of undisciplined eating habits and move into a brand new room full of the graces that come from a strict diet of fasting. In this beautifully decorated room I feed from your dishes Big Eye.

Big Eye, I'm very happy again. I feel like a new man. I'm laughing at St Anselm on the imaginary bulldozer driving rats and mice, and every kind of hidden vermin out of little nests hidden in my soul. I love it. I'm clean. I'm delighted. I give full and total permission to knock every old room in my house that harbours dangerous sharks that spawned everywhere within my sick and sinful mind. St Anselm, drive on. St

Anselm, push on. If need be knock the walls and build new ones. For I see snakes hidden behind stones. As you drive forward Anselm into all the chambers of my intellect I see a massive clear-out.

Big Eye, I never realised that there could be so much dirt inside the soul. I am more than thankful to you Big Eye for sending me a Doctor of the Church like St Anselm to pave the way inside my old derelict soul and clearing it for the rebuilding of fresh and decorative rooms full of new virtues.

O Father, I'm forever grateful. I feel so different. The angry demons bulldozed out of my soul by St Anselm and thrown on the side of the road are angry. Their nests in my head have been destroyed. And they are begging on my soft nature to allow them return. I hear them howling and bawling. But I reject their return. My soul is fresh and clean now with new bright colours and each door into the rooms of my intellect has a new name – a name that is linked to the fruits of the Holy Spirit.

Big Eye, I haven't felt so tranquil for a long time. I'm not ashamed to welcome graceful saints now. The dirty old soul is gone. The dirtiness of my life held me back big time. And this state of being held me back in my friendship with your son Jesus. The state of my soul was so bad that a complete blockage occurred. The flow of grace was blocked by snails, snakes and worms and bits of dirt of every kind. I'm so happy with God's command that my friend St Anselm has powerfully assisted in cleansing my soul and allowing grace to flow freely once again into me. It feels like baptism all over again.

Big Eye

O Liam, you are very naive. The battle is ongoing. The demons hide in debris and could launch an attack unaware to you. You don't want those lovely new rooms of virtues to be invaded by spiders, or snakes or poisonous rats. So I warn you to be on guard and pray at every opportunity.

Liam, you don't know the future. You don't know what's around the corner. You feel good now. And holy work has been carried out on your soul. The advantage you have now is that the supply of grace is flowing freely again into your soul. And together we must prevent a sabotage that may cut you off again in the future. It pleases me immensely Liam to have a holy little man on earth. I know how much you love my Son. And I heard you this morning praying through a miniature version of the Mass as you walked quietly down the road. Liam I am delightfully happy with you.

Liam, I warn though that you stay awake. A surge of bad pressure like weather storms could bash against those new doors of yours and blacken the virtues that are written on the doors of your lovely new rooms. When you see these storms coming, run into the room that has my Peace written in the door. This room is beautiful Liam. You can meet my Son in there. And don't open the door until the storm is gone. I warn you of these things Liam because you are vulnerable. I wouldn't like to see you battered by an ugly and evil storm.

So Liam this is a work in progress. It's not completed. There are many forces to come at you yet and the more perfect you become the tougher are the tests ahead. For my adversary doesn't like losing battles for souls.

Liam, I have a team in place to help you from heaven. I'm aware of your love for and communion with men and women who were faithful to my Son. I had a meeting in heaven with these and all are willing to help. You are connected by the Eucharist and you are familiar with them. I know you love St Anselm so he is on the team. Also on the committee is Fr William, your former Spiritual director. I also added St Dominic whom you loved for his compassion for souls and ability to preach my Truth. Edward your father is on the committee too. He was a good family father and he gave you the seeds of the faith by praying the rosary with you every evening. This father also was a model of good example by attending Mass and confession regularly. Also on the team is St Catherine who has impressed you by her mystical writings that has influenced you. And lastly I include St Patrick to help you because you are Irish and this saint was the voice of the Irish.

Little Man

Big Eye, you are right. My spiritual growth isn't completed. More irritating squibs came my way in the last few hours. I need a good back up team to fight off surges of stress caused by disagreements and selfishness.

Big Eye, I write to tell you because you understand human life and the continual disagreements and breakdown in human relationships through to the strength of each person's free will. Some people are very difficult to get through too. And I know nobody would listen to my words. I believe what I say is important but most people don't want to hear me.

Big Eye, my advice is overruled and that hurts. I'm a man of my word but I had to backtrack and renege on a promise.

The second squib occurred on my way to town for a meeting. I choose a bad route for traffic blocked me in several places. I ran the risk of being late for my appointment.

A red mist attacked my mind and resulted in irritability. I cut corners and blasted with words drivers in my way. There were major traffic holdups and I had to detour. In the midst of the red mist I passed a police car and the possibility of being late incensed me.

Big Eye, I'm sorry. It was a day of two halves. The morning was beautiful. I began my journey content within myself. But the squibs in the afternoon caused flare ups and my peace of mind changed.

Chapter Twenty-Four

Big Eye

Liam, work on your mood swings that go from happiness to frustration in a quick space of time. The world is fine so enjoy the rest of the evening. Your little island on the West Coast of the Atlantic is lovely. The streams flow. The sun shines. The air is clean. Traffic flows. Cities are busy. Workers are on the move. I watch you all. Ireland is close to my heart. In the past generations of Irish people served me faithfully and the remnant of that tradition remain loyal.

But I wonder Liam how many are aware of me. You walk down the road praying to me every morning. You hear cars on the main road travelling in opposite directions. The world of human beings is hectic. But very few seek me. Very few think about me. Very few pray to me. And the few that do give as little time as possible. Yet your country is prosperous. There's plenty of food. Many talented students go through the educational ranks. So who is going to be interested in a religious book? What have you to sell Liam? What I'm trying to tell you Liam is that education is important for students but religion isn't. They all want good careers but I only play a bit role in their lives.

Liam, life without me isn't worth living. I watch all. I see millions of busy souls proudly driving behind the wheel and travelling somewhere. But I see no spark inside their souls. They are weary and tired, and unhealthy due to diet and lifestyle. I love Ireland and all through the century's saints came up from Ireland to heaven. But the present generation forget me. There's no holy man or woman to lead. So I hope your writing might reach a few souls and turn back the clock to the traditions of the past. That is why I include St Patrick on your team for in the fifth century he converted the Irish from paganism to my Son Jesus and the Catholic way of life. I hope your writing might bring back the lost who have abandoned me in favour of a social revolution that excludes my involvement.

Liam, I've travelled with your people like I once did with Moses through their times of hardship. It was tough in Ireland. I've seen your struggles. Things are never perfect. But there are good people among you. And I admire the effort of a remnant making their way on Sunday's to my Son's Church around the country. There's nothing better than to adore the Scared Blood of my Son. There is nothing more worthwhile than to listen to my Son's Word.

Little Man

Big Eye, thanks for keeping your eye over Ireland. I love my green isle. I love the culture and spirit of every Irish person. We are known all over the world and yet we are a small island. We have had great influence. Once we were known in Europe as a land of Saints and Scholars. We have a proud heritage. But it is changing. There are different streams of new philosophies flooding through the minds and hearts of a new type of Irish person. Many of us were reared on a simple Catholic menu of prayers, Mass, and confession. That's gone. It is liberalism, and materialism now. The faith is passed from adults to children anymore.

St Patrick return. My voice representing the voice of the Irish, call you to be with us once more. And your heavenly Father is in favour. We need you. You are needed more than ever. I love this man. Big Eye, of all the holy men and women on earth nobody explained the Trinity of Divine Persons better.

You are big Eye. You are my True God. You are One Person. St Patrick picked up a leaf of shamrock from the ground and explained to pagans in Ireland that you are One God but Three Persons. The shamrock had three petals each representing you Big Eye as a Father, Son and Holy Spirit. I love praying thinking of the image of the shamrock symbol. I love praying to my God as Father and God's Son as my brother and God the Holy Spirit as my inspiration. I love each Person of the Trinity.

Big Eye

Liam, you live in a beautiful land rich in green pastures. Your country has great farmers who are highly skilled with machinery. You have everything – corn, fruit, vegetables, cattle, sheep, horses, pigs and milk.

Liam you have mountains, rivers, forests and exceptional beauty spots in parts of the country where tourists visit every year. I see them visit in hundreds the Cliffs of Moher and the lakes in Killarney.

Liam I see the remnant of a great period in religious worship as Churches dedicated to my Son are spread about in locations all over the land. My Son has Eucharistic Churches all over the land. There are some devout worshippers remaining who represent Anna and Simeon who always prayed in the Temple in your Son's time.

But I'm afraid, Liam, that if you went into a school today and held up a piece of shamrock before students they might laugh at you. These guys are well educated and don't fall for simplistic explanations of the faith. However, I'm fully in support of you in regard to the spiritual, physical and mental health of all citizens in your beloved country.

Liam, I am in talks with St Patrick in regard to this matter. I'm looking at the religious and political leaders in Ireland and the decline in spirituality among your people. Let this issue with me.

Little man

Big Eye, I'm grateful for my life and place of birth. I'm more than grateful for the choice of my parents and grandparents in bringing me up as a Catholic Christian. This is a great country. It's wonderful to be here. And I'm grateful for the break from Great Britain. It's because we have our own culture and identity. I remember the men and women of nineteen sixteen who won our freedom. They paid a price for my freedom with their lives.

Big Eye, I have the freedom to express my faith by sitting confidently in my room and writing. Unfortunately, not everyone would agree with my beliefs. I'm all for you Big Eye. A Nation's strength is in its relationship with you Father as well as with each other in the community.

Big Eye you shine brightly. I see the sun coming up from the east in the morning. It lights up the green fields and shrubbery. It lights up the blue sky. It's magnificent. I'm glad to be alive. Life is marvellous. I hope it will last forever. I'd feel sad if my life stopped. I wouldn't see the sun shine anymore or the beauty of nature.

Big Eye, I wouldn't mind dying though if it meant seeing you face to face and joining with all those who were loyal and made it to heaven. I'd gladly die if heaven is better. I was always amazed with martyrs in the spirit they walked to their deaths at the hands of their wicked persecutors.

Big Eye

Liam. I'd welcome you. I'll take you into my arms. I'm outside your window looking in. You do believe I have a Big Eye and could see everything. Liam, open the window. Let me in. I'll cuddle you. I'll hold you in my arms.

Liam I can do anything. I'm not dead even though you think it is hard to grasp how anyone could live for millions of years. My Love is perfect. Nothing bad comes from me. I'll fill your room with goodness.

O Liam, your smile is lovely. I can see that I make you happy. I like that. All anybody wants in life is a little bit of love. That's why I emphasise the importance of love for each other. My Love doesn't breakdown. But human love does. I think you know that Truth by now.

Liam, be careful for the rest of the evening. You don't know what's around the corner. The unfortunate thing about human beings is that I gave them free will. The reality here Liam is that anything could happen. That's why I tell you to be careful. I respect free will even though wrong choices often result in arguments and disagreements. I see great pain in people that result from a free will making bad choices.

Little Man

Big Eye, can I seize the moment? The experience is electrifying and powerful. I'm in the arms of my Father. I feel his love and protection. Wonderful! It's good for me. It's a really nice experience. I feel every bone and muscle in my body heal.

Big Eye, I recall the Apostles feeling wonderful on the mountain with your Son Jesus. It was really a good experience for them. They felt great about it. I feel great now. I had great walks with my religious brethren on the Wicklow, Dublin and Mourne mountains. On one occasion we watched a cloud descend into a valley between two peaks. There was a hush, hush and amazing silence amongst us. The experience was reminiscent of biblical accounts of a voice being heard through a cloud. I'm sure that was you, Big Eye.

O God, I'm so in love with you. This is magnificent news. You are hot Father. I feel your love and grace run through me. I'm fresh and awake as tiredness and stress evaporate. An experience from a Divine Person like the Father, Son or Holy Spirit is of a magnitude way above and beyond any other experience on earth. Big Eye

I'm about to embark on a mission. My whole being bubbles up with excitement and an awareness of your Presence. I'm going to the best clothes shop to dress my body in such a way that my elegance would indicate holiness, integrity and purity. And my mouth will be like the Golden Mouth of St John Chrysostom in the way I speak about your Son, Jesus Christ. I'm dressing up for a mission.

Big Eye, I'm not bringing food for the poor or clothes for the homeless, or care for the sick. These are important. I bring instead a promise from your Son that where two or three are gathered in Jesus' Name I am there with them. I can have no weak spots in carrying out this mission. I'll dress immaculately and elegantly so that any person who wishes to pray with me will encounter a true friend of yours Big Eye.

Prayer is the heartbeat of the spiritual life. A fake or dud spiritual director wouldn't last long on the circuit. People are not fools. They see through you. Any weakness or slip causes disinterest. Adults turn off if a man of sincerity is bluffing.

Big Eye, my password is desire. I bring that to my prayer session with any person willing to engage in a passion for Jesus. All dry souls, all sad souls, all drowsy and tired souls are welcome. I can bring every kind of a soul away from the drudgery of stress and worry within a family or pressure related to the place of work. All I require is three people and their will be no ambiguity of motives.

Big Eye, I gather people in no other Name except yours. In that way I'm gathered in the Name of Truth. It's not personal for me. It's about love and spiritual direction for each person that avails of praying together. It's about a core concept in Big Eye's Doctrine namely the spiritual care of each person.

Chapter Twenty-Five

Big Eye

Liam. I like your ideas. You are really conforming to My Will. I like it. You are beginning to see in the same way as my Son Jesus viewed humanity. Every person is precious Liam. My son not only noticed the lepers and sinners but he engaged with them. He saw beyond their status. He saw a person. My Son Jesus had pity on every soul that was poor in spirit.

Liam, I'm beginning to see a similar type of mental perception in you towards your brothers and sisters on earth. I have nothing but praise for your mother and father who moulded your faith in me and my Son. The seed of faith is sown by parents. If parents don't pray the children may never pray. Your parents prayed with you. And they heard my Son's Word at Mass. And they received the Body and Blood of my Son regularly. And I'm delighted with your idea to care for each other. You are well grounded in faith. And you accomplished a deepened insight into Catholic Doctrine during your experiences in religious life. And like St Dominic you care for the souls of all.

Liam, I like your sentiment of caring for the souls of others. I can well imagine where you are coming from. It would be sad if your siblings and parents didn't accomplish a place in the kingdom of heaven. And of your clan going back to the first family on earth you pray for their salvation. I'm aware of all your ancestors and due to your prayers for them I intend to shepherd them.

Liam, I like your humility. It attracts me. I'm more than pleased with you. I have at last a man on earth that cares for every soul. Well

278

done! You are now in the kind of territory suitable for gentle lambs called to serve like my Son. You have eyes for the task. I care for the downtrodden. I care for sinners. I care for the sick.

Liam, you have potential to follow the Sacred Way. I have your Mind. I have your Heart. Your desire to please me is sufficient. I accept your credentials and place you among my lambs.

I'm aware of your sincere prayers for all your relations living and deceased. I've heard your prayers for all those you prayed for. People believed in you to pray for them. And I'm satisfied that you included them when you offered prayers to me. That's very important. The living and dead like to be remembered.

Liam, I like that. It was one of the reasons that caught my eye about you. You were willing to give your life to me so that nothing bad would happen to anyone in your family. I accept your life as a sacrifice. The care for souls and the search for Truth lay deep in your character

However, Liam you have your hands full. People drinking alcohol and taking drugs would spit in your face if you try to change them. There's a huge spiritual problem throughout the world. The world has rejected my greatest prophet. The world has despised and turned their back on My Precious Lamb. I see it on their faces and in their body language on the streets. The people are lost because they have stopped going inside my Prayer Houses for gatherings in My Name.

Liam, I am at a loss. I don't know what is going to help. There isn't much more that I can do. I gave my Beloved Son. The Cross of my Son is the only way. It's not too late for conversion. But I can tell you solemnly that dead souls, dead wood, unspiritual bodies and all rejectionists are no good to me. They are scrap. They are cut off from me by their own choice. I gave every person free will. But these angry people blame me for everything that goes wrong. All I can do through your writing is to remind them that the gospel of my Son is there for them if anyone wants to come back to me.

Liam I am happy with you. You continue every day to try and be better. You have come on leaps and bounds. You still have a few bits and pieces to work on. I'm glad that you shun evil. The remaining two stand-out imperfections that you have are bursts of temper and bouts of gluttonous eating outside meal times.

Little Man

Big Eye, I'll try to amend my weaknesses and every other irritation that damage closer union between us. I'll snip the sin. I'll pray for a spiritual wash every morning. I desire to be as white as snow.

Big Eye, can I talk to you? I don't want to come across as possessive or obsessive. But I want to spend time with you. Father, push away the world. I want to be with you. I'm your little bird. I sing in the palm of your hand. Stroke me and hear me chirp. I want to feel your care and love Father. Could I go with you for a spin across the sky and travel into orbit and view the gates of heaven? I'd love a heavenly holiday.

Big Eye, the world is okay. Everyone is busy. There are not many thinking about you. People don't have time. I see them in cars travelling. But they don't know much about you. The human being wants to be independent and self-reliant without any interference. That's not me. I want to be your little bird but sometimes you are not there for me.

Father, do you see my mind, heart and body when I walk down the road. My mind plays like a broken radio. I can't catch any dialogue between us. I'm not aware of my head and what is going on inside it. The same applies to my heart. There isn't any feeling. I should be feeling your love Father.

Big Eye I can understand Jesus' feeling of desertion on the cross. You were not there for him Big Eye. Are you doing that to me? I hope not. I don't like feeling down in myself. I dislike praying when you are not at the other end of the stick. It affects my confidence and doubts arise in relation to wasting my time.

Big Eye, I'm sorry. I'm selfish. I know you can't hold my hand all the time. There are seven billion people on earth. It's healthier anyway and more mature when each person in a relationship has space to stand alone, work alone and pray alone.

Big Eye, I'm mature. It's alright if you pop into a family in Brazil, or work with a Parish in Nigeria. I'm okay about it. You are a God for all. I'm perfectly okay with all the strings you have that are attached to all the Catholic Churches on earth. You keep aflame more than one candle. I love you anyway.

Big Eye I'll try to keep warm when you are not near. I've tasted your beauty and I'll not let it go. I'll not sulk when you are away. I'll light a candle and keep the bright spark of love alive. There's no need for me to blow cold and cry when my beloved is absent. My friendship is strong and permanent.

Big Eye

Hello Liam. It's not an easy achievement for any person to obtain a permanent state of holiness and perfect unity with me. You would be worthy of heaven if you were in that state of mind. Perfect sanctity is only attainable after conquering millions of large and small temptations so as to cling to my Christ and pass from death to a new life in heaven.

Liam, the Way is shown to you. The Truth in regard to what you must do is in my Son Jesus. Eternal Life is achievable through my Son. So I command you once more to Love my Son. What you must do is back off. Don't force yourself on me. It will exhaust your mind. All I expect from my little Lambs are small gentle steps. These listen to my voice. And one major step I beg of you is that you don't judge anyone. You have done that in regard to Muslims and sinners. No one is to be tagged or labelled. For a true to disciple must possess the Divine Doctrine that every person is special and entitle to be loved. You are encouraging the evil of your neighbour into yourself when you criticise or condemn anyone no matter what their crime or sin consists of. I expect an attitude of holy compassion in your conversation with every person belonging to the human race.

Liam, all goodness comes from me. I choose you. You can't make yourself holy. Nor can you make me holy. It's a gift Liam. The man in Supervalu pointed this truth to you. He was a born again Christian. He repeatedly told you that my Spirit is a gift. Everyone following Gaelic games saw him with a poster behind the goals at big matches. He had a quote from St John 3:7 saying that you must be born from above. In other words, you can do nothing without me. All through the history of Scripture you read the acknowledgements of holy men declaring that My Spirit came to them.

So Liam my love is a gift. You can do nothing by yourself. So be grateful. You labour like a slave if I was not working in you. You are an empty vessel without me. It is I that fill your soul with love, fill it with holy compassion and fill it with purity. I know what you need. I pluck thorns out of your mind. I replace hard drives like defiance and resentment with software that is gentle and peaceful and compliant with my Will. I puncture your strong will. I stick pins into it and deflate it. And out of that dead will of yours I blow up new balloons in your mind filled with air that comes directly from heaven.

Liam, all you require for this to happen is a welcome. I can't work with a defiant and cold heart. I like my lambs to be playful and friendly with the spirit of children. I like simplicity. Sometimes I'm met with a barrage of obstacles and worries that fly at me like a shower of bullets when I make contact with some souls.

Liam, I want to teach you a few things. The first lesson I advise for you to comprehend is to regard your mind as an egg. The mind is your communication centre. I'm at work in there once you welcome me. You wouldn't see me with your eyes or hear me with your ears. But I will be at work in the eye of your intellect. This is significant. Your egg the brain must retain my love and knowledge. If there is a defect in the egg, in the brain or in the mind I can't work with you because My Knowledge is lost and wasted. So open up your mind to me and close it to everyone else. I'll give you a code when I knock. You will know that it is me by the warmth of my finger gently tapping at your skull.

Liam, you make me proud and made it worthwhile for me to stand by my world of human life. It's for your kind of response that I regard my Son's sacrifice a success. Liam I can hover around your mind. Don't worry. I created you and I can recreate you. In a split second I could fly from heaven straight into your room. I have delicious gifts for you. I also have good news from your team of Doctors in the sense that they are at the latter stages of putting together a holy package that marks you out as a man close to My Heart.

Chapter Twenty-Six

Little Man

Hi Big Eye! Good morning. I love you. From your message above I must change. I must teach myself to be a lamb and be a threat to no one. I must have the characteristics of a child by being friendly, playful, and unchallenging. I can't be a worrier. And I can't live on an even footing with you, my heavenly Father. I want to be your happy little child. Simplicity pleases you. I don't want to be difficult or complicated. Father, I'm your child. Could I have some sweets? Can I have virtuous sweets like joy, peace, love, purity etc.? I want to be a child forever if it means Big Eye cares for me. I want a new childlike approach towards my Father. By this mentality I'll hammer the aggressive man that is in me. The Father/child model is worth consideration.

Big Eye I know you are a Father figure. And I know your Son is Jesus Christ. But the fact that your Son Jesus taught us to call you Father indicates that I'm a son too. I'm an adopted son. So I can call you my Father too. You are the Father of the whole human race.

Big Eye it is rather soothing to believe and think that I have a Father of your calibre. It's also a scary thought to think that I could find myself lost in the world. So how do I keep close to you Father? I'm here in West Limerick. Where are you?

Father, do you look down from heaven? Or are you sitting on a star beaming into the world? Or are on the moon with a magnificent eye monitoring your favourite creation? Or are you visible at all? I feel your Presence but can never see or hear you.

Big Eye, all I do know is that without you there's sadness in my life and a feeling of worthlessness. I'm nothing but an empty shell without you. But some of those feelings are affected by sin. I have come to believe that sin humbles me. And I add further that sin is in each and every person. The human being is vulnerable to temptation both externally and internally. It's difficult to be good. I could do well for a while and then a big fall happens. And all the grace accumulated runs down the sink. It's gone and I have to rebuild credit again.

Big Eye, I'm worried. Is it true that I'm nothing without you? What does that do for my self-esteem? My life means nothing without you. My mind is nothing other than a piece of trash. There's no love in my heart. I'm just a wild wandering ostrich estranged from the Source of Life.

Big Eye I'm sorry. I'm sorry from the perspective that there are more sins in me than first thought. I caught them at work this morning. My sex drive returned and it drove my mind mental for a few hours. I'm sorry Father. At one stage I had the choice to return to spiritual writing but I indulged further in deep in sensual desire.

Big Eye, I'm ashamed to stand up before you and face you. I don't know why you bother with me. I try to win freedom by following the Way of your Son. But there is more sin in people and in me than I thought. I'm an ashamed child this evening looking for comfort. I don't feel valuable now. I don't feel lucky now. I've slipped back into the mud of the earth and lost my grip on the feet of Jesus hanging on the cross.

Big Eye, godless people are riff raff. These cut themselves of from you. They don't want you. But who am I to judge? I'm nothing so why should I judge. Are unbelievers and layabouts in trouble? What is it to me? I'm no to judge. My brother Jesus did not condemn the woman caught committing adultery.

Big Eye, your son Jesus was the perfect priest. He welcomed and forgave sinners. What about the unrepentant? What about the rapist who was released from jail early and raped again but this time murdered as well? There is no good fruit on these trees Father.

Big Eye how many chances are you going to give us all? I couldn't imagine you cutting down branches that bear no fruit and burn them into damnation. I couldn't imagine you snubbing anyone. The saving from execution of the adulterous woman is significant. Your Son did not condemn a sinner. But he told her to go and sin no more. So I must reset my mind. I must go to you Big Eye and ask to be spiritually washed. I must find clean holy water and come out of the mud. I must jump back into your arms Big Eye and allow myself to be washed and healed. For I have the Truth from your Son that sinners are saved once they repent. And I am sorry for every sin committed in the past up to this very moment, and I intend to follow the holy Way of Life in the future.

Big Eye, will you have me back? I align myself to you. I don't want to be cut off. I don't want anyone to be cut off. It's a shocking realisation to think you might close the door to me. I'm at the latter end of my life and I desire to do something good for you. If I help one soul or one human being by my work in this book I'd be delighted. It's my way of giving glory to you, God Most High.

Big Eye

Liam, that's the spirit I want from my friends on earth. If you save one soul for me, you are fruitful. I hope you are fruitful and beautiful Liam. I'm happy that between us Liam each and every soul maybe encouraged to choose the Way of Life offered by my Son. There are many passing with honours English and Maths tests but failing a Christian test. I don't want to be recalling the issue of judging again Liam. But people around the world need to know that failure to recognise and know my Son is a fatal mistake.

Liam, there are many toxic hearts and minds everywhere in the world today. And the contamination is spreading. And it is difficult to protect the next generation from them. Bad people are not nice and are difficult to live with. These souls bark at you once you mention my Holy Name. They don't want me and they shout you down if you tried to change them.

Liam, have a look at your daily routine and seek improvements. Blessed David rose during the night not once but seven times and honours me in prayer. The Great Moses would express joy in canticles and sing psalms for the victory over Pharaoh and over who kept the

Hebrews in toil and oppression. Liam I desire a triumphant song from you. It's only right to celebrate victory over Satan. It's a matter of great joy to conquer temptations.

Liam in order to succeed it's important to be solid. I know you will fall into the dirt at times. But I can pull you out by the hand and wash you clean once you are sorry for offending me. I couldn't allow bad people to triumph over a sincere soul such as yours is. I work best in weakness. It's when you are vulnerable, embarrassed, or humiliated that my grace works best in you. It's when you think you are great and doing exceptionally well that my grace begins to leak out of you.

Liam, remember to discern the spirit that is in a person. My little lambs are always in danger from wolves. I abhor bad people corrupting little ones. It's wise to pay attention and be on guard against others no matter how sweet their voices sound. So observe yourself. Notice each thought that filters through into your mind. Notice all emotions that filter into your heart. Catch the bad spirit before it pops into your eye. Catch the bad word before it races into your ear. There are innumerable amounts of unspiritual, snappy and irritating souls out there that would need very little encouragement to attack my lambs. Once these bad spirits gain your trust they jump in a split second from a human carrier into your inmost parts. And it could take a mighty effort to shift them once they gain entry.

So rise up Liam. Don't be lazy. This vice is like an open door. It allows every sort of tramp, thug, and imp sleep in your bed. So don't let them in. I'm trying to tell you that every person has the potential to be a carrier of a bug. It's because no one on earth is perfect. I solemnly warn you. Monitor the child. Monitor the man. Monitor the woman. All are infected with the sin of the first man and woman.

Little Man

Hi Big Eye. That was a long piece. I thank you for it. I appreciate your care for me. I know of the dangers and concerns. I've had storms in my head and bad experiences. I know what it is like to receive a battering from raging bulls. I know what it is like to be mauled by a pack of hungry dogs. I know what it is like for a sex shark to encircle me. It's not easy to recover from vicious attacks. Big Eye, bad experiences don't go away that easy. Scars remain. Some are physical. Others are mental. When I try to be peaceful and holy a pack of angry dogs jumps up out of the high grass and tear my soul to shreds. It's not easy to be happy when eaten by evil.

Big Eye, I survived many attacks. A wicked thing was done to me. Psychological knives stuck in my back. Word bullets blew me apart. I don't know how I survived. Or maybe I haven't. I'm affected by wickedness. I can't identify a reason why I was singled out. All I desired was to do the right thing and be good. My stress levels increased to such an extent that a brain haemorrhage is a possibility. Also cancer could originate from my stress levels.

Big Eye, I know how difficult it is to cope with toxic thoughts. It's not easy. Life is cruel at times. Wicked thoughts are like bullets. They kill the inside of a person and demoralise. It's like being paralysed.

Father, what do I do? What do I do when wicked words dent my mind? What do I do when an evil person guns me down? Am I expected to tolerate abuse? All through life temptations and imperfections attack the mind, and cause continuous disharmony in relationships.

Big Eye

Liam, I'm perfect. Humans are imperfect. I sympathise with you. I'm aware of aggression shown towards you. Demons like to bark at you. Wrong doers bite you when you try to correct them. It's tough Liam. My Son can tell you. My Son, my Truth suffered for the wicked and impious. On that awful Good Friday my Son dragged with him every sin committed and nailed them to the cross. It was a great act of salvation. By my Christ being lifted up on the Cross I drew all things to myself. The Crucifix became the focal point. Liam, you know my teaching. But I accept your dilemma. When couples enter into relationships they look with hope into a fruitful future. And what appears to be a flower early in life might very well become an unwanted weed later.

Liam I'd be inclined to advice separation in the case of one lover changing and becoming a nightmare to live with. I couldn't tell a victim of abuse to stick it out. It would be like a dog savaging a lamb every day. I'd be inclined to remove the lamb from the bite of the dog.

Liam, look at the consequences of abuse. I tell you solemnly that each day would be hell. Insult after insult would be hurled at you. You would be snapped at like a dog. And your self-confidence and self-worth would take a nosedive. You would live in fear and be afraid to be heard or seen by anybody. The psychological damage would be similar to your mind been blasted with a shotgun every day.

Liam, victims of abuse struggle to be happy. You can't be yourself. You live in fear. The disrespect dished out keeps you frightened and silent in your own home. The unhappiness of the abuser erupts over the slightest little thing. Many women suffer horrific abuse. The seed of bad relationships are often born from irreligious, non-working and alcoholic backgrounds. These people are selfish and have no respect for anyone. These are like people who rebelled against me in Moses time and their dead bodies littered the desert.

Chapter Twenty-Seven

Little Man

Big Eye, I express my love for you and haven't rejected you. I look up at the stars in the sky at night and wonder are you sitting on top of one viewing your creatures on earth. I see one bright star and wonder are you looking down at me from it. Your creation is beautiful.

Big Eye I cast my eye along the blue sky in the morning and feel nothing but wonder at the loveliness of your work. I see jets flying from the West into the sun at the East side. I think of the people in those planes and the wonder of man in creating a flying machine to transport humans from country to country. I sit on a stone near the sea and reflect on the immensity and beauty of creation. I love watching the waves and seabirds. The world is pure beautiful on sunny quiet mornings when most living things are still asleep. The external world and my mind trying to make sense of it is nothing more than a fascinating study. I admire this beauty. I reflect on myself.

Big Eye, I'm looking for peace and rest. I walk down the road and seek quiet spots where I can be alone and away from the bustle and torments of life. You are my solace Jesus. My Lord and Master bring me away in boats and up mountains like you did a long time ago with your friends the Apostles. I'm fatigued from the burden of issues, interferences and pressures of life. Do you hear me Father? The dogs are after me. They snap at my mind.

Big Eye, I turn to you for help and solace. Please take me for spin and away from the din that overwhelmed me. Please open that eye of yours and look at my plight. I've allowed interferences torment me and I've clashed with female demons.

Big Eye I need you so as to recover. I'm outside your door knocking for help. Do you see me? The others are asleep. It is early in the morning. I sit on a stone waiting for you. Come down Father. I need a thorough washing to refresh me. I feel like a man mauled by dogs and the wounds require help from a Doctor of the Church or Divine intervention from either yourself Big Eye, or your Son Jesus Christ, or the Holy Spirit.

Big Eye, the fault is on my side. I blame myself for this agony. I should have found a quiet spot to pray. I had no help to fight. I left myself open and vulnerable for attacks. I pray now Father. I'm in at surgery having my mind bandaged up from the mauling. I'm in no condition to pray.

Big Eye, prompt my mind and heart to turn to you. I try in earnest to muster ideas about you. I try my best to restore holy thoughts. You are the greatest of all Father. I have never come across anything to give as much solace as you have when I hallow your Holy Name. Come Holy Father! I had a dark night of the soul. I was lost in a storm of worry that battered me with a ferocious onslaught. Why didn't I escape and turn to you Father?

Big Eye can I latch onto Doctor Anselm's masterful acknowledgement that you are the greatest and highest of all? I took my eye of you and it led me into a dark and fearful abyss. Father, accept me back. I shouldn't have strayed. I've got to be clever in future. I'll sneak away for prayerful bites of spiritual food. In other words, I call my Father when I'm running into trouble. I'll ask him to collect me. I'll ask him to drive me away from evil spirits.

Holy Father, you are the Highest of All. I glorify and praise your Sacred Name. You are higher than money. You are higher than imperfect relationships. You are higher than wrong interferences that harm peace of mind. Holy Father, you are the greatest of all. I crave to worship your Son Jesus Christ in a manner pleasing to you. Nobody is greater than you. Nothing is greater than you. I'm so sorry Father for not trusting in you and staying with the lambs in safe zones for protection from wicked demons. I'm bloodied and down but hoping that you Father would hold out your hand to me. I don't know if I can re-join my Christian friends in this demoralising sate.

Big Eye, my wounds are bad. I'm in no fit state to pray this morning. It's time to take stock. I'll have to accept my weakness and sickness. My mind and heart can't feel any enthusiasm for prayer. The energy isn't there. The battery is dead.

I'll call my Doctor. Anselm, will you doctor me? Will you bandage my head and help me restore my dead battery, my dead mind and heart so that I can pray like you to fully understand the greatness of God? I want to restore friendship with you this morning.

St Anselm

The best thing to do when recovering from nasty verbal attacks is to run back to your heavenly Father and get into Church during a quiet time and pray. By doing this you will recover and restore friendship with God. I sought solitude myself and it refreshed me. Nothing is better than to contemplate the Highest and Greatest of All. Your recovery will be complete if you follow my advice.

Little Man

Hello Anselm. Thank you very much. I'm grateful for your advice. But it isn't easy. There's a spirit of irritation in my ear. It's causing contemplative disruption. My intention is good but the overflow into action isn't happening. So I can't lie. I can't act as if I have done what I was told by the Doctor. In other words, I'm been told to meditate. I have to contemplate.

St Anselm, I'm struggling all day. When I use the words Our Father, and hallowed be thy Name nothing seems to happen. And when I try to grasp the magnitude of God's Greatness and that God is the Highest of All nothing happens.

St. Anselm I appreciate that you don't like roguery. And I feel that I'm not good enough for eminent company like you and other saints. But I find a spirit of openness about you that attracts me to you.

Big Eye

Liam, I haven't stopped loving you but you have had a bad experience in the wilderness. Anselm is right. You need to find quiet places and pray to me. What has happened is that you became entangled in snappy feminine spirits and these deflated you and caused you to lose contact with me. These leap into your mind when they don't get their own way with you. It's very important for you Liam not to stand in the way of a woman.

Liam, I welcome you back from the claws of three cats that ate the head of you. I agree that you received a mental mauling and breakdown. I'm aware of your need for a Doctor to bandage up your wounds and return you to my care. I'm your spiritual Father and let it be a lesson to you not to take on females again. I have told you before not to judge or challenge anyone.

Liam, I'm fully aware of your choice for me. My response is reciprocal. What please me most is that you don't want human glory, nor do you want money, or anything that's contrary to my Will and Love. Your intention is honourable. I'll not turn down the love of a human being. But note that tests are in place to prove your loyalty. I saw you struggle to pray this morning and there was deathly atmosphere between us.

Liam, I know that you have picked me and don't want anything else in life. At the same time, you want protection for your family. I grant that. This is one of the benefits from a relationship with me. I protect those who love me.

Liam, very few reach the heights that you aim for. You have put me at the top. There is no higher target. I have demanded love from every person.

Liam I watch my creatures across the globe and all are busy. People are on the move all the time even idlers. I don't expect everyone to drop tools and follow me. Work is to be done. Services are part of living. I observe life in all cities, towns and villages. I look for potential saints. But most of the human race follows a pattern. And they are happy with life on earth. But they are conditioned Liam. They work for money and enjoy a good quality of life with it. Some are very smart and exploit others. And some follow big world events. That's okay. I'm not going to spoil the party.

Liam my point here is that most don't stop and think but you have. You've done a lovely thing by sitting on a stone to reflect on me. You have acknowledged that I'm the Greatest of All. And I am.

Liam I'm unimaginable holiness. No eye can see me. But I flutter around your soul. Keep loyal to my Holy Name. Call me Liam repeatedly. There is Life in my Name. I might not hear you the first time but I will if you persist. Call me Father and Sacred is my Name.

Liam, it takes a man of great prayer to unlock problems and frustrated thought entanglements in your intellectual systems. I'd like you to have a better defensive system against stormy spirits. For I am blocked out from many souls through the strength my rivals grip.

Remember I didn't create the world in one day. The same applies to work on your mind. It takes time to make it holy. Pray to the Doctors Liam. My Holy Apostles and Saints fix mind and heart problems just like a mechanic fixes the engine of a car. I know what I created. I have the power and ability to make your mind as bright as the sun. Saintliness is more than a dream if I am at work in you.

Liam, I think we have enough dialogue. I'll have to think of a role for you. The tasks done on earth for your neighbour and for me are counted as credits for entry into heaven. At the end of the day I'm at work in the world with my Son in order to save as many souls as possible. I'll hold a meeting with my Son Jesus and your team to plan your future

Little Man

Big Eye, is writing not enough? I thought writing for the next number of years was my vocation. I'm working out a way of relating to you. My mind and heart labours night and day in search of your love. I could be jailed or killed if I brought a Christian banner into North Korea of strong Islamic countries. I don't know if I'm willing to die for my beliefs. Yet thousands of martyrs were horribly slaughtered because of belief in your Son Jesus. It shouldn't be that way anyone Father. I don't like bloodshed. I can love the Muslim. Isn't that your teaching Big Eye?

Big Eye, what more must I do? I haven't a platform to help people and I don't belong to any organisation. I have trained my mind to focus on you alone and hope all good things would come from a relationship with the Highest of All. Anyway I can't give what I haven't got myself. If I can't walk into North Korea with Christ's Peace written on my forehead what's the point in doing it. However, I will go if I'm sent. I turned down a chance to go to Trinidad a number of years back. I probably should have gone. I'm sorry Father.

Big Eye I'm concerned now. I'm apprehensive. What roles have you in mind for me? I have a home, wife and family to care for every day. I don't know if I could walk away from household tasks. Children have to be brought to school and fed. I'm sorry Father. I shouldn't complain. Big Eye is boss. I have an obligation to obey no matter what work God our Father maps out for me.

Big Eye

Liam, there is never a dull moment. There's an issue a minute. I'm well aware of your domestic obligations. Why are you panicking? I haven't asked you to do anything yet. At the moment you are dragged all over the place and haven't a good daily schedule in place.

Liam. I tell you solemnly to pray with fervour. I see your attempts with your son every morning and evening. I also notice your prayer walks. But your attempts lack bite and routine. What you are doing is a mix-up. You try praying the Our Father. Then you switch to the title of the Sorrowful Mysteries of my Son's passion and death. Then if you are not connecting to me you switch to my Son. I take offence to that. I am the same as the Son. I glorified my Son. I'm one with my Son. In fact, you should reflect on our relationship. It might unite you to us both.

Liam, you are not praying properly to me. There's a lot wrong in your life that only you can change around. Due to a poor prayer line I can't keep your confidence up nor can assist you in dealing with issues. It shouldn't be like this. Prayer can move mountains Liam. And don't blame others. It is you little man.

Liam I saw you eat three bowls of apple stew and custard. It affected you. You are a diabetic. For goodness sake have you no discipline? You made a glutton of yourself. You ate too much. I'm not happy at all. I expect better.

Little Man

Big Eye, you are right. I respect your judgement. I'm disgusted with myself for harming my body by an intake of high sugar levels. And I'm sorry for my sloppy prayer effort that's all over the place. It's no surprise that Big Eye doesn't listen to half of my prayers.

Big Eye, I pay the price. My indiscipline has no effect on you. I cause my own stress and tiredness. My body has a lot of unhealthy ingredients running through my blood stream. I'm doing my best though to drink more water. But when I'm down or something goes wrong I comfort myself with a bar of chocolate.

Big Eye, definitely poor diet affects my relationship with you and others. I can't fast and there is little of it in the Church today. An unhealthy diet increases blood pressure and this in turn harms peaceful and prayerful focus. I blame myself. Discipline has always been my problem. My prayer life is governed by moods and depends on how I feel. That's wrong. I'm not looking after myself at all.

Chapter Twenty-Eight

Big Eye

Liam, I'm your Father. I care for you. But I need you to listen to my voice. There is hope and don't despair. The prayer connection is vital. I'd love to make a breakthrough with you and cement once and for all a prayerful friendship between my Great Mind and your Imperfect Mind. I can't listen to your complaints and imperfections. The world doesn't want to hear Liam Walsh's faults. Liam, go back to your original idea in writing this book and don't drift away from it. Its theme is a relationship between us.

Little Man

Big Eye, that's fine. I have no bother with writing. I write to tell you how much I love you. One good way of doing this is to concentrate on your Word. I love your Word Father. There's Truth in them. How anyone could not feel cheerful on hearing such words as, "Gather in your Name"? And I like these words too, "If anyone loves me he will keep my word and my Father will love him and we shall come and make our home in him". Jesus' Word is inspiring. I feel something beautiful emanating from them.

Big Eye I know them off by heart. I try to love you Father. I reflect deeply on beautiful Words spoken from the mouth of Jesus. What a man Jesus is! What a Divine Man is Jesus? I ponder his Holy Word. These words are Golden Eggs. I cherish them with all my heart. My quality of life is enhanced by Jesus' Word. I accept fully Big Eye's commandment that all human beings should love Christ. I'm definitely a better person through my decision to belong to Christ.

Big Eye

Liam, now you think straight. Place all your eggs in the basket that belong to my Son, Jesus Christ. Only total love will work. You can't blow hot when you feel like it in your relationship with my beloved Son and then a few hours later go cold while doing something else. You think of my Sacred Name – God the Almighty Father - and then become distracted with a fly or a useless imaginary thought. You walk along the road thinking of me and suddenly you look at a building site and the possibility of you working on buildings again. You think of me and then pass by a tennis court and imagine playing a game. Therefore, Liam there is an imbalance in the control of your thoughts where you drift in and out of your concentration on my Super Son Jesus Christ, the Saviour of the world. You do the same thing in the mornings. You tell me that your first thoughts are about me. But it isn't true. You shave first and listen to the news before turning to me. This has to change. You love my Christ first. I desire permanent love. I'm not a fool. How can you say you love my Son Jesus and you don't look at him properly each day?

Liam, there has to be more of me. There has to be precious memories of me. There has to be a filter installed into your retention centre so that you don't forget quickly my Word when you hear it. The retention of my Word is something that's flawed among the faithful. They are hard of hearing. My Word is forgotten shortly after it been spoken.

Liam I command respect. I Am who I Am. I am Big Eye. I'm your Father. Remember your desire to be a child of mine or a precious little lamb of mine. Unless you grasp my Greatness and that I Am the Highest of All there are going to be hiccups and blackouts in your love and unity for me. I Am extravagantly interested in any man that wants to commit to me. This kind of man has to learn to adore me and reject everything and everyone else. My Big Eye as you call me is always on the lookout for missionaries who might form a new people who might come to belief in the Head of the Church, Jesus Christ. I sent St Patrick to your country centuries ago and his influence is remembered to this very day. Patrick is on your team for I know how much you love this saint. Patrick passes on his greetings to you and to the Irish people whom he loved. Work hard Liam. Tell the Irish today to return to their faith. Pray for priests.

Liam, I love your sensitivity. Today you saw a man on a wheelchair and instantly you knew of my love for weak and vulnerable souls. I bring poor souls to heaven. I also support fully those who care for others. It is the ultimate vocation. I favour the poor and sick above the rich and healthy. You must see beyond the sickness and poverty into the beauty of the person. I'm glad Liam that you had the right attitude and had sympathy for someone less well of.

Little Man

Big Eye I love you. You are author of Creation, author of the Church of Christ and author of our Salvation. Nothing is greater than to belong to your kingdom. I'm more than happy to have found the Source of Unity, Truth and Peace. And I model myself on the words of John the Baptist in that you're Son Jesus Christ may increase in my life.

Big Eye, I pray for a Golden Egg. I want it laid in my mind. That is in the nest of my intellect. Christ must increase. Christ must be born in me. I surround my mind with prayer and manure the Egg. I want to feel Christ's growth in me. I want to feel an increase of your Presence. For that reason, my mind has work to do. My mind has genuine prayer to make.

Big Eye, I'm ready for you. Place the Golden Egg in me. Push it into my intellect. I'll pray and consider how this Holy Egg of the Word of God could increase awareness of you Lord Jesus. I'm open for the challenge. I want Christ in my life so much.

Big Eye I'm going to listen to the Baptist. I'll open up to him and unblock all irritations so that they will flow away into the sewer. I allow you Big Eye full permission to work in me. I'm all for increasing God's Spirit in my life. I invite you, day and night to plant holy Word Eggs into my nest of my intellect. I can see your fingers Big Eye planting eggs in me. They are all different colours with different names.

Big Eye, the nest is comfy for you. I invite your Holy Spirit into my comfy cell so that gifts in the form of eggs are laid. The first egg that I must keep hot in the hope of it developing is John's Word about you increasing in my soul. The egg doesn't become anything unless it is attended to by prayer. I pray therefore Father to keep the Holy Egg hot. It's not a baby robin or wren or blue tit that might emerge from this Egg. What's encased in this shell is energy, a substance that fills up my soul with an increase of Christ's Love and Christ's Peace. The Holy Egg is about an internal development of a growth that allows you Big Eye to increase and take over possession of my soul.

Big Eye, I'm thinking this morning. I'm thinking about how this holy desire can be achieved. I have no objection whatsoever of God the Father, and his Son Jesus Christ and the Holy Spirit increasing their Presence in the nest of my intellect. I welcome with open arms an increase of Truth in me. I relish an increase of my love, my favourite, who is my Lord and God to operate in the home of my soul. Big Eye I welcome this good news. Christ can use my soul to increase his operations on earth.

Big Eye, my soul is ready and I'm fascinated with this development. I'll pray and keep warm this precious Word of John the Baptist that what has to be done for every soul is to increase the growth of your Son Jesus Christ in each one of us. The soul should now be crying out loud, "I want Christ". I want to follow Christ. I want to do what he wants. I want to follow the Way of the Lord. Almost instantly an increase of interest in Christ should flood the mind.

Big Eye, it's like a gasoline pump filling a car tank with petrol. Your knowledge pours into the welcoming soul. Your Word fills the mind. Your Spirit activates the Egg in the nest. I'm so glad to welcome the Gospel of Truth into my comfy room of the soul. I look forward so much to having conversations with Christ in my room just like the time Jesus had with Mary as she sat at his feet listening.

Big Eye, it doesn't matter how old my mind or body is. I can refresh it with prayer. I don't think you would deprive an old man of grace. Neither would you deprive a battered soul an opportunity to turn to you for repair and renewal from a life of anxious drudgery. I know you have the power to repair a bad mind and make it holy. I know you have the power to clean up those who speak evil and make them preachers of your Holy Word.

Big Eye, come to me. I invite you. I call you Master and hope you may teach me, your child to receive every Word of Truth spoken in the gospel. I'm willing to work with you one on one. I'm willing to be called aside and reprimanded. I also accept questioning. Your Son Jesus questioned St James and St John. You bluntly said, "What do you want me to do for you"?

Big Eye, I know what I want from you. I spoke and prayed to you about it on the road this morning. I want Golden Eggs to hatch in my mind. And the first of these is an **increase** of Your Presence in me. I want to be reborn from above. And I want a beautiful batch of eggs to make that happen. My mind can in this way connect to heaven. I'm excited about having a future full of Golden Eggs that have the potential of retaining your Word in me. I can't allow my Holy Words to stray anymore and die under an avalanche of evil smog from forces at work in the world. And can I remind you father of your promise. You said, "If anyone loves you, you would come to him and make your home in him. So I expect you Big Eye to keep your Word. I love you. Therefore, I welcome you to make your home in me.

Big Eye, I'd like to know the truth. Are you calling me? Am I favoured? You magnified Mary's soul. You favoured Holy Mary to carry your Word Jesus Christ into the world. The prayer about Mary's is magnificent. I like it. My soul glorifies the Lord. Indeed, Big Eye you were glorified in Mary's life. It's inconceivable for your Son to come in to the world through a sinful body. I'm kind of praying for a change in me so as to have a body full of grace.

Big Eye, Mary is a model for girls. I love her. You filled her with grace. No one on earth had humility, gentleness, and grace as much as Mary. I'd love my soul to have a little of the sanctity that the Lord's Mother and Queen had. I have nothing but praise for a woman that had the holiest body imaginable. If anyone on earth craves for purity look no further than the Blessed Mother. Mary's baby was a Wonder Child that changed the world for the better.

Chapter Twenty-Nine

Big Eye

Hello Liam. Well done. I'm happy with your progress and the plan to encapsulate my Word in an Egg. I'm in a relationship with believers through that channel anyway although most don't recognise it. It is a brilliant way to keep Christ alive in your mind without having to refer to the gospel.

Liam, I increase the Spirit of Christ in you once the door of your soul remains open to me. I'm fully supportive.

Liam, I'm glad you take St John's words to heart in praying for an increase of me in your mind and heart. These are the two power houses where you can feel my Presence and know about my Presence. I love it when you discard all the information from past generations and look with your own eyes towards me in heaven and cry Our Father.

Liam I'm also glad that you realise the through nature of being a caring Father. There is sin stuck in every person even children. And the really good and holy man receives on a daily basis the thorns of others fired into caring hearts. It's because you care that you are a target for others irritations. That is what happened to my Son Jesus. All the sins of the world followed him because he was so good. He carried bags full of sin and continues to carry them in order to create new life – lives that are dedicated to me.

Liam, I'd like you to communicate with me through your mind. The mouth utters words. But your intellect must calculate their value. It's not enough to use words. Words require meditation and comprehension. So Liam you must decrease. You lack a few virtues. My valuable Word escapes your brain. Be realistic! I don't make mistakes. Your head bulges with pride. You need to deflate – decrease. I, your Father must increase in you.

Liam, I have good news for you. I want you to think of an imaginary trail across the blue sky to where I am in heaven. My Son's Prayer tells you where I am. I'm your Father in heaven. No eye has seen me or heaven.

Liam, your large telescopes can't see where I dwell and yet they can see afar. You can see stars. You know there are other planets. But a vision of heaven is beyond your capability. I recommend a trail of prayer and faith. My Throne of Grace can be sussed out through the eye of the intellect and strong contemplation.

Liam, my home Heaven is magnificent. I see all the fine Churches in the world and they are truly magnificent. I have nothing but praise for the buildings my faithful people have dedicated to me. But heaven is dazzling and beyond what the human eye can imagine. I am pure brilliance and my home is Pure Perfection. It's greater than St Peter's in Rome.

Liam, you can't see heaven but I see everything on earth. Isn't that the theme of your book? I'm Big Eye. I see all as well as each single individual of my creation. I see you on road L0909. I know what is in your mind. I'm aware of your strong determination to show me affection.

Liam. I respond to you. You have desire. And you know all good things come from me. You are defenceless, helpless and nothing without me. Now you know the truth. Now you know that you can't be anything without me. Now you know the meaning of the words you must be born from above.

Liam, the prerogative is mine. I choose you. You cannot in anyway make one single little step in my direction unless I call you. You could bang at my door all night and day if you want but I may not open until you are ready to respect me. I have several ways of connecting to you. I can radiate a beam of love from my heart straight into your intellect. I could ask my Son Jesus to sit beside you in Church and establish a friendship. I could send waves of love from the tabernacle into your heart. I can call you at any moment. I'm the Light of your soul.

Liam, there is one thing for certain though. I'm not going to love you and push away the rest of mankind. My Love is for everyone. I'm sure you are aware of my teaching on loving others. I tell you solemnly that if you can't love those beside you, you are unlikely to love me who you can't see. So love of your family and community is paramount if you want to be in the good books with me.

Liam, that's the track to follow. I want you to love and serve others. Then my gift of grace will increase in you. Then you will be born from above. Then my door will be opened to you. And mix in with that quality of loving others a strong faith and healthy prayer life.

O Liam, there is one more thing. The example of those who did make it to heaven can lead you to me if you read their stories. I know you love the lives of my loved ones – the little children who spread my Word and displayed heroic acts of charity. The saints can inspire you. St Anselm has helped you. My Dialogue with St Catherine has inspired you. So we are all in communion. I have great feasts in heaven when welcoming a new saint.

So Liam, I haven't sealed a connection with you. But I want to. Don't break off. I test you. I drive your irritating imperfections out of your soul. I have to be sure that your love is genuine and that you love increases daily. I'm happy though with your attempts to connect to me while walking in the mornings on road L0909.

Little Man

Father, are you kidding me. Can I attain holiness by my own efforts? Or is it a gift from you? If your love Father is a free gift do, I have to work at all? These are questions surfacing in my mind. What I do know is that I have a warm feeling about you Father. And that for me indicates that we are connected. I'm happy with that. It's the difference between feeling dead, broken or disconnected. What I can tell you is that I love the father of Jesus Christ. I'm in search of this Father for a long, long time. I pin all my hopes in life on you Big Eye.

Father I sort of know what breaks up or interferes with this holy connection. It's proximity with other people. I don't like the imperfections in others. I find their spirits dance crazily around my head and their unhappiness unsettles my attempts to be holy. More than anything else I love solitude. My words seem selfish. But why should I sit peacefully amongst others when they bawl to me for entertainment. I'm here to give my life to you Father. I'm one hundred percent certain that unhappy people are the cause of unrest within me. I crave for quiet places so that I can tune into your holy wavelength Lord. I agree fully that I'm nothing without your grace and love.

Father, how can I tolerate interferences and prevent demands on my time? You are my friend Father. Tell me! You are my Father in heaven. Guide me. Teach me to listen. I desire more than anything to be a sweet little lamb for you Father.

Big Eye

Liam, I love you but you do have to respond to my call. It's not a lazy call. You have to work at your relationship with me. I allow all human beings to sleep and rest at night. But as soon as morning comes I want you up out of the bed praying and writing. I'm not a great supporter of idlers and gossipers.

Liam, a relationship with me is something special. It's unlike any other friendship. I don't like my friends going away on holidays from me. I don't like them forgetting me. It's your duty to fine tune your connection to me. I'm always there for you. It's you that breaks the connection. When that happens, communication lines are interrupted and you can't hear my voice.

Liam, my love is special. And you know it. You have tasted the sweetness of my Love. It is prayer that keeps this channel of love fine-tuned. And offshoots of this magnificent and perfect Love in which I am, are Peace, Joy, and Mercy. The ultimate tickle though of my sensational friendship with you is Love.

Liam, I look forward immensely to your efforts and increase your side of the commitment to love me. I'm your Father. I'm here for you. What you must do is continue to increase your sincere prayer and call me Father at every opportunity lots of times every day. My Perfect Love will flow through you once you oil your body and soul with prayer.

Liam, I'll monitor your effort. I'll view your capability. I have said to you that love for me is on a different level than anything else that can be loved in the world. I'm Big Eye. I'll watch your efforts. I'll observe your prayer. I'll watch specially for frustrations when you are having problems maintaining consistency in your attempts to love me.

Liam, this is only the beginning. I'll decide later what tasks I have for you. I don't align myself to lazy souls who refuse to work and yet complain that they have nothing. My Son Jesus pointed this important feature out to idlers standing around and doing nothing at the market place. My Love doesn't sit pretty in the lives of layabouts. I call them to work. And they must accept. The same applies to you. The world needs holy and hardworking shepherds to care for the flock. And you can do this through the written word.

Little Man

Father, why are you bringing this unemployment issue up? You know me. I've worked hard all my life at everything asked of me. I conscientiously carried out all my duties on the building site, in the priesthood, and in retail. I stood faithfully beside my cheese and fish counters and gave great attention to each customer.

Big Eye, I'm beginning to feel a bit uneasy. I haven't dodged work. I'm not an idler. I want to work. And I have carried out all my duties meticulously. But I do admit that I failed to establish a greater trust and love for your Son, Jesus Christ. It was so hard Father. I couldn't see him in the flesh. It was like having to love and have faith in someone that was dead. And the imperfections of Church leaders left me in an awful dilemma. What does a man do when he isn't rated an equal to other students and a possible intellectual?

Father I always took my studies seriously and served tirelessly in two Churches giving seven years to each. I looked at it as a great honour to consecrate the bread and wine and preach your Word. But I fell back in the pecking order in relation to plans for my future. The Order should have made me feel wanted and signed me in for courses relevant to the needs of the Church.

Big Eye

Liam, I'm happy with your progress now. You would never have achieved anything in the Order. I love your singular devotion coming directly from your mind and heart. I'm fully supportive of one of my little creatures crawling towards me in the hope of finding love. I know your mind and questioning nature. I'm aware of your speculative thinking about the origin of the world and life on earth. I know of your awareness of time since my Son walked amongst you two thousand years ago and whether my Presence could survive that length of time. And you wonder about the way one human being replaces another and that is all there is to life.

Liam despite this thinking I know what you want. You want Truth. You want awareness. Unfortunately, this faculty is inactive in most people. But I love you for one reason alone. You love my Word. And you go to great depths to feel the sense of a Word linked to life belonging to my kingdom. I cherish that in you.

Liam, for that reason I call you because your book is written already. I saw you walking on the road and on the beach reflecting over my Word. I have not forgotten how you wanted my Word written on your forehead and in your heart. You meditated regularly on my Son's Gospel. And I noticed the care you gave to my Son's Word. That's discipleship Liam.

Liam, I like simplicity in studying my Word. I like my followers to squeeze the juice from my Word. I don't want you to write about new life. I want your intellect to explain it. I liked your kneeling by the bedside pondering my Word. You browsed scriptural commentaries for an edge to capture the sense of my Word. And I'd like you to never give up on my Word. It has new life Liam. My seed will grow in a mind that cherishes my Word.

So Liam, I include you on my team. I know you are loyal to the Church, Bishops and priests. I'm one hundred percent certain that anything you say wouldn't harm the Church. And I know your feelings of sympathy for priests who find their workloads stretched to the limit. Liturgical ceremonies can wear you down and some priests are unable to go to a quiet place for rest and to refresh themselves. I might change that scenario in the future.

Liam, I have accepted your desire to write. It's because you have experience of my Word and the Church. And I add that you are committed to me. You can write for me. I'll not stand in the way. Writing wouldn't be demanding if completed through an atmosphere of love. I've found a gem in you. I'm glad that you have offered your intellect as a medium to turn the world towards my Power and Love so as to avoid hatred and human disaster. I'll regard your intellect as a depot to fight a war of Peace and Love for each other.

Little Man

Father, I'd be honoured to do something good for the world. And I am more than willing to give you use of my intellect for a good cause. I'm shocked as I know you are of the horrible events in recent years of suicide bombings that shame our humanity and experience of life.

Father I'm delighted to write for you and there is no question of my will choosing themes. My shutters are open. I welcome your Word with open arms. But please forgive me. I'm excited about my future. I know you will guide me to write to the world and propose a Peace and Love plan that may concentrate on the welfare of each human person alive throughout all countries in the world. I will promise a vow to you Big Eye. I, Liam Walsh, on road L0909 will solemnly commit to obey and write for God Our Father until I'm called to die at the end of my life.

Father, inspire me. I love you. I'm patient and will wait for Golden Eggs to appear in my intellect that has wonderful beauty and possibilities to highlight a Father's Love and Peace for every person and Nation in the world. I'll write letters to every nation like St Paul did for early Christian communities. I have the welfare of the world at heart.

Father, I'm very pleased that you inspire me. I'm opposed to war but I'm at loggerheads within in regard how I should feel about the perpetrators of evil. I know of your teaching Father. I'm to forgive them. I'm to love enemies. I'm to show compassion. But it is difficult to still my mind when it is rocked by bombs that are aimed to kill my way of life and my values.

Father, I'm opposed to war. War has devastating effects on families and communities. It's nothing but an outrage bombing bodies and buildings. But the root cause of war could be deeper where souls around the world suffer from an erosion of spirituality. I see it in my own country where human power has usurped Catholic influences. I'm very disappointed that you Father and your Son Jesus Christ have been pushed aside among today's generation of Irish people. I'm deeply alarmed by the erosion of faith in the minds and hearts of our people. The unspiritual state of people today is frightening. I know Father that you are deeply concerned about the erosion of holiness in families and society everywhere in my country in this day and age.

Big Eye

Liam thanks for your vow to work for me. I'm glad you made a Solemn Vow. You promise to write for me. This is a good vocation. This is a good vow. You broke your last vows of chastity, poverty and obedience. But look I know your mentality. You want to commit to me single-mindedly. You thought the Church was the best way to fulfil that sentiment. But I now know that you want a direct relationship with me. I accept your dedication.

Liam, I support your writing. I'm happy enough for you to try and bring back the spirit of St Patrick and St Columba. Every generation needs renewal. And in your book I want you to tell the Irish people to turn back to me. I haven't been happy with the lackadaisical rejection of my Church. I want all believers in my Son to stand up and proclaim their faith. I'm very unhappy with dead and sleepy worshippers. I want to hear your faith from the rooftops. A little murmur of a voice is not heartfelt worship.

Liam, I am with you all the way in your attempts to revive the faith in your country. I don't want to see bodies littered in houses and fields and around the country due to their rejection of my Son and his Church. Intellectualism will not save you. I'm an old God millions of years old and if I viewed your generation at the moment possibly only ten out of four million might make it to heaven.

Liam, don't bog your mind by becoming stuck in words. I flow naturally. I'd like the same for you. I'd not like your writing if you push me aside. I'm gone from your intellect as soon as you omit me. Our spiritual connection breaks up as soon as you attempt to repossess your soul.

Chapter Thirty

Little Man

Father, I know what you want. It's deliciously desirable too. It's deeply appetizing. It's what I always wanted to do. It's to think sincerely. It's deep thinking, meditation, contemplation. Call it what you like. I think twenty-four seven on Jesus and cherish his Word. That's real food. That's real life. That's highly excitable to think about. It thrills my mind and heart.

Father, I must decrease. It's not want I want anymore. I've emptied my mind to focus on you. I add a crucial statement summed up in your prayer Thy Will Be Done. That's a nutcracker. That's a done deal. It's the difference between the door being shut or open to your Kingdom.

O Father! O Big Eye! O God! It's clinched. The penny has dropped. Inspiration comes thick and fast. I've to know and obey God's Will. I've to pray about it. I've to think about it. It's a three letter word that's in the dictionary of millions of words. I love it. I have to be sure. I can't guess it. What is it?

Father, tell me. What exactly is God's Will? Let me be frank and relevant about this. What does Big Eye want me to do? I hope he doesn't want me crucified like his own Son, Jesus. It's a super question. I want to work for you Father. But that implies doing what I'm told.

Father, the first task therefore is to discover God's Will. This is a work that could take months and years of praying. I have to be diligent about it. I've to be persistent about it. The greatest example of what I refer to is Jesus Christ. In the garden on that fatal day he surrendered his will to his Father when he agreed to allow himself to be arrested so as to save mankind. I must follow Jesus. I allow you Father to take possession of my life so that all that I do or say is in union with my Father's desire.

The second task is to do God's Will. This task isn't easy either. It takes time to figure it out. It will only come through prayer. We change our mind often. A human mind could be in disarray and unsteady. I could change my minds ten times in a day.

Father I have identified two tasks. This is one. I write for you Father every day in order to communicate to the world the importance of your concerns for the human race. And I'll develop and improve my union with you Father as the months pass by. I hope to have a book about my mission on the shelves as soon as possible. I'm definitely confident that my writing will contain God's inspiration. The content of my writings will flow once my soul is clean and my intellect is swamped with God's influence. I cannot stand by and allow a deterioration of Big Eye's presence to be pushed out of the lives of Nations and human beings. Nobody should live for this world alone. Each life is a stepping stone towards death and resurrection. This fact of Christ's death and resurrection should never disappear from the memory of man.

Father, my number one task is writing and the second is meditation. I hope to launch meditation groups everywhere. I think of Meditation Huts in National Parks and places where there are forest walks. Groups, families or individuals could drop in and meditate for a while. I always loved meditation and I facilitated groups in the past.

My intention Holy Father if it is your Will is to pray with people everywhere. I can go to families, communities, schools, senior citizens, Churches, or broken souls and pray with them. I go everywhere and anywhere to pray with others. It's one thing to establish a prayerful relationship with you Father but it is another thing to love and help others. And it is this second aspect that pleases you.

Father, I walk home happy. I loved our chat on the road. Thank you Father. The mist and cloud has lifted from my mind. The sun enlightened my soul. And my love tripled on the way. It's definitely a bounce back from setbacks.

Big Eye

Liam, we blend well now and progress has been made. The pieces of your personality fit better now and I can see a warm heart and lovely mind developing. I'm very happy Liam with you. I can see a spiritual house been built.

Liam I say this to you because reassurance spurs up excitement in you. I'm delighted that your intention is to obey me. And I'm grateful that you love the Gospel of my Word. And you plan to help people pray to me. I like your readiness to aim you're very being in the direction of my kingdom. I look forward immensely to many encounters with you as we dialogue. At last I have a brain on earth that I can trust and work with. All you can do now in the coming years is to remind the inhabitants of the earth that rational souls are made for heaven and not to wallow in power struggles with each other on earth.

Liam, I urge balance and caution in writing as I don't want you to feel like a fish that has to live in the water all the time. I want balance where opportunities are there for you to write, walk and pray. I saw how happy you were after a long walk.

Liam, there is one more thing and it has to do with assignments in Part Two of this book. I choose for you Golden Eggs meditations. These are designed to create permanency in your life regarding love and obedience. It's no use loving me and remembering me for a short period of time. Your love for me has to have steel and strength attached. Otherwise my Word will flow in and out of your mind. The meditations are a deeper way of applying your mind to my Word. It's a way of always valuing me as your Father.

So Liam I pick the Eggs. I don't want them coming out of your mouth without being properly contemplated. The problem in the world today through social media is that everyone is mouthy and speaks loosely with no depth of meaning in their hearts and minds. My Word has the greatest and highest wisdom available to mankind. It will last forever. Nothing surpasses it. It is free from roguery and deceit. It is my Truth. Rogue souls, deceitful souls and dishonest souls will never reach the height of perfection.

Liam, I'm planting Golden Eggs into your intellect for consideration and contemplation. I'm confident that you will hatch them and create newly born holy chicks that have my gene and are on the side of my Truth and Love.

Liam, meditate on the seed that I plant in your soul. All day walk around and seek quiet places in order to keep the Egg warm and that it doesn't go cold.

Think deeply about them. The Egg is my Word in your mind. Liam, feel the shell and rub its beauty. I solemnly tell you that I'm never far away from my Word. The more attention you give to My Word the more I reveal myself.

Little Man

Father, it is late in the evening. Where has the day gone? I remember nothing from it. In the morning I travelled to the city. In the afternoon I listened to a rugby match on the radio. And I watched a Gaelic football game on television. I'm sorry about this Father. I wasted my time. However, I didn't receive any Golden Eggs yet. I had no obligation to dwell on a Word Egg.

Father, I'm sorrow too for eating recklessly. I stuffed myself today. I ate all the wrong stuff. This continuous desire to eat worries me. I'd have food in my mouth before my mind knows it. It's the wrong type of food too which holds a large amount of sugar. I'm sorry about this too Father. The action is not compatible with discipline, sharpness and bodily preparation to dwell on your Holy Word.

However, Father, I've bounced back. St Anselm's book refreshed me. I came across the words admit me into the inner chamber of your love. And my holy friend Anselm also added the words I ask seek and knock. It's just what I had been waiting for. These ideas are encouraging. I like them. I love you Anselm. His words are Golden Egg quality.

Big Eye

Liam, you have a sharp eye. Anselm writes like you in the way you pray the words in a personal way. Also you share the same birthday.

And it's wonderful that you feel close to him. I welcome a spirit of communion among my beloved friends in heaven and on earth. I have Anselm beside me. He is willing to close the gap of nine hundred years that exist between you and work together for the good of your soul and all others that concern you.

Liam it is lovely. I admitted Anselm into the inner chamber of my love. He is a little lamb. He is often in the same room as me and I keep him close to my heart. I'm sure you would like to be with us. And because you are an admirer and friend I invite you into the inner chamber of my love. I can do this for you Liam while you are living in the world if you go into yourself. Do what Anselm did regularly. He shut out everything except me. My room is magnificent and you are welcome to knock at the door. I'll allow Anselm to open the door to you. I guarantee you that you will not be sorry.

Liam. I have a challenge for you. Seeing that you stumbled upon Anselm's words I'm going to give you them as your first Golden Egg challenge. I challenge you to figure out through prayer and meditation what you think is meant by my Words to knock, to seek and to find. I've just planted those three little Golden Eggs into your intellect. Liam, best of luck! I'll check in later.

Little Man

Oh Father! I'm excited by my Golden Egg challenge. I could see you planting them gently in my mind. They are lovely -three little brown nuggets. I don't want to give birth to strangers. I want to know what my little eggs are. I like my first challenge because the Holy Eggs has a substance in them that may connect me to Jesus Christ.

Father the first Egg is I ask. My whole being swivelled with excitement at the thought of cracking open this egg that fundamentally could give me anything I want from you Big Eye.

Father, I'm thrilled with your challenge. I warmly mull over this little brown egg. It activates my intellect into action. I search now for data in my inner rational faculties to analyse the word asks, and come up with a perfect answer. And I am almost one hundred percent certain my prayer is to ask for admittance into the inner chamber of Christ's love. I want more than anything else for Christ to put his arms around my head and make me feel accepted and loved.

Father, I'm thrilled with Anselm for inspiring me. These little words ask, seek and knock are so simple that intellectuals don't bother with them. Father, you prod our conscience. You actually tell me what to ask for, what to seek and the door to knock at. Anselm, you used those very words nine hundred years ago. I use them now in order to discover within myself what matters in life now and what my aims should be.

Father, my Golden Egg is in a nest of unimaginable potential. In fact, Big Eye you are giving me a weapon to torment you with. I could ask for anything. But in general I think I will only ask for what is good for me, for my family, for my community and for my country.

Father, my unworthiness has struck me. I'm overawed by having the door into your chamber of love opened to me. I can't face you. You are magnificent in comparison to me. I'm miserable and sick. I couldn't walk into your mansion and feel comfortable among St Dominic, St Anselm, St Augustine and other loyal servants of yours. I don't deserve a place in heaven. I couldn't relax mixing with distinguished company. I'd feel out of place. I'm a miserable wretch in comparison to beautiful and pure saints. It would be evident straight away that I don't deserve a white robe at the Lord's Table. There is no way that my heart and mind would feel comfortable in the company of St Thomas Aquinas and St Catherine.

Father, I'm unworthy. So I don't know how to approach you. I shudder at the thought of a little unknown man like me feeling at ease among fine virgins, martyrs and saints of the Church. I don't know if perfect servants would shake my hand and embrace an imperfect and unholy body and soul.

Father, I'm utterly humiliated at the thought of my entry into your chamber of love. Your chamber is Sacred and Glorious. Your Holy Place is heaven. I love you Father. I love you Jesus. But will you accept me? I write to tell the world of the importance of loving you and you're Church. Nothing is greater on earth. A nobler task doesn't exist.

Father, I don't mean to be impertinent. I have faith in you. I'm not looking for entry into your chamber of love by the back door or as a favour. I genuinely love you more than anything else.

Father, I'm open to change for I know that my imperfect state requires transformation before approaching the door of your chamber of love. I'm well aware of my weakness. I'm well aware of my bodily and mental shortcomings. I crawl towards your Presence feeling feeble and in awe. But I have hope Father that you can repair broken bodies and fix my blind eyes and deaf ears so that my life becomes holy and pure.

Father, I welcome the tip of your finger to touch me and send sizzling powers of holiness, grace, peace and love through me. I know at this present moment I am unworthy to set foot inside the chamber of your love. I'm unfit to be in the company of your Son Jesus and sit at a banquet full of holy Saints.

Father, what happens if you turn me away for not caring enough for my neighbour, the sick, the poor and the broken hearted. I'd be devastated. I'd be hysterical. I'd regard rejection by you, Father a bitter blow. Therefore, I do declare that my writing is designed to help souls to worship you Big Eye. I've always realised that if I don't have your Spirit Father and your Son's Spirit in me then I would have nothing to offer one single soul on earth. I can't give what I haven't got. So I put the onus on you Big Eye to fill me up like a tank of petrol so that I can move forward with energy to drive your message into the hearts of nations.

Father, I move too fast looking for results based on impatient motivation. I haven't meditated or contemplated properly on the Golden Egg and yet I pressurise God for inclusion into his kingdom. Come on Liam. Cop on! I'm just settling in to nurturing your Word Father that nests in the eye of my intellect. I can't expect instant results. I haven't dwelt on the Egg long enough. I've not done enough intellectual work to fathom what I truly desire from my Holy Father in heaven. So I have to return to the mind, return to the nest and meditate profusely on the Word of my Father that's narrowed down to find out what it is that my souls ask for, or my soul seeks, or where the door to Christ's house is located.

Father, a huge question of enormous importance has risen for me. In what manner should I approach your Throne of Grace? Am I to have a shower and put on my best suit and shoes? I like to feel well and look well every time I attend Church and approach the Holy of Holies for the Body and Blood of your Son Jesus Christ. Or would you prefer if I were casual and word jean and didn't care about my appearance? I just don't know what way you would like me Father. I'm inclined to think that your preference Big Eye is for me to approach the Altar of your Son in a humble and sincere manner like a newly born lamb.

Father, I think this seek question, and ask question and knock question are exceptionally relevant because it's embedded in the early formalities of a soul meeting Christ, your Son. The Holy Golden Egg is about admittance into the chamber of love that is a holy and blessed place. It about finding a treasure that is beautiful and remote from every single eye of each human being on earth.

Father, I humbly approach the door of heaven. I'm knocking now. It doesn't matter whether I dress in an immaculate suit or wear rags. My heart is hot for Jesus. My mind desires him more than anything else. I have no idea whether the door will be opened. But I can only imagine that at the other side is Jesus, or an angel or a saint. And I have come out of seven billion people on the face of the earth to make my way to heaven's door. I could even be met by my father Edward or my friend Fr William.

Fr William saved me before by reassuring me that I had a vocation. And I had a talent after all. I made it to the Altar and blessed bread and wine for thousands of people over fourteen years. And my father Edward sowed the seeds of faith in me by reciting the daily rosary every evening and showing good example by encouraging us to attend Mass and confession.

Father, I'm trembling. Heaven is in the heart and mind of Jesus. I have to go through the crucifix. There is no other route to heaven. And I turned away from my salvation due to clashes with generals that misguided and undermined my talent to work hard for Christ in the vineyard of his Churches. So I plead now for Christ to readmit me into the life of his Body and Blood. I want to draw love from Christ's heart.

I want to draw wisdom from Christ's mind. I hope Christ is merciful and compassionate to me. It would be a terrible thing to be locked out, and unwanted, and rejected by the door to Christ's chamber of love been shut to me.

Father, I'll crawl through all the mud of the earth, and shake of all the dirt stuck in me internally and externally by washing myself with sincere confessions and humble prayer in order to make up for years of mistakes in failing to turn to you Big Eye and sticking with your Son Jesus through thick and thin. I stand before you with legs and arms outstretched in complete surrender for my body and soul to be cleansed and made as white as snow. I confess all my past sins and recent sins because I love you Father. I'm sorry.

Father, I believe you have the power to forgive me. I believe you can transform me. I believe you can wash me clean. But is it enough? I could be outside the door waiting a long time. I'm in trouble for not preaching the Gospel. I walked away due to a pride clash. I believed in the Mass but I couldn't handle the mess of men and imperfections of weak leadership.

Father, I'm not ready to knock at your door. I have done nothing for the spread of your Word across the globe. I tell you solemnly now that I beg on my knees for every person in Ireland and throughout the world to turn to Jesus Christ. I appeal to all those who don't care about their souls to turn to Big Eye, to turn to God, to turn to Jesus Christ, to turn to the Holy Spirit, to turn to the Gospel. If one person reads this and turns to God as a result of it, I could return to knock at heaven's door. And I might be allowed in because I saved a lost soul. I guarantee you that if you could taste the sweetness of the Lord as I have you will not regret your decision to turn from sin and the world and aim for heaven.

Big Eye

Liam, I like your writing written above and it is well written. And I'm happy with any human mind that reflect on my Word and does one's best to understand and comprehend its true meaning in relation to living one's lives. But Liam I highlight the issues for you. I tell you what you are doing wrong. And a big stumbling block for you is worry.

You are not God Liam. Let me do the worrying. Have you ever been short of anything? I provide for you. So stop worrying about your son's education, about what bills are to be paid, about your health, about your marriage, and the things you have to do.

Liam, I know what you need. There is no need for you to be going asleep worrying, or waking up worrying, or worrying about your diabetes and wife's health. And stop worrying about growing old. All you need worry about is your love for me. And after that everything falls into place.

Liam, worry kills a person. So come to your senses and trust me. I love you and there is no fear of my rejection for anyone that desires to write to me every day and proclaim their love for me. I require from your obedience so that you can work on the things you are asked to do. The word, "Ask" can work both ways. You ask me for holy gifts so as to be like my Son Jesus. But when I ask you to make the necessary changes your internal intellectual networks divert away from compliance due to roguish interferences.

Liam, I ask you to enjoy what you are doing and love me. I require concentration on my Word. I'm here to help and not clog your mind up with worry. So be your natural self. I release tension in your body and soul. I remind you once more that my Son Jesus laid the foundations to save the world. It is still valid in your life time. I'm not expecting you to carry a bagful of sins and the workload of cleansing the world from sin. So don't think you are my Christ. You are not. I'm happy for you to be a little gentle lamb. So let your hair down and allow all your worries to flow away into the abyss. I'll stroke the side of your cheek and you'll feel everything is okay. Everything is in my hands.

Liam, my challenges to you is your bread and butter work that earns you credit for participation in spreading my Word. Golden Eggs are challenges. But you will enjoy them because they will narrow the divide between the sloth of a meaningless existence and a desire to climb the steps towards the heart and soul of my Son, Jesus Christ.

Liam, I'm very serious about these Egg meditations. I want my Word in your nest. I want energy put into producing insights and even revelations into the meaning of my Son's Word. When all is said and done and in regard to the history of my Word very little is known about me. There are libraries full of knowledge about me but face to face encounters are rare. There are very few who can see things as they are without been conditioned by culture and education. I hope you have far seeing eyes and see foresee the future of man.

Liam, I have nothing but admiration for you in allowing me into your mind. But as I said before I repeat now this is not a short term arrangement. I do not want huge big gaps in a day where you go missing or your mind goes blank and nothing is happening spiritually or mentally.

Liam, think about my Golden Egg. All day ask for the bread that you need from me. I request from you that you keep alive the words ask, seek and knock. I'd like you Liam to comprehend the nature and significance of Golden Eggs. So sit and kneel while contemplating my Word. Only an idiot doesn't know what to ask for. By prayer Liam you can produce a beautiful new life.

Little Man

Father, I do my best to focus on you and use my underused mind. It is here in the intellect that you Father must thrive and build your home. I'd like my mind to be a spiritual powerhouse. And I might just achieve that if I concentrate on the internal life. It's in the inner self that Golden Eggs are hatched. I know what has to be done. I have the Egg. I have the Word. But where is the chick? Where is New Life? It's in the Holy Word. Think! Think! Think!

Father, I have this beautiful word **ask**. This is your Word placed in my mind.

It's surrounded by a shell. It's a gem in a nut. I have to crack its shell and delight in its taste. I ask for nothing other than you Father. I want to feel your love and care of me. I ask for Holy Bread every day.

Father, I put this word through my intellect now. It's dancing in my brain. It's bouncing up and down like numbers in a lotto jar. It's just a simple word. What's its significance? It's a popular word. It's a word in the dictionary. It's a word used by your Son in the Gospel. I'm advised by Jesus Christ to ask and I shall receive.

Father, I don't want to annoy your Son Jesus by asking for rubbishy things or trivial things. Nor do I want to ask for extravagant favours to fit in with the rich and have plenty. But I do ask for health favours for those I love. And I do ask for acceptance into your circle of friends. And I do ask that I comprehend deep meanings from prayerful thinking on Golden Eggs.

Meditations   Part Two

Meditation on I ask, I seek, and I knock   Golden Egg

St Anselm wrote, *"Lord, admit me into the inner room of your love. I ask, I seek, and I knock"*. I adopt these words now and apply them to my life. The value of the written word is evident here. I meditate now on words written by St Anselm nine hundred years ago. I borrow his thoughts. I learn from his thoughts. In order for me to gain admittance into the holy room and meet Christ certain conditions are required from my intellect. Anselm's desire is like mine. I knock at the door of love. All I want is Christ. In order for this to happen I must train my mind to focus on Christ. I can't allow children to irritate me. I can't allow a woman to frustrate me. I ask for Christ. All I want is Christ.

The Golden Egg that is called **Ask** is my first child. I fertilise it with prayer so that it will grow. I manure the roots of the word. The Egg begins to grow. I have come up through my heart and into my neck in search for a spot in my mind where I could park this Word or this Egg called **Ask**.

Holy Father, I'm beginning to suspect that people use words without understanding their significance and deep rooted meaning. I'm the same. I use holy words with proper comprehension. That's why advice and learning flies in one ear and out the other. Therefore, I pray to you Father that it's understood that I **Ask** for one thing and one thing alone.

Father, the best way for me to remember this Egg contemplation is for me to step out of my own body and look at myself through the eyes of another. I want this Word **Ask** to stake a permanent place in my minute to minute thinking and rest permanently in my memory. And I want it to be noted that I **Ask** for Jesus. I cut out everything except Christ. I ask for Jesus alone. I think this simple little word was the cause of my downfall. In prayer I didn't ask for Jesus enough in my life.

Father I ask for unity with you and Jesus. I'm at the door knocking. Anselm pleaded for admittance into your chamber of love nine hundred years ago. In my lifetime today I want to go through the crucifix and into a holy room where you dwell. I challenge my brain to seek this desire. I want nothing more than your love and intimacy oozing from your heart into mine, and work its way up into my brain of sawdust.

Father, I love the new prayer technique that you have given me. Several times today I walked and thought about what **I Ask** you for. I also sat in a cafe and looked out into the sky and reaffirmed the desire of my mind. **I ask** for Jesus. It's simple. Lots of times throughout the day **I ask** for Jesus. I'm not seeking a millionaire or riches. I know someday I'll die and cannot bring anything with me. And I know also that life now is a preparation for death and resurrection. While in the cafe I saw two women having a chat and another woman on her own. I thought to myself about the value of human friendships. I'm at a loss here as I always pick up irritations and frustrations with people. All I want is to walk, pray and write. And I love the Golden Egg development as I don't have to refer to a book to remember your Word. I have it in my mind instead. As many times as possible now I simply **ask** for Jesus.

Father, I'm extremely pleased with myself. I do not want to talk to a rich woman at all. I want nothing filtering into my mind except to ask for Jesus. In all situations that I find myself in **I ask** for Jesus. It is really helping me to focus. I'm the happiest person on earth due to the creation of new life from the Egg Word. O my God! O my Father! It's a sensational delivery. I have a mechanism that can be applied to all difficult situations.

Father, life is beautiful when loved. There is nothing to outweigh the trust and love a child has for a parent. Nor is there anything to surpass the love adults share with each other. In fact, love of any kind is beautiful and even more so when someone believes in you. True love for each other is beautiful. **I Ask** for Jesus' love.

Father, are the words **I seek** different? How is it different from **I Ask**? When I think about this holy Egg – the second of a trinity of Golden Egg Words I think of a world search. Where is Jesus to be found? He is found in his Word. He is found in the Egg. St Catherine would say he is found in the eye of the intellect. He is found on the cross.

Father, I seek Jesus. A clever University student might say to me that he is dead for over two thousand years. He is history. But I would argue that he rose again and ascended to heaven. And there lies a clue as to where **I seek** Jesus. He sits at your right hand Father in heaven. The Catholic faith teaches this truth.

Father, I set my heart therefore on heaven where your Son sits on the throne at your right side. **I seek** Jesus in heaven. Therefore, I lock this Egg, this Golden Word in my mind too. It's the second Egg. And the new life emerging from this Holy Word is that my mind is fixed on things that are above. Inside the door of heaven is the chamber of love. I have to train my mind to seek Christ. My real life is Christ.

Father, I relish my new self and my new life. I love you Jesus. I'm sorry female. I choose Christ. He excites me in a way that has Sacredness written all over it. Christ is all. Christ is in all. Jesus gives me a buzz while the world is full of fuss.

Father, **I seek** something Sacred – something that scares at the same time. My mind prays for comprehension. **I ask** for Jesus. **I seek** Jesus. These tasks require diligence. These words are special. I pray with great intensity and fix my mind on possible locations as to where Jesus might be found. I can't figure it out.

Father, help me. I physically can't go to heaven until death so is there a spiritual line that can be opened between us. I can think of Christ in heaven. I can think of Christ on the road to Emmaus talking to two sad disciples who didn't recognise the Risen Jesus. I can pray to his loving Sacred Heart. I can receive his Body and Blood. I can mediate on the Gospel. I could travel everywhere looking for the Lord in magnificent Churches throughout the world. And I may never find him.

Father, I think Jesus is found closer to home. I could find him in the hearts and minds of people who pray to him. I could find Jesus in an elderly man or woman. Christ is in people. Christians know each other. There is warmness between them. There is a little light in the mind and heart of each believer that manifests itself like a flaming smile. This is very noticeable when greeting one another during gatherings for Mass and prayer.

Father, **I seek** Jesus. And I'm beginning to think that all three of you Father, Son and Spirit can dwell in the mind and heart of those who welcome you. It's not one or the other. It's all three Divine Persons working in the soul. This is a beautiful thought. This is what I want. This book indicates this fact. I wrote for Big Eye. His Word is in me.

Father, for me to adore your beautiful Mind I must become aware of you in my mind. I'm direct, honest and truthful here. You can't place God's Word in a turnip or in a non-thinking human being. I like this idea. It challenges me to think in unison with the Holy Spirit. I'm attracted to the recreation of my mind that seeks Jesus in heaven. I intend to think more about you Big Eye. In the past I didn't consider your Mind or pay attention to your Word. My mind is so deficient that it can't grasp the enormous magnitude as to who Jesus truly is. The story of this book is about a little man being watched by God, and the development of a relationship. I'm told everything is possible for you Big Eye. The requirement is a little bit of faith and it has the capability to move mountains and the largest of problems.

Father, how come it took me so long to wake up to the enormity of your Greatness. I overlooked the miracles of your Son. And I didn't allow your Word into my inner ear and connect with my mind. I feel like a slow learner. But I'm back now. I've bypassed thunderstorms. I'm on the Golden Egg trail. **I seek** Jesus. I love his Body, his Heart, his Mind, his Word and everything about him.

Father, help me. I'm in a dilemma here in my room. I don't know where to seek Jesus. I use all these words but I don't extract the significant sense from the word seek. I could seek Jesus on the cross. But my heart would go out to him if I was to seek him while suffering. I could seek the Risen Jesus. I could seek Jesus as King in heaven. I could seek Jesus in my mind.

Father, I think you are telling me that I can do all the seeking in the world and yet miss the point of focus. And who am I anyway to force myself onto Jesus. I'm treading on overgrown paths and mountainous wilds. I'm on the wrong roads. I have run into a torrent of emotional drama and found myself lost in a bunch of nestles, bushes and thistles. I'm at a standstill and need to check my bearings. I have to walk and pray and return to the Golden Egg. **I seek** you Jesus.

Father, I'm under duress and can't find you. I can't hatch your Golden Word. It's not warming up and there doesn't seem to be any life in it. The situation concerns me deeply. The wind blows cold. And the problems of kids flood around the Egg, and it has left such a mess that it may take days to recover and find the revelation behind the Word Seek.

Father, I'm utterly lost. The big bad demon sprang into action and trampled over the Egg Seek and left a muddy mind and dishevelled nest. It's a question of repair work now. **I knock** for help Jesus. But where is the door? Where is Christ's chamber of love? It's not a nice feeling.

Big Eye, can you see me? Help! I've been ravaged by a demon and feel abandoned in a mountain bush crying for help. I've lost sight of you, Father big time. Big Eye, stretch out your hand and pluck me from the wild and scary abyss and bring me back to the lambs. I'm sorry. And I pray for a good shepherd to take care of me.

Father, I'm sorry. I didn't trust enough. My prayer was weak. I didn't ask for help in time nor did I know where to seek you in my time of crisis. I'm on the way back to you battered and bruised from my stormy ride and savage demonic attacks. Immediately I meditated and contemplated in order to calm down my palpitating mind. I found a way at last to seek you. I've retrieved the Egg and it's warming up to a reunion with Jesus. **I seek** Jesus in prayer.

Father the next few hours are crucial. I think of life as a maze of doors. I struggle and crawl out of a cold place full of bramble, vermin and bulldogs and open a door into your chamber of love. It feels like departure from a hellish experience. It's feels like shutting a door on angry souls. It feels like running for life from a pack of hungry lions. It's like shutting a door on demons and at the other side is a warm room where Jesus waits for the repentant and humble person to cling to the

Lord for safety. It's the difference between a neglectful shabby and run-down life experience and a warm, welcoming and beautiful room full of Doctors of the Church with Christ as Lord and Master.

Father, **I seek** this holy room. **I knock** at the door. I don't know what swept me away with the tide of evil. I drive now towards the chamber of love with humble reverence and gentle attitude. Hopefully I'll be admitted. Save me Jesus. I knock solidly. I'm outside the door. I'm looking for you Jesus. I mediate on this desire. I contemplate quietly and beg admittance into your heart of love. I pray in bed and on the road, and seek quiet places so that I can keep knocking at the door of your love.

Father, it has been an awful struggle for me over the years fighting my demons that stood in the way of my love for you. It looks as if I had a lot of doors to go through before arriving at your house of love. I tried the door of sport, the door of romance, the door of comfort, the door of sloth, and the door of disarray. I have gone through a lot of doors and now I arrive at the house of Christ. I long for reunification with sincere priests and the faithful people that attend Christ's house every day.

Father, I have no other desire. **I ask** for Jesus. **I seek** Jesus. **I knock** at the door now. I don't care about anything else. I've lost my love for money, fame and sensual sniffing. I deeply plough into a world of exploration into the mysterious power behind the Holy Eggs of asking for Jesus, seeking Jesus and knocking at his door. I'll wait for as long as it takes for heaven's door to open to me.

Father, I know these steps are preliminary. And I know that these steps are continuous action. There's life in these Holy Words. I don't want them to ever die within me. I'm the worker that must cherish them in my mind by prayer.

Father, your Son is hiding on me. I can't find him. I've gone through three mind storms in the last three days and it has devastated my peace of mind and cut off my supply of grace. I challenged a sleeping demon. I stirred up a sleeping devil in another soul and there was a fierce scuffle. I can't seek Jesus in this condition or state of being. I was unable for the strong demon.

Father, I'm going through a rough time. I hear of cancer. I saw a dead cow in the field. I hear of brain tumours. And I hear of sickness. I hear of people having only a few months to live. I should really care for people instead of seeking Jesus for myself. Am I selfish? All I want to do is declare and proclaim my love for you Jesus. And in using the words **I seek Jesus** a realisation has dawned on me that your Church doors are open to everyone every day. I should be going to Mass and praying with Christian believers. I have to go to the place where Jesus is. This truthful realisation triples the importance of the Church and the role of pastors who care for their lambs. At every opportunity the sheep of Christ should make their way to Church.

Father, I adore dialogue with you and feel at times sensational as a result. The thought of Jesus loving me is a great feeling. I love him in return. This friendship makes me happy inside. It changes my evening. It changes my life. I know by the level of joy in me that my union with Jesus is as it should be. I feel Jesus around me and my appearance radiates into the eyes of others.

Father, that feeling happens when I feel good by being with your Son through a proper disposition of gentle respect for his Holy Name and humble approaches through the right kind of prayer. The sweetness of the Lord run dry when I listen to games, read newspapers, visit shops, and do nothing. And I'm tossed into the wild ocean when mind storms blow through my brain and heart killing every attempt to pray. So there is no point in blaming Big Eye or anyone else for my failure to remain calm and find quiet places until the storms pass by.

The love of Christ is everything. It surpasses all trials and tribulations. There's no life in temporary pastimes and yet over half of the world indulge in human achievement events that create a different kind of glory than that which comes from befriending Christ Jesus.

Father, I have come to the end of my First Meditation on a Golden Egg challenge. I'm happy but with my mind changing regularly like the weather it isn't easy to consistently maintain concentration levels necessary to create long lasting revelations. I add that the mind goes asleep a lot too. And I further add that problems hamper growth. So I have work to do. I have challenged myself to nurture the seeds of these

Holy Words by asking for Jesus more regularly, and seeking Jesus at every opportunity until I have the door to the inner chamber of Christ's love opened to me. Amen

A Letter to Politicians

Dear Politicians

God asked me to write you a letter. He wants me to ask you a few questions. Why have you become so irreligious? I love Ireland. I love its people. I love its culture. I love its Church. Ireland has been a beacon for the world. Ireland is a small country. Yet it has shone brightly for centuries. But all that's changing in recent years by greedy politicians and by an irreligious agenda.

Therefore, I write this letter to you. I criticise decisions to legalise same sex marriages. Woe to you for changing God's Law. In the whole of the Bible with a history of over three thousand years not once did any Leader of a Nation legislate for same sex marriages? And now your little country has led from the front in classifying two men or two women as having a right to marry each other.

I write on behalf of God. I speak for God. I solemnly tell you that God doesn't approve. The reason is very simple. It's so simple that intellectuals might bypass its simplicity. I'll tell you the truth. This is it in a nutshell. A man is not made for sexual activity with a man. And a woman is not made for sexuality activity with a woman. This activity between humans is a deviation from God's Plan. That's why I'll never classify a gay marriage as a marriage. It's wrong. The argument is over. I'll accept no protests even if all humans disagree with me.

I repeat just in case you can't comprehend this truth in relation to what Constitutes a marriage. A nut fits into a bolt. They become knotted together. These two match – the nut and bolt. Two bolts can't unite. It's a mismatch. Neither can two nuts. It's a mismatch too. The bolt is the man. The nut is the woman. Only these can marry. I solemnly condemn politicians in Ireland for agreeing to gay marriage. Russia banned it. I'm proud of them.

Woe to you politicians. The consequence of your decision has long term effects. It increases the gay population. It teaches children that same sex relationships are normal. It creates a divide between Church and State. It damages moral standards.

I'm sorry gays. I do love you. I don't hate you. But you have no future together. Your relationships are not part of God's Plan. I can't ever see Christ accepting you at the altar to marry. It's not good news for faith in the future. It's not good news for the country. But you do exist. And you have the right to exist.

A separate State Law should have been enacted to recognise your relationship. It should not have been tagged to marriages between a man and a woman because it really is something else and very different.

Meditation on Choices

Every individual, every family, every parish, every community, every household have opportunities to choose. Every boy, girl, teenager, man, woman, single person, married person, old men, old women, and all have a capacity to choose. Choices make us what we are.

There are thousands of choices to make every day as well as throughout a life time. In one day alone many choices are made. It could be washing your teeth. It could be anything. Choices are personal. Sometimes external factors like neighbourhood, families and environment come into play.

Let's look at a few choice types. What do you prefer? To go to Mass on Sunday mornings! Or to lie in bed on Sunday mornings! To read a good book! Or to listen to a boring priest! How many have made this choice?

Everyone has. You either lie in bed or go to Church, or do something else. What do you do on a Sunday morning? Some families lie in bed. It's rest day. Others might attend a sports game. Only a few attend Church.

Let's analyse this choice. What's best for the soul? Think carefully. What value has Church? What's value has resting in bed?

My Choice

I prefer to attend Mass. I never miss Mass. I'm a Catholic and believe in God. I've gone to Mass all my life. My father did too. So does my mother. I was brought up that way. I firmly love the Church. It's one of the only few free places a human being can visit in the world. I do not intend to change. This choice is beneficial. I feel better after it. I hear God's Word and receive the Body of Christ. It's better than a football match or any other type of activity.

Sunday worship is required from all believers. The practise of faith benefits family and community.

God has a Big Eye. He sees. Why aren't children at Mass? I see mostly elderly people. Church attendance is sparse. God's house or the Parish Church is there for everyone. It's a house of prayer. It takes forty minutes a week. God's Word is heard. The Body and Blood of Christ are received. Prayers are offered for everyone living and deceased. The community gathers. Christ blesses us. I wouldn't miss it for anyone. It makes me happy. It's the greatest event of all. There's no charge at the door.

On the other hand, and it is a majority lie in bed, or attend some other activity. The father might not believe. The mother doesn't bother. The children lie in bed and watch television. There's no interest in God's house. Faith has faded.

Big Eye sees. He knows every family in the Parish. He sees the lack of parental influence. Little children suffer. Prayers like the Creed and Our Father are unknown to kids.

Parents beware. Big Eye will hold you responsible. You neglect the faith of your children. They will grow up strangers and not know Jesus. You failed to pass on the faith. It's rapidly dying. Your country will never be the same.

This choice is simple. It's best to go to Mass. It prevents laziness. It keeps you in God's family. It avoids time wasting on television. You believe in God. You worship God. It's an honourable choice. It's the best thing to do. God appreciates families making an effort on Sunday mornings by going to Church and listen to God's Word and receive Holy Communion. It makes children happy.

Choice Two

What's best for human beings? Pornography or virtues! How many people have access to pornography? If you have the internet you have easy access to pornography. What has pornography to offer the soul? Does it affect the soul? Do images of sex affect the eye? If pornography causes you to have bad thoughts and seek pleasure than pornography definitely does serious damage to you. An unhealthy interest in sex makes the soul impure. Pornography makes the mind filthy. Dump impurity. The world of pornography leads to corruption and a compilation of evil thoughts that may lead to rape, sexual abuse, and all sorts of sordid behaviour. I don't like corruption. I'd have grave concerns about anyone with a filthy eye whose vision is filled with pornographic images. For those viewing pornography stop. You do serious damage to your soul. It isn't easily cleaned out.

I pray for girls to have respect. Stop stripping for money. Stop having sex for money. Stop allowing a camera film you while making love.

There's no heaven for filthy men and women who strip for the camera and appear on the internet. These have no moral conscience. It's despicable selling your sex for cameras. Not only do you do harm to yourself but all those who look at the images are damaged too.

How many prefer Jesus Christ who is the Way, the Truth and Life. Who prefers holiness and virtues? The way of Christ is better. Virtue, purity and holiness make the soul beautiful. Choose holiness. The choice is easily.

I'd prefer the good Catholic girl who is graceful, kind, virtuous and modest. The example for us Christians is Mary. She's full of grace. Future girls, I pray for you. Model yourselves on Mary. You would have a happier life. You would gain more respect from your husband. Mary is the purest Lady that ever graced this earth. Choose virtue. Choose holiness. It's a better choice. Go to church. Kneel and pray. Modesty is the best policy.

Girls choose! Choose respect. Choose decency. Choose natural beauty. I guarantee you that it pleases God more to be pure and graceful. It's the best choice to fill the mind with gifts from God than trash from hell.

Choice Three

Think of another choice! Sugar versus fasting! At major Christian festivals like Christmas and Easter we celebrate substantial doctrines of faith. At Christmas we celebrate God becoming a Man. At Easter we celebrate the Passion, Death, Resurrection and Ascension of Christ.

How do we celebrate? Apart from beautiful liturgies to commemorate fundamental Christian feasts we turn the events into huge commercial parties. Look in Supermarkets and Shops at those times. It's huge. It's massive. Chocolate! Chocolate! Chocolate everywhere! Shelves are full of Easter eggs. Shelves are full of selection boxes. Thousands upon thousands are sold. And not only is this a fact but all year round we consume many foods that are full of sugar. We have a huge obesity problem. We also have a high percentage of diabetics. It costs the Health Services millions.

So the choice I promote here is a balanced diet. It's fasting versus fatty foods. It's water versus fizzy drinks. It's sugar versus discipline. It's health versus flab. I recommend an aspect of Christianity that's hugely overlooked in modern times. It's something that Jesus did. It's something that John the Baptist did. It's fasting. Both powerful religious leaders fasted forty days. It's a way of mortifying the body and crucifying the flesh. We would have a better mind and body if we fasted.

We must control diet in our lives. We eat too much. We drink too much. We are always looking for something nice. These bad habits affect happiness. Most of us are overweight. It harms our health. It makes us grumpy. It makes us lazy. It affects relationships. It affects study.

Think about it! Eat a massive dinner! Drink plenty of fizzy drinks! Then try to write and think. We can't. We become groggy. Overeating is gluttony. It's also comfort eating. After eating and drinking excessively we need a rest in bed or a slouch on the couch before the television.

There are two serious human faults combined here – gluttony and sloth. We need to wake up as a Nation. Sugar is killing our nation and making us fat. We need foods that are laden with sugar taxed. Or if we heed this book we might make healthy eating and drinking choices.

So instead of eating a doughnut eat an apple. Instead of eating a nougat bar choose an orange. Instead of drinking a can of Coca-Cola drink a bottle of water. Instead of eating ice cream try a few grapes. Instead of buying Easter eggs opt for a healthy sandwich. Instead of a selection box eat cream crackers and cheese. Instead of eating lots of chocolate narrow it down to a tiny piece.

The other choice is to do what Jesus and the Baptist did. Fast! Do without things. They were healthier, happier and more in control of their mind and bodies. Traditional fasting days in the Catholic Church are Wednesday and Friday. We could cut down on food those days as a start.

Remember times were different in Jesus' time. Obesity wasn't a problem. People walked everywhere. There were no cars, trains, buses or aeroplanes. Nowadays people walk little. We use cars. Therefore, physical exercises are limited. Also there wasn't the same amount and variety of sweet foods available.

So another healthy option is walks. Pray and walk. Exercise every day. Drop into the Church for a prayer instead of the pub for a pint.

So stop overeating and drinking. The quality of life changes once we are fit. It's weighed down, unfit and sluggish when intoxicated with large amounts of sugar. We can change. Our religious leaders showed us the way. Pray for a holy alert head and slim body. Fight the good fight. Fight the flab.

You have great optional choices here. Its discipline and fasting from this on! Say no to chocolate, ice cream, crisps cake, and fizzy drinks. It's our responsibility. We are in charge. Nobody else! Nobody forces us to eat chocolate. The discipline of fasting will bring about great rewards in mind and body. It drags us away from the couch and lazy style of living. Fasting brings sharpness of mind that's opposite to feeling tired all the time.

Fasting also has the advantage of adding years on to life. Bodies full of sugar and obesity kills quicker. A slim fit body is better. We can sit straight with spine erect and meditate. Fitness keeps us alert. The healthy choice brings about a new way of life. Instead of carrying around a heavy sugary body we feel great internally and externally by the healthy choices of food we use.

Unfortunately, sales for unhealthy foods and drinks would drop, and with that job losses. So what? What's more important? I'd prefer to be healthy than keeping a person in a job. But look! The Health Services gain. We would have a healthier Nation. There would be less people in hospital. It's far greater to have healthy human beings than sick bodies. That is the truth!

Hospitals are full. There's no shortage of unhealthy bodies. This comes about through years of abuse. This comes about through unhealthy lifestyles. This comes about through bad eating habits. This comes about through gluttony and alcohol abuse. This comes about through a lack of exercise.

The choice is war here. Talk to the whole family. Bin bad foods. Identify them. Parents don't blame children. They don't buy groceries. Don't bring sweets into the house anymore. Make a stance. It will be tough. But get used to it. It's water from this on. You'll notice the difference in a short period of time.

This is war. This choice is the best one that you'll ever make. You'll feel a new body. You'll feel better inside. You wouldn't be as lazy. You wouldn't be obese. You may find it hard. There will be a longing for sugar. If you give in so what! Get up again. Start again.

Success here is sublime. The mind and body would feel, fresher, lighter and brighter. This discipline of fasting and exercising moves the body and mind into a new level of experiencing yourself. It's a move away from sugar intoxication. You will feel better. You will feel as if you are on cloud nine.

This is fantastic news. This is a great choice. This has the greatest benefits. Fasting helps the body and soul to squeeze out sugary junk. It's in a better place now. The whole intellect now is in a better condition to contemplate Christ. The body isn't drowsy anymore. It isn't sick. It's fully alert. The soul is ready for Christ. God's delighted. Already there are benefits. Eat no more corrupt fatty bread. God will fill the void with spiritual things – the Bread of Life. So wage war now. No more doughnuts Mister. No more bars Miss. You have made the greatest choice of all.

Meditation on Migrants

In recent weeks' thousands upon thousands of people flee a civil war in Syria. Men, women and children flee in boats. These are packed to capacity. Some boats sank and people drowned. A little child's body was found on the shore.

It's a horror story. It's an evil story. It's wicked beyond belief. All wars are evil.

The consequences of war affect families who flee the war zone areas in order to salvage what's left of their family. The people flee in packed boats into neighbouring countries as well as fleeing on foot on long arduous journeys into Europe. If these people remain at home, they could die.

Why in this day and age are people cruel to each other? Religious messages haven't been understood. Islam is peaceful. Christianity is peaceful. So why kill in the name of God? Killing is against God's Law. Moses has it written down in fifth place on the tablet, "Thou shall not kill". You are wrong all who kill.

I solemnly tell you that none of you have a right to kill another human being. It's evil. It's corrupt religion. I condemn the murder of human beings. I condemn the hardship caused by war that has driven people from their homes. I condemn you for your cruelty towards human beings. But I wouldn't kill you. I'm peaceful. I know my faith. It's to love every human being no matter what their religion. Terrorists have nothing to do with God?

Let's get this message clear once and for all. Anyone who is filled with hatred is not a friend of God. Note the word hatred. This is a condition of the mind and heart. It's a form of evil. It's severe and anyone filled with hatred is not fighting for God. It's a deadly disposition. If it is extreme, it results in murder. A whole nation could be affected by it. Or it could be one singular act of hatred.

What's horrible is the human tragedy. It doesn't matter if you are Islam, Christian, Kurd, Sunni or Shiite. What's horrendous is the suffering caused to people? International Community struggles to help. Nations struggle to cope.

God observes. The Son of Man has responsibility. It's a test. Who will help? What Nations will open their doors? We witness a great tragedy. Who will help? God takes note. The Son of Man has authority in heaven and earth. Christ watches the response of nations. This is an opportunity for love. This is a time for caring. This is a time for generosity. It's not a time to lock up borders and shun the plight of children, mothers, fathers and the elderly who were forced to flee from wicked evil.

Germany, France, Greece, Turkey, England, Italy, Ireland and many more have responded to the plight of a poor people. Is it enough though? Is help moving fast enough? God ticked the boxes of caring Nations, and marked X after those that don't care. An opportunity to do well comes from evil. Nations have a chance to enact the message of Christ and care for one another.

My writing is not an attack on anyone. I accept authentic beliefs. I believe in God – the same God that Islam and Jews worship. I believe in submission and obedience to God. I believe in the First Commandment to worship God. I believe in Abraham as our father in faith. I believe Muhammad received a Divine revelation and proclaims God's Word. I accept Muslims worship at Mecca.

Muslims accept Christ as a major prophet. But they don't believe he is the Son of God. God is one! He can't be divided. God doesn't have a Son. He doesn't have a Mother.

But I'm a Catholic Christian. I believe Jesus is the Son of God. I prefer my religion. But look! I see Muslims as human beings first. All are created by God. There shouldn't be divisions in religion. There shouldn't be hatred. I hate no human being. From a Catholic perspective I have no problem with Muslims. They worship God. I worship God. There is no problem.

I have drifted a bit from the plight of migrants. My heart goes out to them. The future is unknown. Religion doesn't matter. People's needs come first. Migrants are first and foremost children of God. Oh, world where is your sympathy? O Arab world where is the spirit of Muhammad! Hold out your hands! Help your brothers and sisters? Your people have fled across Europe for help.

Christian families open your door to these poor people. Don't turn them away. Trust them. Stop fighting. Stop the war. It's not worth one life. Shame on you! Muhammad and Jesus don't accept evil. Believe me! These two powerful leaders of world religions preach peace. My leader Jesus commands us to love enemies. How radical is that?

Jesus Christ loved every human being. He accepted gentiles, foreigners, Jews, and the poorest of the poor. Nobody was excluded. The criteria in Jesus thinking operated on one thing alone – you qualify for God's care once you are a human being.

Global leaders, where are you? You have a duty to care for refugees.

You are all aware of the history of prophets. They were despised. Muhammad was despised in Mecca. He had to move his family to Medina. Jesus was despised by Jews. They crucified him. Many prophets came to speak God's Truth. They were unpopular. Many were killed. Prophets opposed ungodly, oppressors and exploiters. Here is a saying that you can judge by, "The godless finds the virtuous man annoying because he opposes their way of life".

So what's to be done Holy Father? Please influence killers to stop. Islamic State stop! Taliban stop. Al Qaeda stop! We are all one race. It is evil to kill a human being. Stop! Stop! Stop! You see the misery of migrants. You see all those who were drowned in packed boats fleeing the war. World leaders, will you ever learn? Educate the world! It's time to look at our history and learn from it. War is nothing but an attack on human life. It blemishes us forever in the Book of Life. Please pray with me for refugees.

Meditation on Irish Faith

O St Patrick I start with you. You did so much for the Irish. You did it a thousand years ago. Your feet graced our land. You prayed on mountains. You believed in the Trinity. You're a man of great calibre. You were a bright light in our land. You changed us. You sowed seeds of faith. You spread faith in Christ to people that didn't know God. What an honour! You brought Christ to us. You brought something special to our shores. You blessed us. You baptised us. You imprinted the Sign of the cross on our foreheads. I'm very proud of you. St Patrick, I salute you. I'll never forget you. I'm a lucky man. I owe my faith to you.

Father I celebrate a great Saint. He was a great man. He prayed day and night in all sorts of weather. He explained the mystery of the Trinity through the shamrock better than anyone else. I'm grateful to be Irish. I see St Patrick as my father in faith just like the Israelites saw Abraham as their father in faith.

I feel a real sense of communion with St Patrick. And he would like to warn the Irish today not to abandon faith in the Church. There are political moves in recent years to weaken the Catholic Church in Ireland. I would rather die than live in a secular and godless Nation. I pray for a new Bishop and a new Saint Patrick to re-evangelise Ireland today.

After St Patrick we underwent fierce persecution by Vikings, Anglo-Normans, and English Kings and Queens. Monasteries and Churches were looted. Altars were desecrated. Monks, religious and priests were murdered.

Father I pray for those who lost their lives through persecution. I pray for all poor souls – all the forgotten who were bludgeoned to death savagely for being Catholic. Their spirits and what they died live on. I can hear Martyrs screams. I can hear those who died for Christ with dignity.

Holy martyrs! Holy monks! Holy clergy! Holy people of God! Pray for us. Your reward was great. You spilt blood for Christ. You witnessed to Christ. Your lives and work are not forgotten. Ireland lost you. You are missed. But you found a better home with Christ in heaven. You spilt blood for him.

Your monasteries were samples of Christian living. You set up centres for Christian learning. You led Europe in Christina art, culture and literature. You shone a great light across Europe. You became a great

Christian haven for God. You wrote a national treasure - the Book of Kells.

O Father, forgive those wild Vikings and Normans who attacked us. O Father, forgive Oliver Cromwell and his cruel Parliamentarians who attacked and slaughtered without mercy whole towns of Irish Catholics. This man, O Lord desecrated Churches, hounded bishops and priests and killed them. Mass was forbidden. Catholic lands were confiscated. Protestants were colonised

O Father, forgive Henry V111 too. How did we survive? I'm grateful for our Catholic forefathers who struggled through centuries and cling to faith in God. Many great and ordinary Irish people unknowns to us died through those turbulent years of persecution. I pray for them Father.

Father, I mention specifically Bishop Nicholas Walsh from Kilkenny who was martyred 1585. He maybe a distant relation! I pray to him for Ireland today. He worked on translating the Bible into Irish. He was another great Irish scholar whose live was taken from him. Father I recall Blessed Terence Albert O Brien too. He was executed in 1651 for being a Roman Catholic. I remember too Saint Oliver Plunkett, Primate of All Ireland. He was executed in 1681. Saint Oliver was the most famous Irish martyr. He was hung for promoting Roman Catholic faith. When his sentence was announced Saint Oliver said, "Deo Gratius".

Modern Ireland! Politicians! Are the lives of these men in vain now? These men died for us. How could you bin them? How could you ignore them? These men are our legacy – Irish martyrs. How could you downplay and reduce the influence of the Catholic Church in Ireland. I don't like your new legislation. I don't like your plans to push down Catholicism and upgrade Islam and other religions. You can support other minority faiths but not by side-lining the largest faith of our land that I'm proud of. I'm proud of my roots. I'll never forget those who died in Ireland. I'm a proud Roman Catholic. I love my faith. And I'm saddened by our present Government in the way they treat the Catholic Church today and legislate for all sorts of anti-Catholic Amendments and new Laws that in the long run will harm the fabric of our culture and country.

How could this Government push a thousand years' history of faith and politics aside? I'm dumbfounded. It's like cutting out the soul of the Nation. Modernisation isn't worth that. I want loyalty to the men and women of Ireland who died for their country and faith. I appeal to the electorate not to vote for irreligious, humanistic, liberal and unchristian candidates. These exist in the present Government and are anti catholic.

O Government! How could you forget the work of great Irish leaders? The English suppressed the Catholic Church. The difference now is that it comes from within. Daniel O Connell fought for Catholics. He was an intelligent Irish political leader. He fought for the rights of Catholics. He fought for religious tolerance. It's not shown now to the Catholic Church. This does not imply that I'm against minority faiths. I'm against legislation that's harmful in the long run for our people.

Father I pray to all Irish Martyrs who died for their beliefs. Tell them Father, that this man on road L0909 appreciates them. I'm a proud Irish man. I'm more than grateful for those who shed blood for God and Ireland. Let's remember them with a lighted candle. Remember Bishop Nicholas Walsh, Blessed Terence Albert O Brien, Saint Oliver Plunkett and every single person who died for Christ, for belief in his Church, his doctrine and teaching.

Why do I write this stuff? Why do I recall the past? It's because I shouldn't forget. They died for Truth. They died for me and Ireland today. They died for Catholicism – the official religion connected to St Peter and Christ. I can't forget those whose lives were ended prematurely because they were Catholic.

Father, it makes me feel good inside. It's because I remember our dead of the past – each one of them. I connect with those who are forgotten. These are Irish martyrs. They are precious. Every person slaughtered in Ireland by English Kings and armies continues to remain valuable to all of us today. In a similar way to St Patrick these men, women and children contributed to our culture, heritage and freedom to this very day. I immensely honour them – the least as well as the greatest of our martyrs.

But was it worth it? Catholics today don't care. We live in different times. We live in a competitive world where money and business comes first. We live at a time where religion isn't the number one priority anymore. We live in a time where leisure and sport has more followers than the Church.

It hurts. Father in heaven! It hurts! We have lost our soul. Memories are lost. It's all education now, progress, achievement, and success. What's overtaken us? Selfishness! Greed! St Patrick must feel aggrieved. He once heard the voice of the Irish calling. And he responded. I hope Patrick you hear me now. Come again and live among us. I'm afraid of losing our soul. I'm afraid that we will be less Christian in the future. And I have a son and possible his children to live in this country in the years ahead. I'd be devastated if he lost his Catholic faith.

O Father in Heaven, teach us a lesson. Help me! I want so much to highlight the value of our fathers, grandfathers, and great grandfathers going back to the time of your beloved Son Jesus. I want to acknowledge every generation of Irish people. This piece of writing is a memento for the forgotten. This piece of writing is a conscience recall. I recall and pray for the repose of the bodies killed in Ireland from years of persecution. I decorate with flowers each soul lost during those terrible years. I stand up and clap for every soul who would not disown Christ. These are our National jewels. Through their Angels they can descend again and restore Ireland to its former glory – that is a land of Saints and Scholars. We achieved a high standard of moral and Christian living while persecuted so why can't we achieve it now when free.

Meditation on The Son of Man   Golden Egg

Thanks Father! I look forward to the challenge. I love it. God has laid a big Egg in my mind. I grapple with it. I'll be busy. In this challenge, in this Golden Egg is a Messianic title. I'm to study it. I'm to meditate on it. I'm to contemplate it. I'm to gain self-knowledge. I'm to hatch a revelation. By this piece of writing I hope to comprehend an attribute of Truth about God. The Gospel Words are, 'Son of Man'. So I meditate now. This Golden Egg is mentioned by St Mark and Prophet Daniel. It's a beautiful title. I love it. Daniel wrote, "I gazed into the visions of the night and I saw coming on the clouds of heaven one like a Son of Man".

I love this quote. I see a visionary. I see a man deep thinking and gazing into the visions of the night. I see Daniel. I walk myself at night and gaze at the sky wondering if it was possible to see God Our Father or Mary Queen of heaven.

However, I ask a question. Questions are direct. Who is this Man that Daniel saw coming on the clouds? Is this man God's Son? Is this Man something more than human?

I think so. The words are lovely Big Eye. I like them. The Son of Man is the Messiah that is to come into the world. I'm not a fool. Daniel foresaw the coming of the Son of Man. Do I understand? Not at all! I see no chick yet.

The blind beggar man called Jesus Son of David. That's another Messianic title. What's the difference? Is there any? Is the Son of David the same as Son of Man? I don't think so. I prefer my Golden Egg words. There is something mysterious and exciting about Son of Man. I want to grasp it Father. I mull over the words. I work on them. I'm anxious with excitement.

Son of David help me. I pray to you. Who are you? Why did a blind beggar call you Son of David? Oh! I have the answer. Thanks Lord! It connects you to a royal line. It connects you to King David. It connects you to the House of David. It links you to Kingship and the most revered and honoured royal house in the history of Israel. But also and significantly more important is the linkage through blood. The Son of David is connected by blood to the House of David. Wonderful! Christ is in line for Kingship. But the human connection is not what I am after. I think Son of Man has a different interpretation. And that's what I am to explore through prayer, meditation, and writing.

Meditate Little Man! What do you think? Very few scholars gave time to this Golden Egg of great significance. It has a Divine gene. I wouldn't pray to the Son of David. I'll pray to the Son of Man. I'm thinking Big Eye. I'm running the words through my mind. Jesus, you have many names. Do they all mean something different?

Who is the Son of Man? Big Eye, tell me! Is this the Son that you sent to men?

I better be inclusive here. Is this the Son of Man that you sent to the human race – men, women and children? Your Son came down from heaven. You interfered in human life. The situation was so desperate on earth that you sent a Saviour. You are God over the whole of human life. You are the God of yesterday, today and tomorrow. You sent the Son of Man into the world though as a once of intervention. You care for every human being born. You cared for the first man Adam. You are there for man today. And you will be there for the last man.

Big Eye, you sent a Son of Man. Why was that? Are you aloof? Where is your Body? Have you tasks outside of earth? You have responsibility for us. You created us. Did you place the Son of Man in charge of human life? Christ has all authority on earth. Why did you do that? Why did you become human?

St Anselm asked you that question. Remember he queried your reason in the eleventh centenary. He asked the same question I ask now. Why did God become man"?

Let's be clear. I pray for answers. I don't need a theologian, a scripture scholar, a philosopher, a professor or a teacher to interpret a Divine title. I interpret with my own mind. It's a beautiful Golden Egg. It will be in my mind for some time. I might learn a new way of honouring God's Son and knowing his unique role in the world. I pray to a Son of Man. method.

I carry those words around with me. I think of them while working, walking, relaxing and while in bed. I pray to you Big Eye. I love the focus on this title. **Son of Man!** **Son of Man!** Father, help understand. I'm shocked by the disciples. They heard Jesus refer to himself as the Son of Man. Yet they argued about their own status. I'm interested in God's intellect. I'm interested in the role he gave to the Son of Man. I try to figure out if Christ is the Son of Man for Catholics only, for Christians only or for Muslims too and the whole human race.

What way will I figure it out? I'm the son of a man. So what's different? I'm the son of a woman. Jesus is the Son of a woman. Both mothers are called Mary. So what's different? So why didn't Jesus call himself Son of Woman? He had a more direct gene. Interesting! The Son of Man!

Think Liam! Keep going! I call myself a Little Man. There's no comparison though. I'm insignificant. I'm someone among billions made of the same stuff. I'm a man in the sense of being part of the human family. The word 'Man' that refers to Jesus has a universal interpretation. Jesus is Man for the human race. Jesus always existed. Jesus came into the world to do a saving task. Jesus accomplished his task and departed.

I'm a different man. I was born of woman too. But I haven't a Divine gene like Jesus. My father and mother created me. Both were one hundred percent human. Jesus wasn't. His Father is God. It's an unusual arrangement. The fact that he had human form makes him fully human too. I'm contradicting myself.

There's another difference too. I'm born from nothing. I began my life as nothing. I'm finite. Christ is infinite. Daniel saw the Son of Man coming on clouds from heaven before he was born. So the Son of Man is from heaven. The Son of Man pre-existed. He came from God. He is the God Man. His portfolio is support for the whole world of humans forever.

But I struggle. How can I perceive, comprehend, sniff out the sense, extract the meaning, the essence and mystery of such a sophisticated title like Son of Man? How do I pray to a Son of Man? What image is there? Daniel's vision attracts. But I often look towards the sky and see nothing like a Son of Man.

Should I rely on Scripture for my knowledge and faith? It becomes a scriptural Son of Man then. Look again! I scrutinise closely the word Man. My mind has to work here. It's is a Golden Egg meditation. The Egg is nested in the mind. Proceed calmly. Relax. Think of Daniel's vision.

The Son of Man has Authority, Glory and Sovereign Power. Wow! Wow again! These words throw more light on Christ's title. Wow! The Son of Man has Supreme Power. I'm right so. This is a Man above all men. All Nations are under him. All peoples have an obligation to worship him.

Definitely Jesus is unique from other men. I try to visualise a picture of this Man. I worship him. I adore him. I must write. I must have an image like Daniel. O my God! Christ continues to come. I worship a King. King David wrote beautiful psalms in praise of God.

Now I have attributes of the Son of Man. He has Supreme Authority. But it is up to us little men to recognise it. Christ's authority could pass unnoticed in human minds and hearts. It's because we have a human agenda. We are snug in the world.

Notice the interaction between Jesus and his disciples. He calls them. He asks them a question. What were you arguing about? They wouldn't answer. Jesus refers to himself as the Son of Man and that he has to suffer. They didn't understand him. But they had respect. Why do I say that? They were afraid to ask him who's the greatest. That's good. Fear is an aspect of respect.

O Little mind! O Little Man! What have we here? O dull brain! Nobody understands Scripture. It has to be revealed. Big Eye reveals. Take me for a ride Big Eye? Take me across the sky. I look for the Son of Man. Our Creed tells me he sits in heaven at your right hand. Is that true?

Come on Little Man! What's in the Egg! What's inside the shell? Keep it warm with prayer. Sit on it! The shell will break. The truth will come out. I'll capture the sense of Christ's description of himself.

Hatch! Meditate! Hatch! Pray! Meditate! Pray! Son of Man! Who are you? Where are you? Daniel's vision was a long time ago. St Mark's Word was a long time ago. Could I have a new vision of you? Are you a Man on a cross? Are you the Man on the crucifix? Are you a Man above the world now? Do you sit beside God the Father in heaven? Whose Son are you? Questions! Questions!

What about Daniel's Man! It's a lovely vision. Where did that Man go? He hasn't been seen for a long time. Are there any more revelations or visions? I like the vision of the Son of Man coming on the clouds of heaven. Is it an end of world vision? It's heartening Jesus might come back into the world on clouds at the end of time. It might be advisable to work hard for God.

Come on Liam! Come on Liam! Stick it in the mind. It's an Egg. Its content is a powerful Messianic title. Hatch it! Hatch it! It's not a dream. Work intellect! Don't let the Golden Egg die. There must be an experience. The title Son of Man must mean more than words.

I'm not comfortable Father. I don't understand the title. It's not an attractive title. I could pray to Jesus. But I don't feel right saying, "I love you Son of Man. How do I picture or view you? Are you a big Man? Are you a special Man? Where's your Office? How can I grasp it? Work brain! Work! Maybe I'm tired. Maybe I force the issue. Maybe I'm unfair to God. I must be careful. I can't bully God. The Father of All can't be forced to enlighten me?

Muslims don't accept the title Son of Man. In their faith Jesus isn't Divine. Daniel's vision is exceptional though. It identifies Christ as above all other humans being of every age. Son of Man has all the hallmarks of a Divine Being. Christ is Top Man. Big Eye sent him to save us. Big Eye put him in charge as the Man above all men. Why though? What was his worry?

Big Eye had grave concerns about his favourite creation - the human being. Evil spread in them. He saw how bad human beings had become. So Big Eye acted. He sent his beloved Son to save the world from corruption. God loved his creature so much that he sacrificed his own Son to bring as many as possible back onto the straight and narrow road mapped out by his Son through faith in the Crucifixion.

The Son of Man is a Saviour so. But I can't understand how custodians of religion could be bad and evil. The Son of Man did not get on well with Jewish religious leaders. It baffles me. Jesus, Mary and Joseph, it baffles me. How were Pharisees and Sadducees bad? These leaders of Old Testament religion rejected the Son of Man and had him crucified.

Okay! Okay! Hatch the Egg! Pray the Words! Kneel! Concentrate! Raise eyes to heaven! The sky is blue. Do you see a Son of Man anywhere? Is the experience of this mysterious person in the Words? I can't grasp it. I can't comprehend. Come on Lord! You promised. The last Golden Egg challenge proclaimed, "Ask and you shall receive". I'm receiving nothing. Help Holy Spirit. I want to know. Am I not privy to such knowledge?

I sit at my desk. I scratch my head for answers. It's not looking good. The meaning of three little words confounds me – Son of Man. Oh! Scripture tells us that the Son of Man will be delivered into the hands of men. So it is Christ I ponder. It's Jesus. O my God! Why call yourself a Son of Man?

The title has consequences. In fact, it's a fatal revelation. You tell your friends that you wilfully intend to hand yourself over to men that will kill you. This is a horrible story now. This is absurdity beyond reasoning. Holy Father, what's going on here? Your Son states that he's the Son of Man – a Divine Person. Then he declares that he wilfully intends to allow evil men plot his death. What! This is mad religion. No wonder St Peter remonstrated with him.

How could this happen? The Son of Man is Divine. He can't die. This is the greatest Man ever to set foot in the world. Religious leaders intend to kill him. Why? Why? Why? Look at his good work! Look at his miracles! Look at his wisdom! Look at his teaching! Look at his care for the poor! What's wrong Jesus? You can't be serious. Is this a game? You predict your death. You know the killers. You walk into your killer's hands. What's wrong with you Jesus?

What will the disciples do? Who'll be in charge? The Son of Man can't manage his followers if he hangs dead on a Cross. Is this a game? Is Jesus playing around with the emotions of his disciples? O I forgot! His men don't understand. Nobody talks like that. It's a new experience. The Son of Man, predicts his suffering, predict his death, and unbelievably predict his resurrection three days later. Come on! What's this? Is this a madman?

Poor St Peter and his eleven friends! What are they facing? Their leader agrees to die at the hands of those who were supposed to be minding shop – supposed to be looking after the people of Israel. These are ordinary uneducated followers – fishermen and tax collectors. These are ordinary down to earth individuals. What's this talk about dying and rising in three days? It's a game. Jesus playing a game with their minds!

So where am I? I afraid Daniel St Mark's words are realistic in hindsight. I like your vision but Mark's Son of Man is the Christ who suffered, died and rose again. It is this journey alone that leads us to the mystery of the Golden Egg. My Son of Man is none other than Christ hanging on the Cross. It is also the Son of Man that rose again. It is also the Son of Man that ascended to heaven. And it is this Son of Man that sits at God's right hand in heaven.

But I also add that there are hidden implications. He is in sole control of the Universe and life of humans. God gave him Supreme Authority. From my part I revere him. He is my Son of Man. I visualise him at God's right hand. I give him my Will and entrust him to guide the rest of life into his control.

And because the Son of Man has such power and authority I beg him to care for my gene on earth. In that statement I pray for the death and resurrection of my family. I don't mind death if I come out at the other end alive. I put my trust in Jesus. I hope my mother, brothers, sisters, all relations living and deceased are nurtured by the Son of Man and brought to heaven when they die. I'd like us all to be reunited in heaven with the man who started me out on the religious route – my father. Amen.

Meditation on Nations of the World

Big Eye, I look at the world through your eyes. You have made me a prophet for a day. I'm to address all Nations on earth. Oh! What an honour! I'm above the sky sitting on a star watching all Nations in the world. I send a message of support to leaders of powerful Countries who refrain from war and conflict. I congratulate Governments who make good decisions for people and care for their needs.

Big Eye, I'm your prophet for the day and my task is to point out political mistakes across the globe and to highlight the decline in moral erosion. Political decisions made today may affect future generations. I have a right to speak whether you listen to me or not. I'm not a voice in the wilderness. I'm not a voice from the past. I'm a voice concerned about the here and now.

Father, I think you are Truth. Therefore, I dislike humanistic thinkers. I dislike nihilism. I distrust liberal thinking. I'm my own man with strong beliefs. I dislike pressure groups too. I dislike intellectuals influencing moral decisions favouring anti-God legislation.

Big Eye, I know you watch the earth and you gave authority to the Son of Man to teach all Nations a Way of Life that is pleasing to you. It's is that Way that I recommend for every human being on earth. In this Way of Life respect and love for each other are leading lights in promoting joy rather than pain for each individual.

Big Eye, I hope to please you and write well. I don't like any political decision that differs from your Will. My Way is God's Way. I'll not give in even if the whole world disagrees with me. I'm all for promoting morals, goodness, virtues, manners, respect and love. I'm against all forms of interference in human nature and experiments. I oppose hatred and war. It's a disgrace and shame on humanity when bombing people occurs whether by terrorists or State.

Big Eye, I recommend prayer, justice, love and truth for every person. I oppose dirt, laziness, negligence, deceit and selfishness. I abhor bad management of a Nation's wealth. I detest pulling wool over people's faces to cover up white collar crime. I condemn increasing public pensions when the poor have no homes. I loathe wastage of land and buildings that are an eye sore throughout many rural and urban areas. I criticise fat cats and high paid consultants and Chief Executives who receive a salary of over a quarter a million a year.

Big Eye, I pray for change where the welfare of the human being is put at the centre of life going forward. I've prayed long and hard about life. I search for Truth. You are that Big Eye. I'll tell all Nations in the world what you would like to be communicated. I'm all for United Nations helping where there is suffering and atrocities. On your behalf Big Eye, I congratulate Countries that supply and help those who are in need of shelter and food due to natural disasters or war.

Big Eye, there's a lot of pain and suffering. I hear of many cases of suicide, lots of sickness and a Nation struggling with high levels of sugar consumption, drugs, robberies and sexual perversion. I thought a lot about spiritual poverty. I pray to you Big Eye for guidance. A revolution in life style is required. For poor health is often caused by what we eat and drink every day.

I have set out my stall to advice Nations. And my inspiration comes from the Father of the universe. I've prayed and thought deeply about the word Father a lot in recent years. Switch off if you like. I don't care. I love my heavenly Father who cares for the whole world and every person in it. I've made a breakthrough. I feel connected to the Father. The Highest and Greatest of all is in heaven. And I feel privileged by signals recently that a little man like me has won favour. I've set my mind on the Father, and the Son of Man. I trust Jesus. He keeps to his Word. What God says is true and there is not an inkling of deception in his promises. The Words of Jesus are truth. Remember Truth doesn't lie. So listen to his Word when he says, "If anyone loves me he will keep my Word and my Father will love him and we will come to him and make our home in him". That's beautiful. I trust his Word. O my God! The Promise by the Lord has sent a surge of great joy through my mind and heart. I can't see God through my bodily eye. But I know him through the joy in my mind. So I firmly believe God's love is in me because I love the Father of Our Lord and saviour Jesus Christ. I have a right therefore to speak on behalf of my Father. And my interest is not personal gain. It's to do with the world and the behaviour of human beings. It's to do with Governments, Presidents, Kings and Leaders of Nations.

Big Eye scans his powerful eye across the world. He gave authority to his Son and accredited him with the title Son of Man. I have many meditations above on the title Son of Man. Briefly this title signifies that Jesus has authority over the affairs of Nations and every person on earth. I have agreed to work with the Father and Son so as to be a voice like that of a prophet to both inspire and correct National Leaders throughout the planet in their responsibilities towards human beings and the welfare of the earth.

Big Eye runs the show. He supplies the world with natural resources like rain, light, heat, air, earth and water. Every day for millions of years these resources are available for the growth and sustenance of life. The whole world has been explored and major cities and towns are awash with progress as economies thrive with multiple business adventures and trade across the planet.

Big Eye is proud of the industrious nature of man. And good Governments and Political Leaders deserve credit where it is due. It's a huge responsibility caring for four million people, twenty million people, or seventy million people. On a smaller scale it's a task in itself for a father and mother to care for smaller groups like family and children. Leadership is required there too, and political decisions can help in the role of the family. However, political decisions might not boost unity in the family. Instead of supporting the most powerful unit in society like families they throw inducements to single parent families.

Big Eye, I pray for Governments. The Leaders of Nations must not act alone. Neither should they make new Laws alone. A think tank team should always be set aside to consider better ways of serving a Nation. That's what politicians are elected to do. All political issues should be reined in, thrashed out, and solved. The target all the time is to serve people and Country. A desire for personal gain should never be in the forefront of a politician's mind.

Big Eye, I have great faith in you that you can expose corruption and reduce the influence of community leaders that lack in providing care for every citizen under their stewardship. And I have great faith that the humble man may rise to the top in society and show strong spiritual direction and expose wrong doing particularly all fat cats who don't care for the people they purport to serve.

Big Eye, I pray to you. I pray for discretion and prudent care of people. There's much that can be done to improve physical, mental, emotional and spiritual well-being. People are not happy. It's largely their own fault. It's also the fault of the habits and culture of society. It's also the fault of materialism. There's too much temptation and sugary foods thrown into our faces. Health is wealth. Therefore, the future is about training people to adopt good habits in eating and drinking.

Big Eye, guide all Nations. A Nation's workforce generates wealth. Income must balance expenditure. The Public Accounts Book must balance revenue with spending. Bad management cripple an economy. Wastage cripples an economy. Corruption cripples the economy. Exploitation cripples the spirit of a person. Bad economic decisions cripple the running of a country. The general rule for all politicians is to serve. A genuine leader of a Nation with his Cabinet of Ministers must put the country and the welfare of its people first. The desire to serve struggling families and communities has to be at the heart of every politicians' portfolio. Elected representatives are there to serve.

Big Eye, I love your Son Jesus. This holy soul curbed human ambition. He taught us to serve. If anyone desires authority, he/she must make themselves last of all. If you want to be a great husband serve your wife. if you want to be a good father look after your children. If you want to be a good politician serve the people. Politics is about providing services that help a Nation to prosper and grow. There are many Departments that require astute and diligent management like Education, Employment, Agriculture, Justice, Health, Transport, and Finance.

Big Eye, I'm not doing well for the day. I'm not a good prophet. I must pray to you Father, and to the Son and to the holy Spirit. I'm supposed to be a prophet for the day to advise all nations on earth. There's no point in pointing out the obvious. We all know Departments has to be run. We all know that we are human. We all know mistakes are made. And we all know people complain no matter what's done for them. I'm after something different. I'm after the welfare of the human being in today's world spiritual poverty might be on a scale never witnessed before. I'm sure millions of people don't bother with a commitment to Jesus.

Big Eye on the other hand the world seems fine. The birds sing and praise nature and seem happy. The green grassy fields look splendid as cow's graze contentedly. There's a transformation in the countryside as everything grows. This is you Big Eye providing. I can see you in heaven observing developments. It's great that Nations are by and large at peace with each other. But all life is lost until they find you Big Eye. It's marvellous to see big events like the Eurovision Song Contest where we see glorious performers singing for their Nation. It's human glory. It's the best available. But so many lose hope. So many don't believe in a resurrection. There's a Darkness into Light event now every year to highlight support for suicide awareness.

Big Eye, I worry about Nations bulging at the borders with human beings having nowhere to go due to the constant multiplication of new life through sexual connections. It's a worry. The world has to provide for a larger family. Man has been hugely successful and industrious in using resources on earth. He has made use of materials to build aeroplanes, trains, cars, skyscrapers and millions of useful gadgets. I think of human beings on the face of the earth in the same way as an army of ants at work underneath a mound of clay. People like ants work and work oblivious of the prospect of eternal life and heaven.

Big Eye, human development and world progress is one thing. Nations are busy building their economies, their arsenal of weapons, their production of foods, and their transport systems. But there are huge flaws in big cities with robberies, accidents, murder, and rape. The quality of the person or the integrity of the person has been left behind as businesses strive for financial greed so as to enjoy buying holiday homes and lapping it up under rays of a hot sun.

Big Eye, life may seem magnificent in big cities like Tokyo, London, Paris, Madrid. You must be happy Father. There's skilled men and women for everything in every Nation. There are priests, plumbers, carpenters, electricians, postmen, doctors, block layers and specialists in everything and anything. You must be proud of the human race Father. All workers are there to provide a service.

Big Eye, I don't know how you sustain the universe with heat, air, water and earth year in and year out. The feeding of people is challenging enough. All the people in Russia, Nigeria, America, Korea and Argentina and the whole world has to be fed. You provide for all Nations. I don't know what the overall story is, and the future of the world. I can't image tripling the population and maintaining control and peace throughout the world. I fear illness and war will break out if Nations exceed population growth.

Big Eye, Leaders of Nations need to plan. Sixty years ago County Councils built crooked, windy and bumpy roads not thinking that they would be death-traps years later due to everyone owning a car and using roads. Bad planning and poor hindsight from Governments has a lot to do with deaths on the road. The world need visionaries in all

Political Departments. I've seen County Councils building houses and knocking them down again because they were declared unsafe thirty years after erection. If I were to plan for the next one hundred years, I would tackle population control and the welfare of each person. I would create a Health Plan, a Crime Plan, a Road Plan, a Housing Plan and others necessary plans that would visualise a future generation of needs to serve a Nation. I would also include a Religious Plan and Educational Plan. It is wrong for any Government throughout the world to take religion out of politics. A nation that doesn't include God in their politics heads for ruin.

Big Eye, I can identify with your sentiment and desire for the spiritual welfare of each person. I feel a deep concern when pagan intellectuals encourage and dictate legislation that reduces your teaching Father in the influence of a Nation. I think a world without God turns in on itself. Off all the millions of people existing on earth how many are aware of the Presence of God, a Father figure who invites us onto a new level with a possibility of a home in heaven. I wouldn't like God to be reduced in my Country. And that has happened. My advice as a prophet for today is to encourage every person on earth to use their individual right to worship in Spirit and Truth the One True God whether you are Catholic or Muslim. It breaks God's heart to see perversion in religion. Diversity is evident in religion. But that does not give Governments the right to bully Catholics for the minority. Muslim Countries don't bend backwards to accommodate Christians. I speak for Christians to stand up for their faith but not by suppressing another's beliefs. It's when religion goes bad or the lack of practise that erodes the spiritual fabric of a Nation.

Big Eye, tell me what to prophesy. I'm your prophet for the day. Tell me what you want said. I'm isolated anyway so I can't suffer consequences by condemning greed, exploitation, spiritual poverty, and the decline of worship. It's not a question of whether you are a Muslim or Catholic. It's rather a question of a person's level of worship whether it is at rock bottom or high up on the scale of commitment. Although I'm not going to compare the two religions. I'm a catholic and proud of it. I love Jesus Christ and his teaching. I love the Father of Jesus

Christ. I love the Catholic church and it magnificent houses of worship throughout the world where Christians can gather to pray and worship.

Big Eye, I'm opposed to war. I preach Peace for all Nations. The killing of people is never a satisfactory solution to a crisis. But I think war breaks out when people become bad and full of hatred. War breaks out too over greed for money and oil. Powerful Nations would kill if their livelihood was threatened.

Big Eye, I pray to you. Are you watching me? Please don't kill millions of human beings through World Wars and Health epidemics anymore. I don't know what you are going to do Big Eye when people go bad and live as if you don't exist. I pray and warn them in this book to change and turn to you. Faith in you is the only bit of consolation left to us. I find it myself when I sit in a Church for an hour and pray. I come out refreshed and different. Please listen to me. I'm a prophet for a day and I urge you on my knees to turn to Jesus and his Father.

Big Eye, I'm sure you have plans for the earth and for the human being who is the most intelligent and most capable of all your living things. But I don't know your Will. And I query whether sexual activity and population growth as well as resources in the future have consequences for future generation. For man rapes the earth for materials. And man abuses the earth for scientific knowledge. I refer to the drilling into the earth for a few kilometres. And I refer to nuclear testing underneath the ground. I condemn any interference in nature. The earth should be adored, loved and respected for it is the home of humans for as long as there is life on earth and sexual activity between males and females who fall in love. I hope climate warming doesn't result in flooding of cities and lie lowing parts of the earth. I hope human beings have respect for their bodies by rejection of drugs and alcohol. For I would not like to see God losing patience with humanity and carry out the sense of the words in Scripture where it says a time of unparalleled distress may shake the world.

Big Eye, I love you deeply. I agree with you fully that you are a One True God of Muslims, Jews and Catholics. I for one would like to change the world and put up a strong defence or resistance against racism, bigotry, and hatred. Why fight? Why kill? Why hate?

These qualities are not attributes of our heavenly Father. Instead these qualities have in some way filtered into the minds of people who are misconceived about the characteristics of a Father who loves every child born on earth. I'm a prophet for the day. I offer help for bad minds, sick minds and evil minds. I offer a change of heart. I sow the words of Jesus Christ where there is hatred. I blast a shot of a powerful sermon into their mixed up attitudes that read, "Love your enemies". I pray for a cleansing of the mind, and for the removal of mixed up oils of impure unadulterated from clean oil. There can be no ambiguous thinking about the Father's command to love.

Big Eye, I write to National Leaders and Governments throughout the world. I'm a miserable prophet. No one will read criticism. I'm only a little man on road L0909 with no opportunity to influence powerful men who govern huge countries and populations. I don't think for one second that Putin in Russia, or Cameron in Great Britain, or Ayatollah in Iran would listen to a voice crying for a better policy of awareness of God and a better policy of care for each person in their jurisdiction. I'm saying nothing worthwhile for National Leaders.

Big Eye, I'm fearful and frightened of things going wrong in the world that could plunge Nations into a crisis. At the end of the day the World is One. What happens to one Country affects all. The whole world pleases the Father of all Nations by helping to clean up from devastation caused by earthquakes or war. That's the spirit that God wants.

Big Eye, I'm concerned about forces at work that squeeze you out. I dislike the spread of worldly ways and the infiltration of evil into the heart and soul of life experiences. I'm conscious of the fact that the Son of Man had a stable and cradle of straw for his birth. And I'm further concerned that the only place the world was prepared to give Jesus was on a stake stuck in the ground in a humiliated position. So as a prophet for the day I condemn godless Nations who suppress individual freedom to worship. A State should not persecute religious liberty, especially if it is no threat to peace in the country. And I also support conversion from one faith to another if an individual desires change.

Big Eye, Governments must not change the Law of God. Future generations pay a heavy price for bad decisions. Anything that differs from God's teaching and has over a period of time damaged relationships between Big Eye and Man should be rejected. I dislike politicians who hire consultants to find a way around pressurised human demands to legislate bad laws for the Country and are on a collision course with God's Will. I'm sure Big Eye doesn't agree with two men marrying. I'm sure the Father of All Life wouldn't agree with abortion as it is the ending of a life that God created. I'm sure selfish Governments are under wrap from Big Eye's vision of inequality of Governments increasing State Pensions while the poor are homeless.

Big Eye, I pray for the creation of a New Man throughout all Nations in the world. The politician that please the Lord of Life is the man or woman that displays sincerity in their words and actions by getting things done for the people. Political rogues should not be elected for public service. And the right man/woman for public service should both have political and religious education. The New Man suitable for politics should be religious, honest and cloaked with integrity. The question people ought to decide when voting for a candidate is whether they want pagan intellectuals running the country or keep to the traditional Catholic culture that has served for centuries through tribulation and persecution. A Government running a Nation without God is like a man trying to drive a car without petrol.

Big Eye, I looked out the window last night and I saw a solitary star through it. I thought of you looking at me from that star. And I thought that there isn't much wrong with the world. I don't want to come across as a man full of criticism of Nations, Governments, and the media driven reports of evil incidents around the globe. I want to think of the world as a happy place end enjoy the life given to me. Therefore, on beautiful sunny mornings I like to praise you and sing like the birds. It was a glorious day.

Big Eye, on the other hand covering up cracks and faults paint an unreal reality. It's not enough to put plasters over cuts and bruises. It's unacceptable brushing faults underneath the carpet. An innumerable amount of incompetent decisions can't be ignored. I pay a price if I mismanage my family account. I can only see Truth if I don't dump pooh and there is a lot of that in all of us. Corruption is pooh.

Big Eye, I attack mismanagement and wastage of public funds. I don't like corruption in politics because it contributes to ordinary people suffering. I don't like corruption at all and I condemn those who make money by ruining the health of people through, drugs, alcohol and cigarettes. Fat cats have no sympathy from me. The ordinary eye of ordinary people doesn't easily see corruption. Deceit and lies don't have a body. But eventually avarice shows. For what is in the heart of man will come out eventually.

Big Eye, I abhor exploitation, extortion and cronyism. Over the years I saw

Commissions, Enquiries and Tribunals set up to investigate corruption within politics and it has cost the tax payer millions of euro. I'm very disappointed Father that in the centenary year of the birth of our Nation many greedy politicians shamed the men and women who died for freedom.

Big Eye, I may not have touched on what you want said to Nations and their Rulers. I've tried my best to be a prophet. My concern is our world and the future. My desire is to follow the Christian Way of life. Christ's teaching is a super model for living. I want to finish by thanking Jesus and his Father for the world. It's a beautiful place. And I want to play my part in challenging every man and woman both living in the world now and in the future to turn once more to God. It breaks my heart to see people in droves drifting from their faith. I finish by appealing to all Governments in the world to keep God in their Constitution and encourage people that no money can substitute for Love, Peace, Justice and Truth. That's the end of my prophet's day with the Son of Man. Amen

Meditation on Thy Will be Done   Golden Egg

Hello Big Eye. I've chosen **Thy Will Be Done** for my next meditation on my third Golden Egg challenge. I like it. It appeals to me. The petition is a beautiful few words coming shortly after greeting you Father and acknowledging the Sacredness of your Name. I like the word Will. And I pray for understanding that my life on earth and my life at the present moment is lived in a way that pleases you Father. I have no other desire except to please you.

Father, I observe a problem in every person in that we want to live without you and do what we want. This thing is very noticeable in children too. The rebellious and disobedient mentality is evident throughout the whole of our history. We strive for independence and sort of take offence to anyone wanting to change us, and not allow us do what we want. So I think Father there is a kind of a person that don't want you, and don't want to listen to you.

Father I observe this defiance and wicked reaction sometimes in children when an adult chastises them for being bold or for not showing respect. The human beings' stubbornness to get their way is very strong even in children. They cry and bawl when they don't get what they want. I can see you challenged Father. If children don't have respect for parents, it is likely they will ever respect you Almighty God and Father. I don't mix with many people anymore for this reason. I don't waste words on people. It's because they throttle my views. I can see Father why you wouldn't trust yourself to many. People don't want a Father telling them what to do. Minds puffed up with pride treats others as idiots. I'm great but you are an idiot. Father, you have a tough task in converting this lot. The rebellion against you continues.

Father, I love you. I'll listen to you. I'll obey you. I'll try to please you for the remainder of my life. I adore you. I'll hammer my will power every time it surfaces to question you or differ from you. I want heaven. I want Jesus. I want God. I'll allow that sentiment to survive. I'll only fuss about one thing and that is to kneel before you Father, and obey your wish for me. And I hope

Father I know things go wrong. They went wrong for your Son Jesus. He fell three times climbing Calvary with a heavy cross. But he kept going. His endurance lasted. Most of us become depressed when things in life go wrong. We curse ourselves. We take our unhappiness out on others. We blame everyone. But the real culprit is the self. It's because we go astray and rely on ourselves instead of you Father.

Father, I firmly believe I chose with your help a fantastic Golden Egg challenge in sifting through the mind for anti-God sentiments based on a selfish will. Life is all about pleasing the Father. It's about doing what we are told. It's about doing what is right and just. It is about being like Jesus. It is about being an obedient son or daughter. This is a serious Christian task. Go away if you don't believe me. I want to be left alone. These words, 'Thy Will Be Done' are Spirit and they are Life.

Father, I think about you first thing in the morning. I think of your Will being done on earth. I think of your Will being done in me. I think about these holy words every morning. That is what a Golden Egg challenge is. It's praying around a beautiful Egg. It's a fascinating challenge. I look towards the sky as I walk and think about the magnificence of creation. I look towards the sky and think of your dwelling place Father. And I sometimes ask myself why aren't I happy and praising my Almighty Father with songs of joy.

Father I ask for enlightenment. I'm frightened of sickness and death. I saw a dead cow. I saw a dead dog. And I hear a lot about cancer where body parts go bad. Is there any cure Father? I trust you who made the body can cure the body. I pray for enlightenment. My friend St Anselm did the very same thing nine hundred years ago. He was fascinated by the brightness that came over him from the brilliance of your light Holy Father.

Father, I'll be your holy child and obey you. This is real serious stuff. By this holy prayer to do God's will I must kneel at the feet of Jesus bowed in humble submission to his leadership. If I'm given a cross to carry I must bear it and refrain from complaining. I trust God. There is nothing new in Big Eye's viewpoint of earth as he is well aware of sickness and death every day.

Father the important thing for me is to do what I'm told. It's not easy to trust my freedom to another. For I don't know where they will take me. But I trust God my Father. I'm in safe hands with God. Truth does not lie. There's no deception in God. In fact, by being close to my Father everything corrupt in me would be exposed. The bright light of God's Presence would expose everything.

Father, it's not an easy step to go out into deep water with you. The fear factor creeps in. But I must trust. O Father, this is a tough call to relinquish my will to you. I know there has to be changes within me. Instead of becoming bullish, confident and arrogant I must allow Christ to train me to have the characteristics of a lamb. In that way I am more acceptable to people by listening to problems and offering peace and love in places where there are hurt and anger.

Father, it has also come to my notice that I can't gain access to you except through Christ your Son. It would be impossible to find your will therefore unless I go through Christ. I think maybe the approach to you Father is best served by praying like St Catherine in referring to you as a Blessed Eternal Trinity. I might find your Will for me by addressing you as Father, Son and holy Spirit. I like saying the prayer anyway of Glory be to the Father, and to the son and to the Holy Spirit.

Father you fill my soul and in order to do your Will I must hunger and thirst for you as often as possible. The Will of a person is a powerful faculty. It has the power to block another person from doing something. It has the power to prevent someone from doing something in a different way. It has the power to block progress.

Father, I'm shocked by the power of the Will. And I'm convinced that you Father have techniques to bring a person to their knees by a succession of things going wrong. I'm completely humiliated at the moment and my Will is at the mercy of God. I'm like a child that needs his Father due to the amount of things going wrong. I often curse my luck when things go wrong. But this time I'm accepting a series of serious incidents of bad luck. I had an operation on the back of my head, my wife is quite ill, and my car broke down on a visit to my sister in Galway.

Father, I'm taking the knocks like a man. And I remain obedient despite the pain. I remain fully focused. And I beg you not to allow my wife suffer. It would be excruciating pain seeing her suffer just like the way you saw your Son suffer during the last few days of his life in the flesh amongst us.

Father, this is a very serious prayer from me. I remain steadfast in prayer.

I must obey and keep strong. But it is so hard Father. I must accept suffering and your Will to test me. It's a factor of this Golden Egg challenge. Obedience! Obedience!

Father, I understand the message clearly and it could change my life. But at what price. I was once asked to go to Trinidad and do missionary work for your Son Jesus Christ and I turned it down. At the time my mind wasn't prepared for it and I felt it was a punishment for hassling Superiors for their lack of catering for my spiritual needs and theological development. I wanted a study challenge. But I wasn't rated intellectual enough for that to happen.

Father, I hope you wouldn't hold that decision against me. I took a vow of obedience and reclined from an offer to go abroad and serve Christ. I think for God to take the heart out of me by striking at my health, and my wife's health, or economical setbacks has the potential to sink me. I'm sure Big Eye has a bigger picture to worry about rather than my narrow perspective. Pope Francis addressed seventy million Catholics in America recently and surely they are more important than a little man on road L 6134 in Ireland is. The Will of God and the cooperation of the American people gives the faith a great chance of surviving. It's fantastic that Thy Will Be Done is surviving in the minds and hearts of the faithful through troubled times two thousand years after Christ's crucifixion. When faithful mouths proclaim the Lord's Prayer the Will of God is not far away.

Father, I'm happy with the Golden Egg Words embedded in my mind. I keep the Words warm by prayer. I turn to the Words when things go wrong, when it rains heavy, when storms blow and when kicked by others. I accept Christ and feel nourished by his Word as well as his Body and Blood. Father, I accept your decisions for me. All of me loves all of you. Thy Will Be Done. I tumble every little nuance connected with these Holy Words upside down and inside out in order to extract their golden and spiritual meaning.

Father, help me. I'm dealing with something that isn't revealed to ordinary little people especially one like me. I'm a nobody on the earth. But I want to prove to you that I love you. I pin all my hopes on you. If you have a message to transmit today to the world I'm there to help.

You can use my writing or my voice. I don't mind. I'm not a liturgical priest but I have a commitment to you and your Church.

Father, I'm not trying to speak louder than the Church led by Pope, Cardinals Bishops and priests. But I do want to add my voice. I don't want to leave the earth without voicing my love for you Father. I belong to Christ too. I'm a member of your faithful followers and have a great interest in encouraging those who lost heart and desire a fresh approach to renewing their love for Christ and his Church.

Father, I know my prayer is big and maybe outside the ambit of a human being. I seek the Father's Will for the present and future generations of human life. I'm a small little man attempting to bypass education, bypass the history of human life, and bypass influences by professionals and see for myself the magnificence of the world with its billions of living things and their reason for existing. And above all I want to figure out for myself the reality of knowing and loving a God in whom Jesus taught me to call Our Father. That is the goal and drive of my ambitions.

Father, I address my writing to you. The power is in the Word. The power is in the prayer. The power is in faith. There is no other way to find the Father that I adore. God is not found in any other way. He is not on top of Mount Everest. He is not dining with the Pope in Rome. He is not in a plush hotel with the richest person on earth. God is found by prayer and faith in humble and sincere adoration. It is the eye of the intellect that tunnels its way through the debris of life into the parlours of heaven where Our Father dwells.

Father, I'm grateful for this chance to write in praise of your Holy Word and Name. And there is no way that I undermine the role of your Son Jesus Christ in establishing a love for you. Everything that Christ did and said had all the hallmarks of a masterpiece of revelation where nobody can go to the Father except through the Son. All peoples on earth and that includes every human being in every country has the chance to worship Christ in Spirit and Truth. Nobody should feel alienated no matter how poor or ugly. The Father's first call of duty to each of his beloved children is to love one another.

Father, the barriers of division and hatred continues today as it did in your Son's day and in Pharaoh's day when intolerable suffering was dished out to those that were not Roman or Egyptian. However, amid the struggles of life and the presence of evil inherent within the human being a chance has been given to everyone to choose the kingdom of God.

Father, I ask for your love. I ask for strength when things go wrong and my life falls apart. I cannot stay down and curse my luck. I'll rise from suffering. I'll get up even if I fall twenty times. I'll try and burst forth in prayer amid huge surges of misery, failure and horrible events that hit me. I strive for the Word in the Golden Egg. I run into my Father's arms when I see the black evil beast rampaging towards me. I'll cling to the Holy Word, **"Will"**. Out of all the words in the Bible I pray for clear insights and directives into Christ's advice that may make me into a human being that complies with learning and doing his Father's Will.

Father, I look for you. But I find you through obeying your Son's cousin. The way has been pointed out to us. There are no excuses. It's like a see-saw. We either go up towards the things of heaven or go down towards the things of earth and hell. St John pointed the Way. In each soul every day the Father must increase. The Way of the Father, the Love of the Father and the Truth about the Father has to be every person's fight in the climb towards holiness.

Father, I wholeheartedly agree and give full consent to your power to tear to pieces and shred ruthlessly all traces of pride stuck in my head. You can rip it out of my system. For I know there exists evil in everyone. Unfortunately, it's part of the human condition. The words increase/decrease comes from a massively important contemplative in St John. The increase and decrease of the Father in each of our lives every day is a fluctuation process. It's a measurement of the amount of grace in the soul. It can go up or down in conjunction with our actions or lack of them.

Father, I'm terrified of more attacks from Satan. I hate and reject his involvement in human affairs. I detest the Devil. He causes awful evil, heartache and wicked suffering. I definitely desire your Will and protection Father. And I'll thread carefully. For I don't know where Satan's next trap of evil will spring from. All I can do is acquire good habits and pray. It's important to use our faculties to choose and control all activities including little things like eating sweet cake. For it often happens to unthinking people that something is done and we wonder why we did it. Spontaneous actions are not helpful.

Father, I don't want my work to be pie in the sky. On one hand I write about doing your Will but all the activities and decisions of each day and are something other than this holy sentiment. It may be a question of bridging the gap between a Sacred Intention and Practical reality. I do know that some of the Saints endured awful human suffering and pain in order to follow a holy way of life. And it so happens that in tolerating our daily crosses without complaining is a trait lined with holiness.

Father, I choose to remain faithful despite setbacks. I question my motives each day. I watch my problem with fasting for my Lord and God. I must imagine that the thorns pressed down on Jesus' head is a replica of what should be felt inside of us. The thorns are symbolic of bursting sins in the mind especially the sin of pride and selfishness. And the lashes on Jesus' body are symbolic of sins of the flesh.

Father, I desire insights and Truth. I'm conscious and alert. The sun will shine after I've died. Therefore, I'm not important. But it is coming clear to me from the Father whom I love that I need to turn my attention to the plight of peoples throughout the world. I can't live in a cocoon as if nothing outside of myself matters. I do care for the people of Russia, Syria, Korea, and Europe. I'd like every person on earth Father to love you and worship you as our universal God who provides for the earth on a daily basis. Unfortunately, the majority of human beings live unconsciously of you your involvement and Presence.

Father, an awful lot has to do with the human mind in making adjustments in our lives to turn, and turn and become conscious of you as the Father of Our Lord and Saviour Jesus Christ. There are two things in which the swivel of the human will must turn to and that is towards love of you Father first and secondly love of others no matter what their religion or background.

Father, for my part I must make the right choices to pursue your Doctors of the Church and learn from them. I don't want to live as if my brain is dead. I intend to use it to learn from the great teachers that led exemplary lives throughout the centuries in their love of heaven and the kingdom of God. Nothing is greater than a mind fixed on God. After all I address all my writing to the Father and Big Eye.

Father I choose to read about you every day. I choose to go to Church with the people and hear your Word and receive the Body and Blood of your Son. I have to deal with the knockbacks that come my way every day. I'm on course to obey and do your Will. Or maybe there are more demands. I may not be giving up everything. I may be hiding little nest eggs – little pockets of money, or little bits of freedom that shut out the Lord. I am by no means perfect. And I've done very little in the line of charity and help in serving those who are spiritually poor.

Father, I pray for this Golden Egg challenge of **Thy Will Be Done** to bulge into life in my mind. My choices must be holy. I can't allow things to happen without careful consideration. I can't allow Satan to laugh every time he bangs my head of the ground and drives nails through my good intentions by knocking any trace of love or peace out of my character.

Father, it's not easy to follow the Truth, the Way and the Life when I have huge commitments towards a wife, a son and home to use up my energy and time each day. I can see the sense behind the words of Jesus that if someone wants to follow the Lord in complete commitment he must leave practically everything. So father I feel this Truth is a setback. I'm working off limited opportunities to do your Will.

Father, this is dangerous ground. I'm unsure of your demands. Surely you wouldn't expect me to walk out on my sick wife and young son and abandon my commitments in order to change course and fully give all to you. I often hear people say to me that priests should marry. I don't think so. The commitment to Jesus is a greater responsibility that commitment to a man or a woman in marriage. I also don't want to live a double life where I'm committed to Christ while writing and committed to marriage when my wife and son require my time.

Father, I must be realistic about my freedom and intermittent double life where I can't give all to Christ while I'm dragged here and there, and everywhere by family commitments. I may be wanting to commit completely. Also I might be afraid of you Father in the sense you might ask me to do something that I block mentally and feel reluctant to commit.

Father, I think you are demanding and expects hard work from followers of the Way, Truth and Life. What do you want me to do big Eye? Do you desire that I leave my family and be free to cross the border into Iran and other Muslim countries and preach the Gospel of Christ, your Son? Do you desire I preach the Word of God in my home city and plead with people to change and turn to you Almighty Father?

Father, I know your Will is done in heaven. Everyone adores you and loves you in heaven. There's no trace of evil whatsoever. Jesus taught me this Truth. Earth is a different kettle of fish. There's a lot going on that has nothing to do with your kingdom Father. Unfortunately, the human mind and heart and go bad and carry out despicable crimes. There's a lot going on that does the opposite to God's Will that make him unhappy with us.

Father, it's certainly against your Will when suicide bombers blow up the lives of human beings because of hatred. These people are filled with evil and bring great joy and laughter to Satan in hell. Any person that blows up people do not belong to Allah of the Muslim world or God of the Christian world. All acts of evil where people are killed, or assaulted, or exploited, or abused are on the opposite side to you Father, and they can be rightly classed as disobedient and ungodly.

Father, I'll finish this long Golden Egg challenge by urging people to follow the Ten Commandments and form their lives into doing God's Will on a daily basis. The strong emphasis in Jesus' teaching is to love each other, to love your neighbour, to love your community, and to love your enemies.

Father, choices for love and choices for doing good are central in this Golden Egg challenge. Each human being should opt to please you father in everything done throughout each day. The hunger to practise what's good must be each individuals desire. The way to heaven is sorted out in the human mind. The route back to the Father and the rising of the soul towards God is based on the hundreds of little choices made every day. Father, I love you. I'll do my best to follow the example of my own words now.

Father, no progress towards heaven is forthcoming among those who make bad choices. All who are filled with hatred hasn't a hope in hell of escaping hell. Only those who turn to the Father and the teaching of Christ receive the key to the kingdom of beauty and eternal life.

Father, therefore I offer a choice to every human being. The words Thy Will Be Done on earth as it is in heaven cannot be ignored by the citizens of the planet. The mess is in the human mind. All who are intelligent have an obligation to enter the debate within oneself and examine one's conscience so as to sift through 'bad will' and 'good will' choices at every opportunity throughout each day. The mind has to be focused and trained to opt for the love of our heavenly Father. The teaching of Jesus Christ is paramount. The Lord is the Perfect Doctor. All interactions must stem from the knowledge and teachings of Jesus. It is the Perfect Way. It is the only Way. It is the Truth. Amen

A Love Letter to God Our Father

Father, I write this letter to tell you that I love you more than anything else in life. I seek your Presence and Truth after a few wild years searching for meaning in the things of the world. I was around twenty at the time shortly after my father's death. All I want is you. And I want to follow the Way your Son Jesus pointed out to me during his time amongst us in the flesh.

Father, I cherish and delight in the Way that your Son Jesus taught me to pray. I love it when he tells me to call you Father. I'm so pleased to know that you are my Father too. I'm not out of order in calling you Father. It's wonderful in this little part of the world and in a quiet place on this island to raise my heart and mind in prayer to you Almighty Father. And it gives me great pleasure to know that you are there to care for me.

Father, I'm happy to call your Name every day. And I take literally and understand that I'm a child and you are my Father. And I wonderfully rejoice in the fact that you are awesome and that you are perfect. I pray sincerely to you. I love you with all my heart. I adore your holy Name. My letter of love to you begs for forgiveness if I have ever overstepped my place or acted as if I was above you. I'm a child if you are my Father. And I pray to you for the grace to recognise my lowly position and show respect at all times.

Father, I declare unreservedly my love for you. With strong feelings I think of you every morning, during the day and every evening. I concentrate with great depth the words of your Son when he taught us to call you Our Father. I dwell on such beautiful words. But I understand that you are a Father to all not just me. However, that doesn't stop me from loving you personally.

Father, the whole of human life is your family. I'm one of your children. I cannot see you nor comprehend you. But I can pray to you and the humbler I approach you the greater is the chance that a love union might occur. I long for that Father. I know Father that you love everyone, and that you care for everyone, and that you feed and clothe everyone. But I want more. I want to embrace you in prayer and faith. I want to feel your warmth and love for me.

Father, I don't want to die without leaving a letter of love behind me to tell the rest of mankind how great you are and that I did my best to love you. I know I'm not perfect. I've many faults. And I've contributed very little to the work of your Son. I'd be devastated if you cut me off. I approach you through prayer. I call you every day as is expected from a child who needs his Father. I hallow your Holy Name. I ask to be part of your family. I pray to obey your will.

Father, I love you deeply because I benefit from your compassion and mercy. I'm privy to your great Truths. I'm in touch with a Father that has the power to shower great graces into me. My Father transforms me and helps me be a child of God. I'm thrilled and lucky to know my Father so well.

I love my Father. I love him. He provides for me. He makes me smile. He makes me feel good inside. I love this Father more than anyone else in life. God is my number one. As I have said I don't want to die without writing you this letter. I hope it will be posted and reach every country in the world. I'd like people to read it. I'd like to give people hope. For my Father is your Father too no matter what your religion is. All you have to do is learn Jesus' prayer and call God your Father.

Father, I feel very strong about my next point. It's about focus. It's about finding what matters. It's about stilling the mind. It's about shoving aside every other word and every other activity and concentrate on calling you Father. You are in heaven and Jesus sits at your right hand. It could be the start of something special. It could be the start of a love that cannot be surpassed or bettered in this life. I declare from the depths of my heart my love for you Father, the Father of Jesus Christ.

Father, I want to spend time with you. You are my perfect soul mate and you would never hurt me. But I'm sure to be tested. A day doesn't pass by without trials and challenges. I must jump over them and don't look back. I love you Father, I do my best to understand your nature. I treasure your Holy Name. I'm interested in Divinity – things beyond the mind of man. The earth means nothing. I follow gospel precepts to avoid anger, endure evil, avoid love of pleasure and money. For I have to do my part in order to love my Father.

Father, I desperately need your love. I can't run away from everyone so as to be with you. It's a beautiful day but I can't enjoy it. I'm weighed down with worries. Father I long for your embrace and reassurance.

Father, I thank you for my life. I don't want you to think that I'm ungrateful. I love life. The cows graze in the fields. The birds sing cheerfully. I hear the lorries and cars moving on the main road. Everything goes well. I thank you for my life and in the way you provide everything. All I have to do is train my mind to appreciate you more and more each day. I can't walk along with my head down and carry unnecessary worries in my heart and mind.

Father, I long for Mass each morning and for the opportunity to receive worthily and consciously the great mystery of my faith – the Body and Blood of Jesus. In doing that each day I can love you more. Mass must not become a chore. I approach the Sacrament of Life fresh each day.

O Father of love, I am so lucky to have you in the same way as I have my son. I console him when he cries. I help him when he worries. I kiss him and tell him he is the best boy in the world. I do things for him all the time. O Father will you embrace me, and pick me up when I'm down. I'll try to please you and do what you ask. O God Our Father correct me when I lose patience and bark. Your Almighty hand held against the side of my face would quell my irritations. I can fight my demons by filling myself up with the food of Life and the drink of Life. It's all about making room for Christ within my most inner parts.

Father, this is no joke. I'm deadly serious. I'm never to approach you or your Son with the mind of a rogue or tease your seriousness. You are my Father. Your Son Jesus is my brother. I adore and worship you.

Father, I know you are in heaven but you have a way of been present to me now. I want to think about you and feel your Presence all day long. I imagine myself sitting with you, walking with you, hearing you, and feeling you. I can't wait to see you face to face after my death. I don't expect a revelation now, or a transfiguration. But this obscure relationship wouldn't stop me from loving you.

Father, I agree and consent to be your child. It's my desire now to do your Will and become part of your kingdom by belonging to the family of saints and holy souls. I trespass against no one by minding my own business. I wouldn't trespass against you either Father. Once I receive a piece of Bread each day that is linked to the Body and Blood of your Son than I'm happy. I'm humbled to be fed by you Father.

Father, I feel wonderful. My connection to you feels like a bucketful of grace has been thrown over me and it seeps through my whole being. It's a beautiful feeling. But I'm aware that on the other side there are some dirty places and pockets of resistance thwarting the influence and spread of holiness.

However, Father I welcome you with an open heart. I welcome your Son too. I'll delight in the shower of grace as it oozes through every vein, muscle and bone in my body. This is holy oil. This is holy stuff. It is the stuff that enables me to love you in return. All I have ever wanted once I tasted your sweetness is to love you.

Father, I'm well aware of your deep concern for the human being especially from the point of view of their ability to love you. It seems that dirty oil has filtered through each soul and has left them in a mess spiritually. I'm well aware to that I'm dealing with my Father who commands the love of every human being. And before I finish this letter to you I express my struggle to love.

Father, the main difficulty preventing my love for you is original sin. I'm convinced there is plenty of badness in people including myself. And while in this life I can't be rid of it. There's no perfect human relationship and that includes a love for you Father. There's hurt and suffering everywhere.

Father, I do my best. I'll wait at the water well in Syria for Jesus and talk to him. On that day so many years ago Jesus enthralled the woman from Syria as he told her how to worship in Spirit and Truth. It made her very happy. I'd love that same chat with your Son, Father. I think of other chats that Jesus had too.

I want holy grace to run into my heart. I want Jesus' Word to well up inside of me. Father, I want our hearts to unite. Let the holy stuff ooze into me. I've waited a long time for you Father. My human father had this desire many years ago. He loved you. I want to follow his example.

Father, I hope you will accept my letter. I'll increase my prayer to you. I'll obey your command to love others. But I need your help. Satan batters me every time I try to love you. He beats me up and knocks me back. I need the effects of the last two petitions in your Son's Prayer to work. Protection from evil is vital. Satan has to be beaten out of my head. I emphatically reject him. I want you Father. My soul seeks you. I pray that I may know you and love you. You are all that matter. I hope to live up to this desire to love. I'll not run away from you Father like Adam and Eve did in the garden. I'll walk towards you like the prodigal son and beg for you to hold me in your arms and love. Amen

Meditation on the Body and Blood of Christ
Golden Egg

Big Eye, I find it is hard to make a connection with you. So I focus on your Son Jesus. I focus on the concept of an Eternal Sacrifice. The Son of man died for sinners two thousand and fifteen years ago. It was a single act. But it is eternal in nature. It has lasted so long. Thousands of sacrifices occur around the world today.

Big Eye, are you watching? I notice the words in the Mass. I notice the blessing. I notice the Holy Spirit called upon the bread and wine. I remember your Son's words. This is my Body. This is my Blood. I connect with God through this Body and Blood. Wonderful news! The celebration of the Eucharist is the heartbeat of a priest's life. The Mass is the life of the community. All the faithful hear the Word of God and receive Holy Communion. The more that participate the better the quality of life in the community.

Big Eye, watch me! I feel embarrassed for you. I wouldn't have done it. I'm a Father too. I wouldn't agree with sacrificing my son's life for scoundrels and wicked sinners. Big Eye you are mad. I thought you had Supreme Intelligence. The killing of your Son to save us was a crazy plan. You know as well as I do human beings can be cruel and ungrateful.

Big Eye, come on! Who would die for adulterers, rapists, paedophiles, murderers, thieves, drug dealers, abortionists, exploiters, and pornographers? What are you trying to do? Are you trying to bring hardened criminals to heaven? No wonder the Jews tried to kill you and eventually did through crucifixion.

Big Eye, what's in your mind? What were you thinking? You turned religion upside down. You bashed and attacked religious leaders in favour of sinners. You demanded obedience from your Son by asking him to accept being crucified. Big Eye, are you crazy? No father couldn't stand by and watch their son been beaten, mocked, scourged, stripped and crucified. Are you heartless?

Big Eye, you saw a bigger picture. The world of humans mattered deeply to you. You loved us very much despite corruption and wickedness that's widespread in our mixed human state. You wanted to redeem us. You wanted to save us. And the sacrifice of your Son mapped out a way for each one of us to return to God.

Big Eye, I appreciate your love for me. I couldn't imagine a world without Christ. I would have no way back to God. I'm fascinated by Christ's love for me. I'm grateful that the Son of Man left his presence behind in the world by the sacrifice of his life witnessed every day from the altar.

Big Eye, it is the Body and Blood of Christ. You gave your Son to us to eat and drink. In that way Christ is in us. The priest consecrates the bread and wine using Christ's words. The bread and wine change into something new. Christ is Divine. If Big Eye creates from nothing surely he can change something already existing into something different. It is faith that understands this.

Big Eye, I love the Catholic Eucharist. It's the only religion and Church in the world that believes in the Real Presence. And a big part of that belief is the faith of the person. I'm sad though that there exists a decline in worship. I ask myself on Sunday mornings where are the families of the community? Why are they not going to Church to hear your Word and receive the Body and Blood of your Son? Unfortunately, thanksgiving is short lived. Memories of Christ's love for us fade and die.

Big Eye, I pray for a new Master and new Shepherds to care for a world that hasn't you Big Eye and your Son Jesus Christ at the centre of their lives. More and more people are descending into a state of spiritual poverty. I'd love my book to spark of that renewal. By and large priests are available to celebrate Mass but large numbers of the faithful don't bother attending.

Big Eye, I believe leaders of the Eucharistic celebration require enthusiasm and inspiration for what they do. The whole community require awakening. It saddens me attending dead ceremonies where lifeless bodies don't profess their faith with eagerness and joy. Why are they so dead in themselves? For goodness sake, the Lord's Word should inspire and his Body and Blood enthral every soul.

Big Eye, congregations are far too casual. The Holy Spirit is in their midst as the unique act of Christ's sacrifice is re-enacted before our eyes.

Come let us worship. Why is there a lack of enthusiasm in proclaiming the prayers? The Our Father and Creed are powerful opportunities to speak up and be heard. The priest forgiving sins and the Peace Prayer before Holy Communion are unbelievable and consoling religious acts of devotion. Come on Christians! Wake up! It's a unique opportunity to have Jesus Christ in our midst.

Big Eye, help me. I address the faithful. Come on! Mass is sacred. It's holy and inspirational. It's us that are dead. We moan and complain. The Mass is Holy. An opportunity for contact with Divine Life is near at hand. I'm rather sad that people prefer to sleep and do other things. I beg you in God's name to go to Church and hear things and receive a Sacred Host that could change your life.

Big Eye, I'd like to tell people to pray. They depend too much on the priest to pray for them. Every mind and heart must pray. Every head at Mass must rise to the occasion and add something to the quality of worship. All must pray for their individual needs as well as the needs of the community. All Churches must seek ways of enhancing the Spirit of God. Wake up Christian! Stand up for God. Adore Jesus Christ.

Big Eye, I feel work has to be done. People receive the Body of Christ casually. That is an insult. It's disrespect. I say this because I mean what I say. I speak the Truth. Remember Peter falling at the feet of Jesus. Peter knew of the greatness of Christ. So I ask for prayers before meeting Christ in Holy Communion and after it too. It's only proper that each individual respect Jesus Christ.

Big Eye, remember my Golden Egg meditations. I pointed out the importance of asking, seeking and knocking. What do I ask for? I ask for Jesus Christ in Holy Communion. I ask for his Holy Word in the Scripture readings at Mass. I ask that wherever you live you stop and think. I ask you to stop moving for a while. And look up at the blue sky and say I seek God. I ask you to rise from your beds and go to Church as often as possible. The Lord will welcome you. The doors are not closed to you.

Big Eye I want to help. I feel like knocking at the door of every house and inviting those who are poor in spirit to return to Church. I feel like travelling through every village to welcome the lost back to the Christian community for worship. I want to walk across hills and mountains to seek out the abandoned and lonely in isolated homes and let them know that the Good shepherd has not forgotten them. I want to tell them that Christ is still alive and if they need help it is available where neighbour care for neighbour. I pray that the elderly and lonely are brought to Mass by caring and loving friends of Jesus.

Big Eye this is a selfish age. The kids want entertainment. Adults are busy earning money. Don't disturb signs are up. And the smart phones are more precious than a human being. New and modern friends are televisions and computers. But one thing is certain. Forget God and Jesus Christ at your peril. At the end of the day I cannot resurrect myself. I depend on God. The fact of death comes to every person. And it is there that Jesus Christ is supreme. I depend on the prayers of the Church and the Eucharistic Prayer to deliver my Passover. It is in this mystery of living a life, dying at some stage and rising to life again that makes me trust in Jesus more than any other religion in the world. These events are all covered in the celebration of Mass. And many of the elderly know that belief in Jesus and the Mass is their insurance policy for a place in heaven.

Big Eye, I love this Sacrament, Corpus Christi. I value it. I loved been a priest and celebrating Mass. I loved the consecration part. I love the whole structure of Mass. I blessed bread and wine. I ask for forgiveness for sins. And I prepare for the reception of the Body and Blood of Christ. I pray for children to understand the Mass. I pray for parents to teach them. My son Luke never misses the celebration of the Eucharist on Sunday mornings. I choose the Church instead of rugby for him. I encourage him to say Jesus five times before receiving the Sacred Host.

Big Eye, I love St Ambrose's prayer in preparation for Holy Communion. He has the right ideas like make me clean in soul and body; give me grace to partake worthily, banish evil thoughts etc. I just love it. O Sacred Banquet I love my sacred Meal. O dear! What precious food it is! What a joy on earth for those lucky enough to participate in God's Life. Now I see why you sacrificed your Son, Big Eye.

Big Eye, I taste heaven on earth through this Holy Meal. It sets of a struggle in us to reject sin and evil. You have showed us the Way. But why is man so dull? Why are we so stupid? God is on our Altar and most of the world is blind and deaf and can't grasp where the source of life is located. Many people prefer a few pints than the Blood of Christ? Others prefer a sports match than the Body of Christ? O silly man! Do you not know silly goose that the way we live in this life depends on our entry into heaven? The world of humans is watched closely by Big Eye and the Son of Man.

Big Eye, reality bites in. I can't go anywhere without the power of God. Inhabitants of the planet make a huge mistake. They are crippled with weak faith, bad faith and lost faith! Why reject Christ? Why reject the Church? I beg you not to allow a bad priest to damage your faith and use it as a reason to endanger your soul. It does your life more harm than good by turning your back on the Church. I cannot see any hope of heaven for godless people. What's left for the godless? Plenty of rest in bed! Plenty to eat and drink! Plenty of relaxation and sport! A great time on earth! Tons of pleasure! Loads of money!

Big Eye, I'm concerned. I'm deeply concerned. Families ignore you and reject practising their faith. It's as obvious as day that a large percentage of families have dropped away from Sunday Eucharist. I can't understand it that little children are deprived from the Body of Christ due to negligence of their souls by parents' decisions.

Big Eye, I am glad you asked me to do a meditation on the Eucharist. I have a strong love for it since my time walking the streets with Bishop Brooks carrying the sacred Host. It is a Golden Egg. Big Eye, bless everyone who adore the Sacred Host. I contemplate Christ on the Cross. St Ambrose and St Thomas Aquinas wrote prayers on this subject. There devotional prayers are found in the back of the Divine Office.

Big Eye, I feel Divinity touches me every time I receive the Sacred Host. I have searched the earth for Truth and found nothing except the Son of Man to satisfy my desire. I hear his Word and receive his Body and Blood. As Saint Anselm wrote there is nothing higher or greater than our Supreme Father with a Golden Eye that watches carefully for the good of each of his faithful children on earth. Amen

Acknowledgement

This is for my wife Deirdre whom I thank for her patience and support while writing this book. Without her help this work would not be possible. I thank my son Luke too for his kindness and patience with me through this work. They both gave great joy and support. I thank I Universe too for their help and for publishing my book.

Printed in the United States
By Bookmasters